AFTER SCHOOL
NIGHTMARE

Story and Art by
SETONA MIZUSHIRO

8

go!comi

Translation – Christine Schilling
Adaptation – Mallory Reaves
Production Assistant – Suzy Wells
Lettering & Retouch – Eva Han
Production Manager – James Dashiell
Editor – Brynne Chandler

A Go! Comi manga

Published by Go! Media Entertainment, LLC

Houkago Hokenshitsu Volume 8
© SETONA MIZUSHIRO 2007
Originally published in Japan in 2007 by Akita Publishing Co., Ltd., Tokyo.
English translation rights arranged with Akita Publishing Co., Ltd.
through TOHAN CORPORATION, Tokyo.

Visit us online at www.gocomi.com
e-mail: info@gocomi.com

ISBN 978-1-933617-63-3

First printed in August 2008

1 2 3 4 5 6 7 8 9

Manufactured in the United States of America.

Koukoku Senior High School

Table of contents

AFTER SCHOOL NIGHTMARE

Our Story So Far

Mashiro Ichijo is a high school student whose body is half female, and half male. One day, he's called down to a secret infirmary to participate in a "special class" he needs to graduate. He learns from another student, Kureha, that each person takes on their true form in this class. When each student reaches their personal goal, their most heart-felt dream will come true. Mashiro decides to use this class to become a true male.

But when another dreamer – a merciless knight – exposes his body's secret and Kureha's tragic past, Mashiro vows to protect the weaker dreamers.

Who is the real person behind the knight? While trying to identify the real people behind the facades, Mashiro is accosted by Sou, a male student he doesn't much like. Sou tells him "you're a girl" and then forces a kiss upon him. Wondering whether Sou could be another dreamer, maybe even the knight, Mashiro becomes obsessed with Sou.

But when Sou's sister, Ai, reveals that Sou is the knight, Mashiro is stunned. Vowing that he'll never forgive Sou, Mashiro tries to free himself from his confused feelings by spending a tender night with Kureha.

Soon, Kureha tells him she wants to break up now that she sees what is really in his heart, and returns to her parents' house.

At the end of his rope, Mashiro finally confesses to Sou that he loves him, but what does that really mean...!?

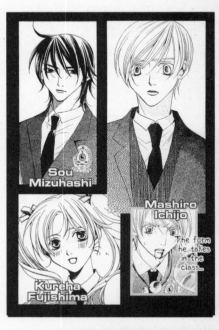

Sou Mizuhashi
Mashiro Ichijo
The form he takes in the class...
Kureha Fujishima

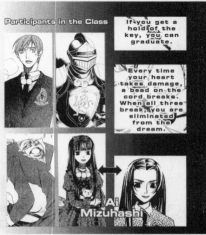

Participants in the Class
If you get a hold of the key, you can graduate.
Every time your heart takes damage, a bead on the cord breaks. When all three break, you are eliminated from the dream.
Ai Mizuhashi

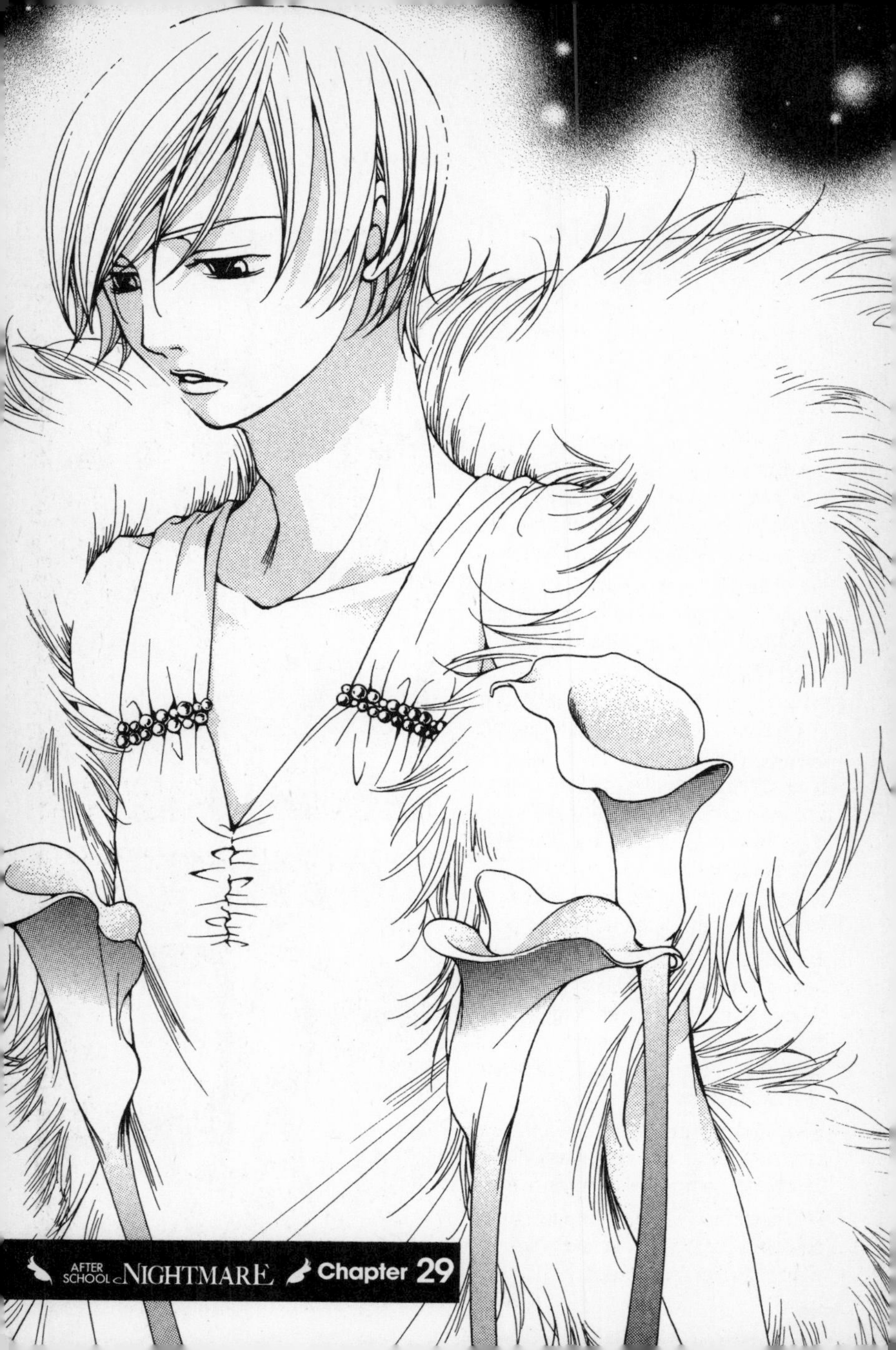
AFTER SCHOOL NIGHTMARE
Chapter 29

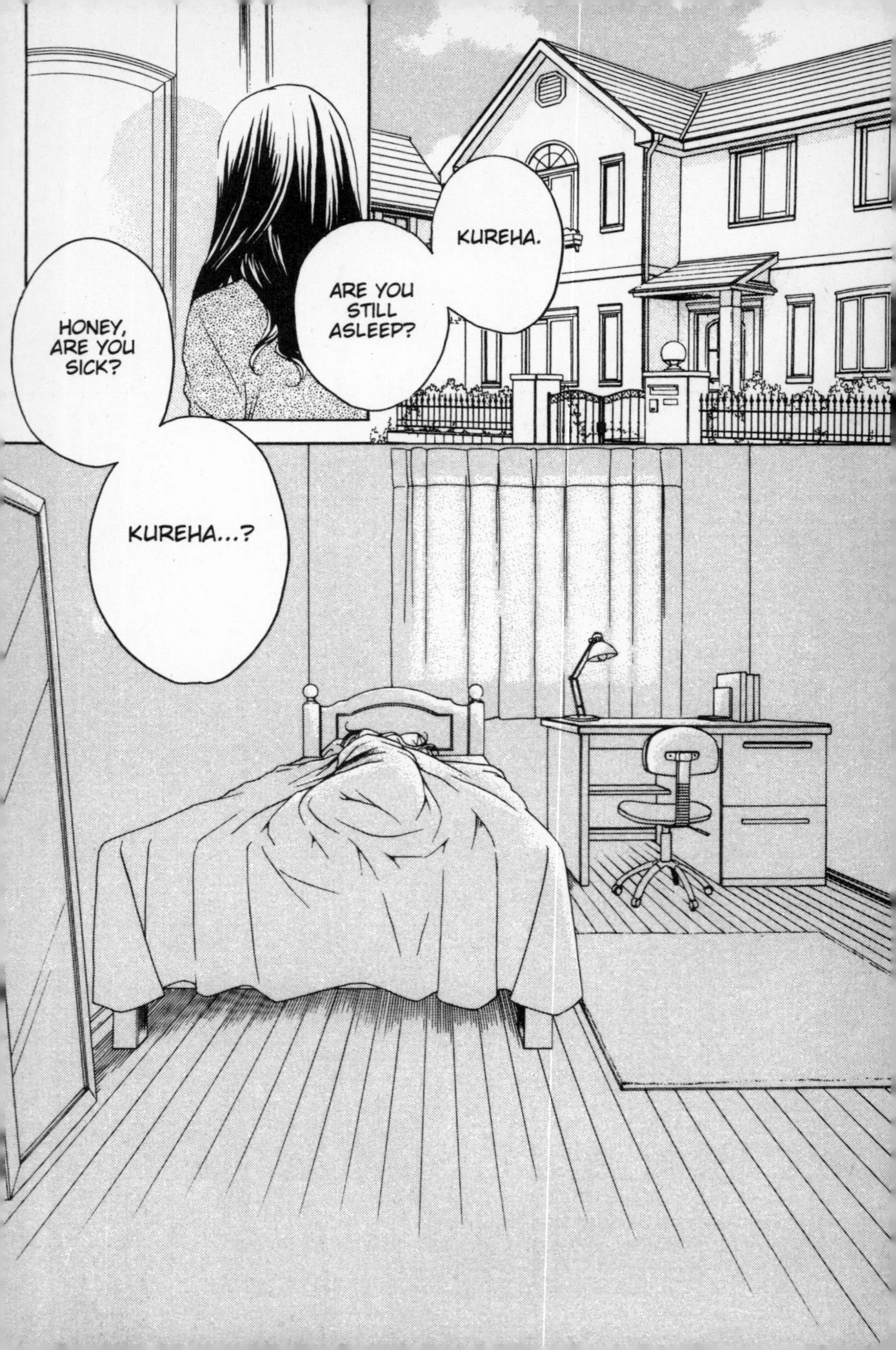
KUREHA.
ARE YOU STILL ASLEEP?
HONEY, ARE YOU SICK?
KUREHA...?

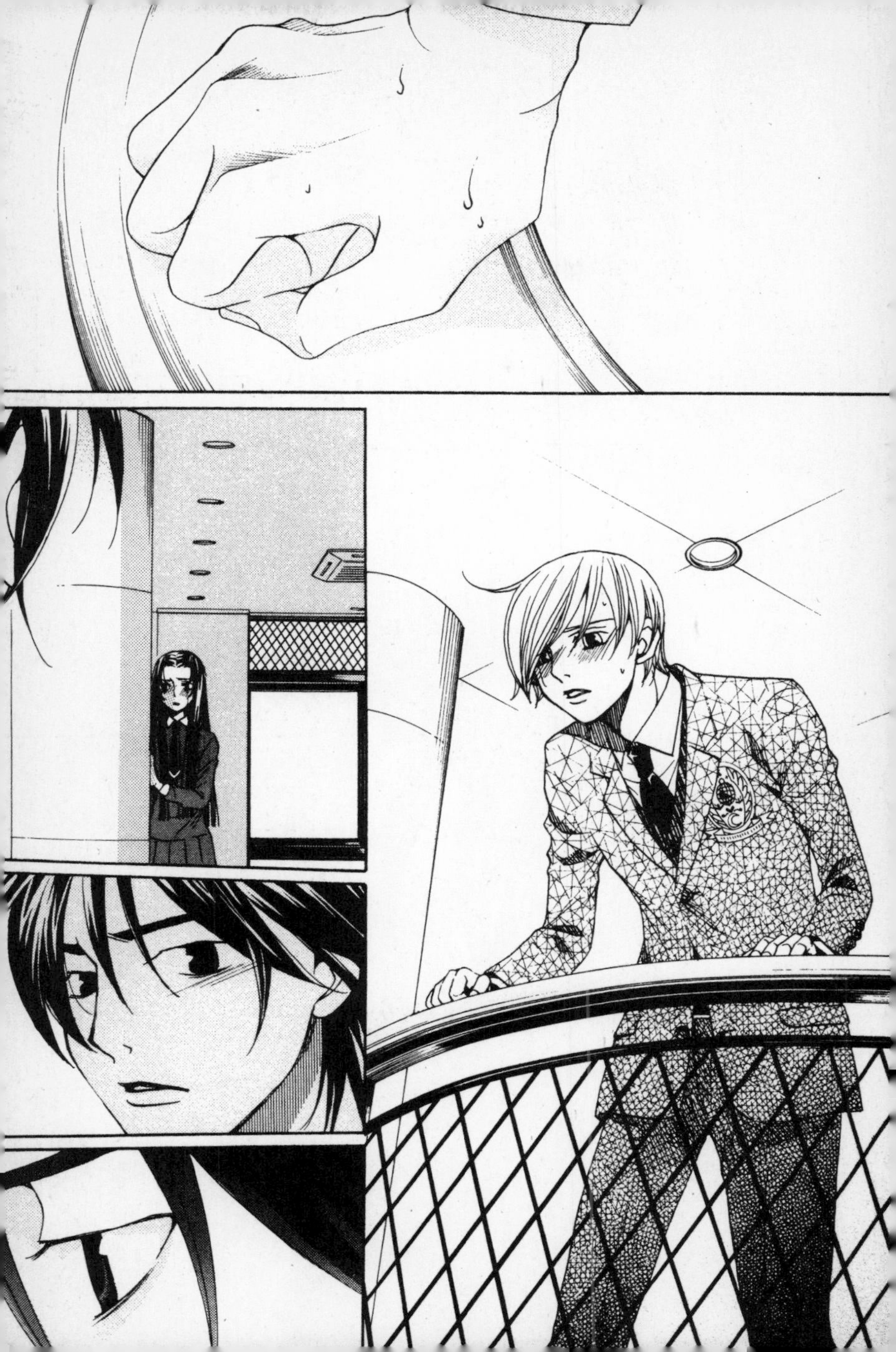

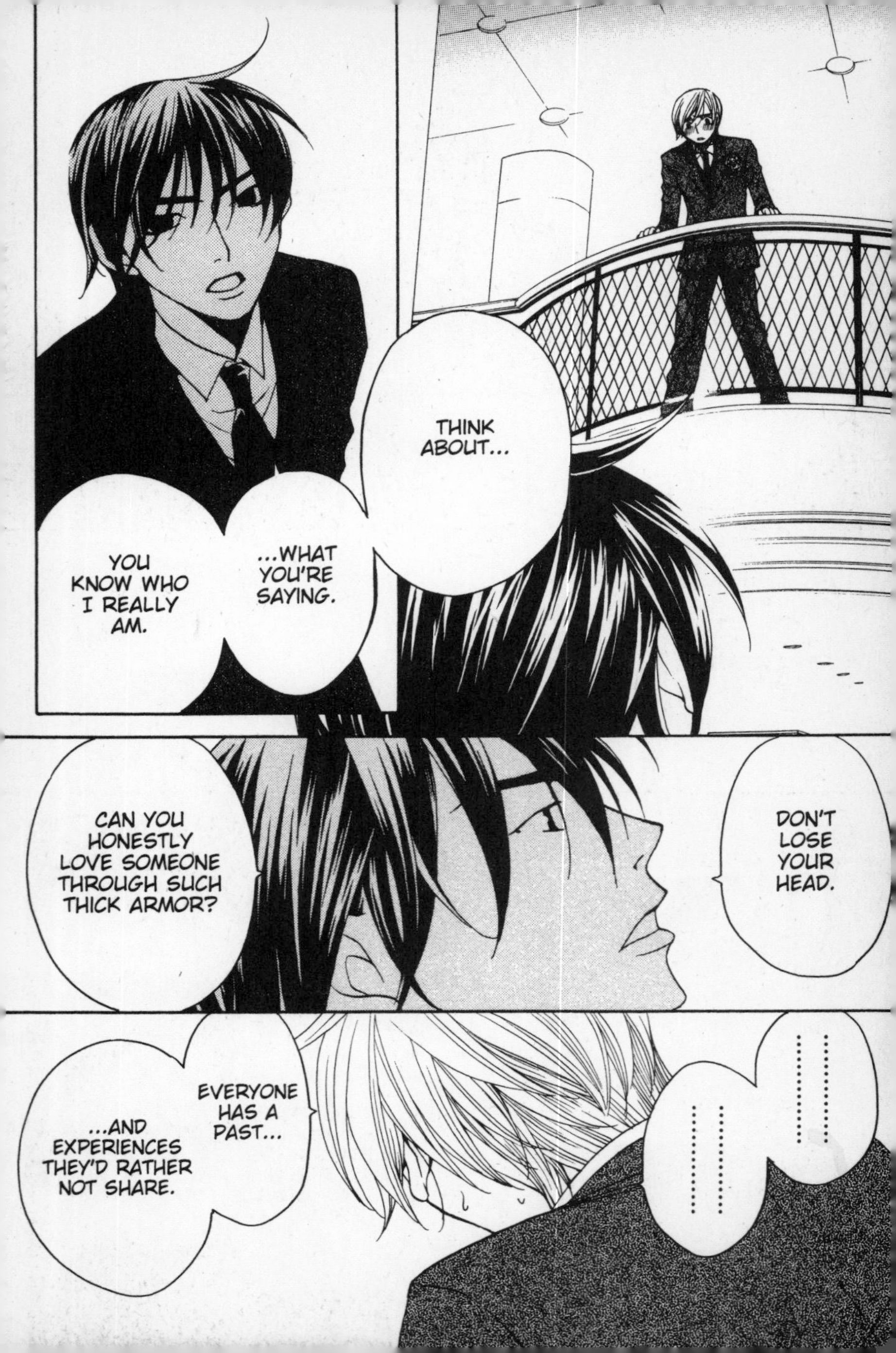
THINK ABOUT...
...WHAT YOU'RE SAYING.
YOU KNOW WHO I REALLY AM.
DON'T LOSE YOUR HEAD.
CAN YOU HONESTLY LOVE SOMEONE THROUGH SUCH THICK ARMOR?
......
EVERYONE HAS A PAST...
...AND EXPERIENCES THEY'D RATHER NOT SHARE.

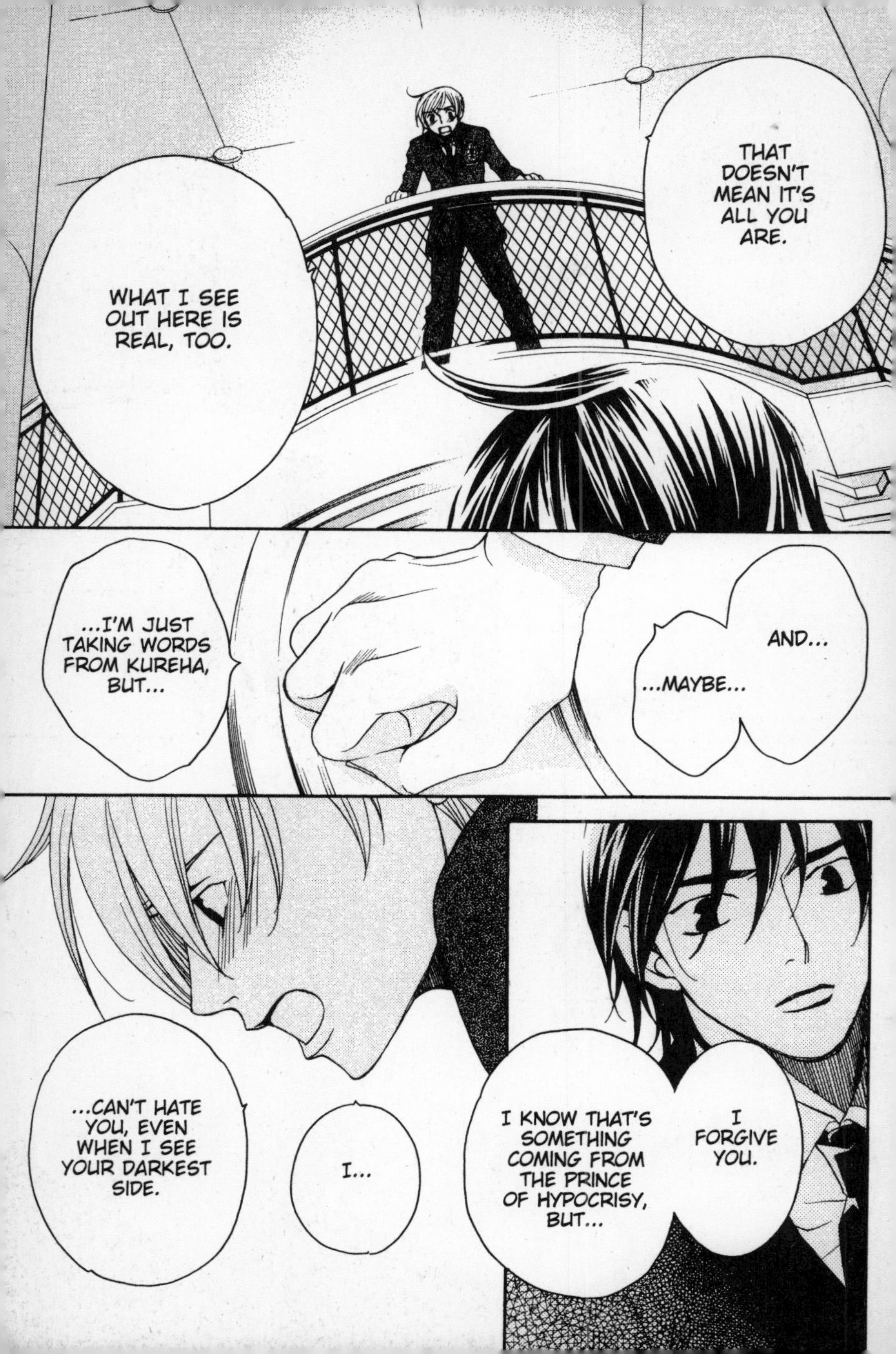
THAT DOESN'T MEAN IT'S ALL YOU ARE.
WHAT I SEE OUT HERE IS REAL, TOO.
AND... ...MAYBE...
...I'M JUST TAKING WORDS FROM KUREHA, BUT...
I FORGIVE YOU.
I KNOW THAT'S SOMETHING COMING FROM THE PRINCE OF HYPOCRISY, BUT...
I...
...CAN'T HATE YOU, EVEN WHEN I SEE YOUR DARKEST SIDE.

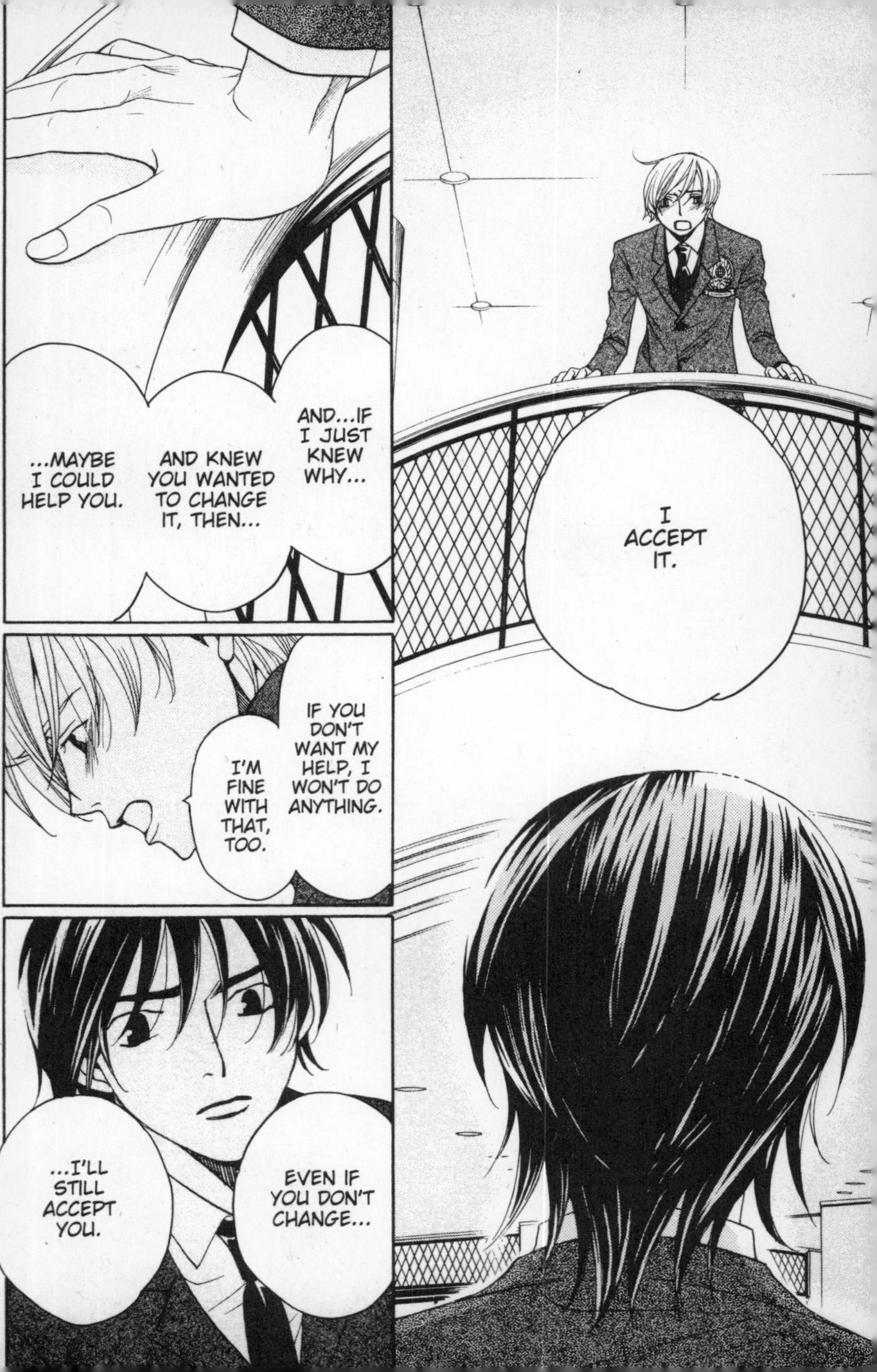
I ACCEPT IT.
AND...IF I JUST KNEW WHY...
AND KNEW YOU WANTED TO CHANGE IT, THEN...
...MAYBE I COULD HELP YOU.
IF YOU DON'T WANT MY HELP, I WON'T DO ANYTHING.
I'M FINE WITH THAT, TOO.
EVEN IF YOU DON'T CHANGE...
...I'LL STILL ACCEPT YOU.

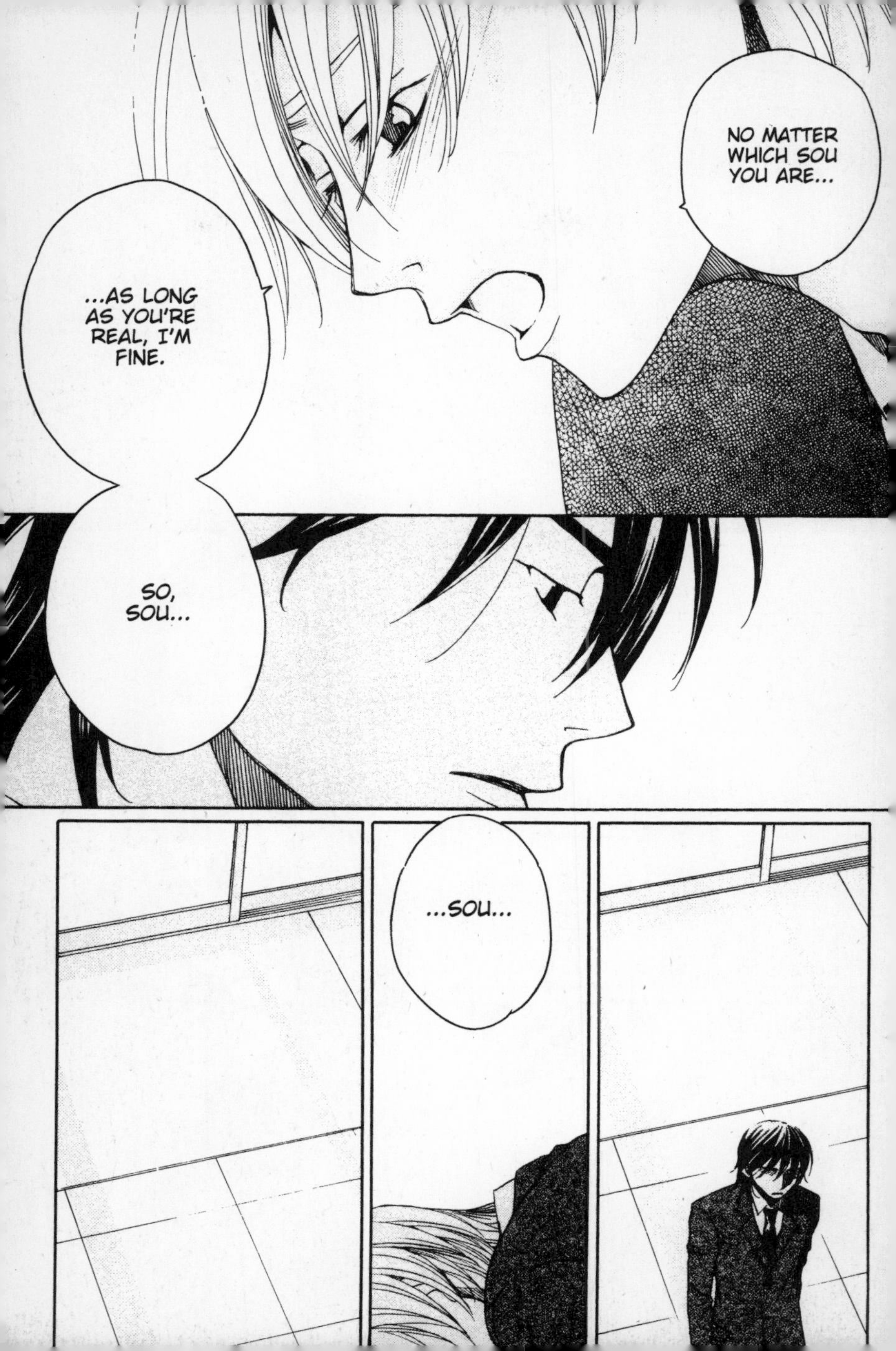
NO MATTER WHICH SOU YOU ARE...
...AS LONG AS YOU'RE REAL, I'M FINE.
SO, SOU...
...SOU...

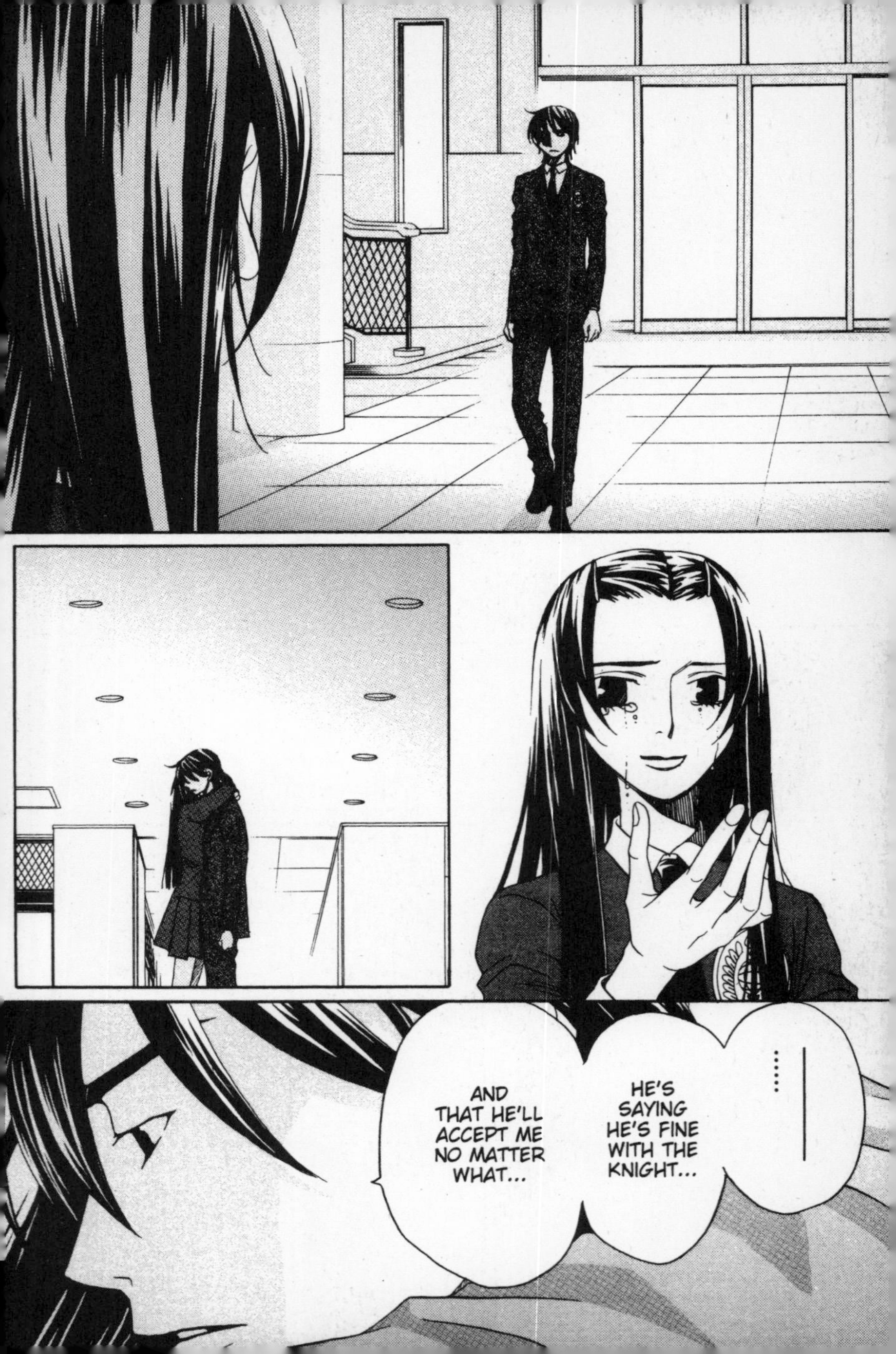
......
HE'S SAYING HE'S FINE WITH THE KNIGHT...
AND THAT HE'LL ACCEPT ME NO MATTER WHAT...

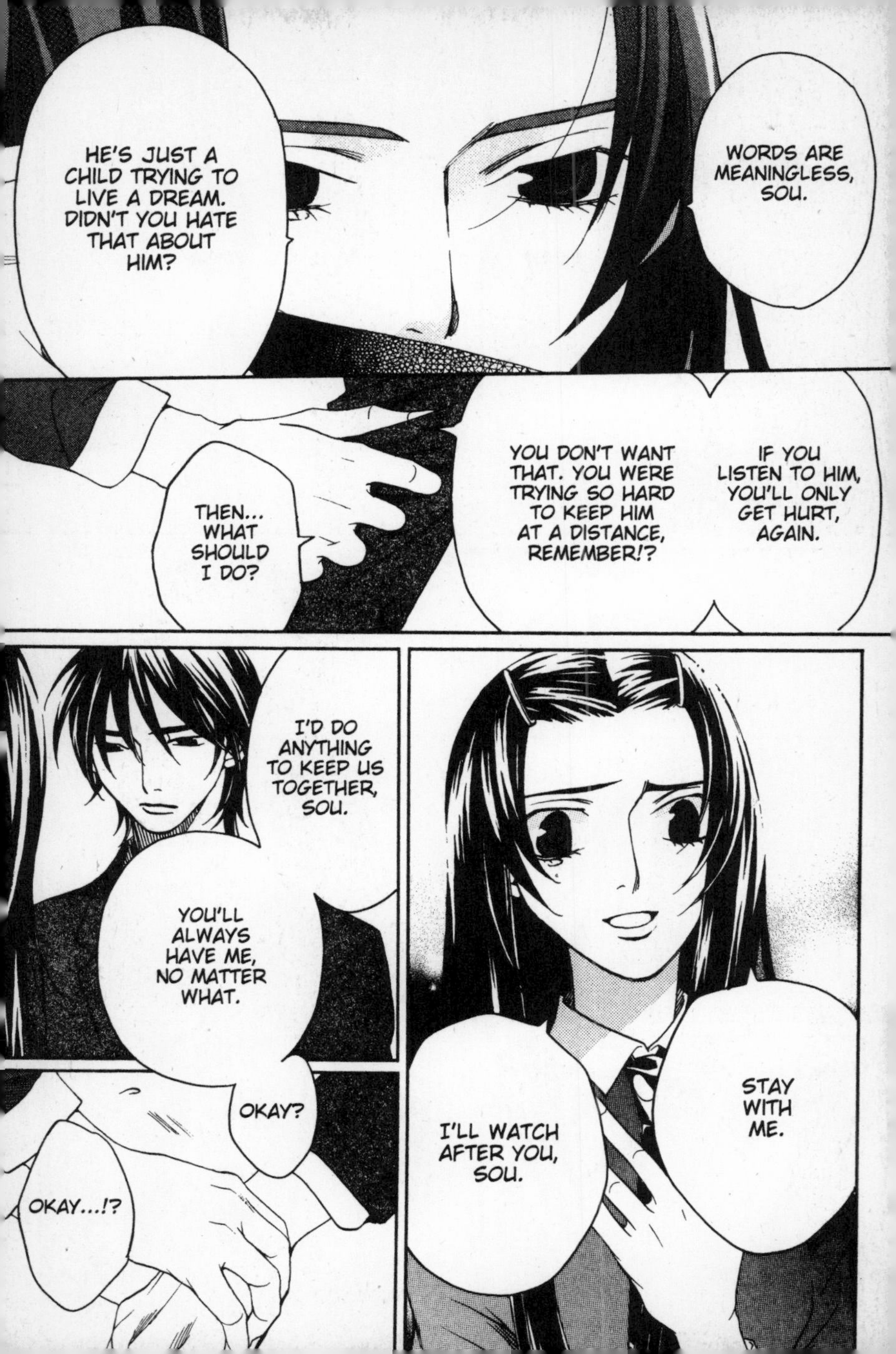
WORDS ARE MEANINGLESS, SOU.
HE'S JUST A CHILD TRYING TO LIVE A DREAM. DIDN'T YOU HATE THAT ABOUT HIM?
IF YOU LISTEN TO HIM, YOU'LL ONLY GET HURT, AGAIN.
YOU DON'T WANT THAT. YOU WERE TRYING SO HARD TO KEEP HIM AT A DISTANCE, REMEMBER!?
THEN... WHAT SHOULD I DO?
STAY WITH ME.
I'LL WATCH AFTER YOU, SOU.
I'D DO ANYTHING TO KEEP US TOGETHER, SOU.
YOU'LL ALWAYS HAVE ME, NO MATTER WHAT.
OKAY?
OKAY...!?

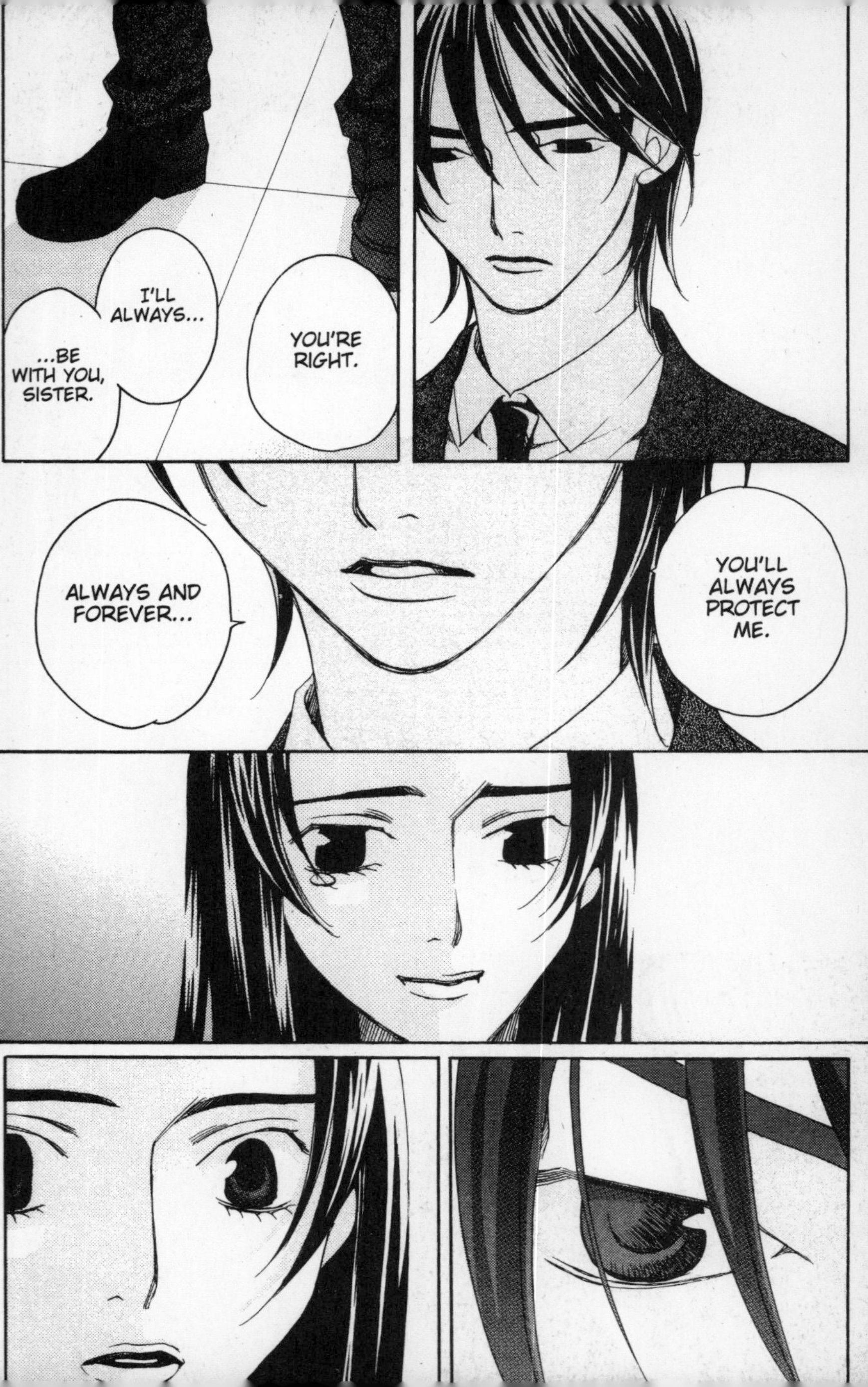
YOU'RE RIGHT.
I'LL ALWAYS...
...BE WITH YOU, SISTER.
YOU'LL ALWAYS PROTECT ME.
ALWAYS AND FOREVER...

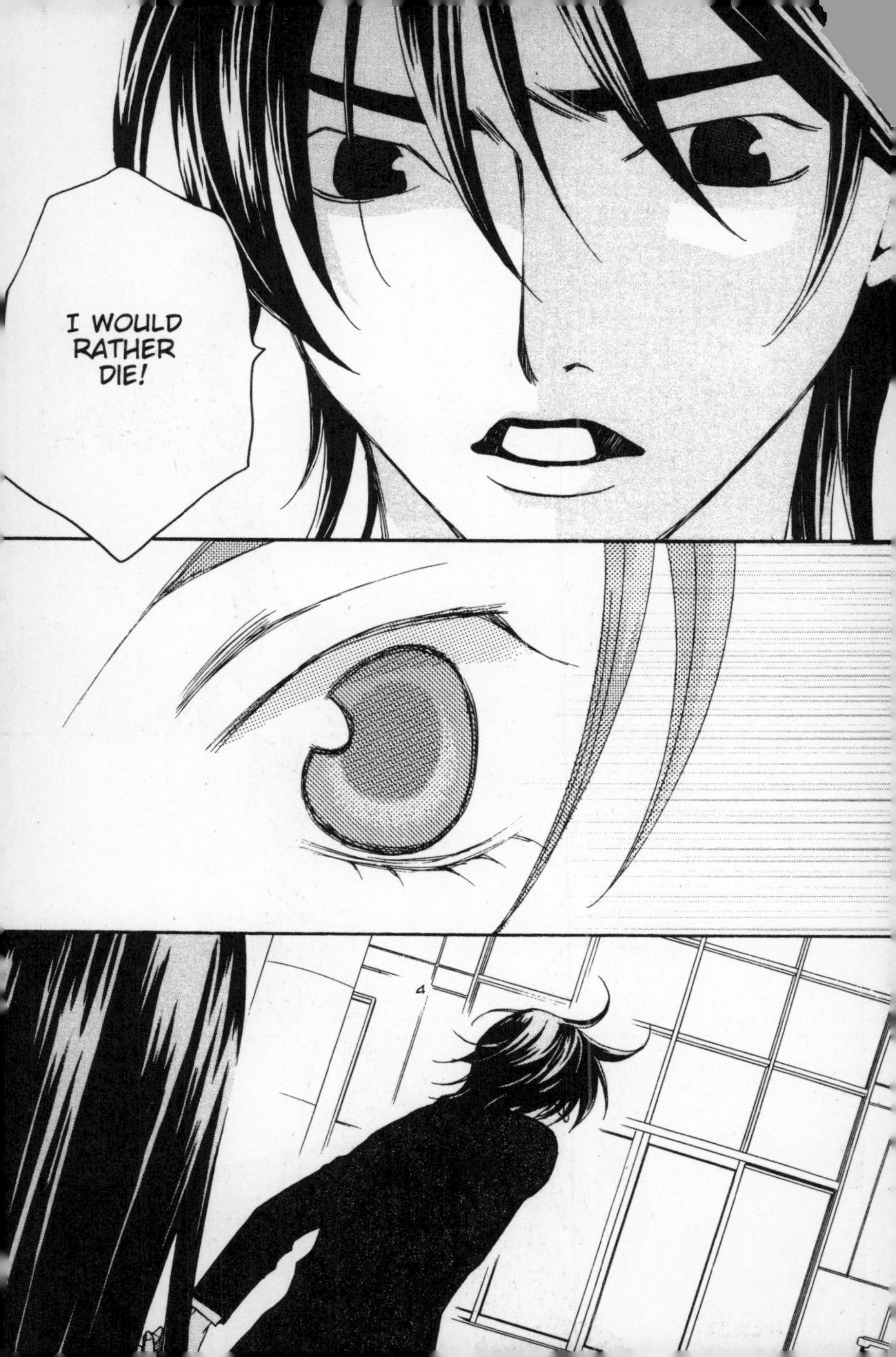
I WOULD RATHER DIE!

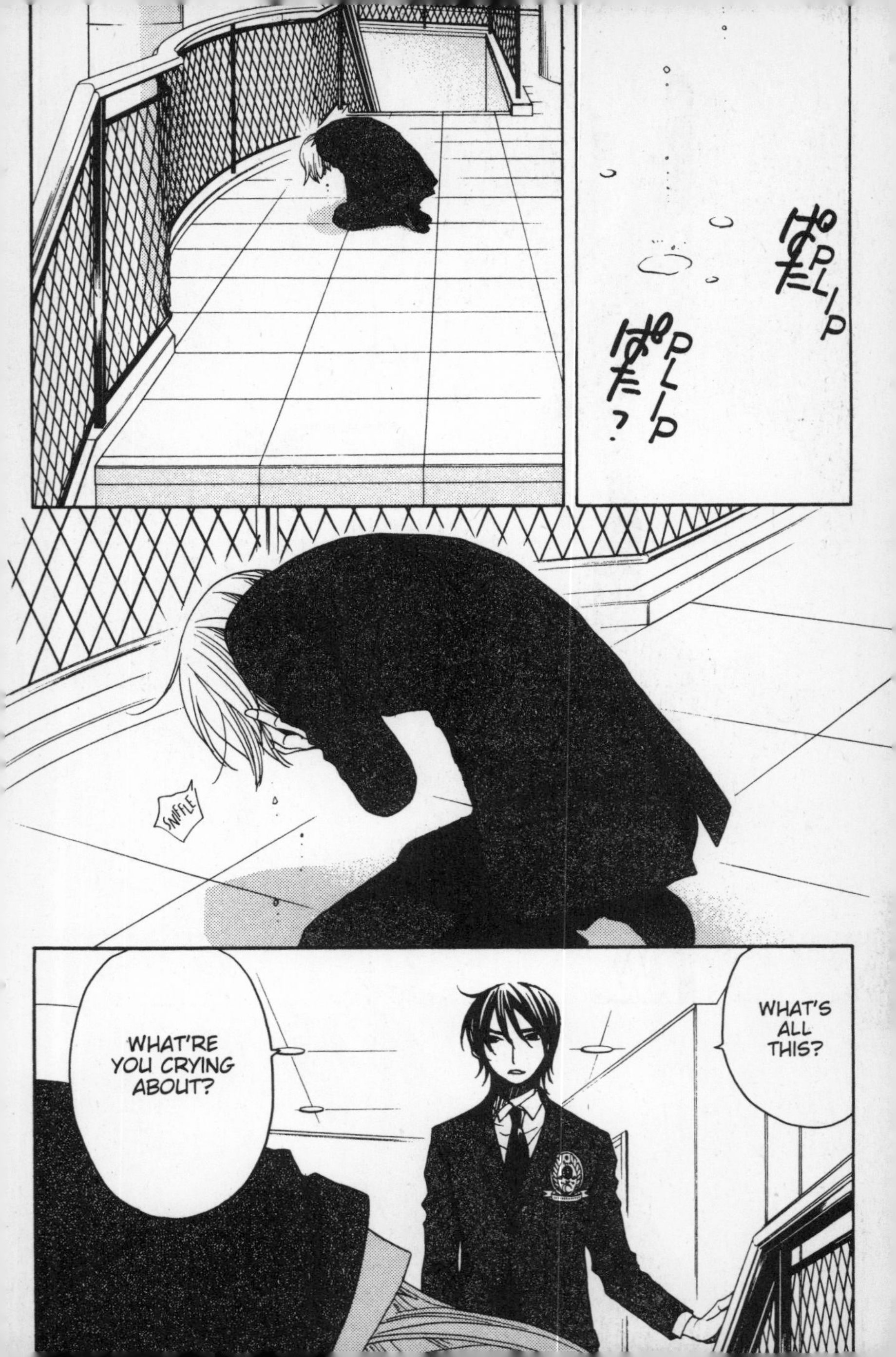
PLIP
PLIP
SNIFFLE
WHAT'S ALL THIS?
WHAT'RE YOU CRYING ABOUT?

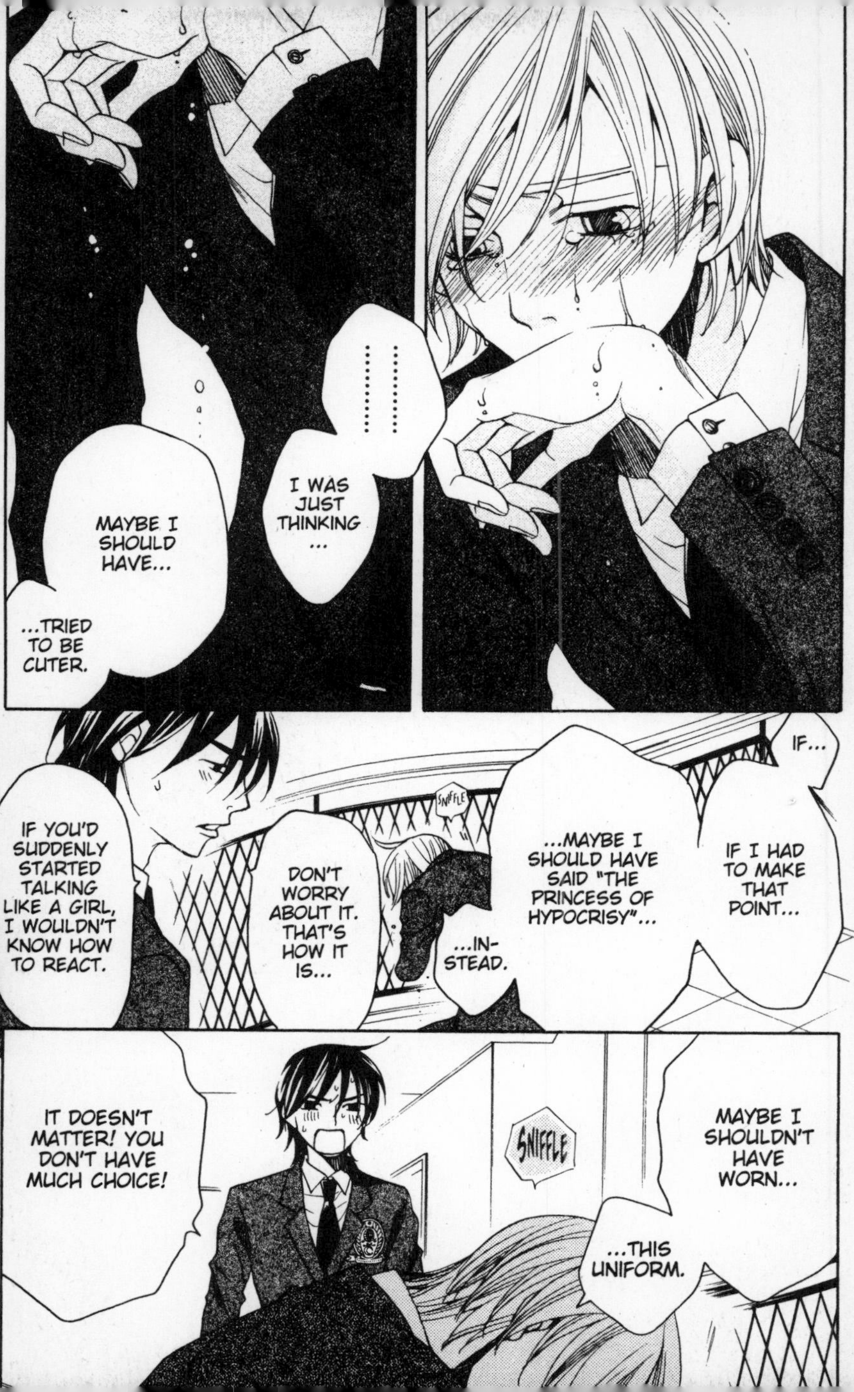

......
I WAS JUST THINKING...
MAYBE I SHOULD HAVE...
...TRIED TO BE CUTER.
IF...
IF I HAD TO MAKE THAT POINT...
...MAYBE I SHOULD HAVE SAID "THE PRINCESS OF HYPOCRISY"...
...IN-STEAD.
SNIFFLE
DON'T WORRY ABOUT IT. THAT'S HOW IT IS...
IF YOU'D SUDDENLY STARTED TALKING LIKE A GIRL, I WOULDN'T KNOW HOW TO REACT.
MAYBE I SHOULDN'T HAVE WORN...
...THIS UNIFORM.
SNIFFLE
IT DOESN'T MATTER! YOU DON'T HAVE MUCH CHOICE!

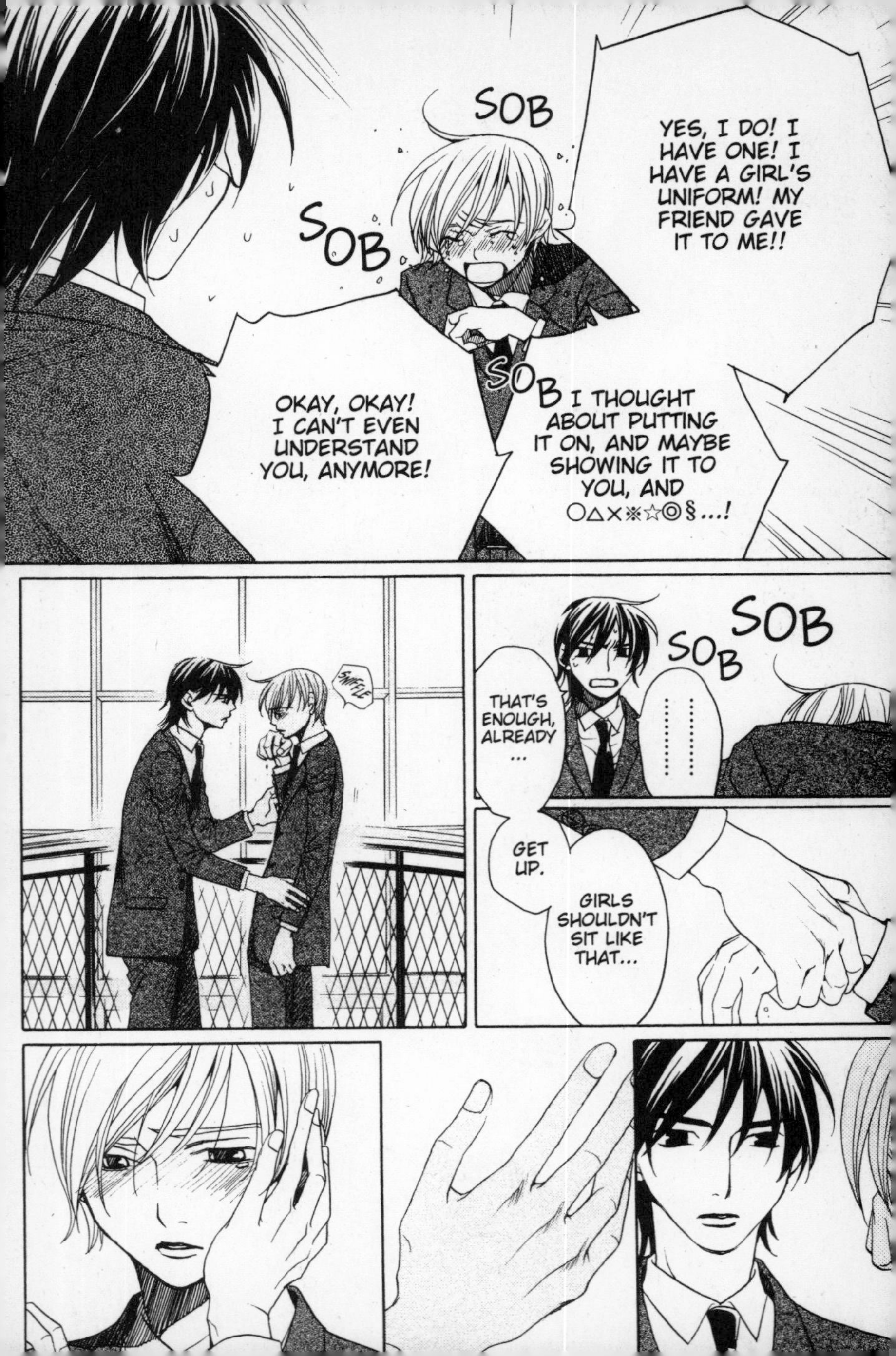
SOB
YES, I DO! I HAVE ONE! I HAVE A GIRL'S UNIFORM! MY FRIEND GAVE IT TO ME!!
SOB
SOB
I THOUGHT ABOUT PUTTING IT ON, AND MAYBE SHOWING IT TO YOU, AND ○△×※☆◎§...!
OKAY, OKAY! I CAN'T EVEN UNDERSTAND YOU, ANYMORE!
SOB
SOB
......
THAT'S ENOUGH, ALREADY ...
GET UP.
GIRLS SHOULDN'T SIT LIKE THAT...
SNIFFLE

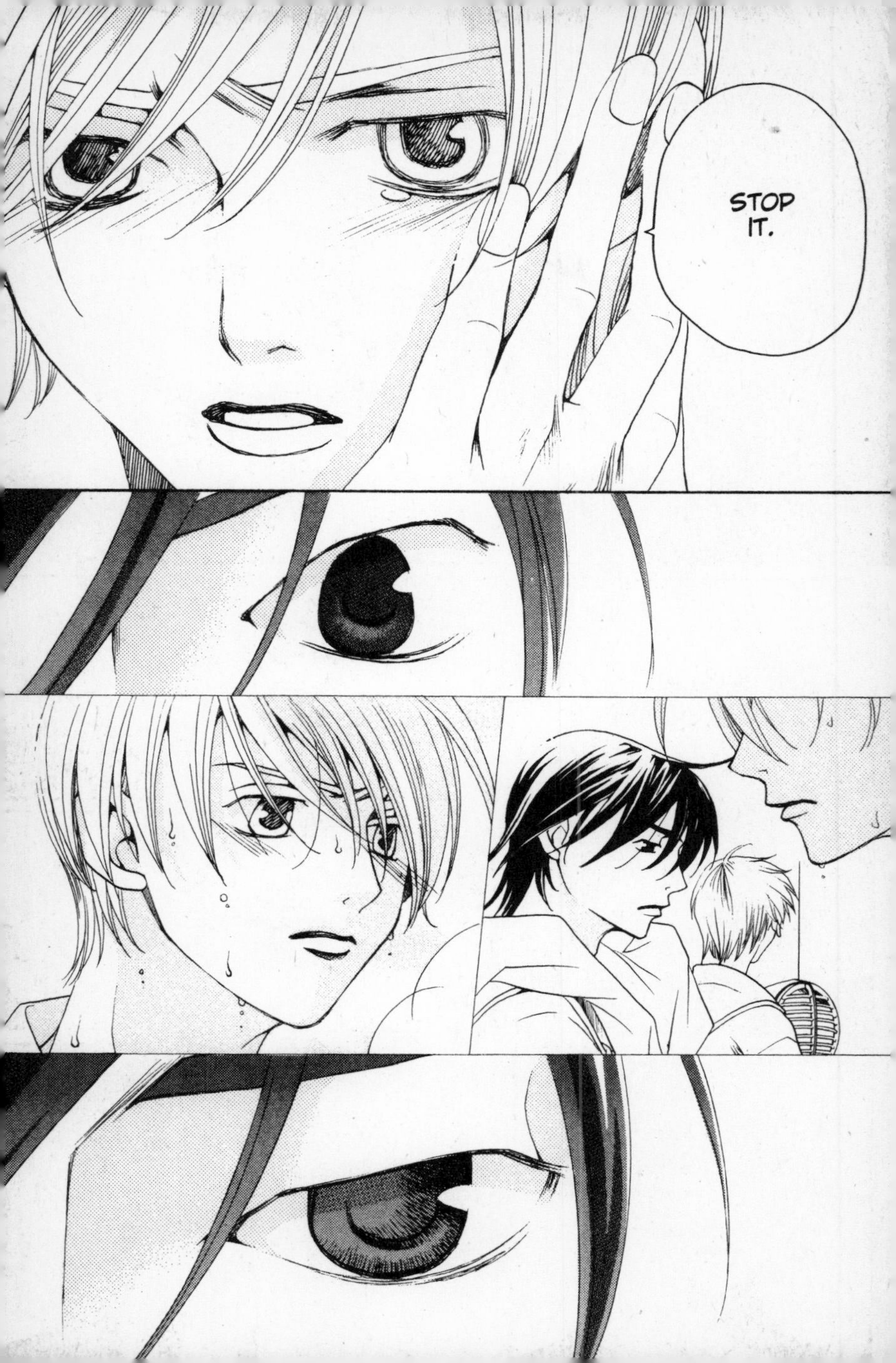
STOP IT.

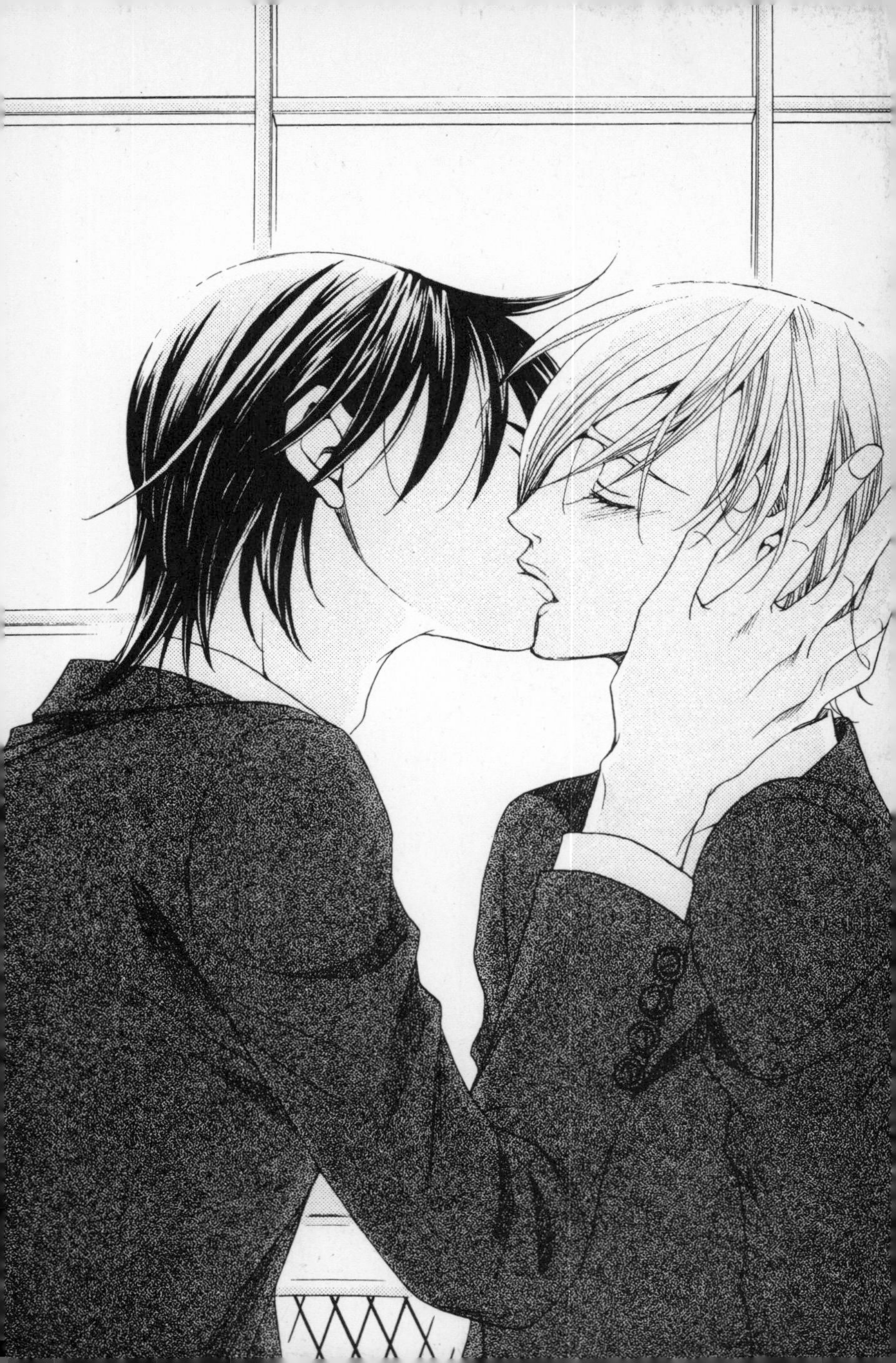

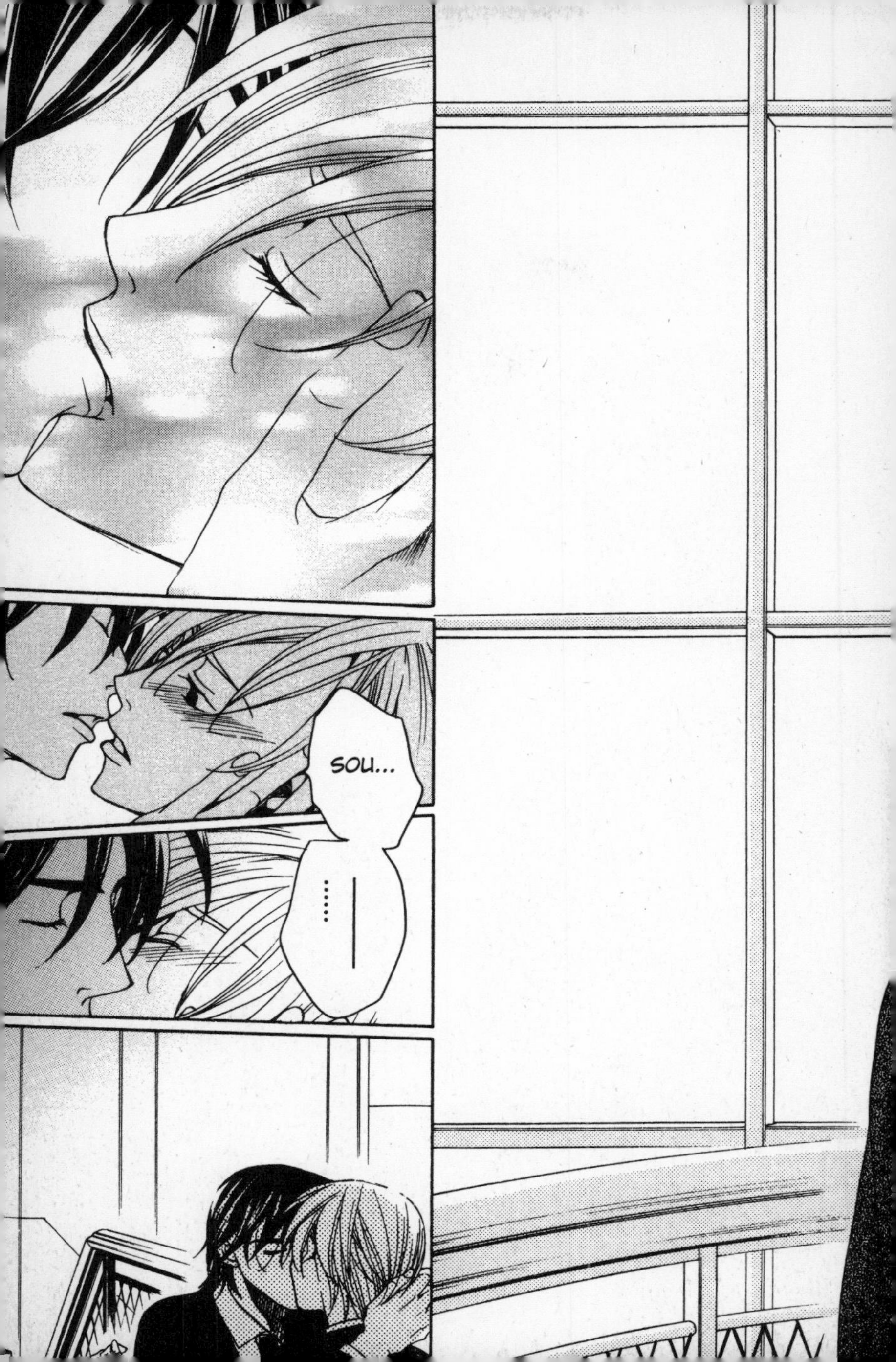
SOU...
......!

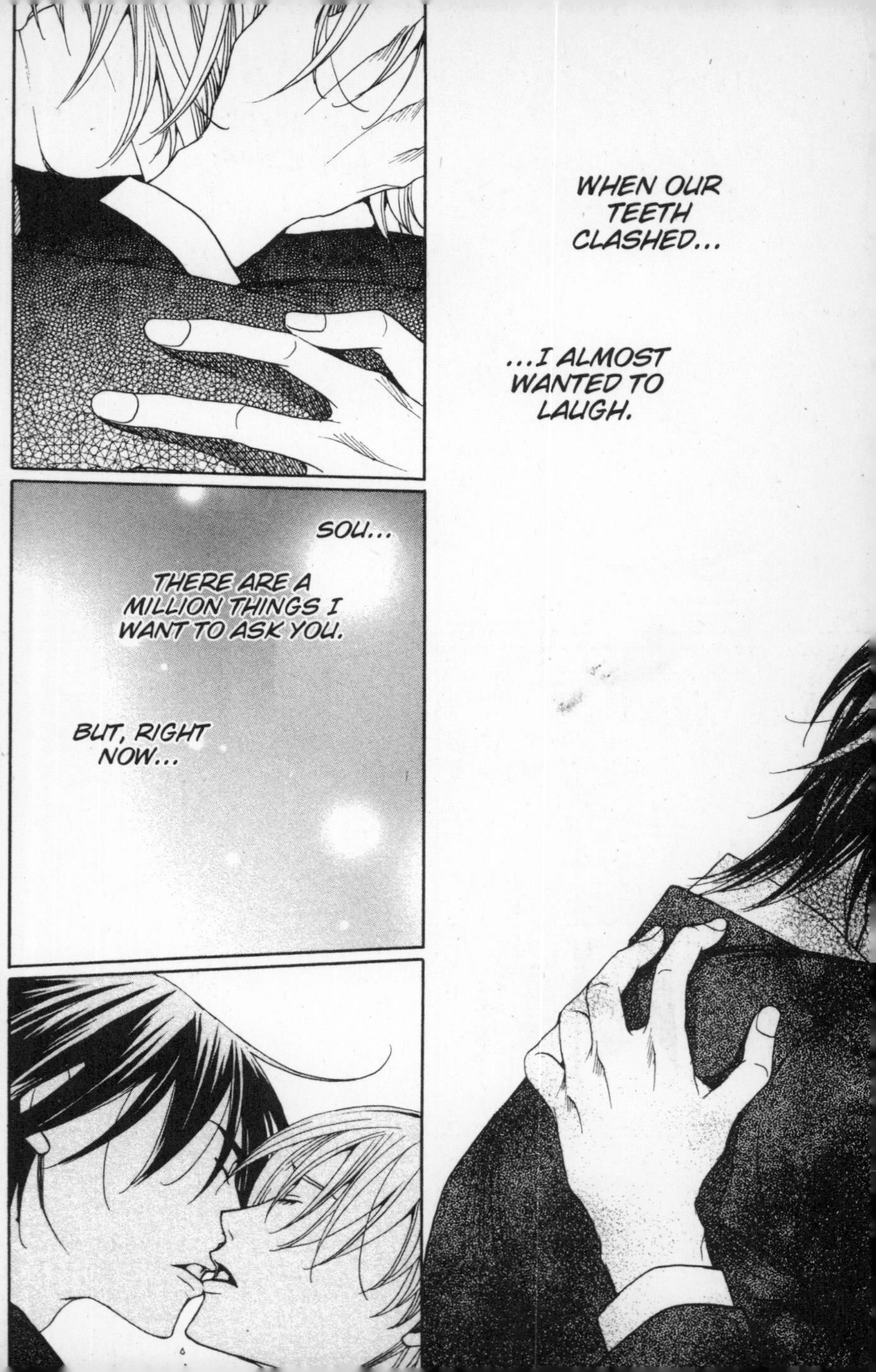
WHEN OUR TEETH CLASHED...
...I ALMOST WANTED TO LAUGH.
SOU...
THERE ARE A MILLION THINGS I WANT TO ASK YOU.
BUT, RIGHT NOW...

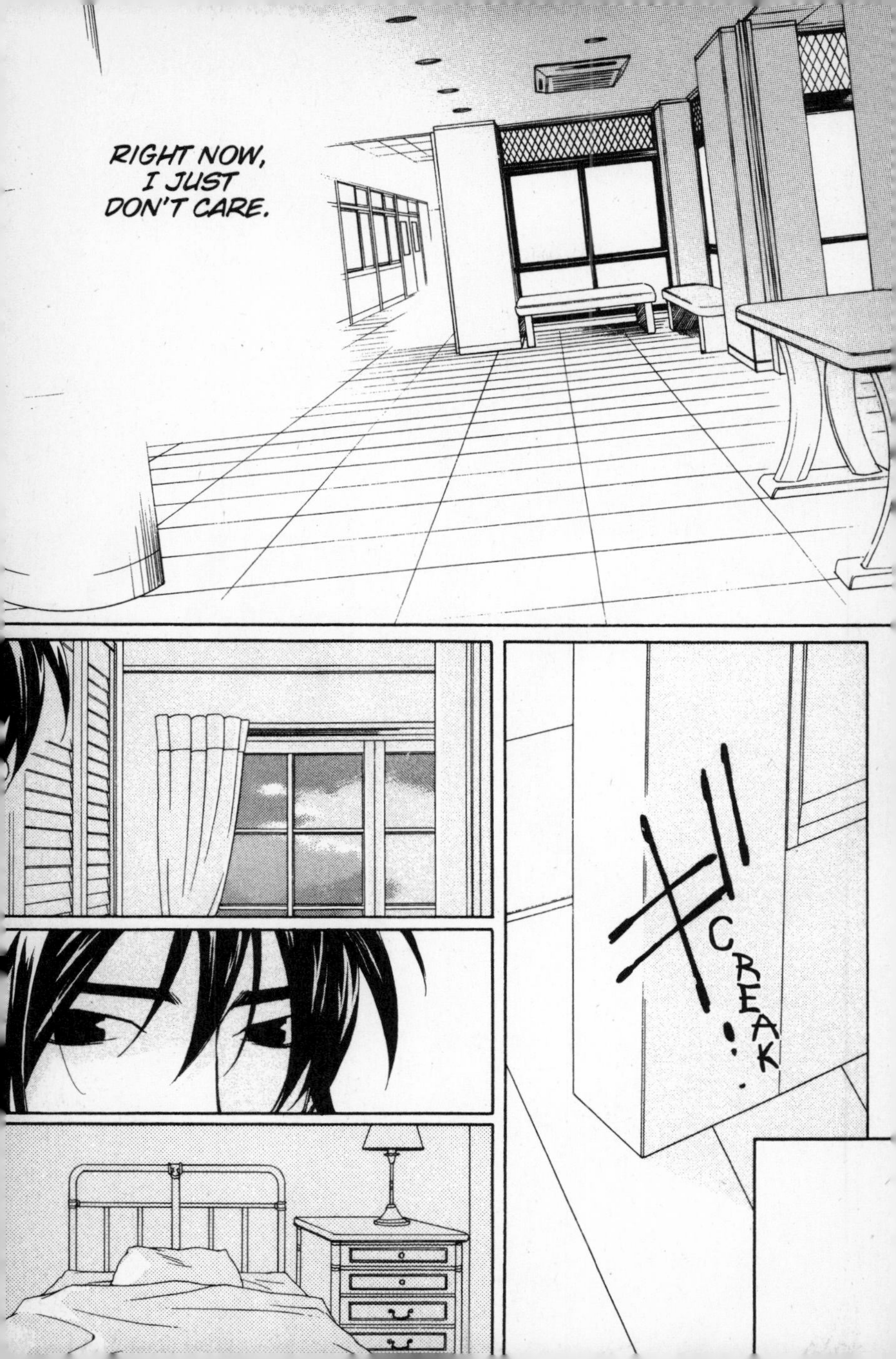
RIGHT NOW, I JUST DON'T CARE.
CREAK...

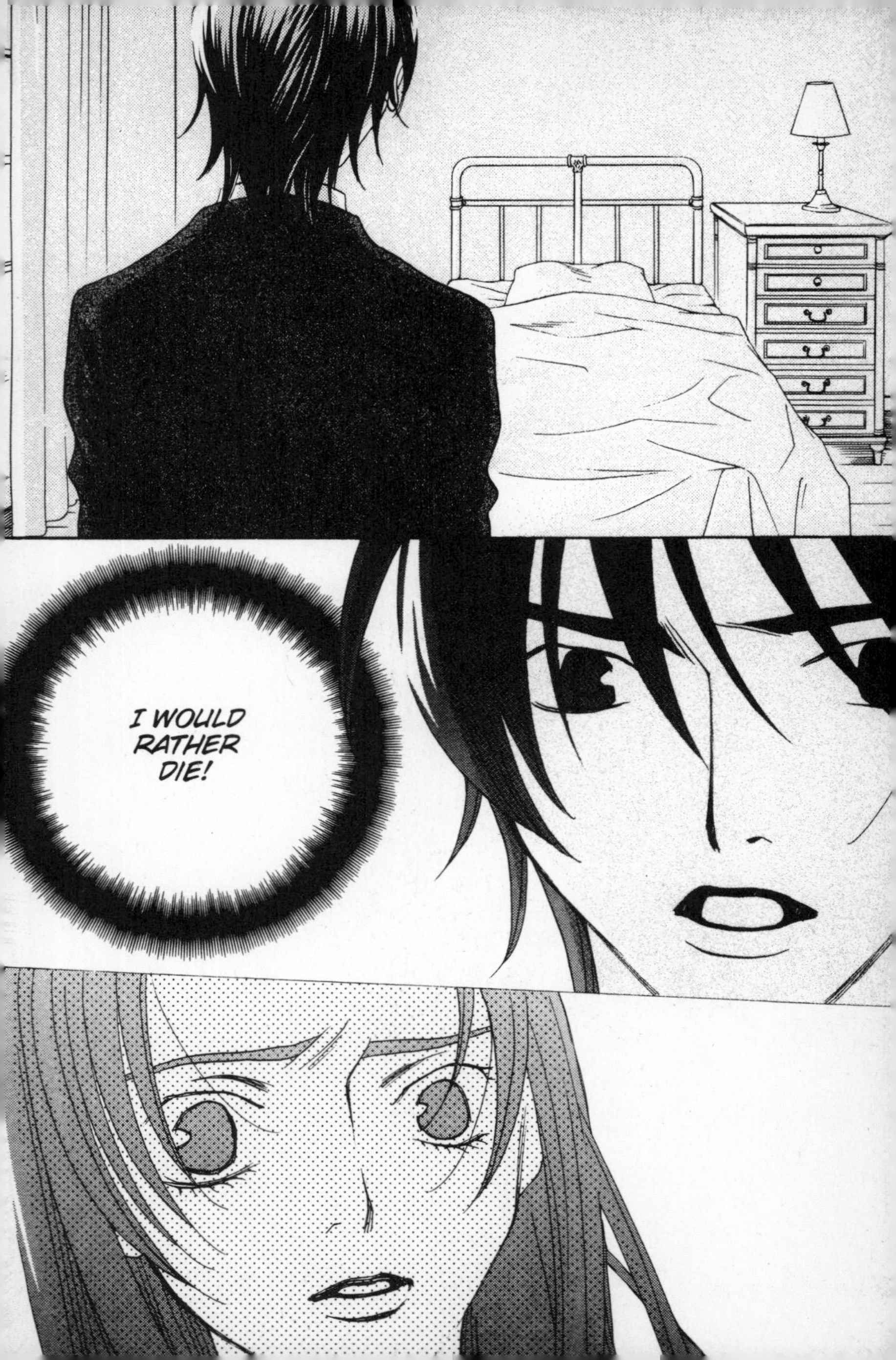
I WOULD RATHER DIE!

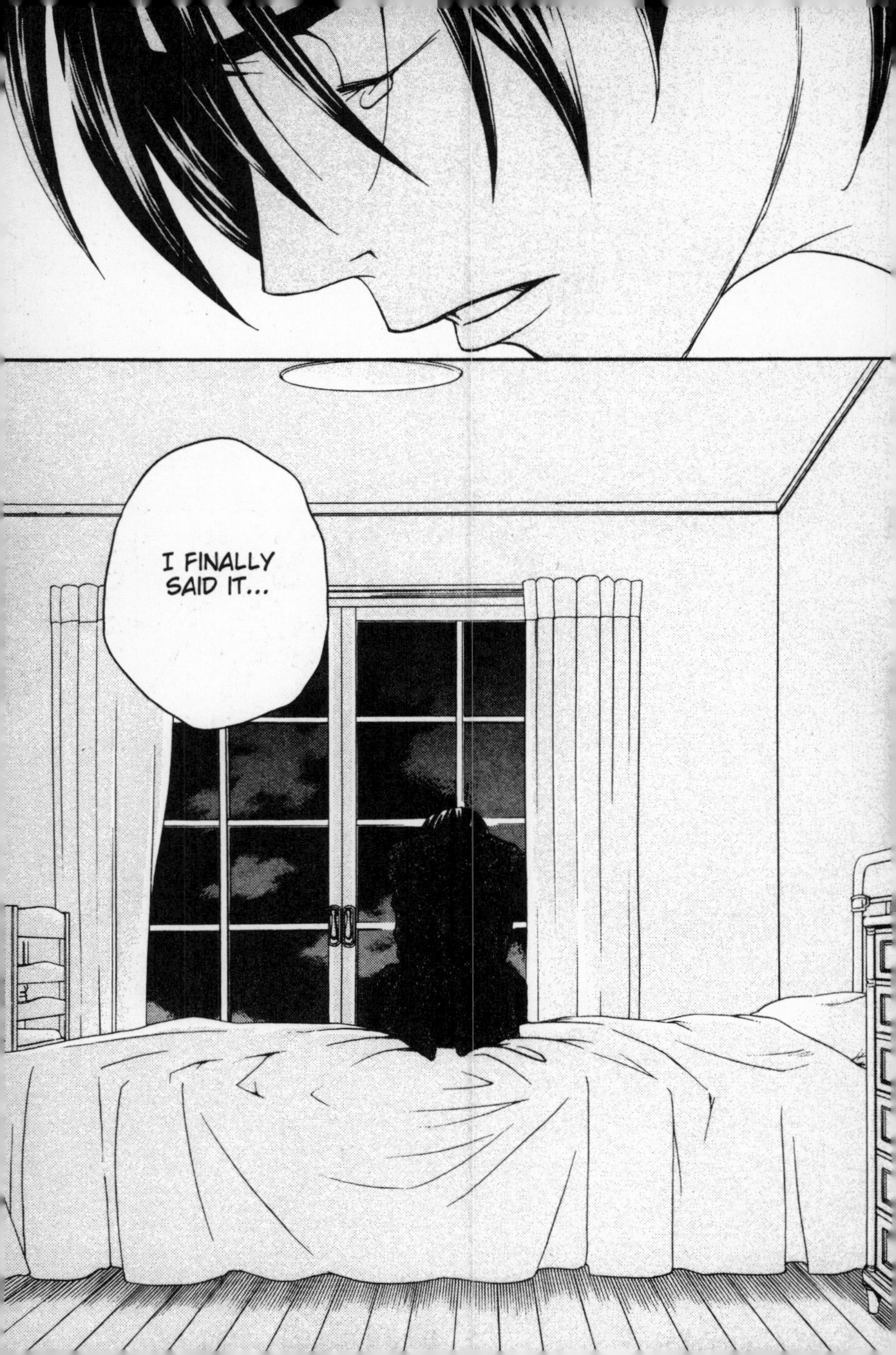
I FINALLY SAID IT...

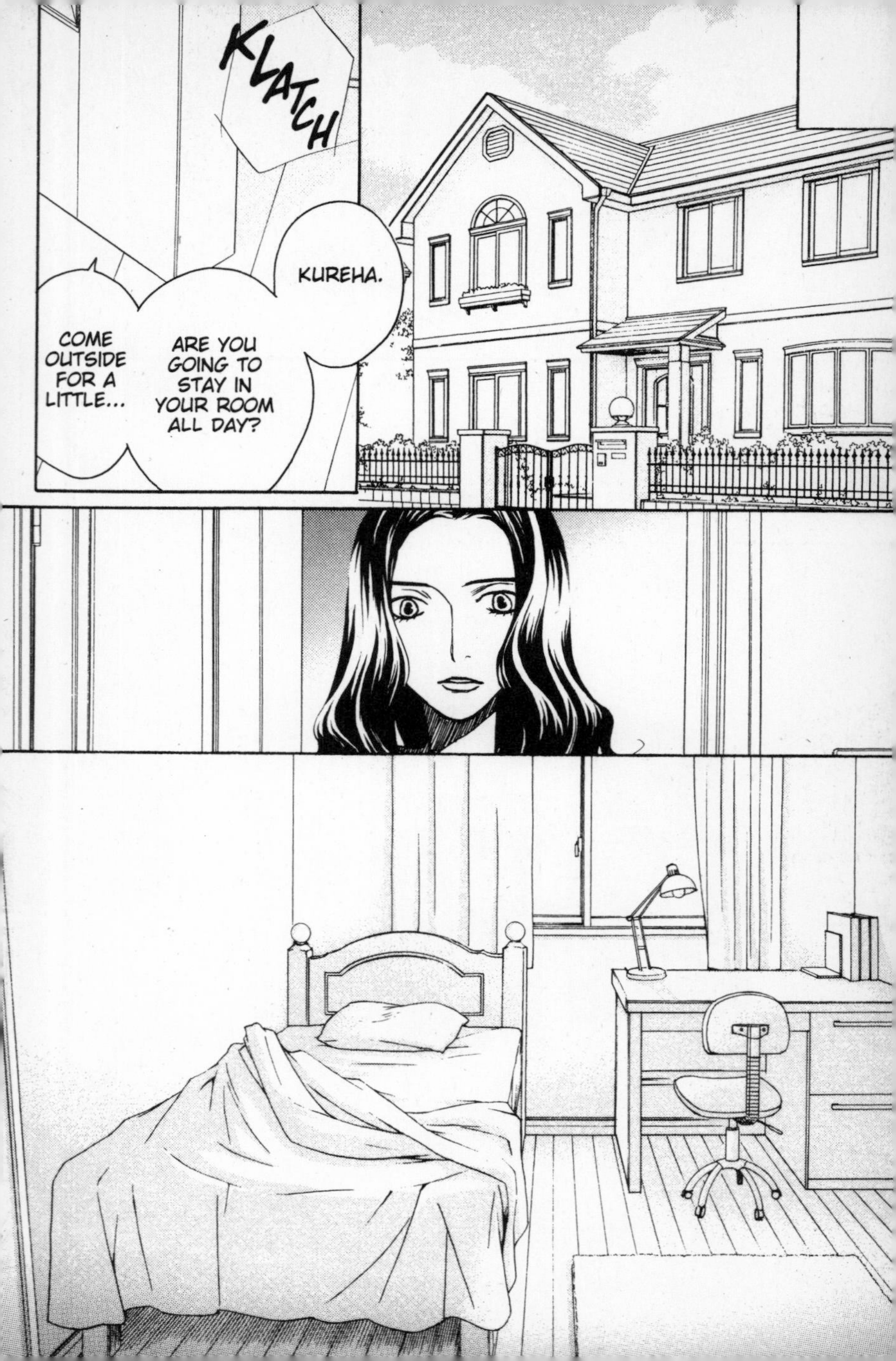
KUREHA.
ARE YOU GOING TO STAY IN YOUR ROOM ALL DAY?
COME OUTSIDE FOR A LITTLE...
KLATCH

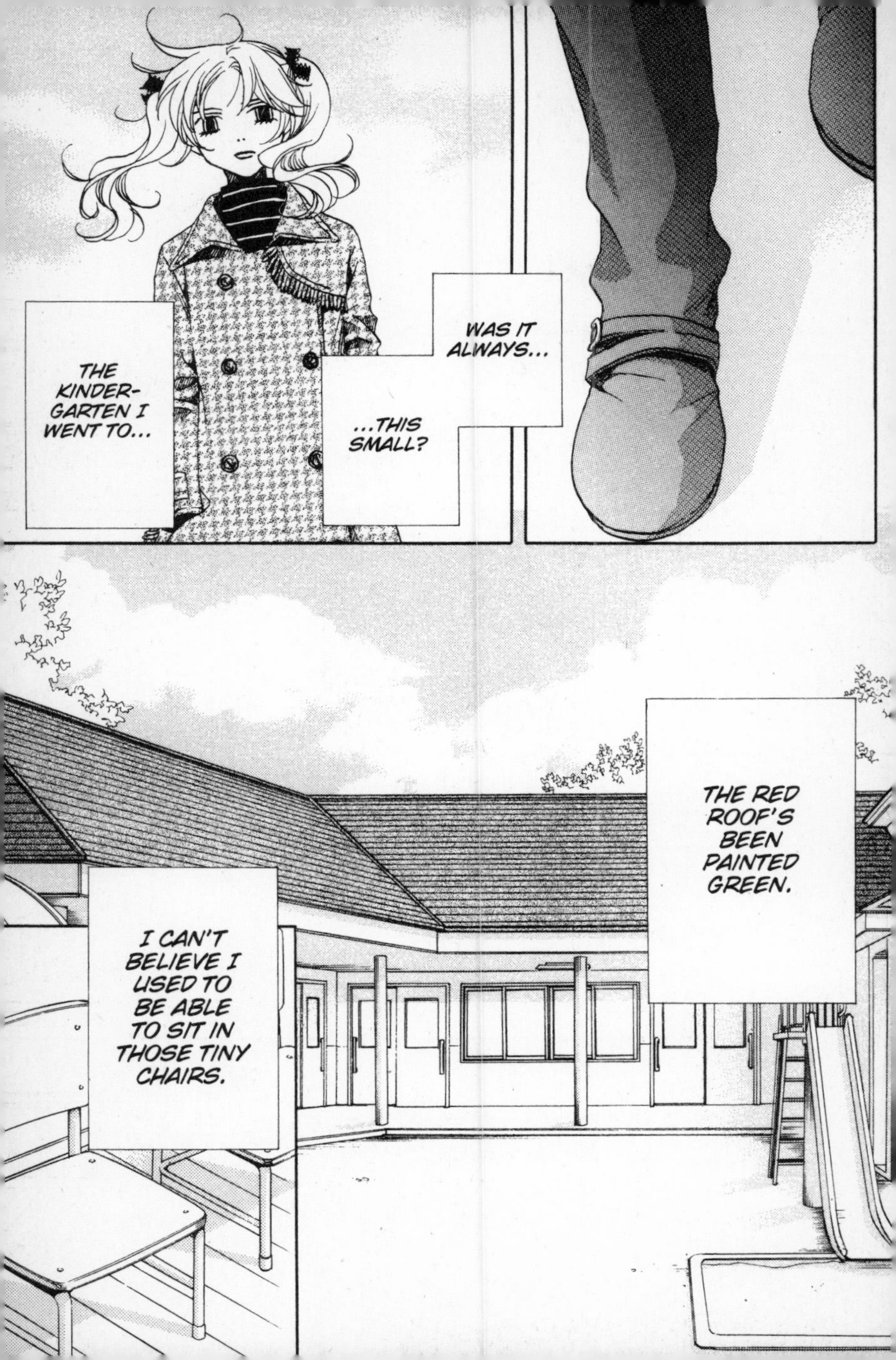
WAS IT ALWAYS...
...THIS SMALL?
THE KINDER-GARTEN I WENT TO...
THE RED ROOF'S BEEN PAINTED GREEN.
I CAN'T BELIEVE I USED TO BE ABLE TO SIT IN THOSE TINY CHAIRS.

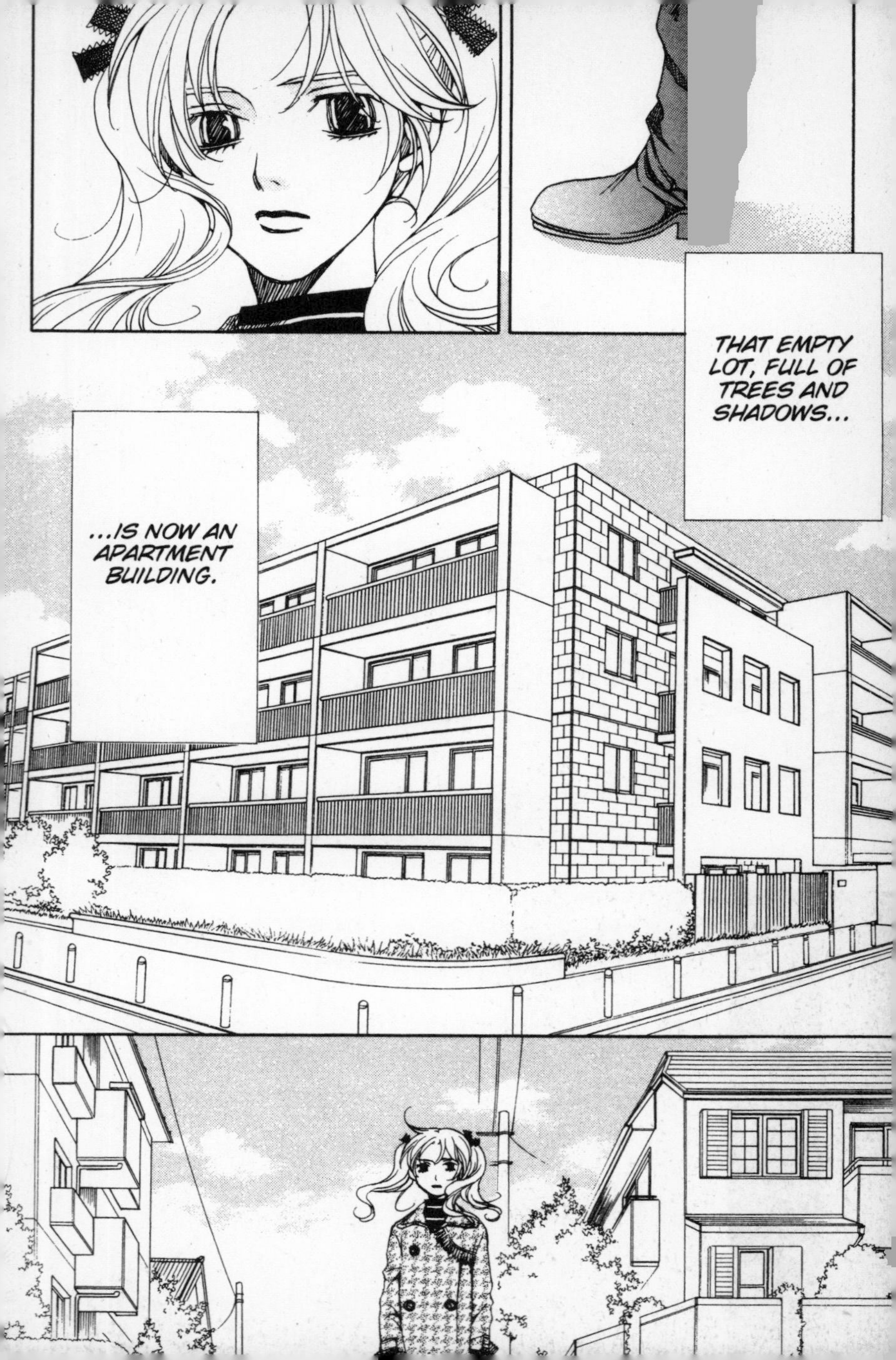
THAT EMPTY LOT, FULL OF TREES AND SHADOWS...
...IS NOW AN APARTMENT BUILDING.

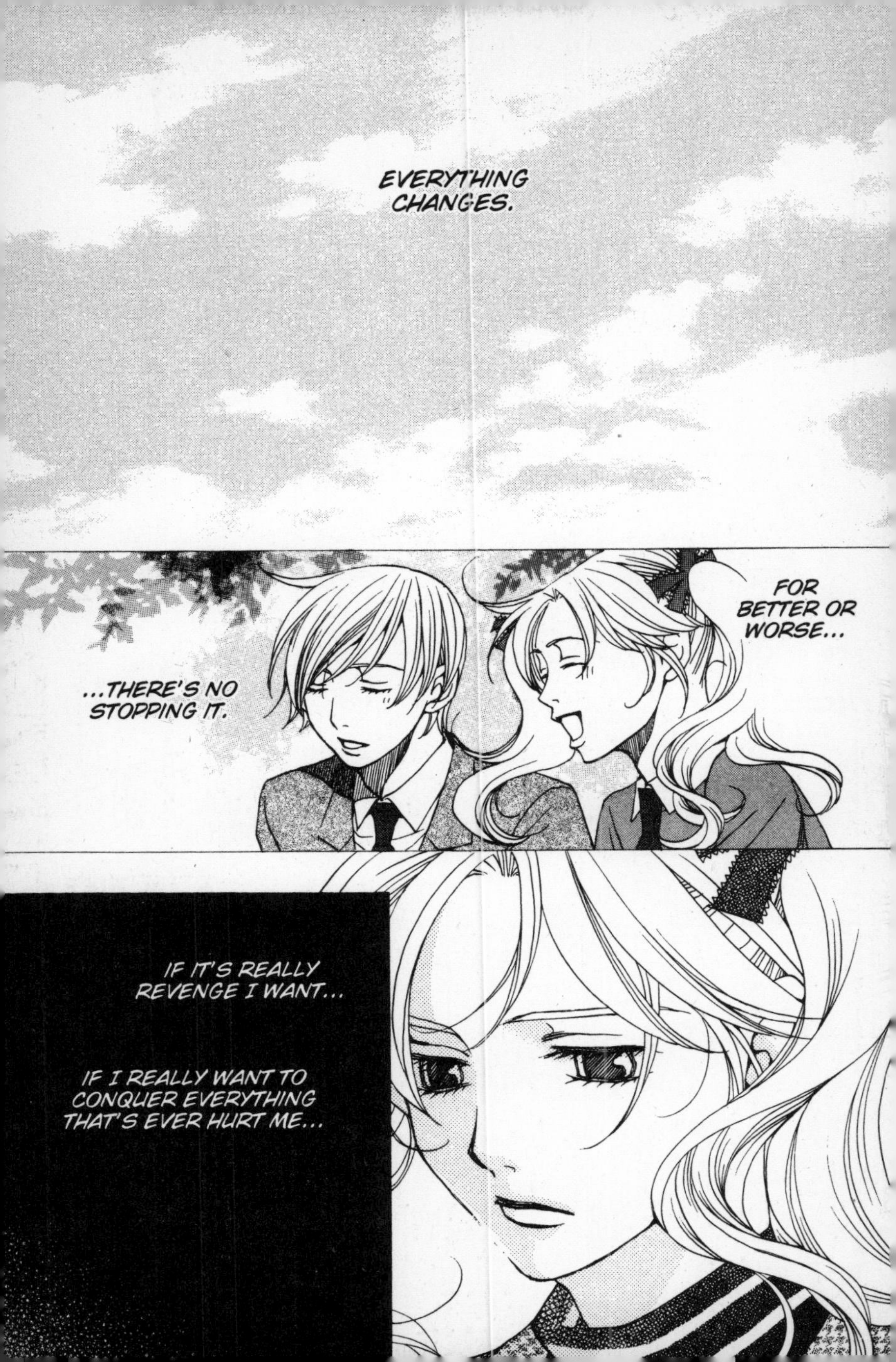
EVERYTHING CHANGES.
FOR BETTER OR WORSE...
...THERE'S NO STOPPING IT.
IF IT'S REALLY REVENGE I WANT...
IF I REALLY WANT TO CONQUER EVERYTHING THAT'S EVER HURT ME...

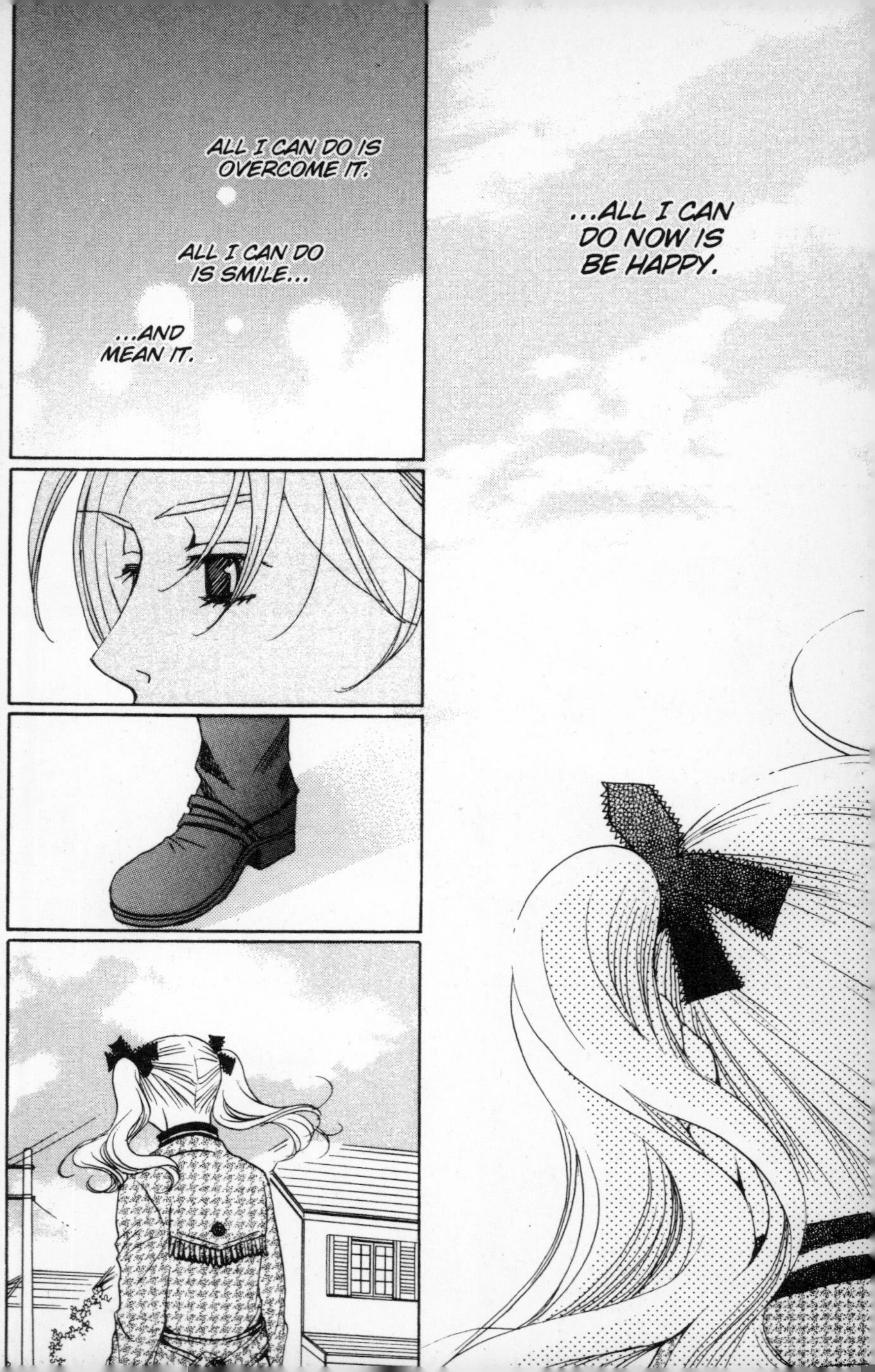
...ALL I CAN DO NOW IS BE HAPPY.
ALL I CAN DO IS OVERCOME IT.
ALL I CAN DO IS SMILE...
...AND MEAN IT.

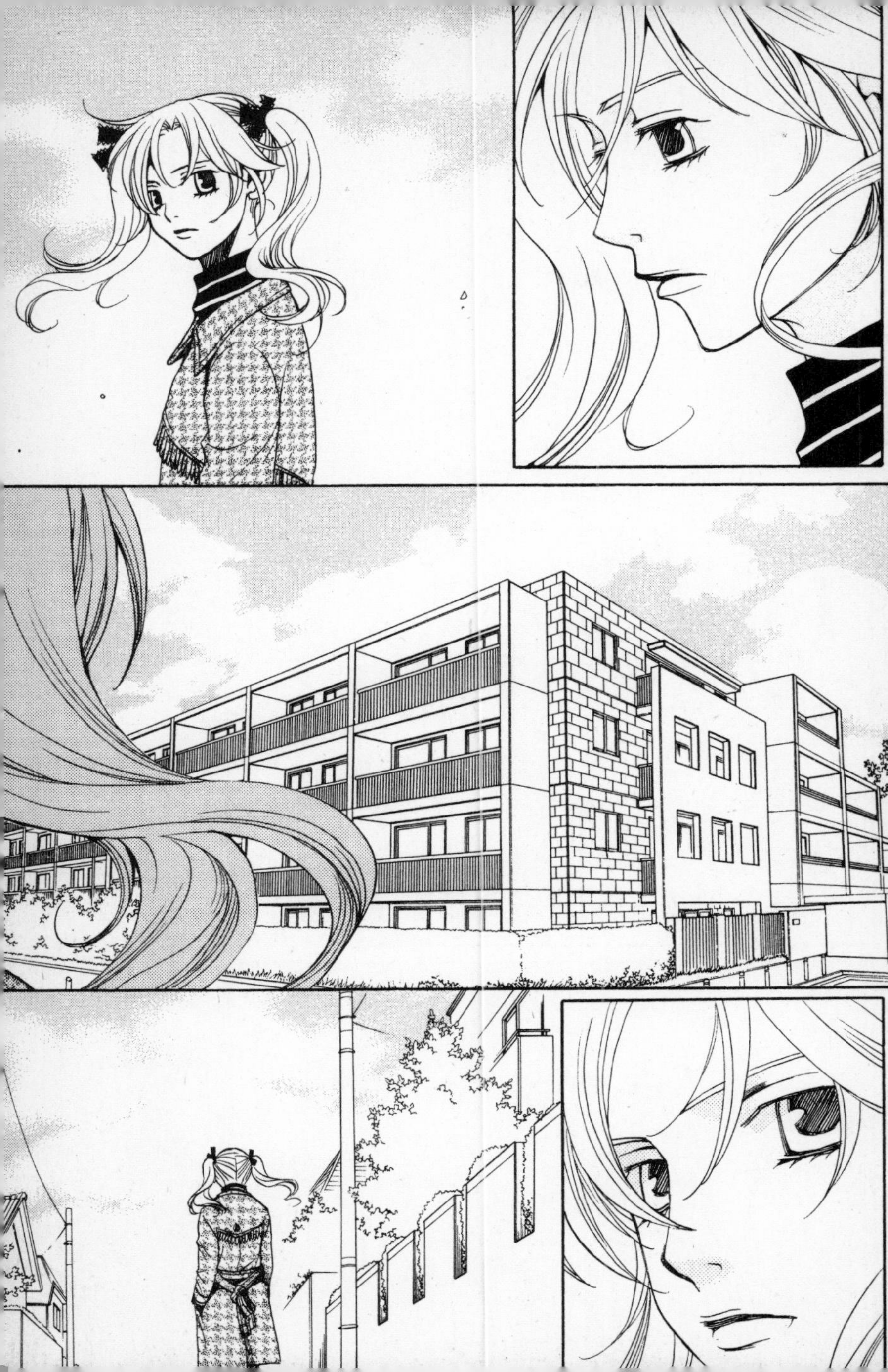

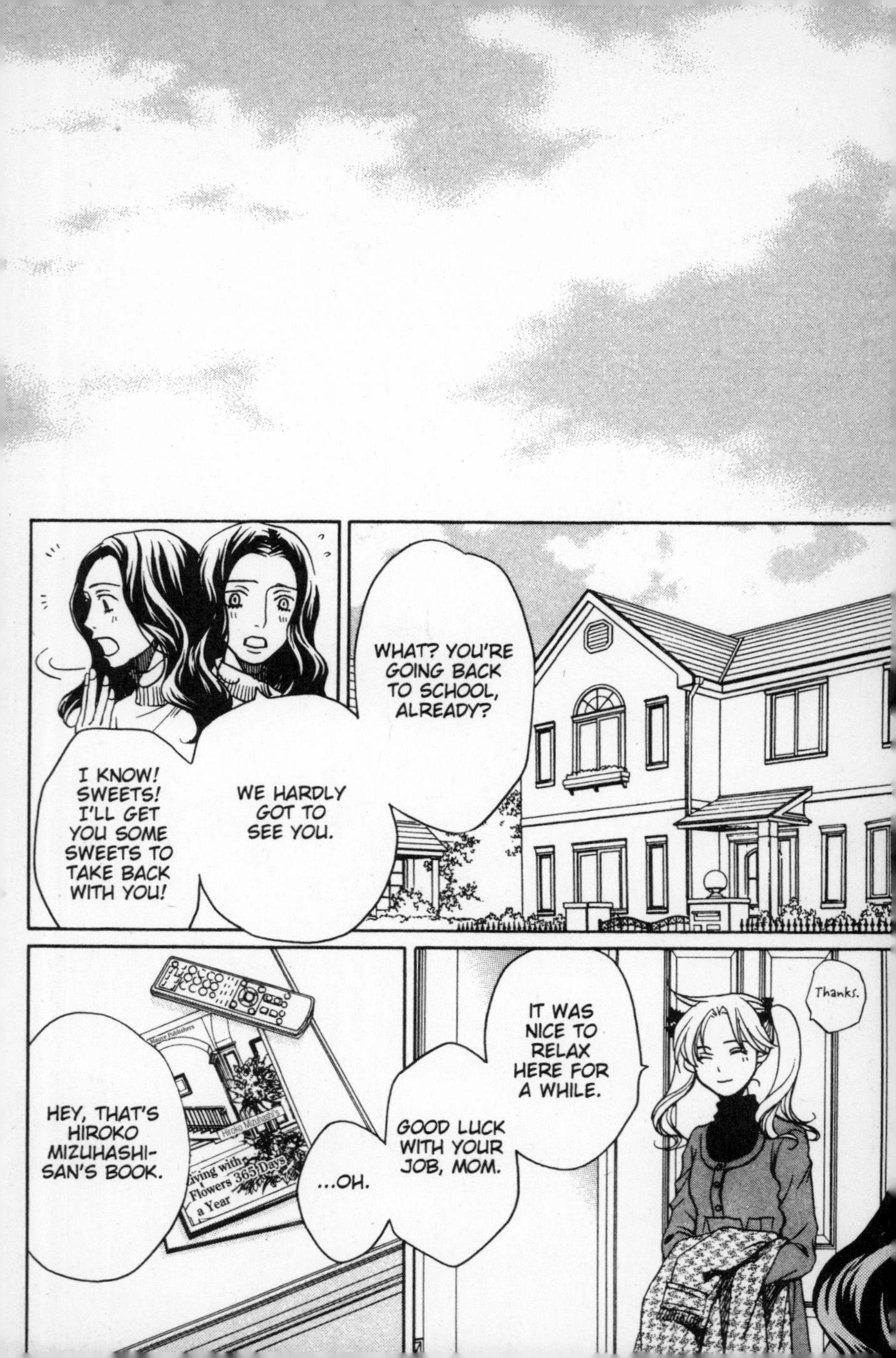
WHAT? YOU'RE GOING BACK TO SCHOOL, ALREADY?
WE HARDLY GOT TO SEE YOU.
I KNOW! SWEETS! I'LL GET YOU SOME SWEETS TO TAKE BACK WITH YOU!
Thanks.
IT WAS NICE TO RELAX HERE FOR A WHILE.
GOOD LUCK WITH YOUR JOB, MOM.
...OH.
HEY, THAT'S HIROKO MIZUHASHI-SAN'S BOOK.

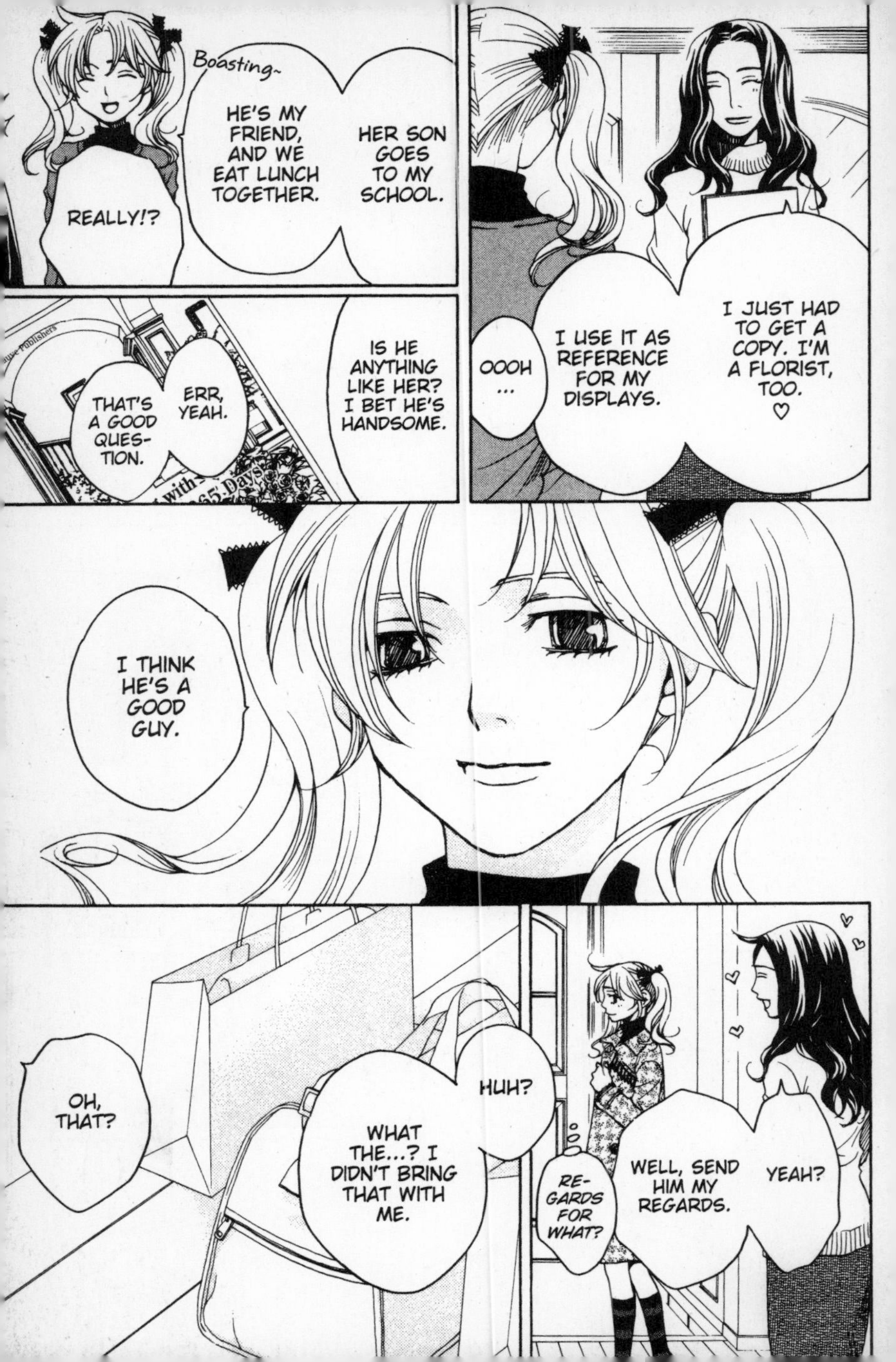
I JUST HAD TO GET A COPY. I'M A FLORIST, TOO. ♡
I USE IT AS REFERENCE FOR MY DISPLAYS.
OOOH ...
HER SON GOES TO MY SCHOOL.
HE'S MY FRIEND, AND WE EAT LUNCH TOGETHER.
Boasting~
REALLY!?
IS HE ANYTHING LIKE HER? I BET HE'S HANDSOME.
ERR, YEAH.
THAT'S A GOOD QUES-TION.
I THINK HE'S A GOOD GUY.
YEAH?
WELL, SEND HIM MY REGARDS.
RE-GARDS FOR WHAT?
HUH?
WHAT THE...? I DIDN'T BRING THAT WITH ME.
OH, THAT?

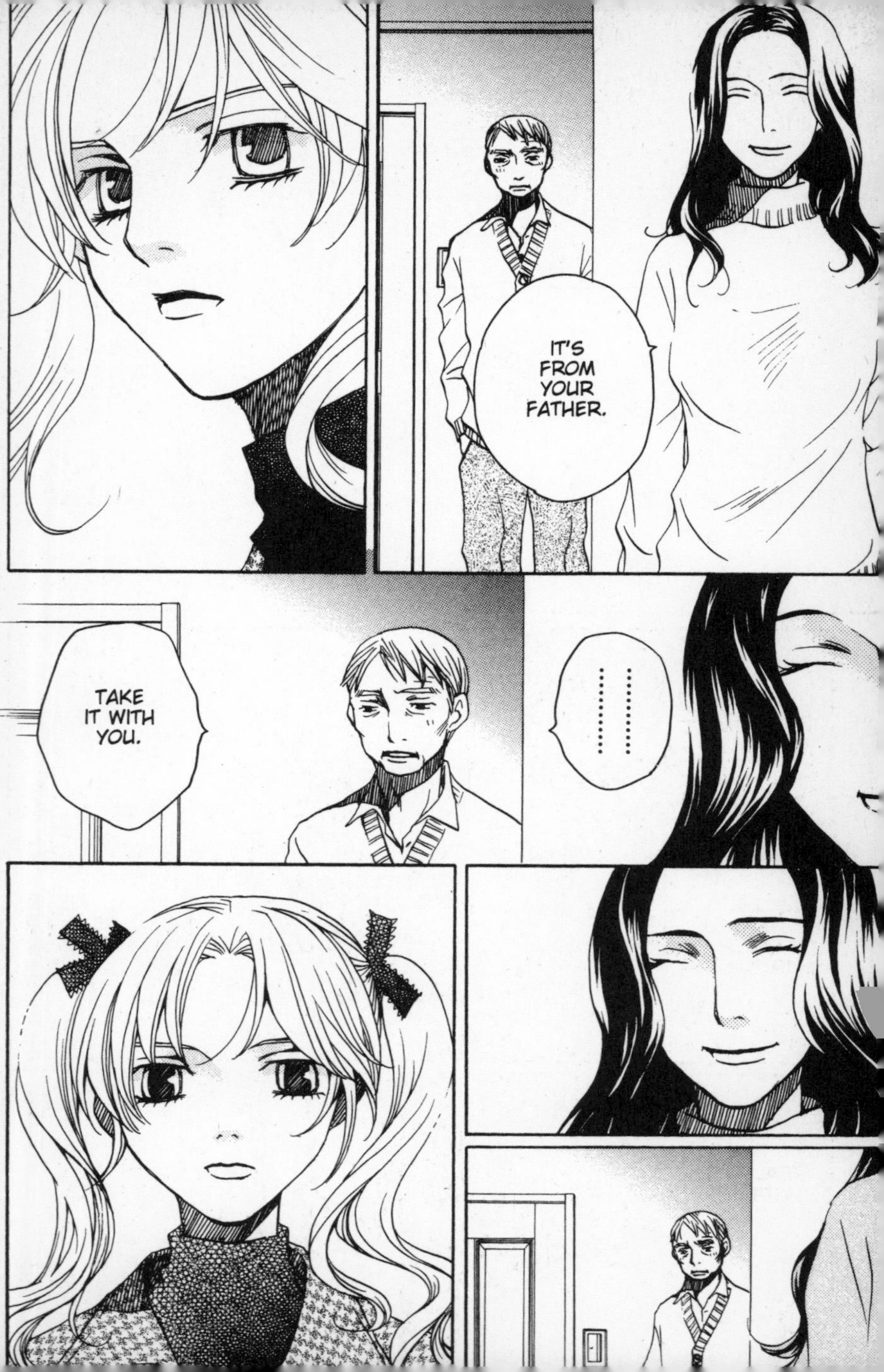
IT'S FROM YOUR FATHER.
TAKE IT WITH YOU.
......
......

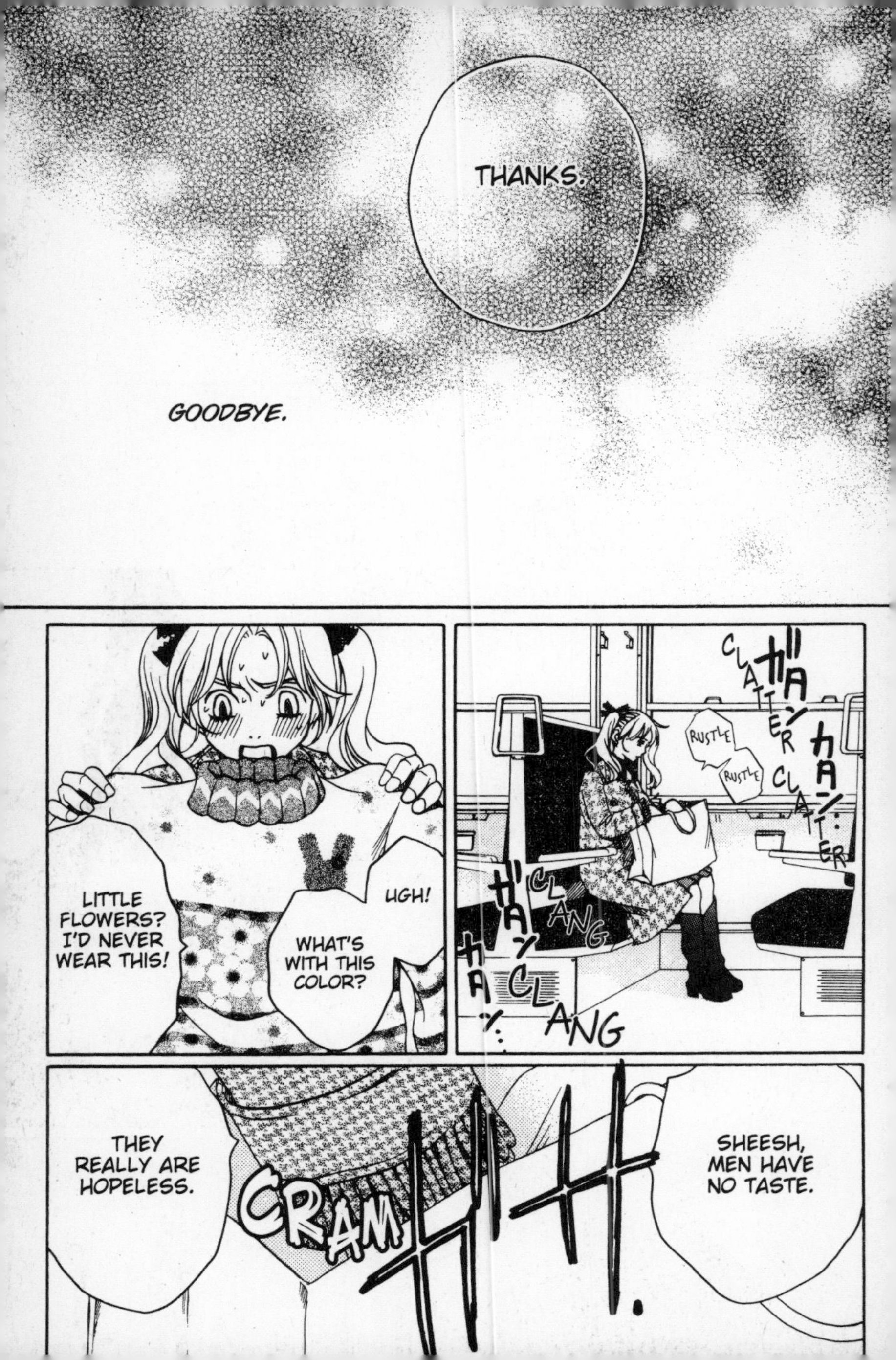
THANKS.
GOODBYE.
CLATTER CLATTER
RUSTLE
RUSTLE
CLANG CLANG
UGH!
WHAT'S WITH THIS COLOR?
LITTLE FLOWERS? I'D NEVER WEAR THIS!
SHEESH, MEN HAVE NO TASTE.
CRAM
THEY REALLY ARE HOPELESS.

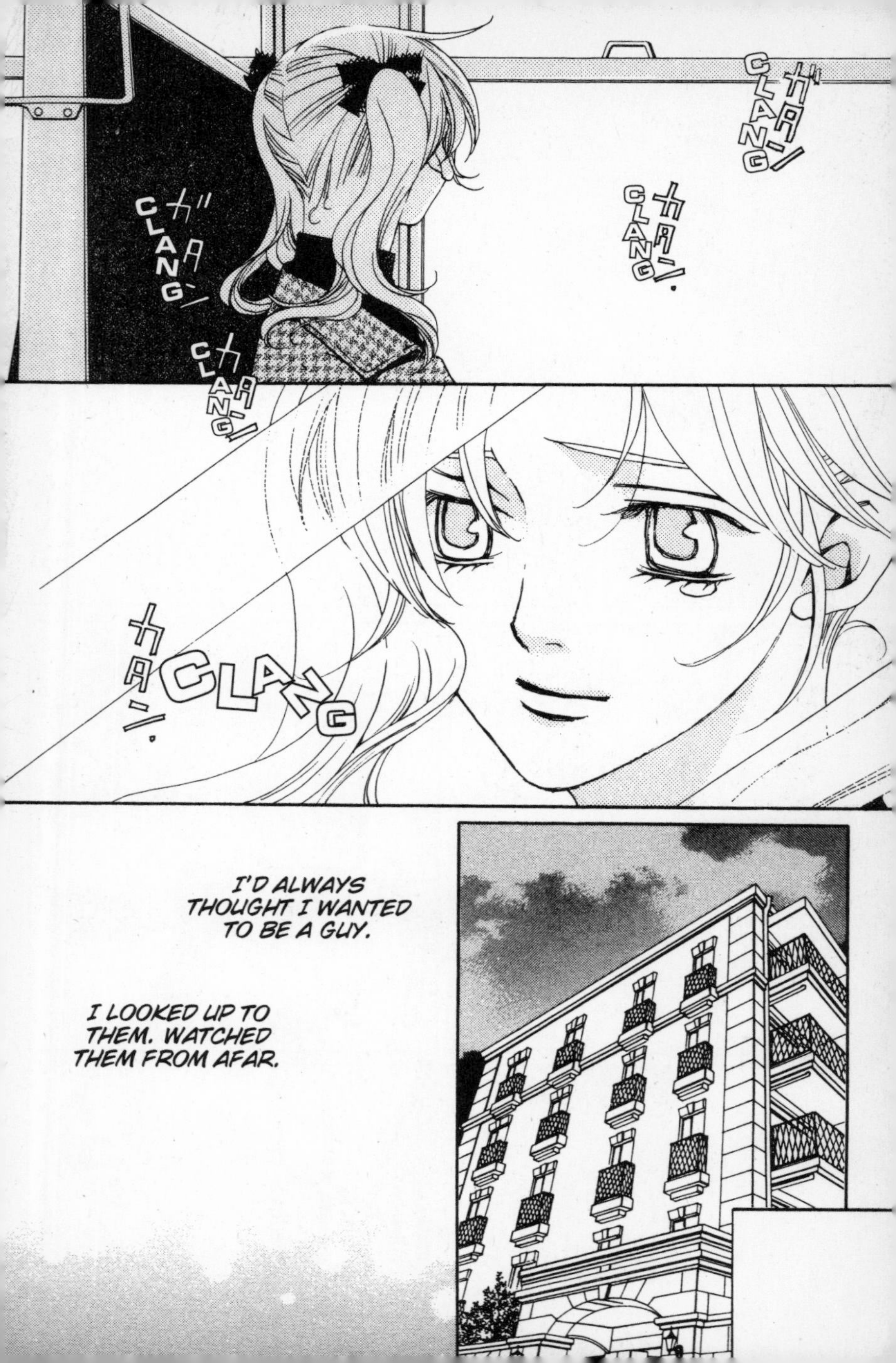
CLANG
CLANG
CLANG
CLANG
CLANG
I'D ALWAYS THOUGHT I WANTED TO BE A GUY.
I LOOKED UP TO THEM. WATCHED THEM FROM AFAR.

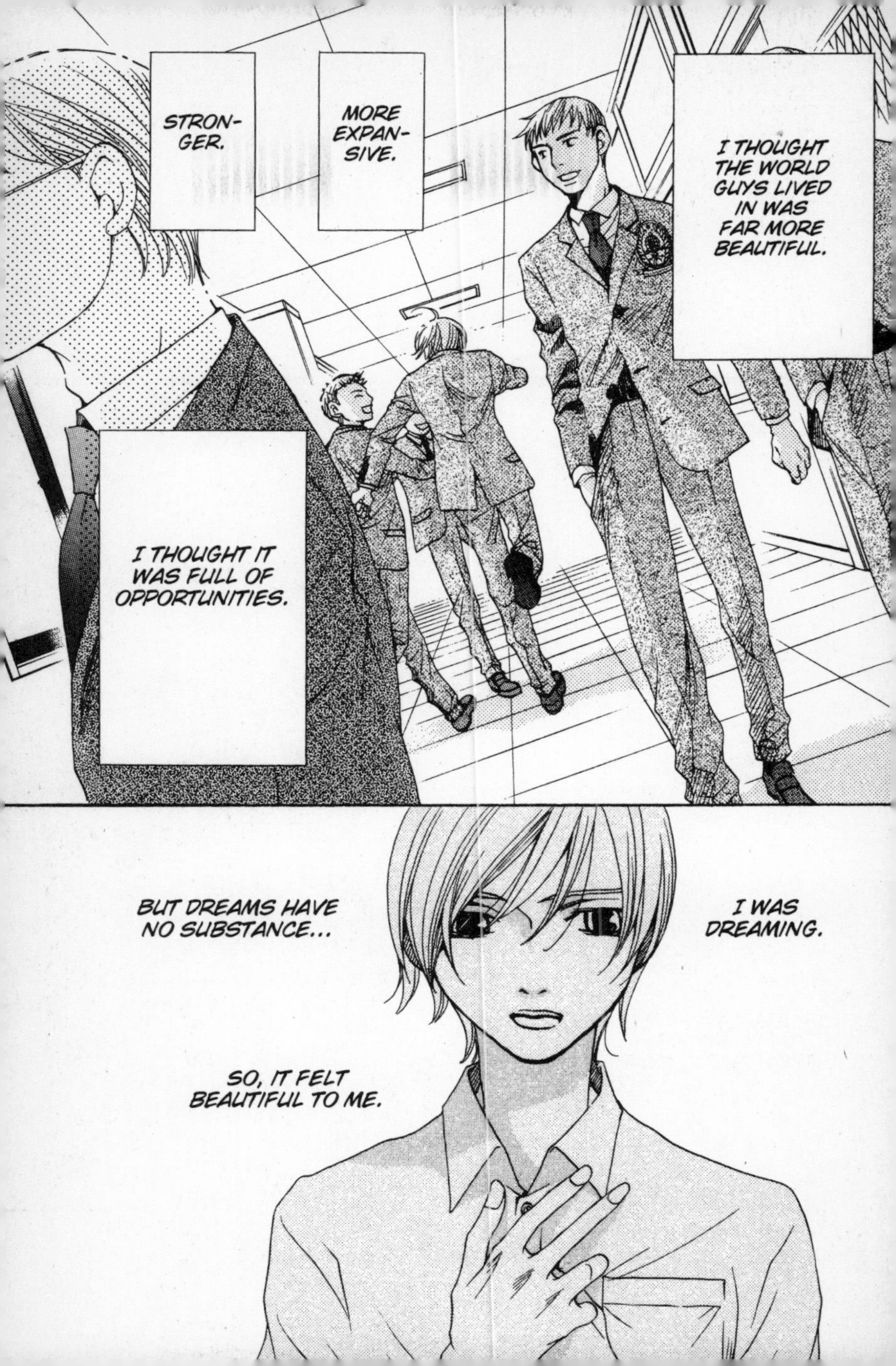
I THOUGHT THE WORLD GUYS LIVED IN WAS FAR MORE BEAUTIFUL.
MORE EXPAN-SIVE.
STRON-GER.
I THOUGHT IT WAS FULL OF OPPORTUNITIES.
I WAS DREAMING.
BUT DREAMS HAVE NO SUBSTANCE...
SO, IT FELT BEAUTIFUL TO ME.

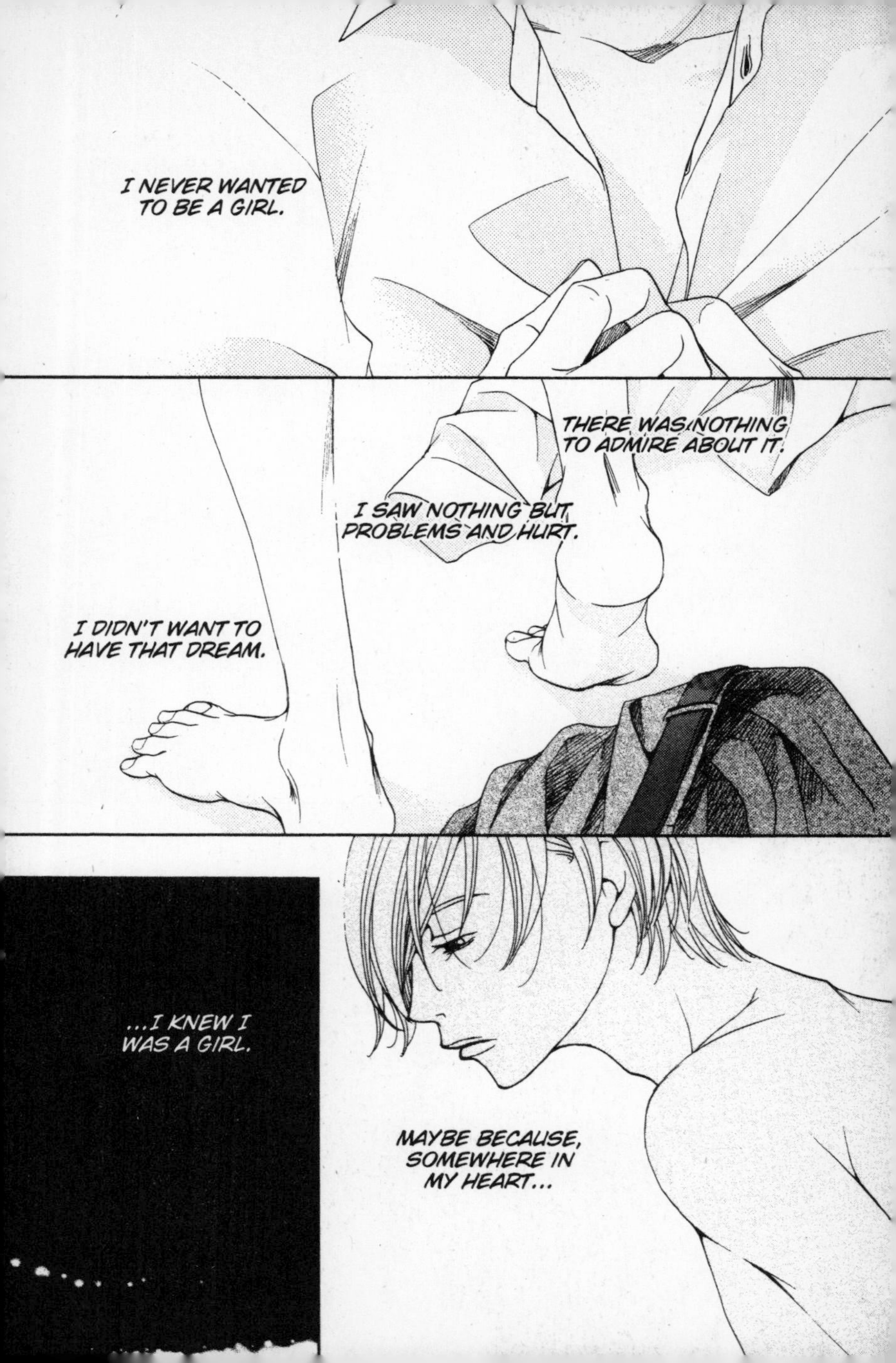
I NEVER WANTED TO BE A GIRL.
THERE WAS NOTHING TO ADMIRE ABOUT IT.
I SAW NOTHING BUT PROBLEMS AND HURT.
I DIDN'T WANT TO HAVE THAT DREAM.
MAYBE BECAUSE, SOMEWHERE IN MY HEART...
...I KNEW I WAS A GIRL.

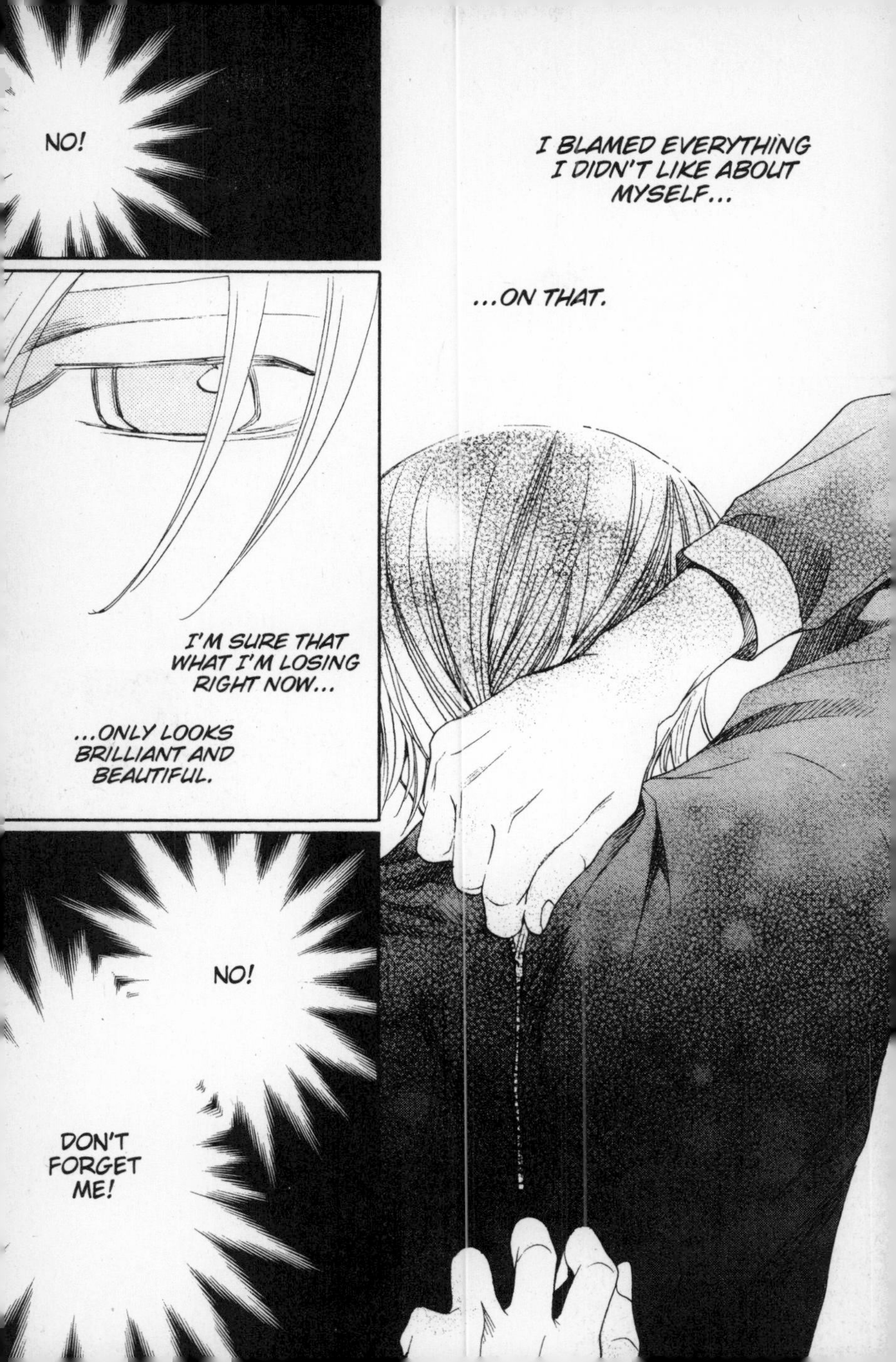
I BLAMED EVERYTHING I DIDN'T LIKE ABOUT MYSELF...
...ON THAT.
NO!
I'M SURE THAT WHAT I'M LOSING RIGHT NOW...
...ONLY LOOKS BRILLIANT AND BEAUTIFUL.
NO!
DON'T FORGET ME!

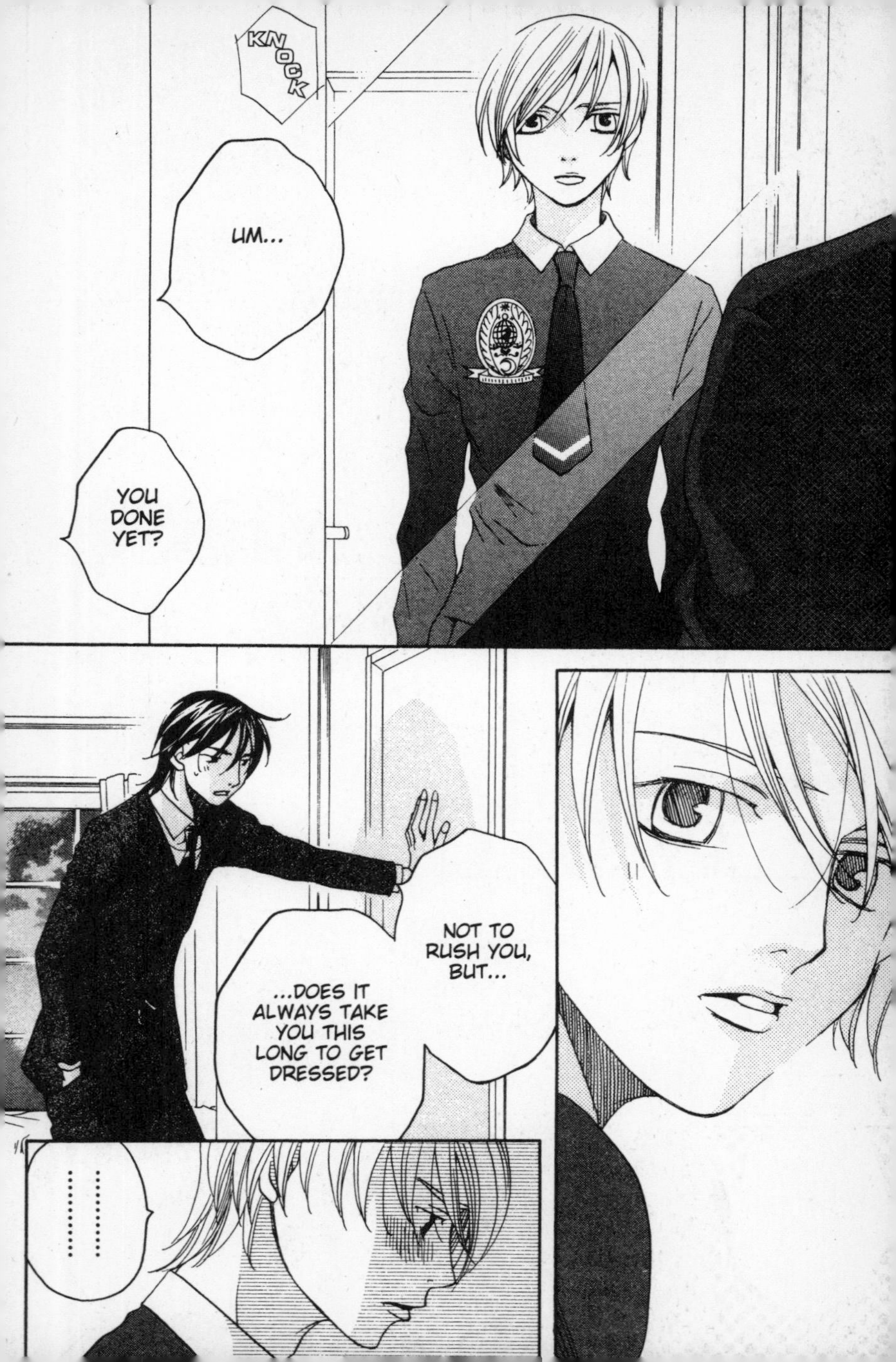
KNOCK
UM...
YOU DONE YET?
NOT TO RUSH YOU, BUT...
...DOES IT ALWAYS TAKE YOU THIS LONG TO GET DRESSED?
......

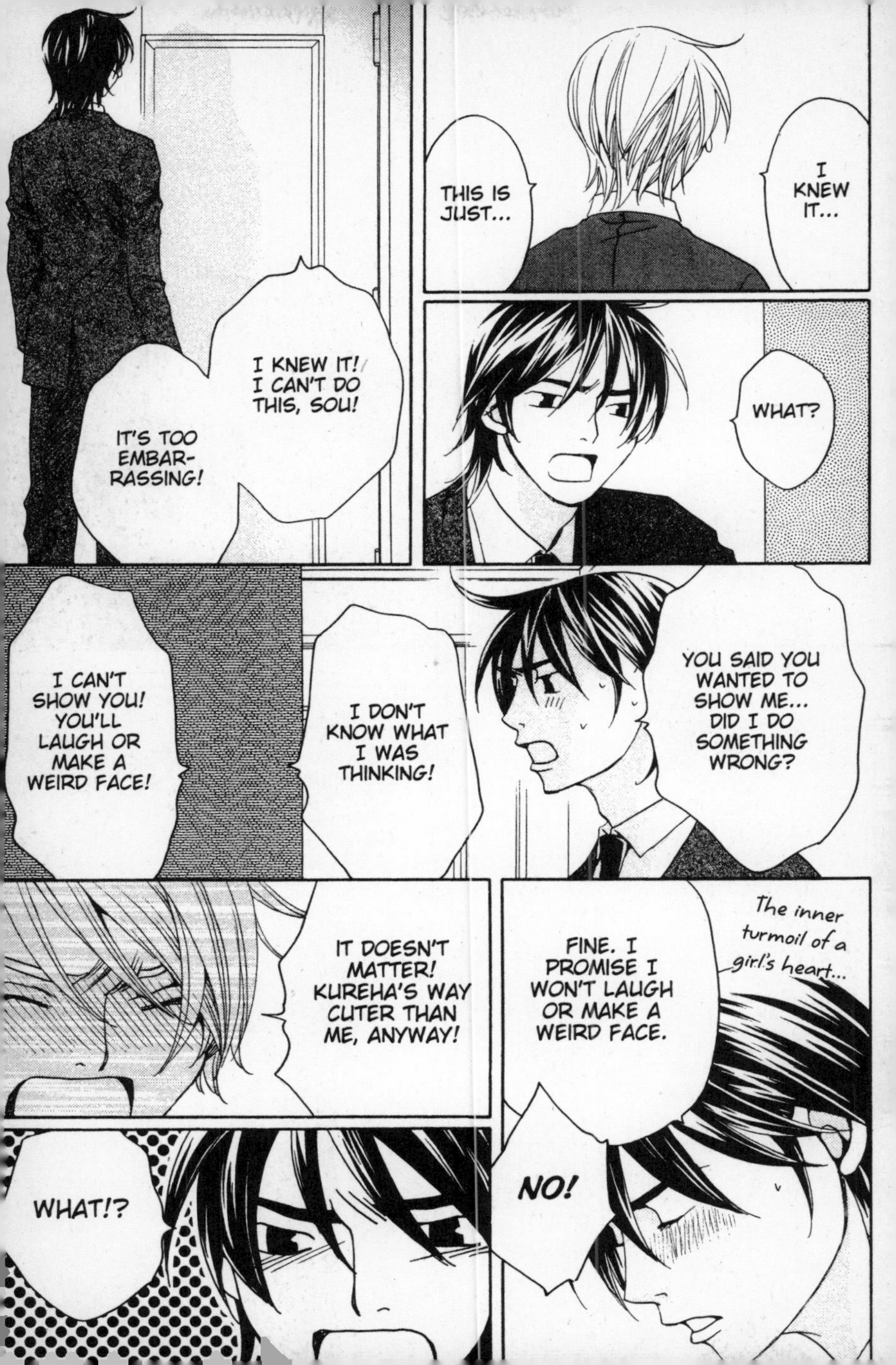
I KNEW IT...
THIS IS JUST...
WHAT?
I KNEW IT! I CAN'T DO THIS, SOU!
IT'S TOO EMBAR-RASSING!
YOU SAID YOU WANTED TO SHOW ME... DID I DO SOMETHING WRONG?
I DON'T KNOW WHAT I WAS THINKING!
I CAN'T SHOW YOU! YOU'LL LAUGH OR MAKE A WEIRD FACE!
The inner turmoil of a girl's heart...
FINE. I PROMISE I WON'T LAUGH OR MAKE A WEIRD FACE.
NO!
IT DOESN'T MATTER! KUREHA'S WAY CUTER THAN ME, ANYWAY!
WHAT!?

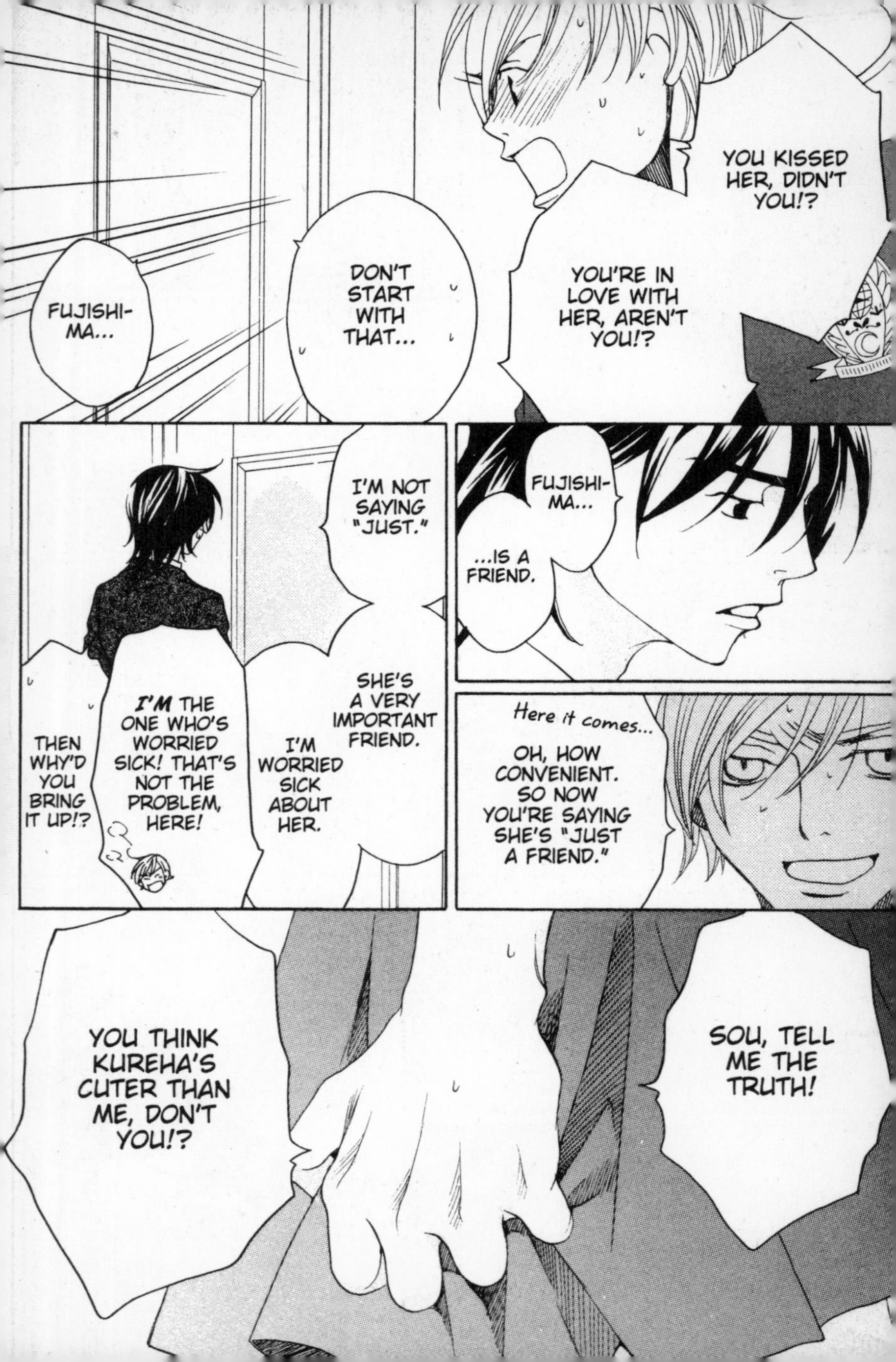
YOU KISSED HER, DIDN'T YOU!?
YOU'RE IN LOVE WITH HER, AREN'T YOU!?
DON'T START WITH THAT...
FUJISHI-MA...
FUJISHI-MA...
...IS A FRIEND.
Here it comes...
OH, HOW CONVENIENT. SO NOW YOU'RE SAYING SHE'S "JUST A FRIEND."
I'M NOT SAYING "JUST."
SHE'S A VERY IMPORTANT FRIEND.
I'M WORRIED SICK ABOUT HER.
I'M THE ONE WHO'S WORRIED SICK! THAT'S NOT THE PROBLEM, HERE!
THEN WHY'D YOU BRING IT UP!?
SOU, TELL ME THE TRUTH!
YOU THINK KUREHA'S CUTER THAN ME, DON'T YOU!?

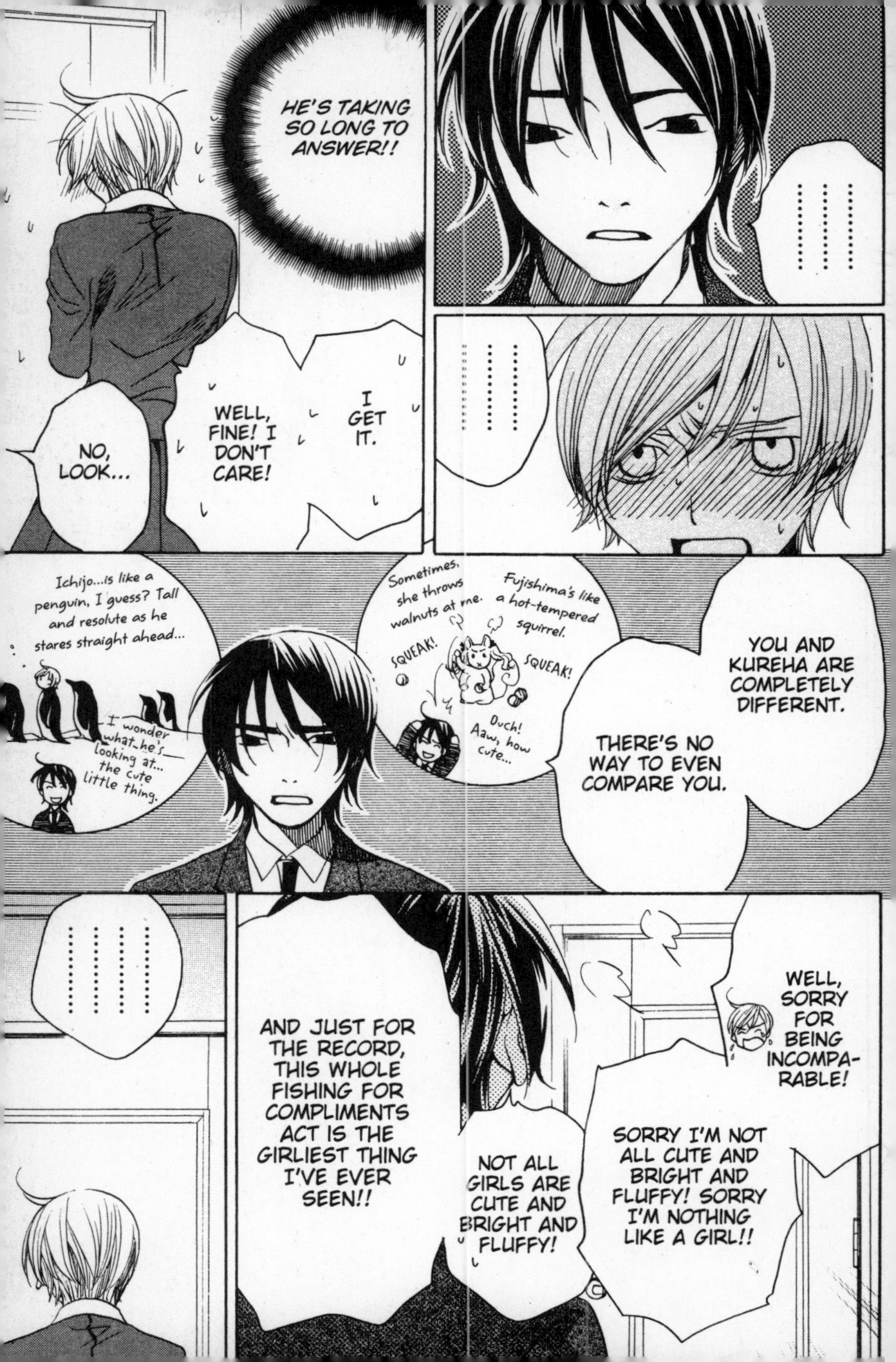
......
......
HE'S TAKING SO LONG TO ANSWER!!
I GET IT.
WELL, FINE! I DON'T CARE!
NO, LOOK...
YOU AND KUREHA ARE COMPLETELY DIFFERENT.
THERE'S NO WAY TO EVEN COMPARE YOU.
Fujishima's like a hot-tempered squirrel.
Sometimes, she throws walnuts at me.
SQUEAK!
SQUEAK!
Ouch! Aaw, how cute...
Ichijo...is like a penguin, I guess? Tall and resolute as he stares straight ahead...
I wonder what he's looking at... the cute little thing.
WELL, SORRY FOR BEING INCOMPA-RABLE!
SORRY I'M NOT ALL CUTE AND BRIGHT AND FLUFFY! SORRY I'M NOTHING LIKE A GIRL!!
NOT ALL GIRLS ARE CUTE AND BRIGHT AND FLUFFY!
AND JUST FOR THE RECORD, THIS WHOLE FISHING FOR COMPLIMENTS ACT IS THE GIRLIEST THING I'VE EVER SEEN!!
......

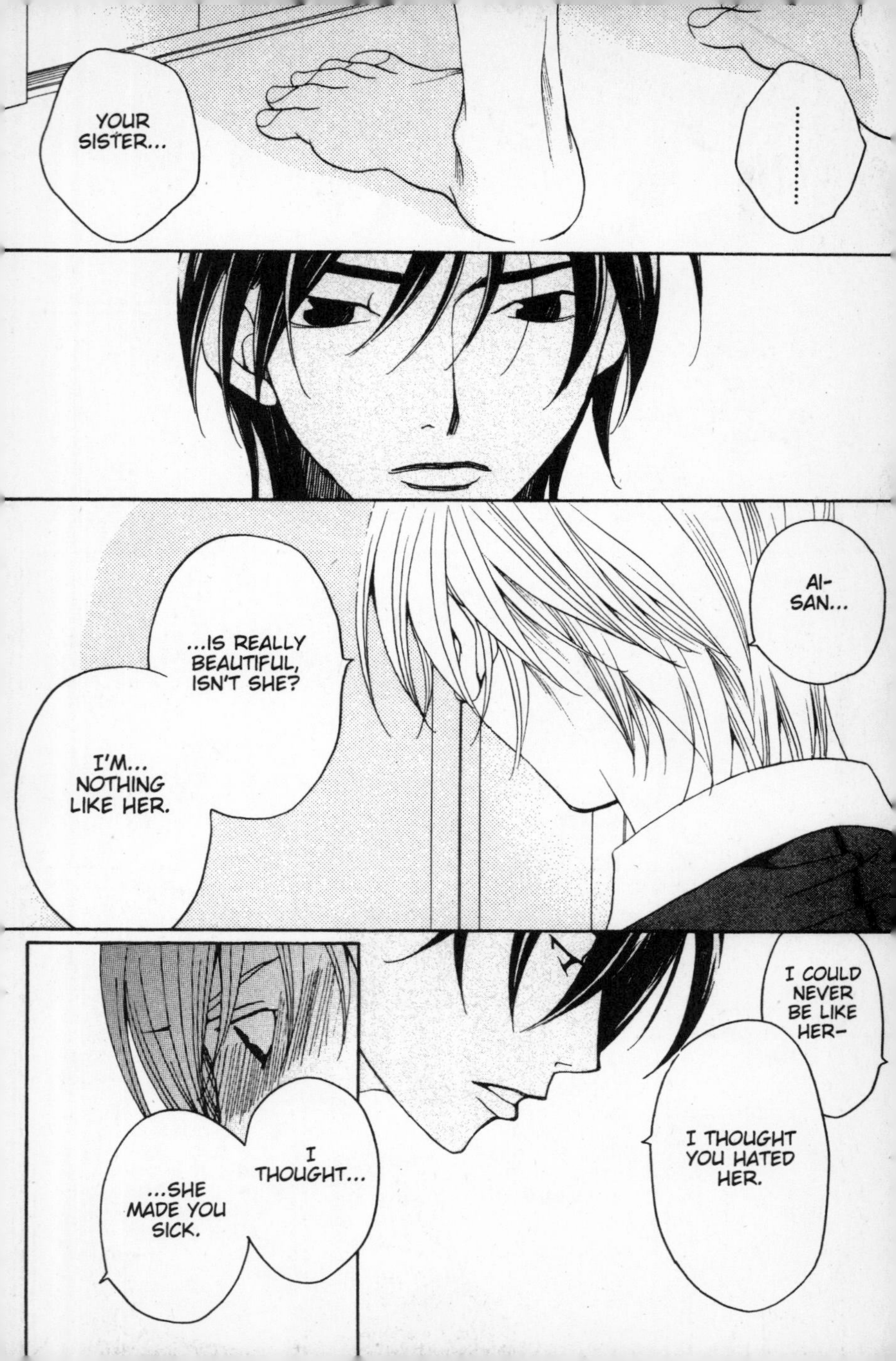
......
YOUR SISTER...
AI-SAN...
...IS REALLY BEAUTIFUL, ISN'T SHE?
I'M... NOTHING LIKE HER.
I COULD NEVER BE LIKE HER—
I THOUGHT YOU HATED HER.
I THOUGHT...
...SHE MADE YOU SICK.

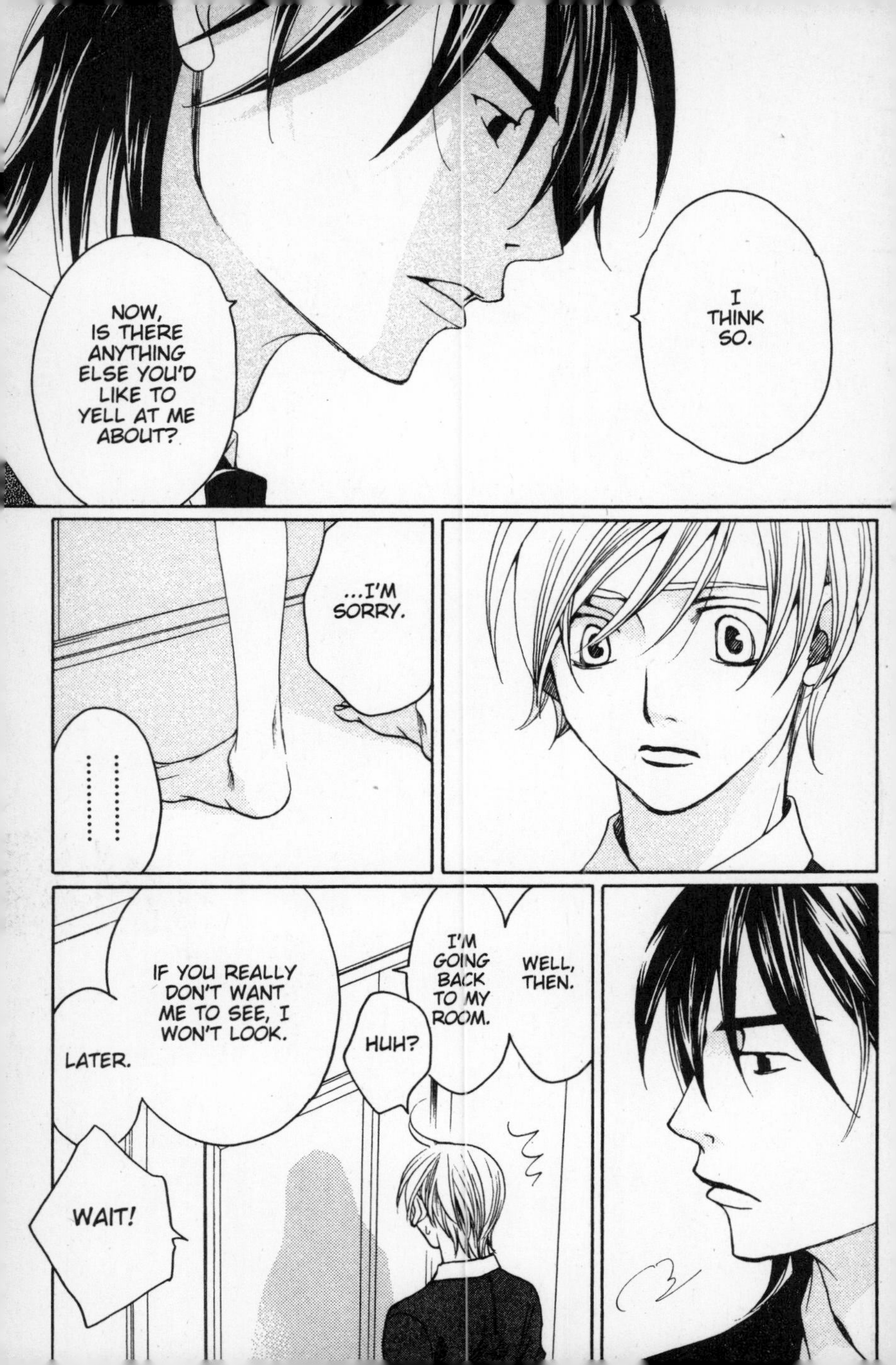
I THINK SO.
NOW, IS THERE ANYTHING ELSE YOU'D LIKE TO YELL AT ME ABOUT?
...I'M SORRY.
......
WELL, THEN.
I'M GOING BACK TO MY ROOM.
HUH?
IF YOU REALLY DON'T WANT ME TO SEE, I WON'T LOOK.
LATER.
WAIT!

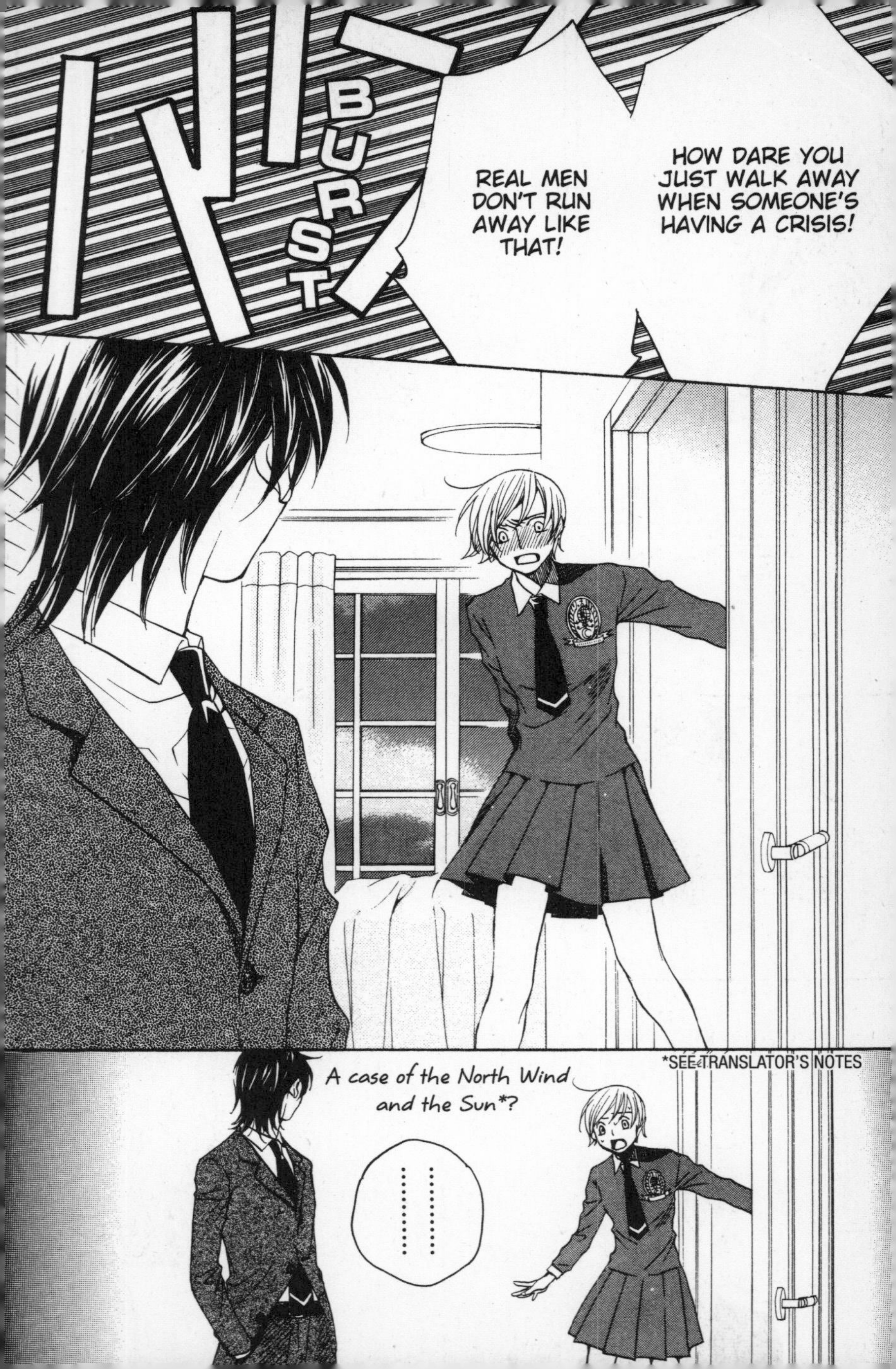
HOW DARE YOU JUST WALK AWAY WHEN SOMEONE'S HAVING A CRISIS!
REAL MEN DON'T RUN AWAY LIKE THAT!
BURST
*SEE TRANSLATOR'S NOTES
A case of the North Wind and the Sun*?
......

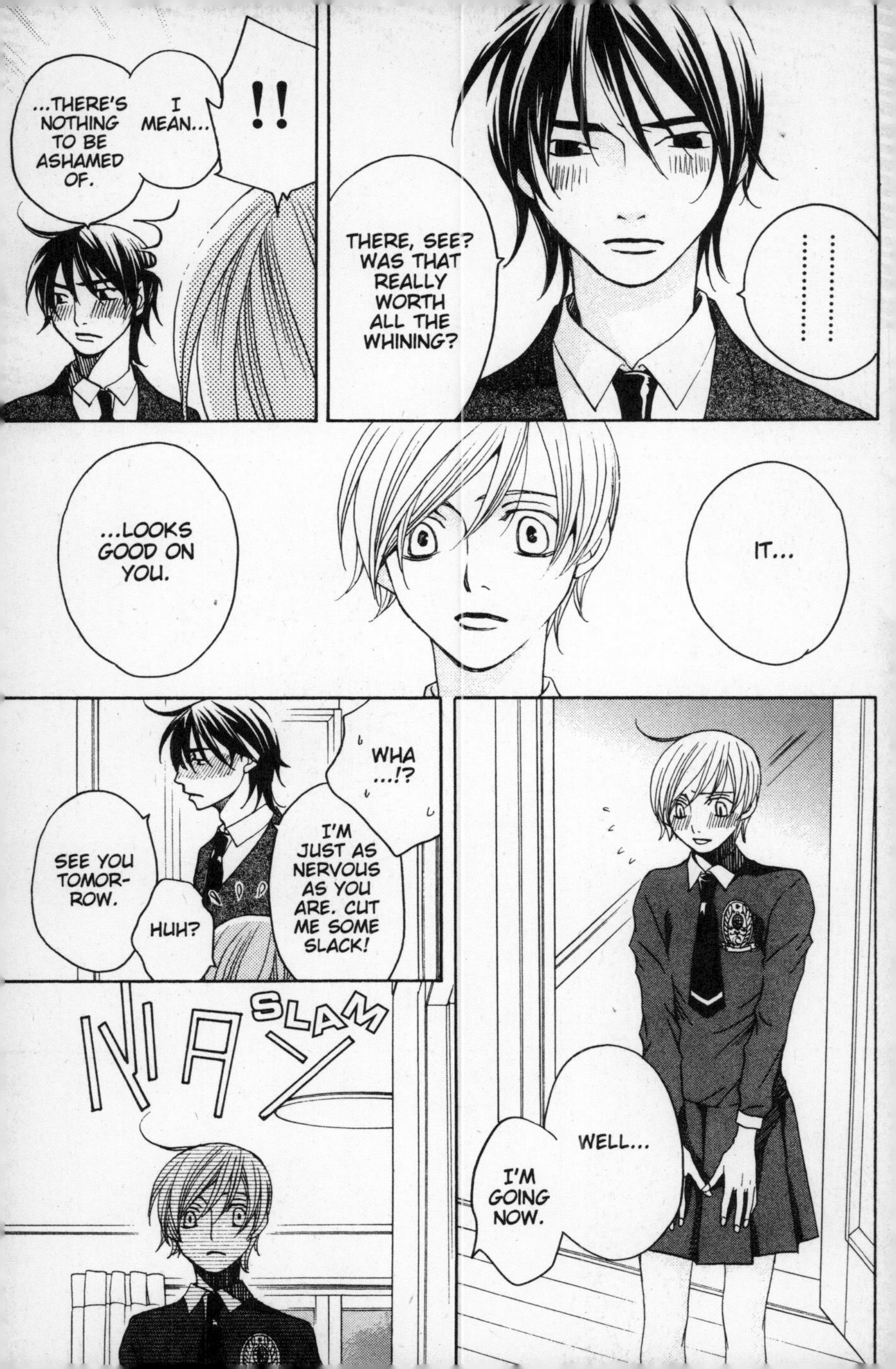
......
THERE, SEE? WAS THAT REALLY WORTH ALL THE WHINING?
!!
I MEAN...
...THERE'S NOTHING TO BE ASHAMED OF.
IT...
...LOOKS GOOD ON YOU.
WELL...
I'M GOING NOW.
WHA ...!?
I'M JUST AS NERVOUS AS YOU ARE. CUT ME SOME SLACK!
SEE YOU TOMOR-ROW.
HUH?
SLAM

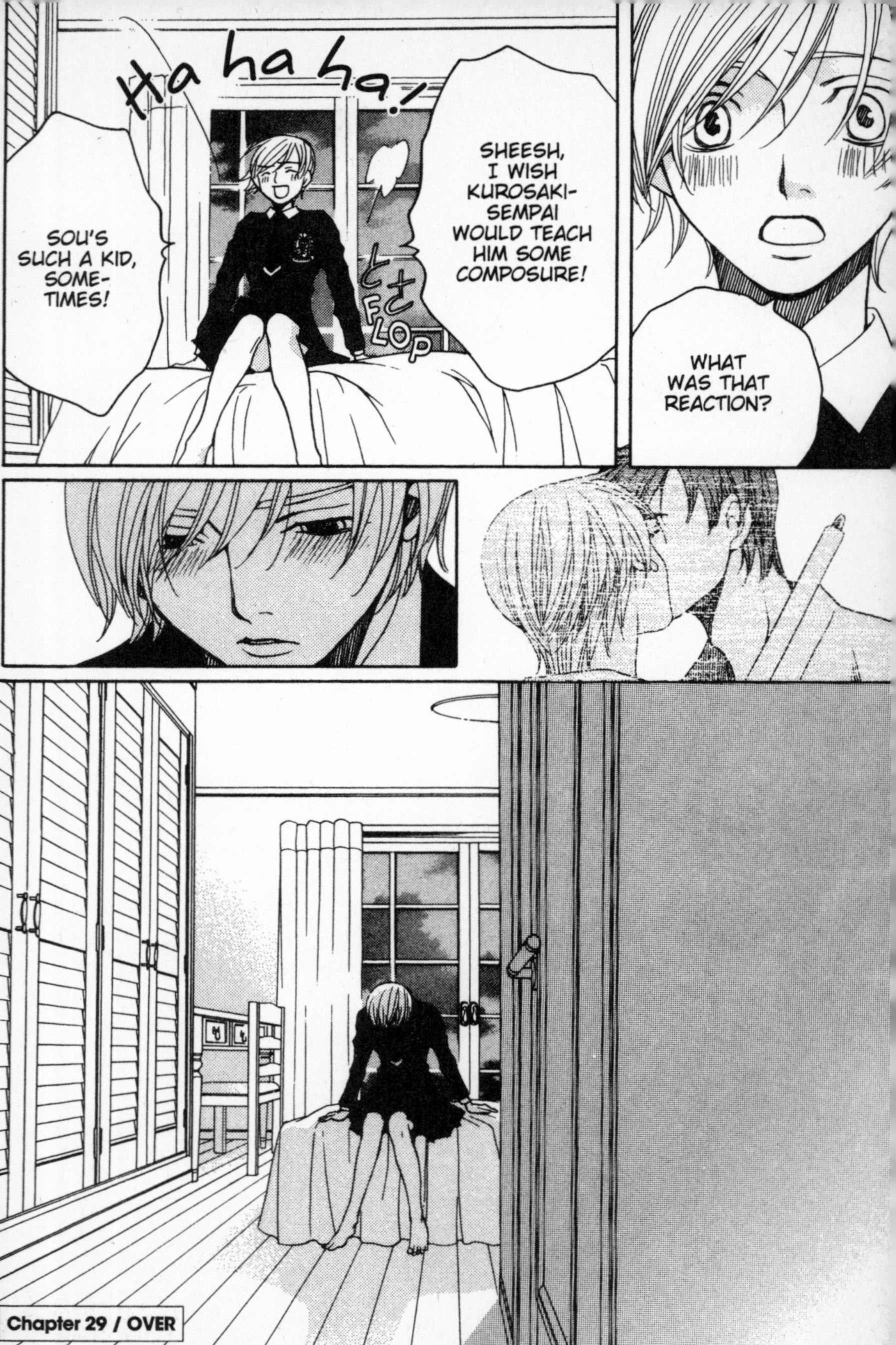
WHAT WAS THAT REACTION?
Ha ha ha!
SHEESH, I WISH KUROSAKI-SEMPAI WOULD TEACH HIM SOME COMPOSURE!
FLOP
SOU'S SUCH A KID, SOME-TIMES!
Chapter 29 / OVER

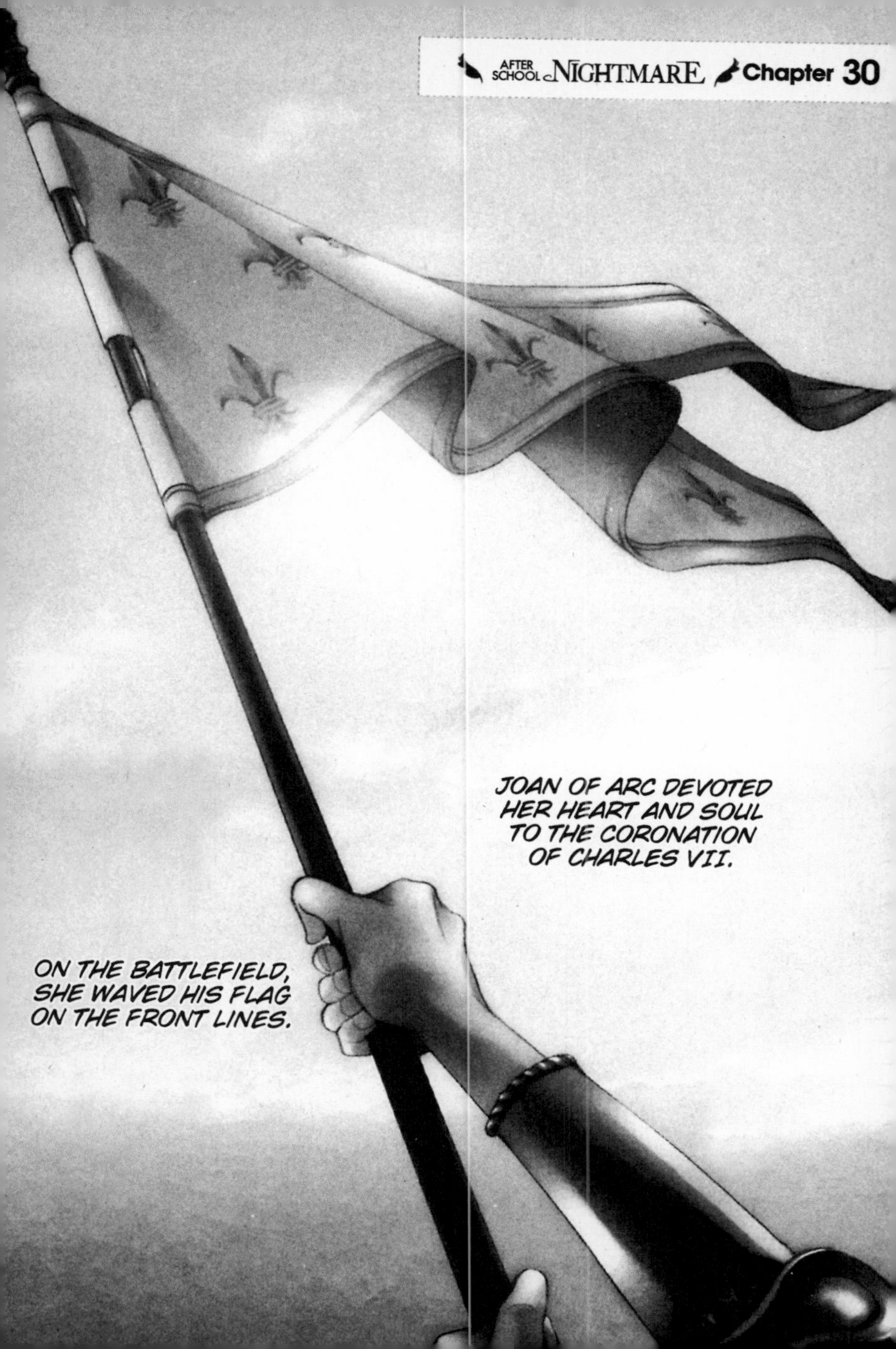
AFTER SCHOOL NIGHTMARE Chapter 30
JOAN OF ARC DEVOTED HER HEART AND SOUL TO THE CORONATION OF CHARLES VII.
ON THE BATTLEFIELD, SHE WAVED HIS FLAG ON THE FRONT LINES.

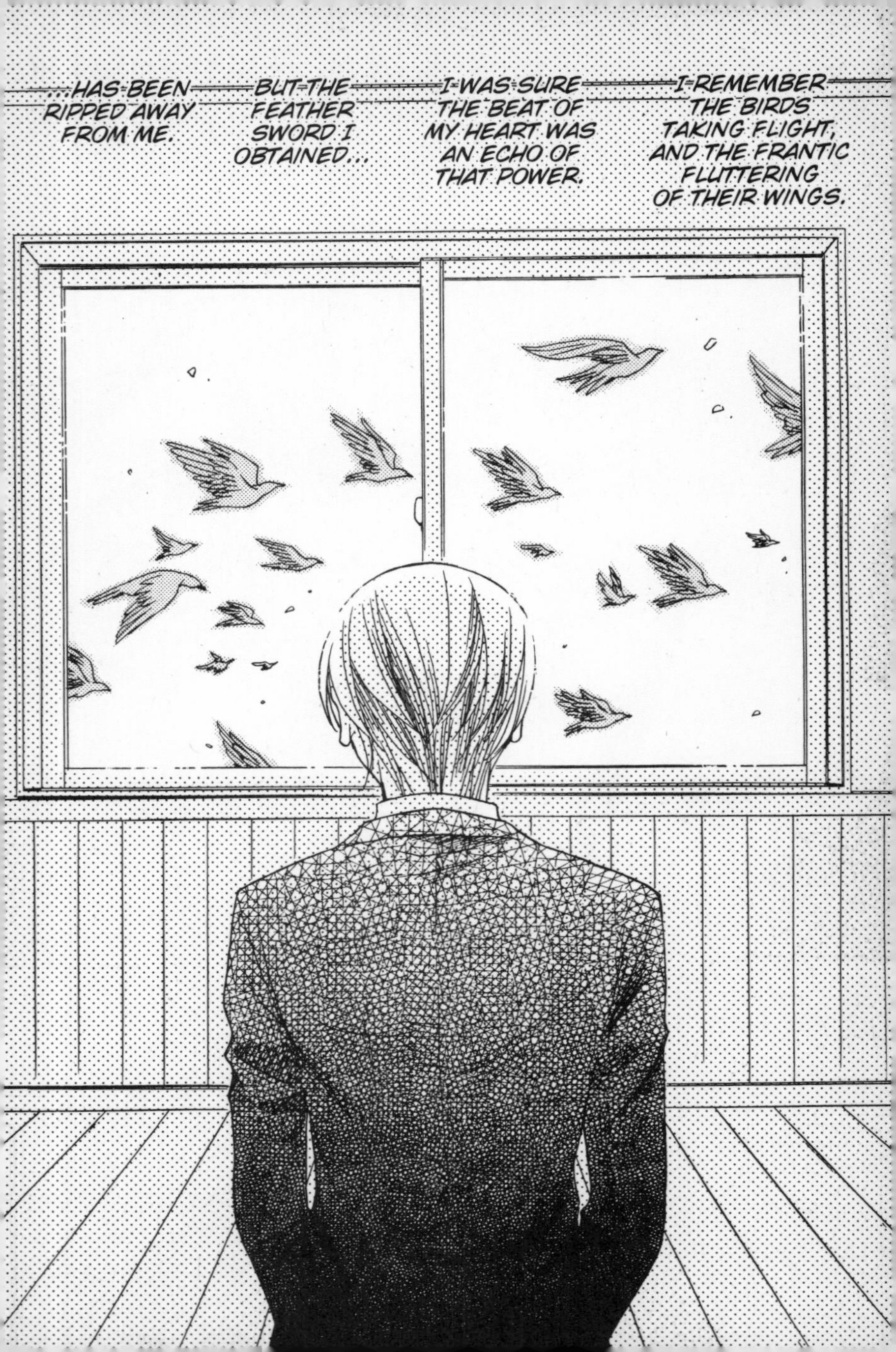
I REMEMBER THE BIRDS TAKING FLIGHT, AND THE FRANTIC FLUTTERING OF THEIR WINGS.
I WAS SURE THE BEAT OF MY HEART WAS AN ECHO OF THAT POWER.
BUT THE FEATHER SWORD I OBTAINED...
...HAS BEEN RIPPED AWAY FROM ME.

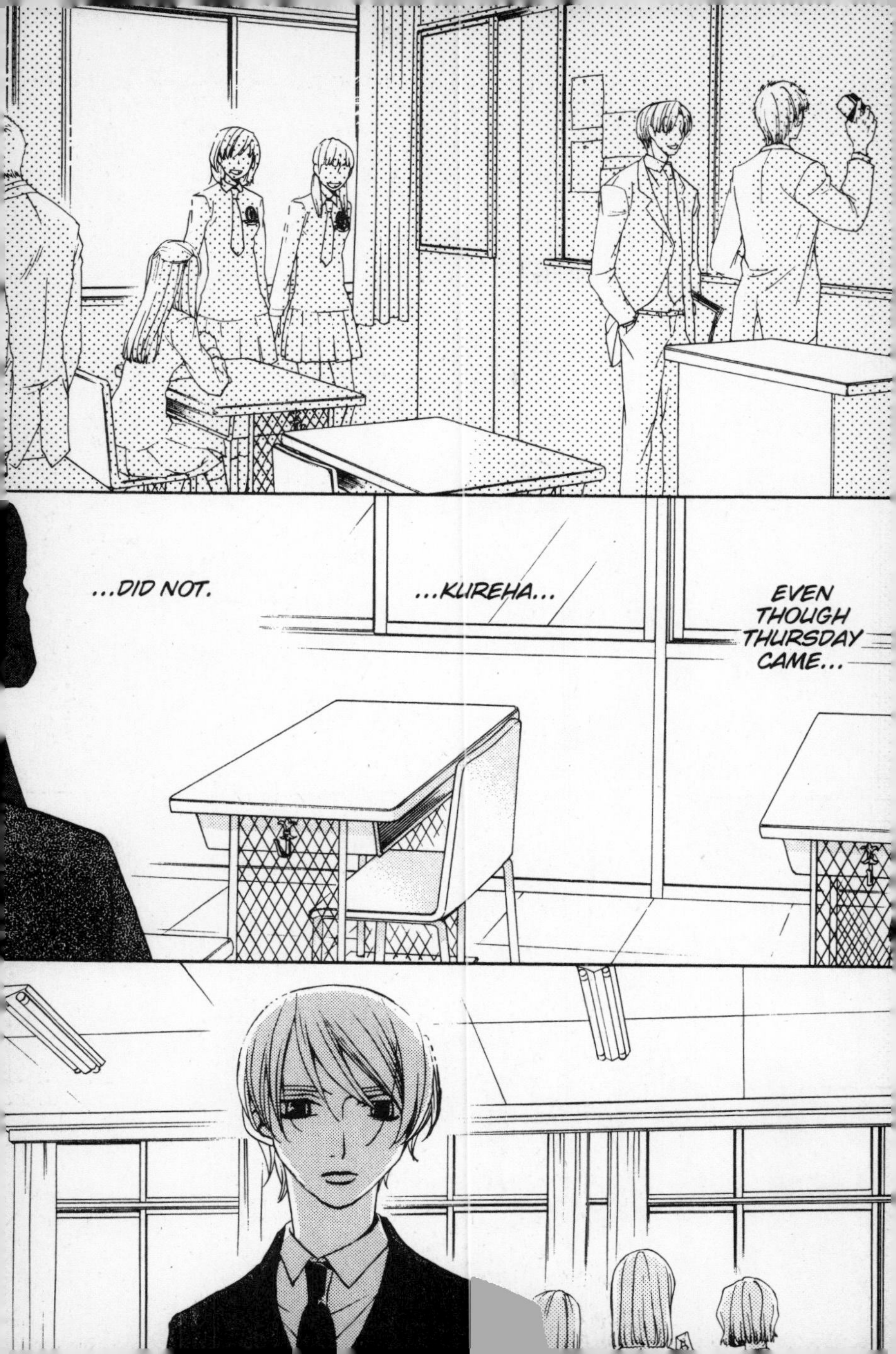
EVEN THOUGH THURSDAY CAME...
...KUREHA...
...DID NOT.

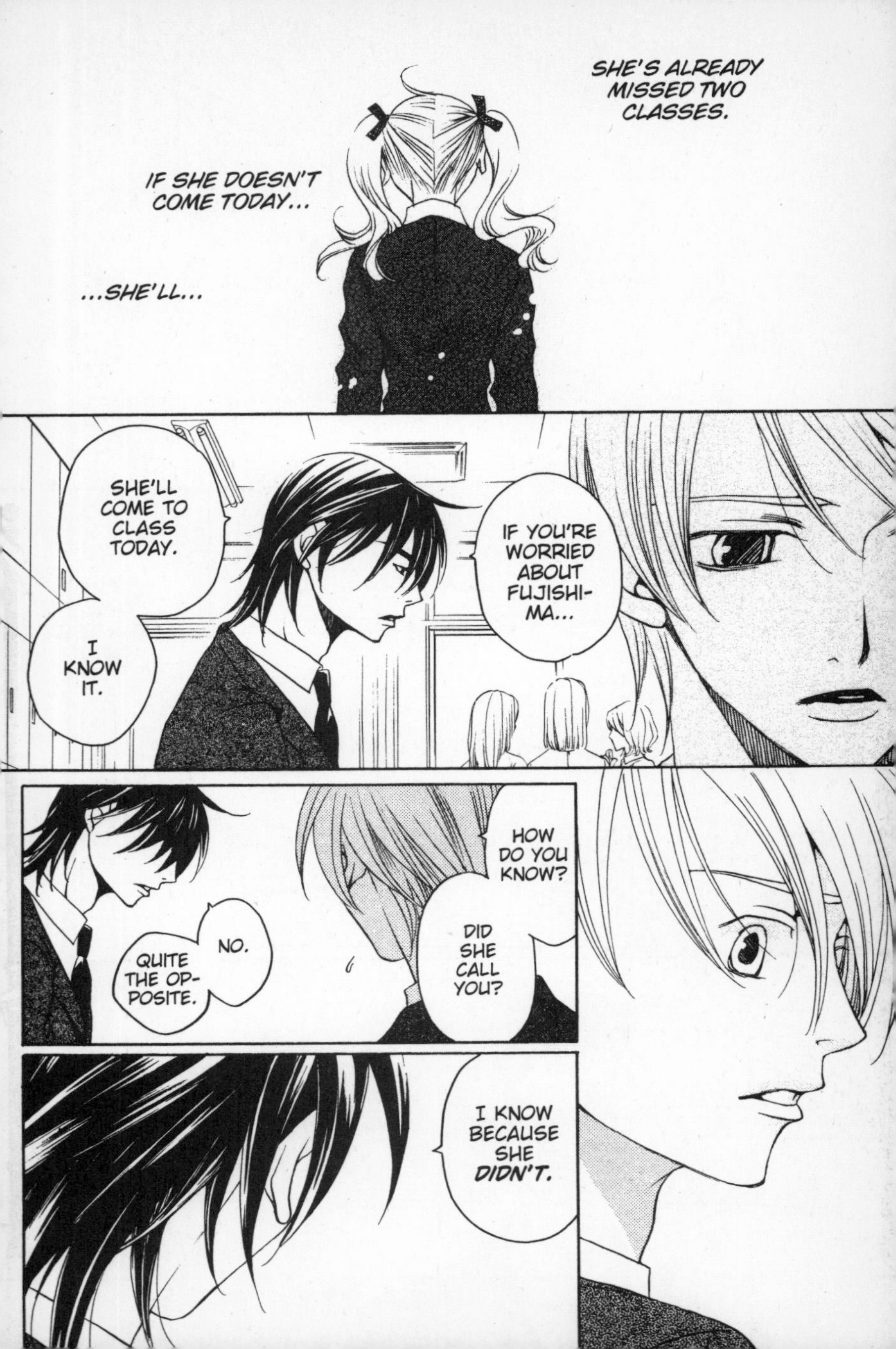
SHE'S ALREADY MISSED TWO CLASSES.
IF SHE DOESN'T COME TODAY...
...SHE'LL...
IF YOU'RE WORRIED ABOUT FUJISHIMA...
SHE'LL COME TO CLASS TODAY.
I KNOW IT.
HOW DO YOU KNOW?
DID SHE CALL YOU?
NO.
QUITE THE OPPOSITE.
I KNOW BECAUSE SHE *DIDN'T.*

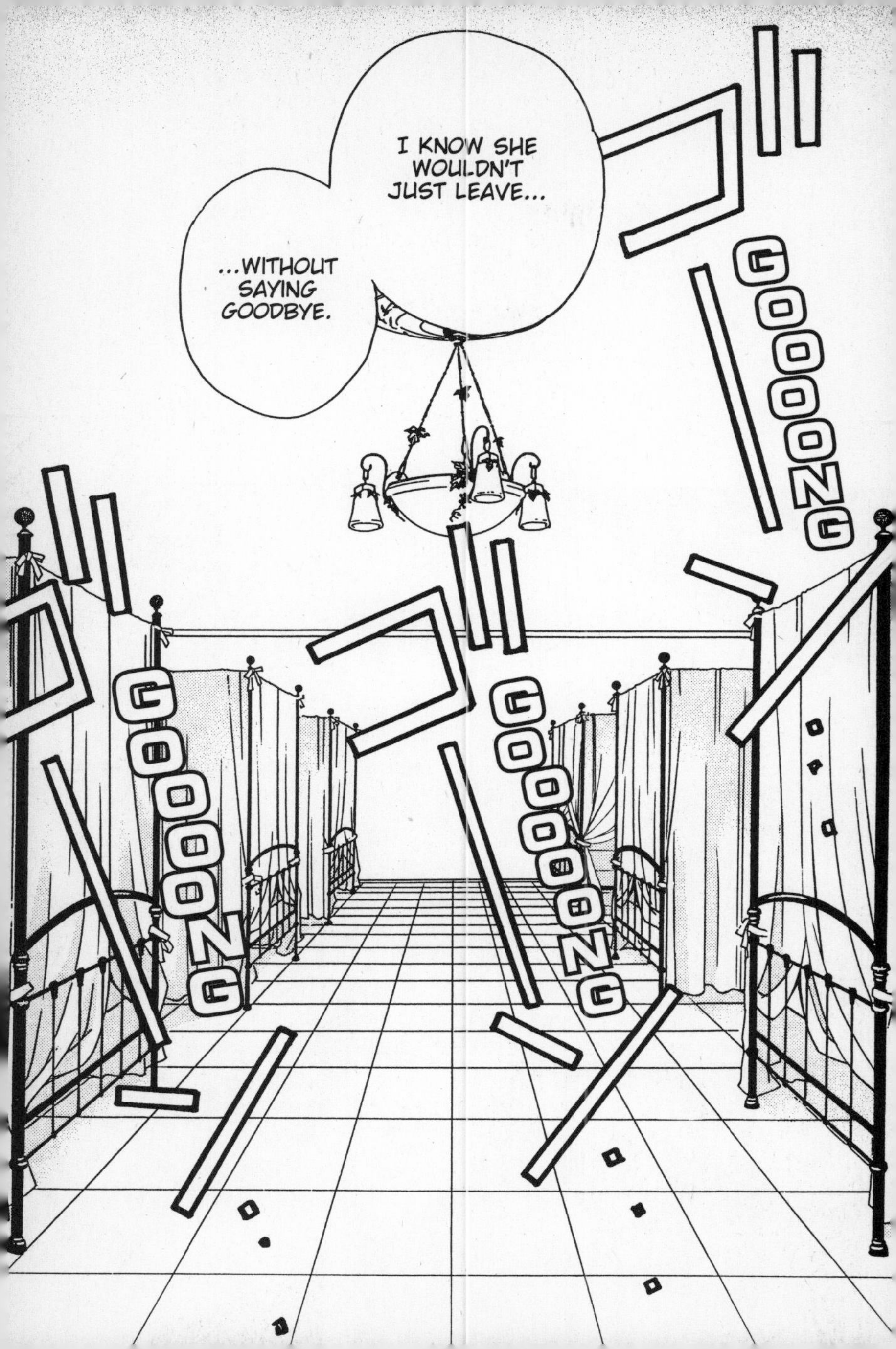
I KNOW SHE WOULDN'T JUST LEAVE...
...WITHOUT SAYING GOODBYE.
GOOOONG
GOOOOONG
GOOOONG

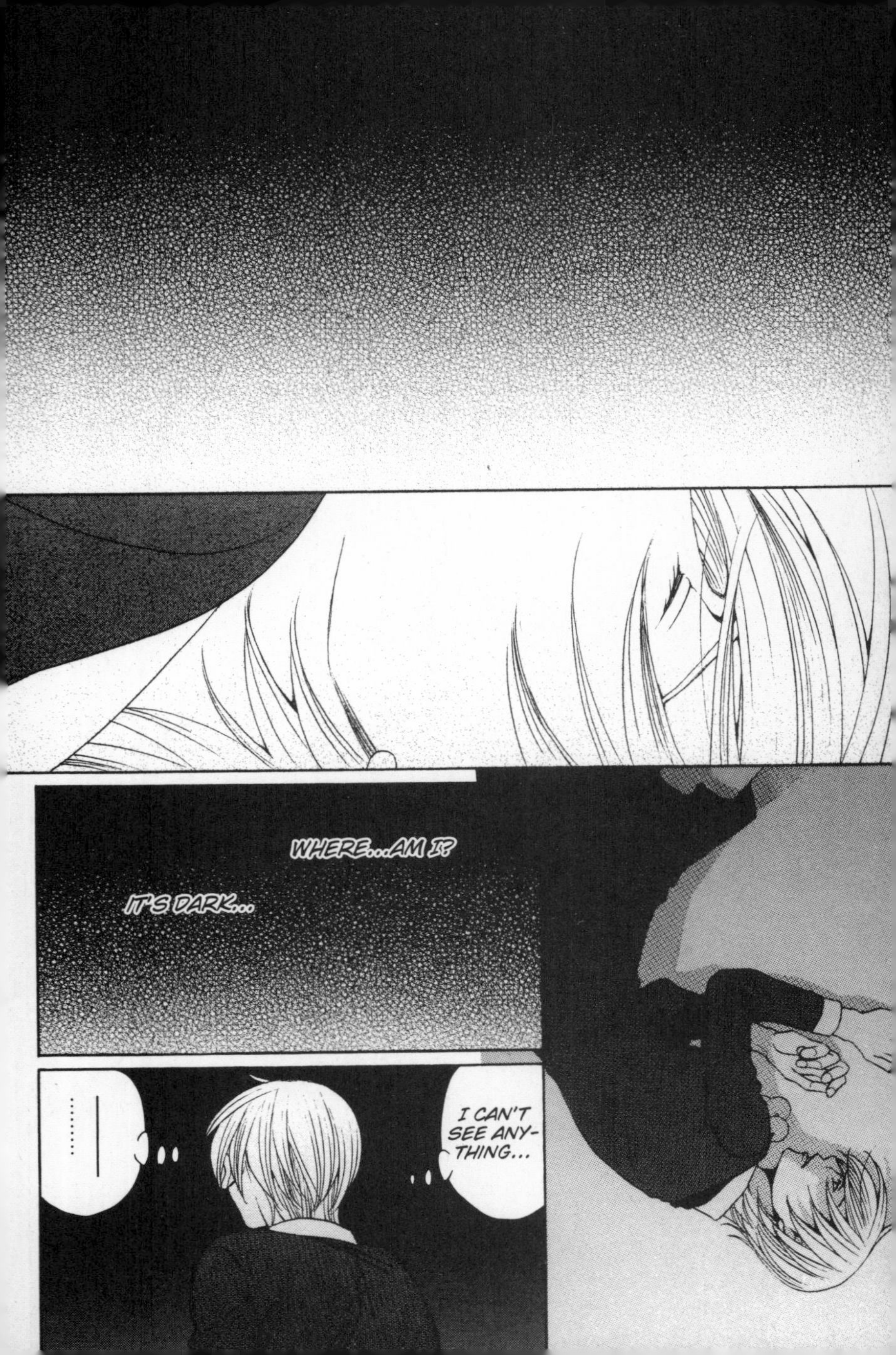
WHERE...AM I?
IT'S DARK...
I CAN'T SEE ANYTHING...
......

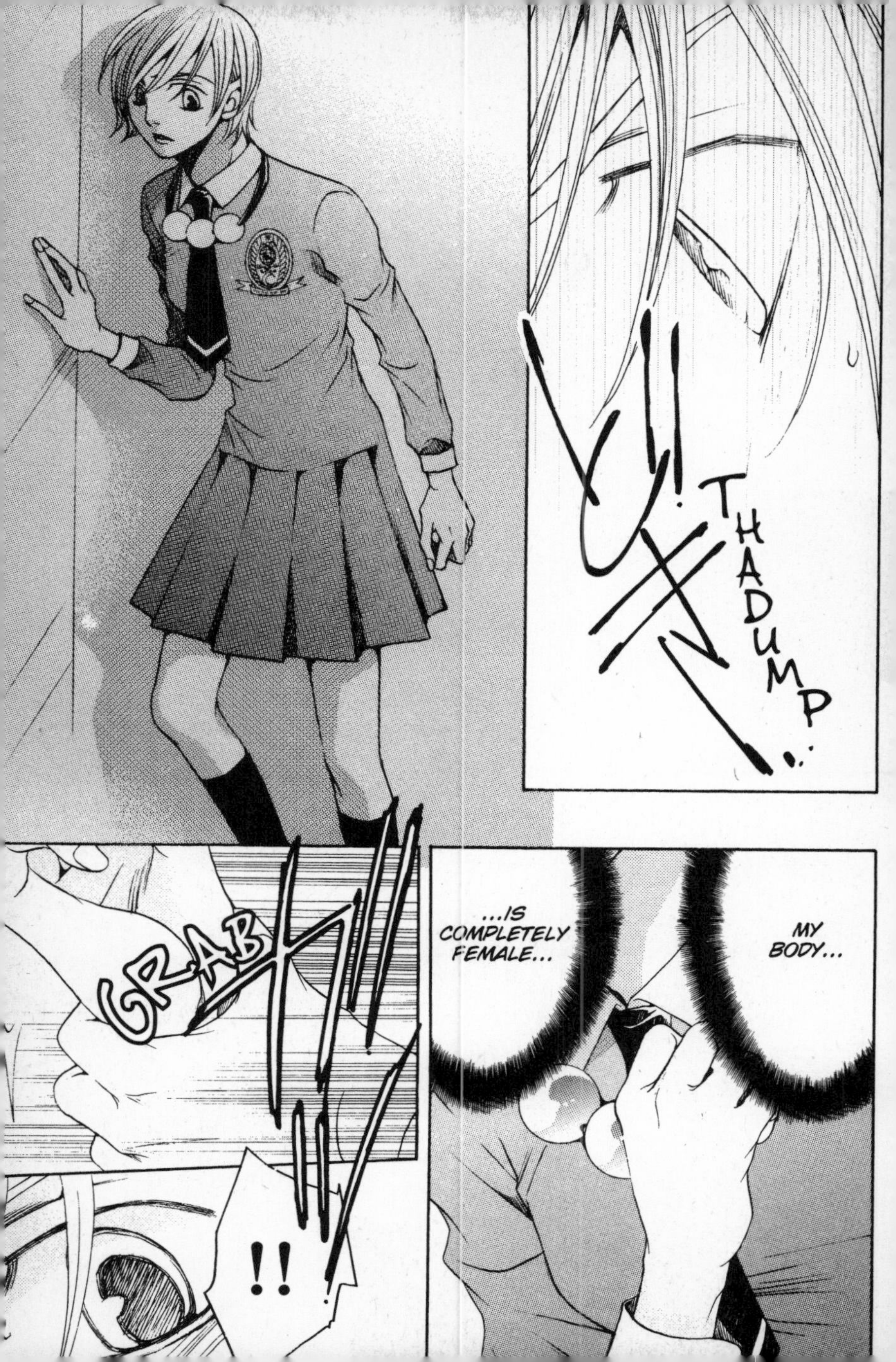
THADUMP..
MY BODY...
...IS COMPLETELY FEMALE...
GRAB
!!

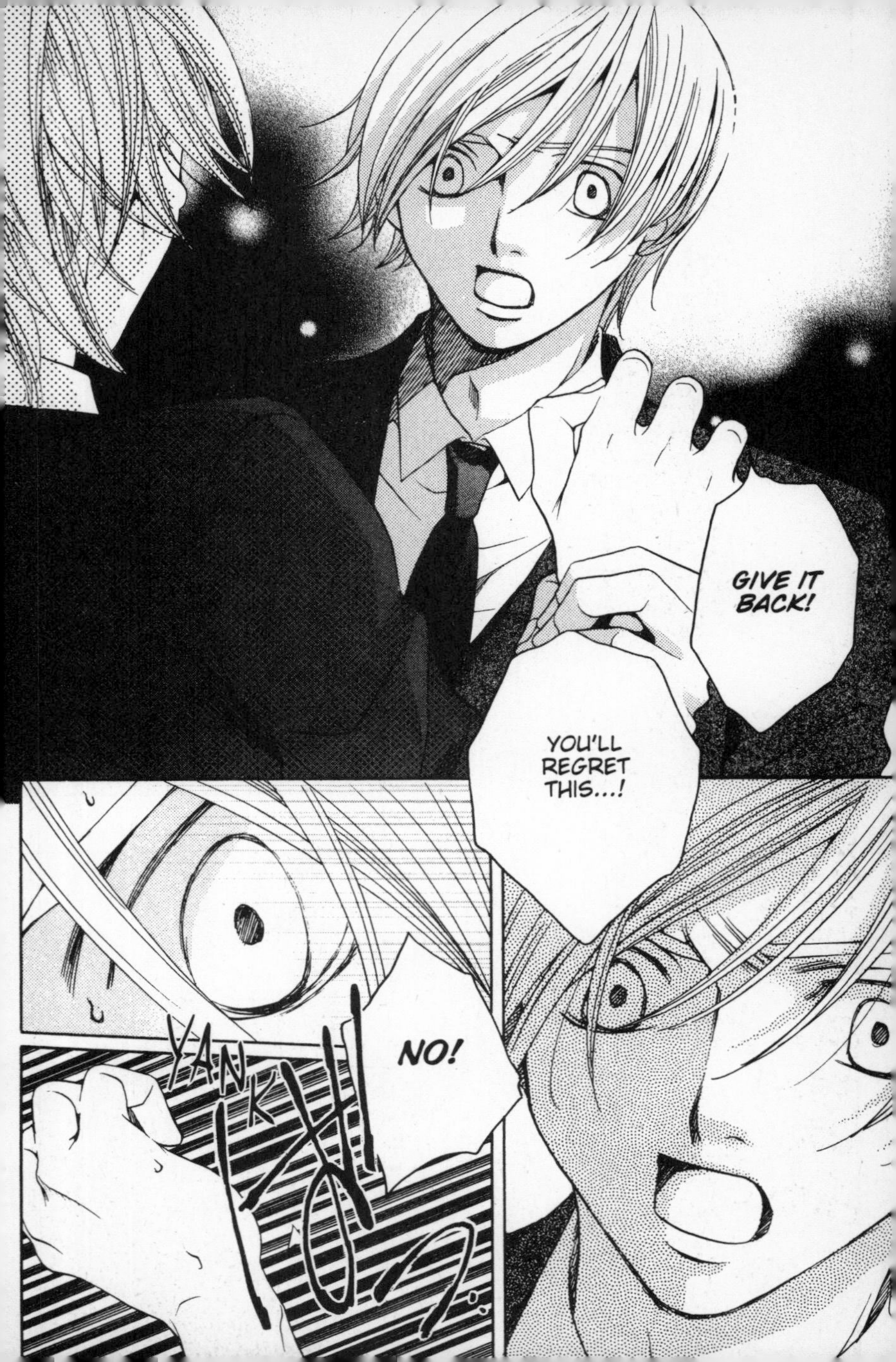
GIVE IT BACK!
YOU'LL REGRET THIS...!
NO!
YANK

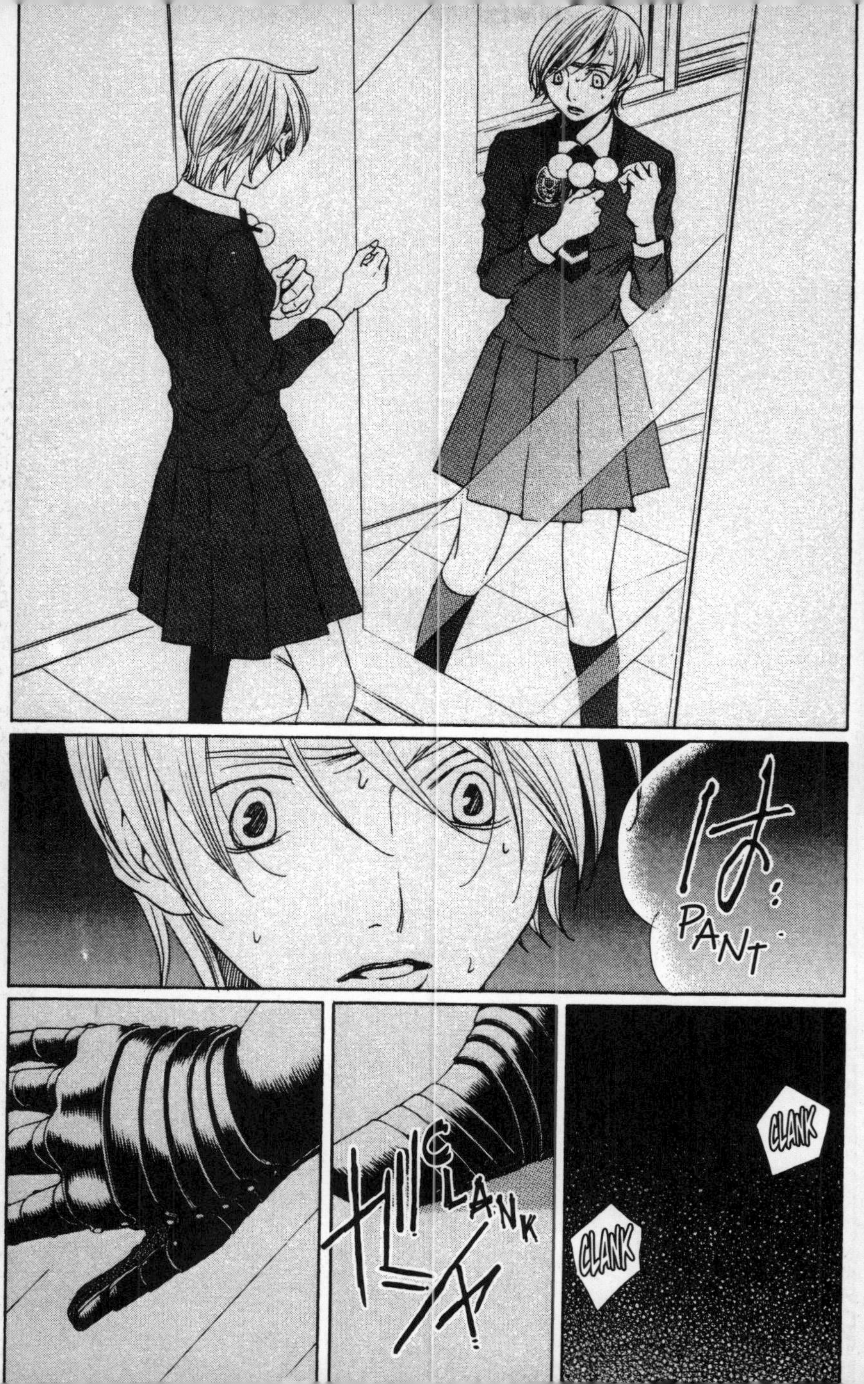
は
PANT
CLANK
CLANK
CLANK

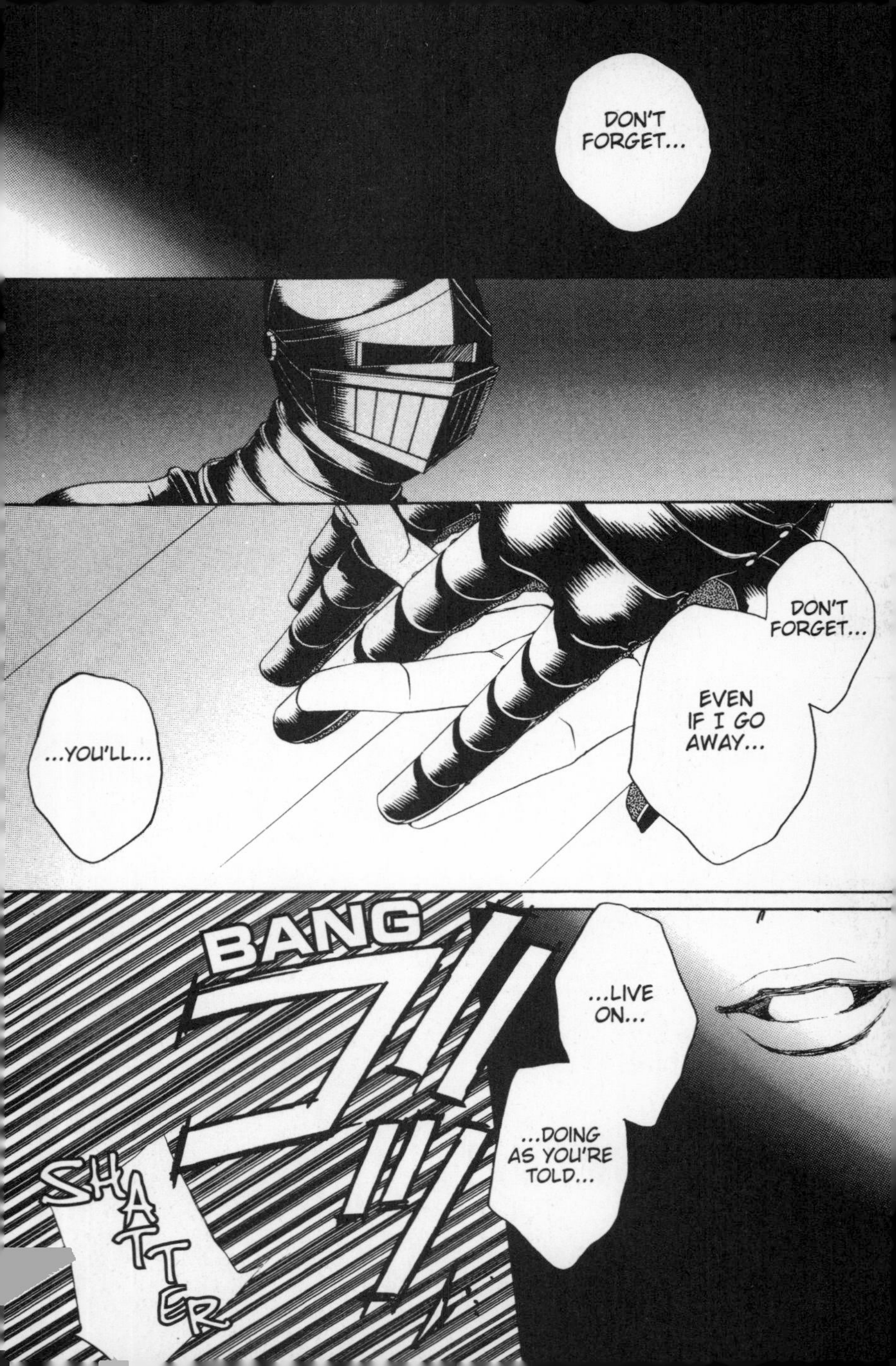
DON'T FORGET...
DON'T FORGET...
EVEN IF I GO AWAY...
...YOU'LL...
...LIVE ON...
...DOING AS YOU'RE TOLD...
BANG
SHATTER

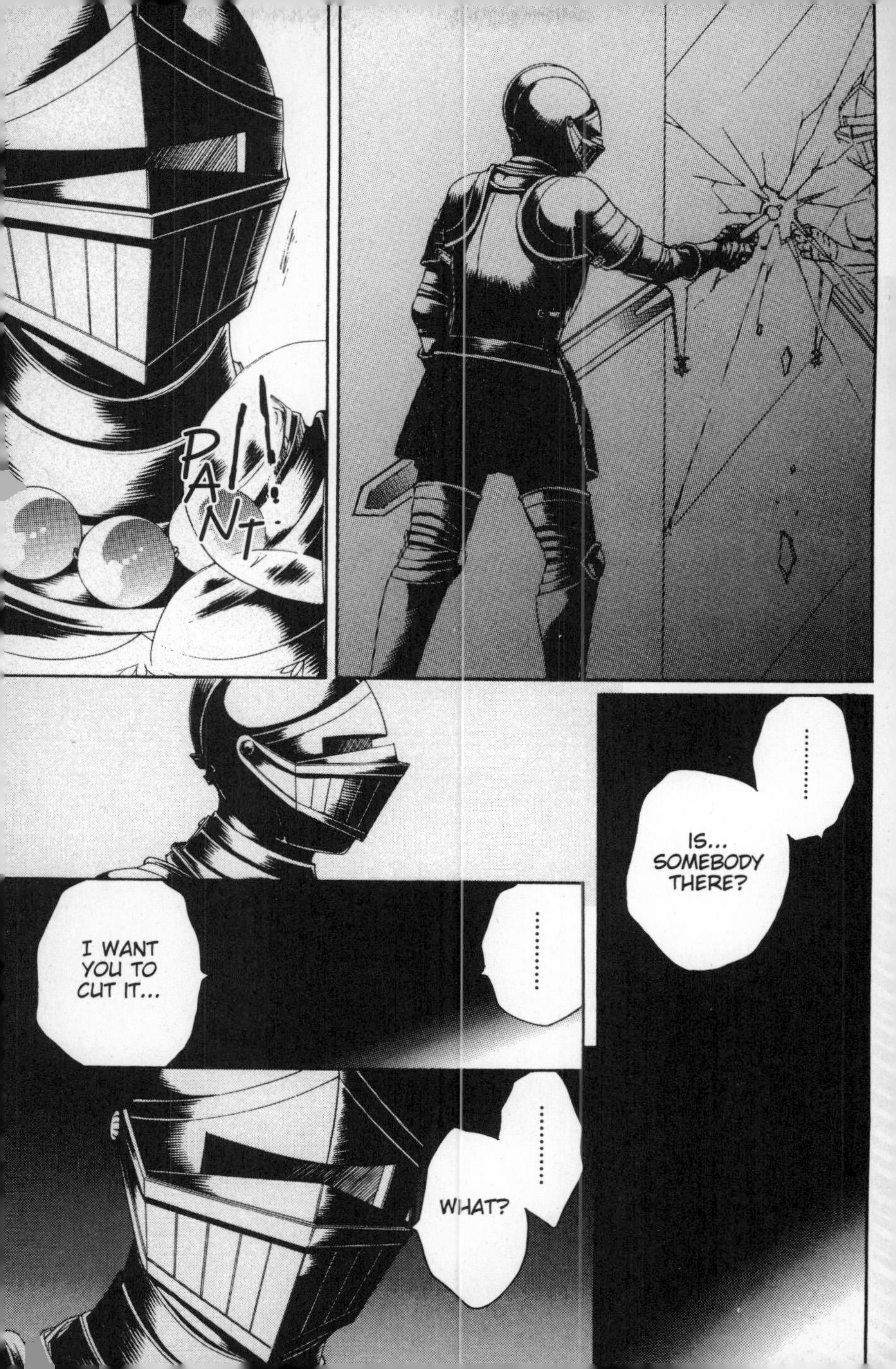
PANT!!
......
IS... SOMEBODY THERE?
......
I WANT YOU TO CUT IT...
......
WHAT?

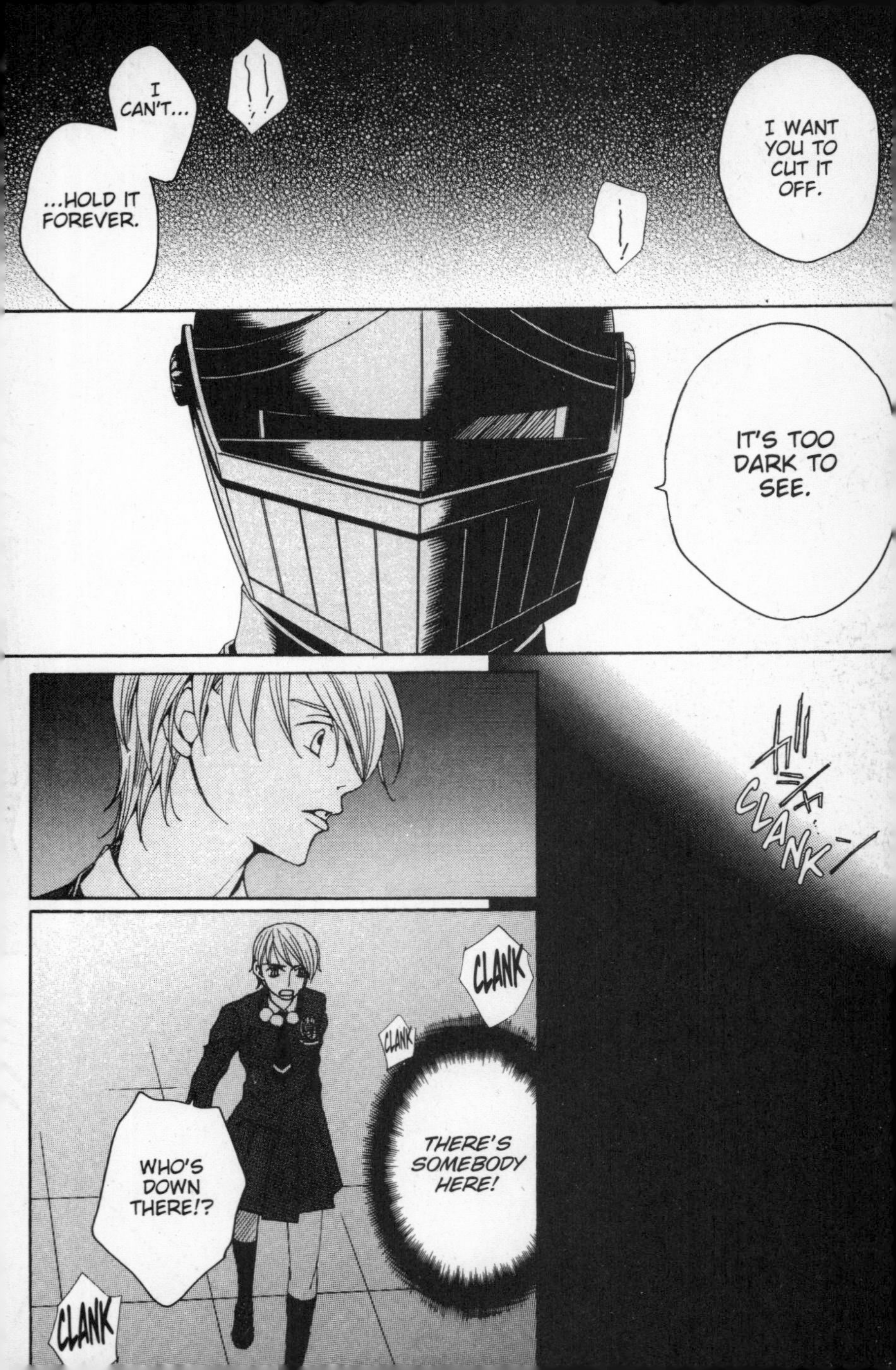

I WANT YOU TO CUT IT OFF.
!
!!
I CAN'T... ...HOLD IT FOREVER.
IT'S TOO DARK TO SEE.
CLANK
CLANK
CLANK
THERE'S SOMEBODY HERE!
WHO'S DOWN THERE!?
CLANK

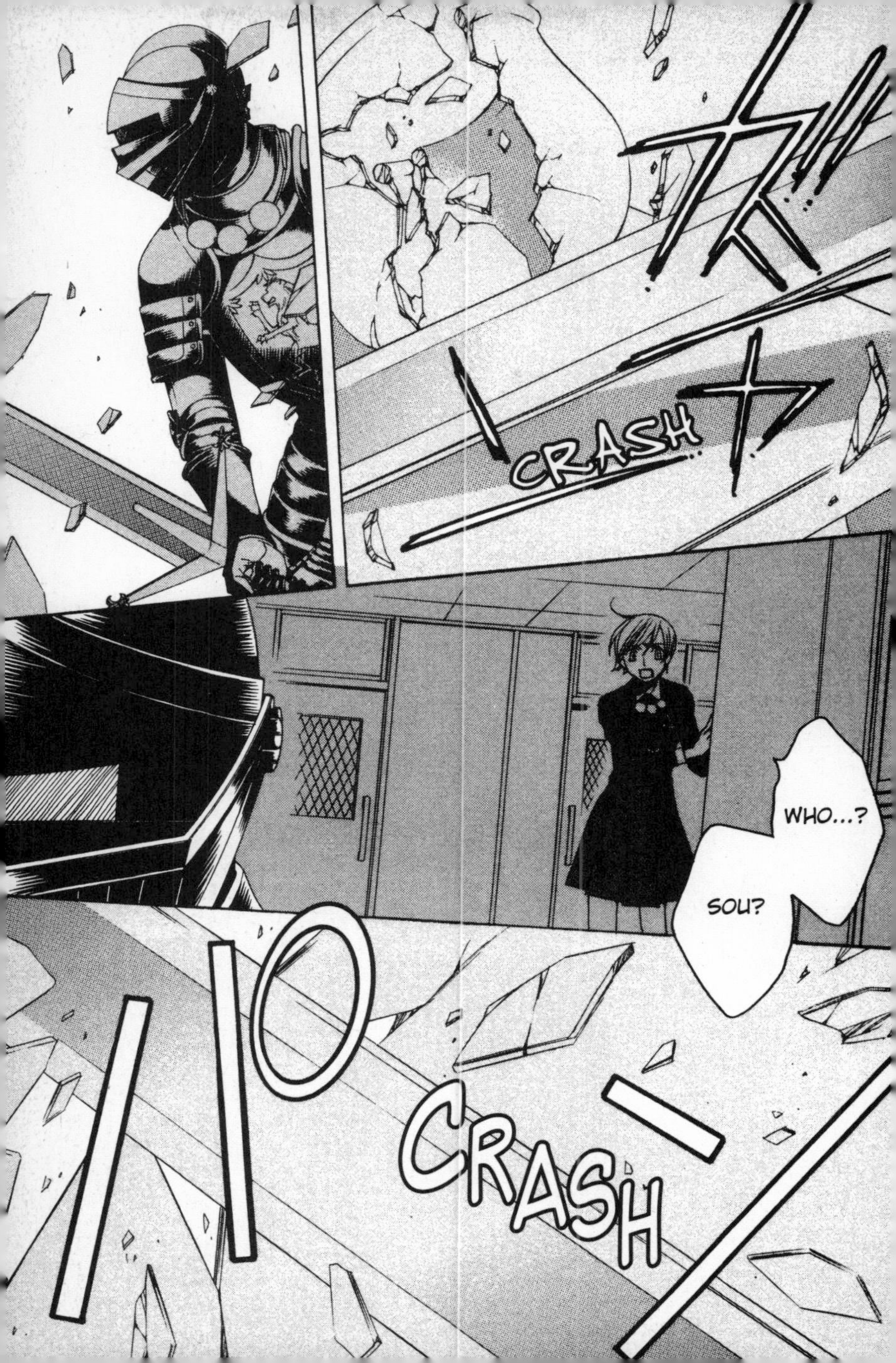
CRASH
WHO...?
SOU?
CRASH

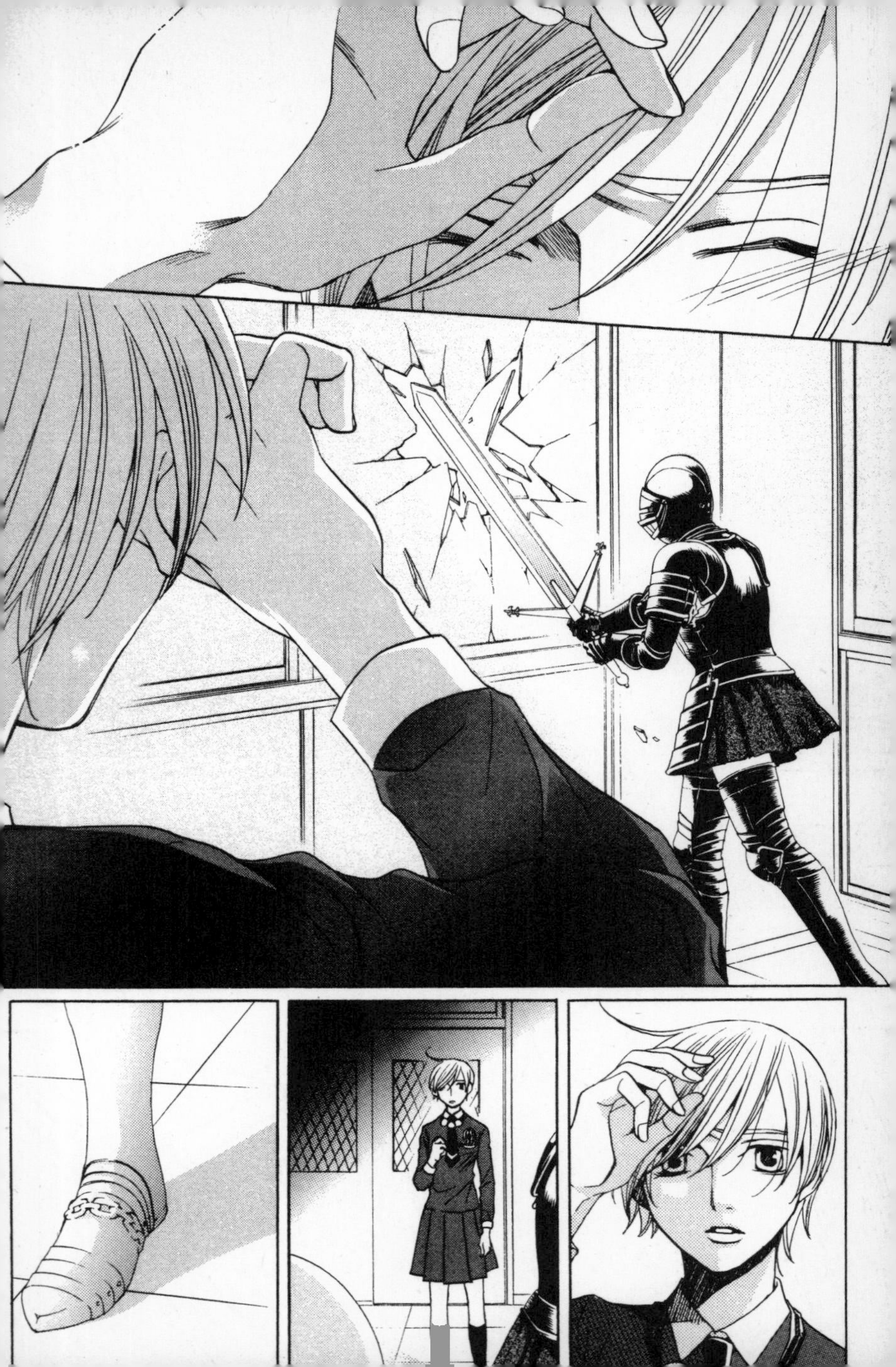

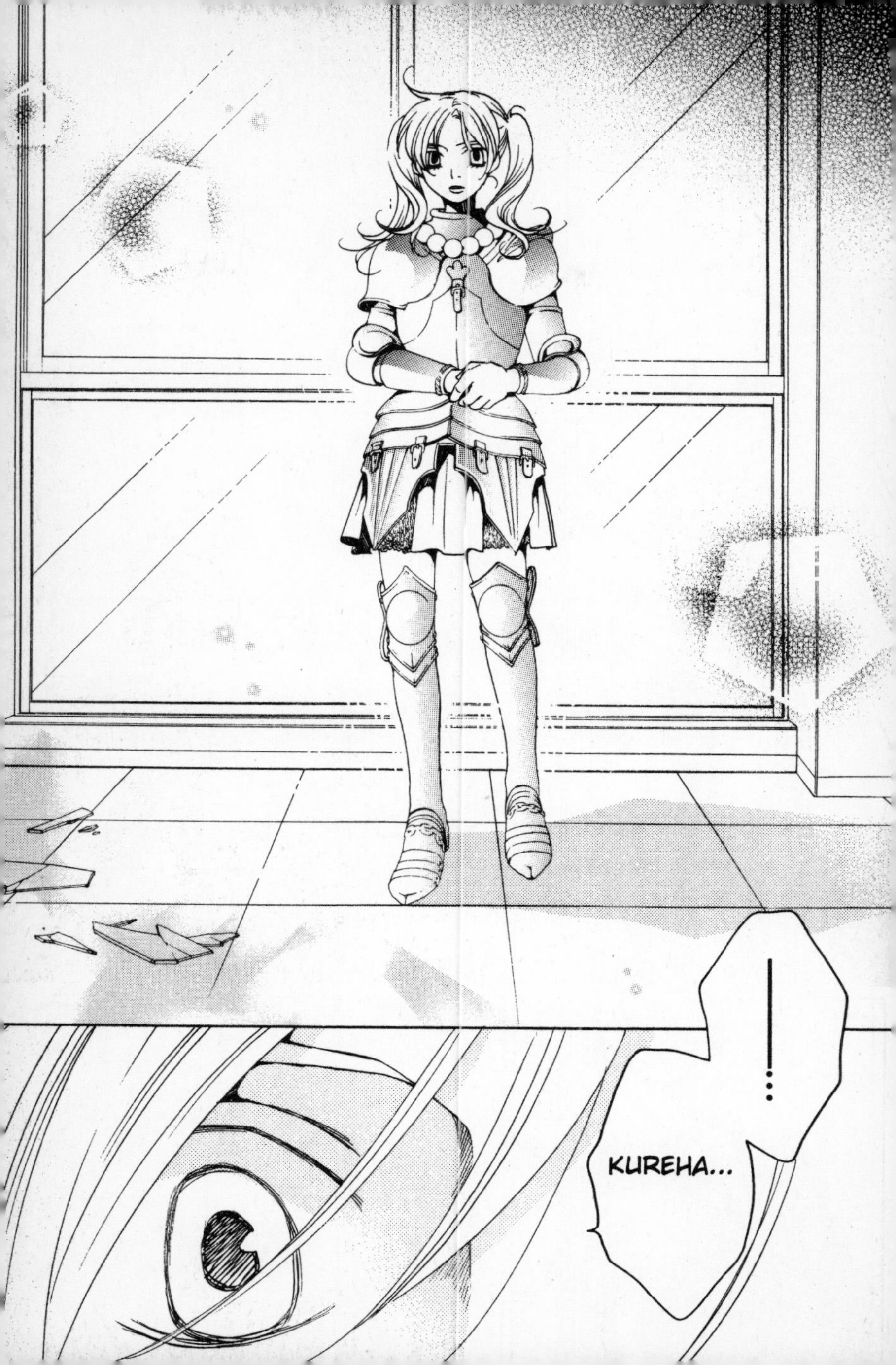
!...
KUREHA...

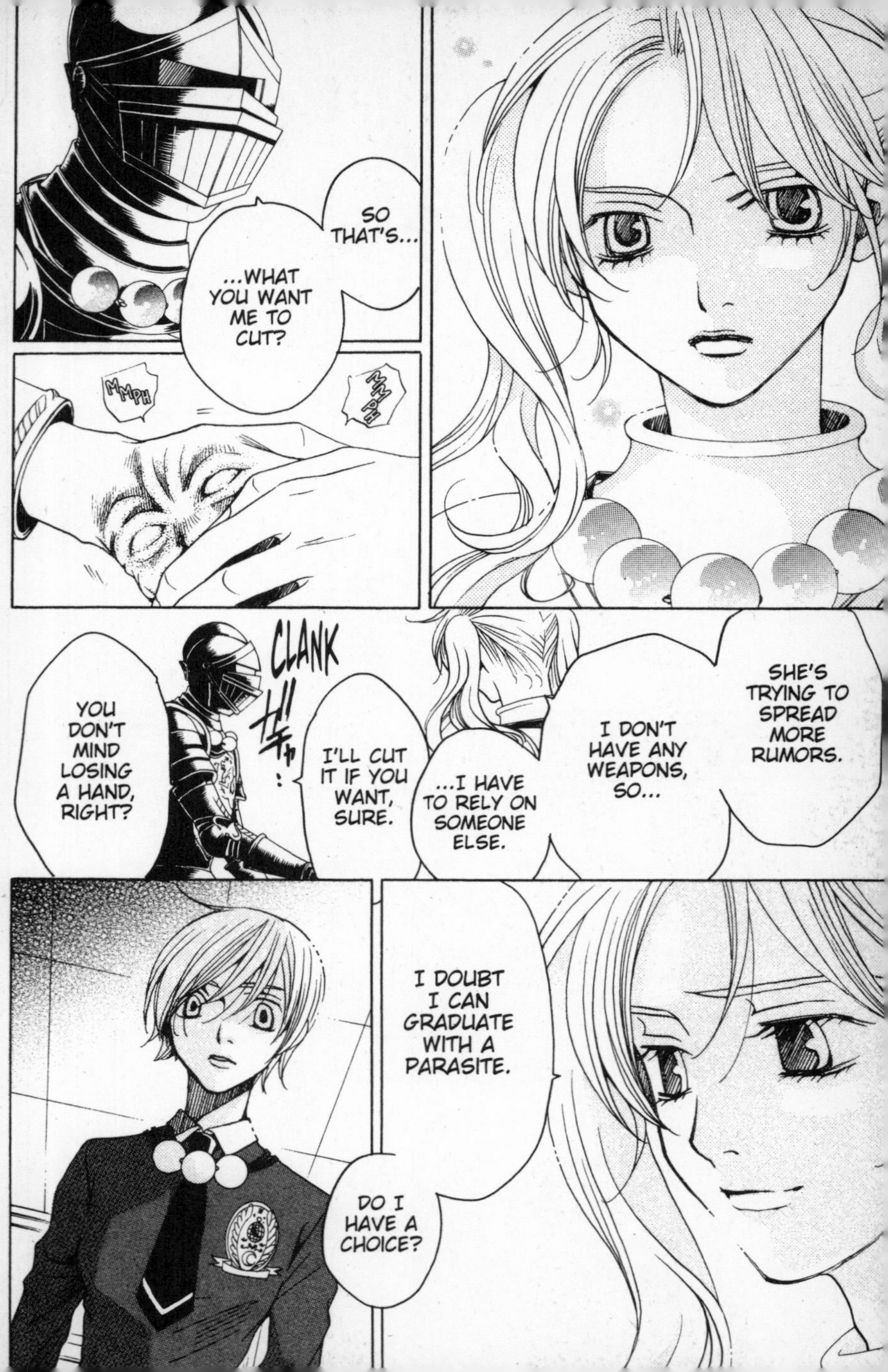
SO THAT'S...
...WHAT YOU WANT ME TO CUT?
MMPH
MMPH
SHE'S TRYING TO SPREAD MORE RUMORS.
I DON'T HAVE ANY WEAPONS, SO...
...I HAVE TO RELY ON SOMEONE ELSE.
I'LL CUT IT IF YOU WANT, SURE.
CLANK
YOU DON'T MIND LOSING A HAND, RIGHT?
I DOUBT I CAN GRADUATE WITH A PARASITE.
DO I HAVE A CHOICE?

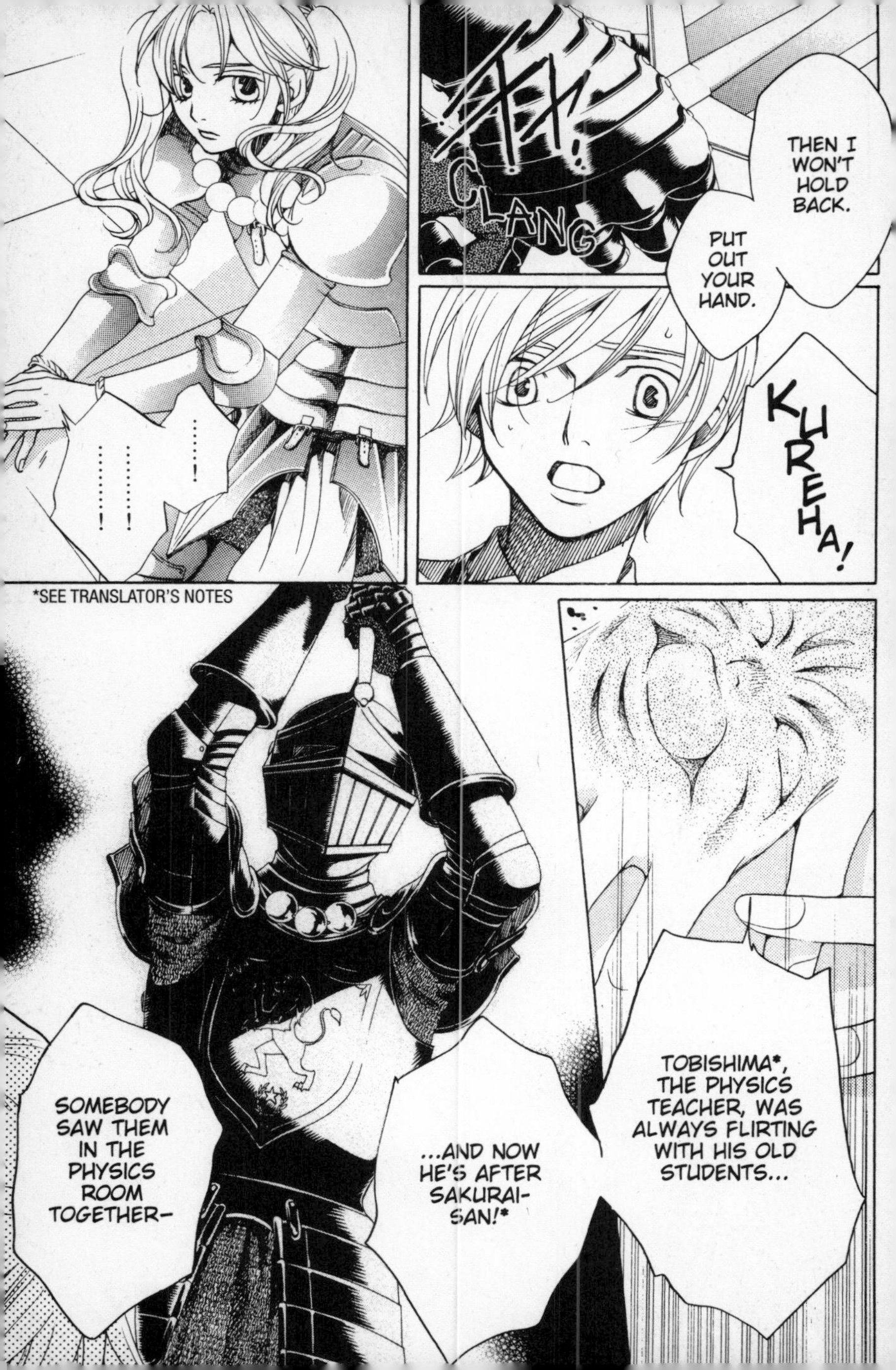
CLANG
THEN I WON'T HOLD BACK.
PUT OUT YOUR HAND.
KUREHA!
......!
......!
......!
TOBISHIMA*, THE PHYSICS TEACHER, WAS ALWAYS FLIRTING WITH HIS OLD STUDENTS...
...AND NOW HE'S AFTER SAKURAI-SAN!*
SOMEBODY SAW THEM IN THE PHYSICS ROOM TOGETHER–

*SEE TRANSLATOR'S NOTES

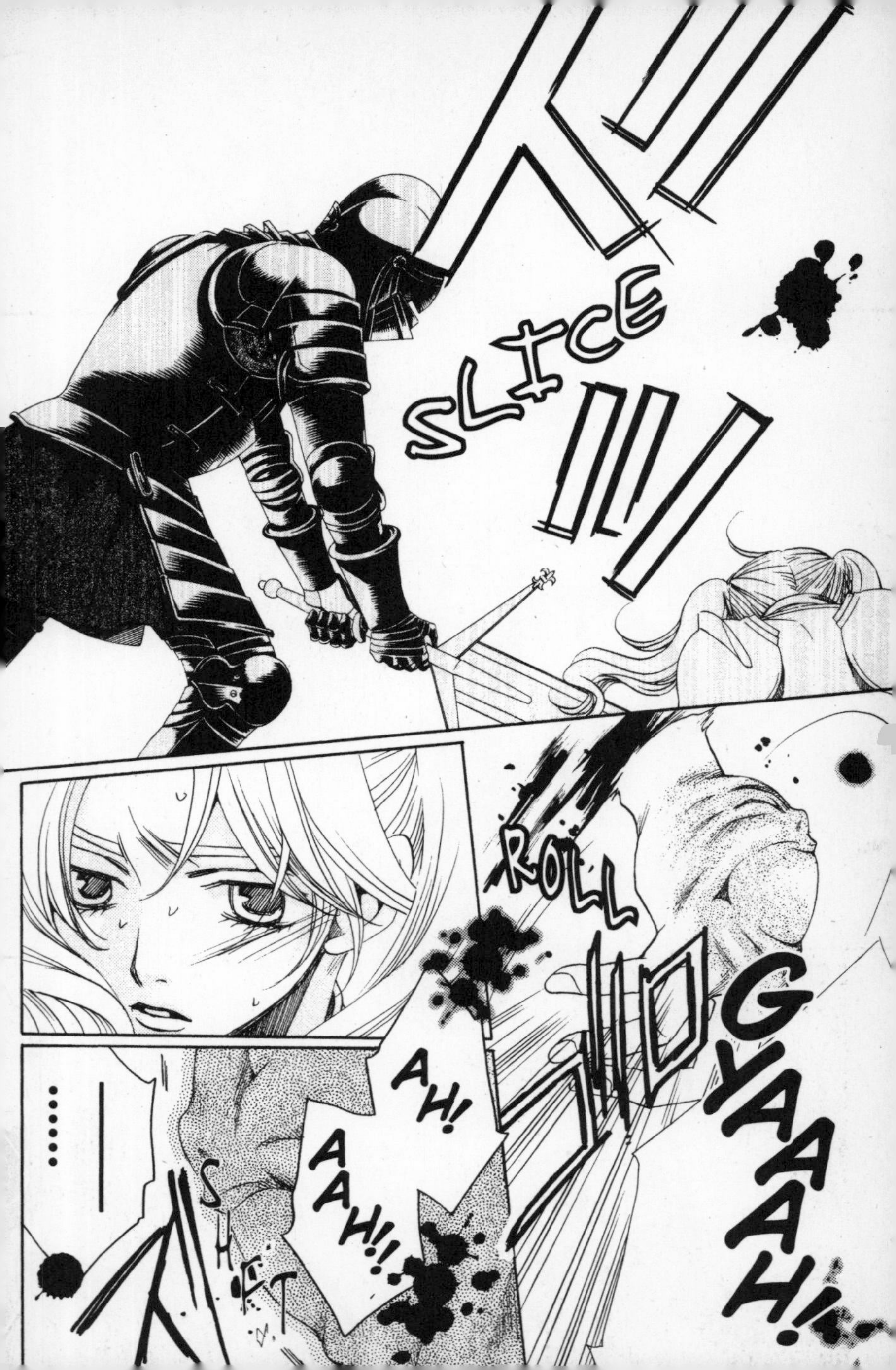
SLICE
ROLL
GYAAAAH!!
AH!
AAAH!!
......

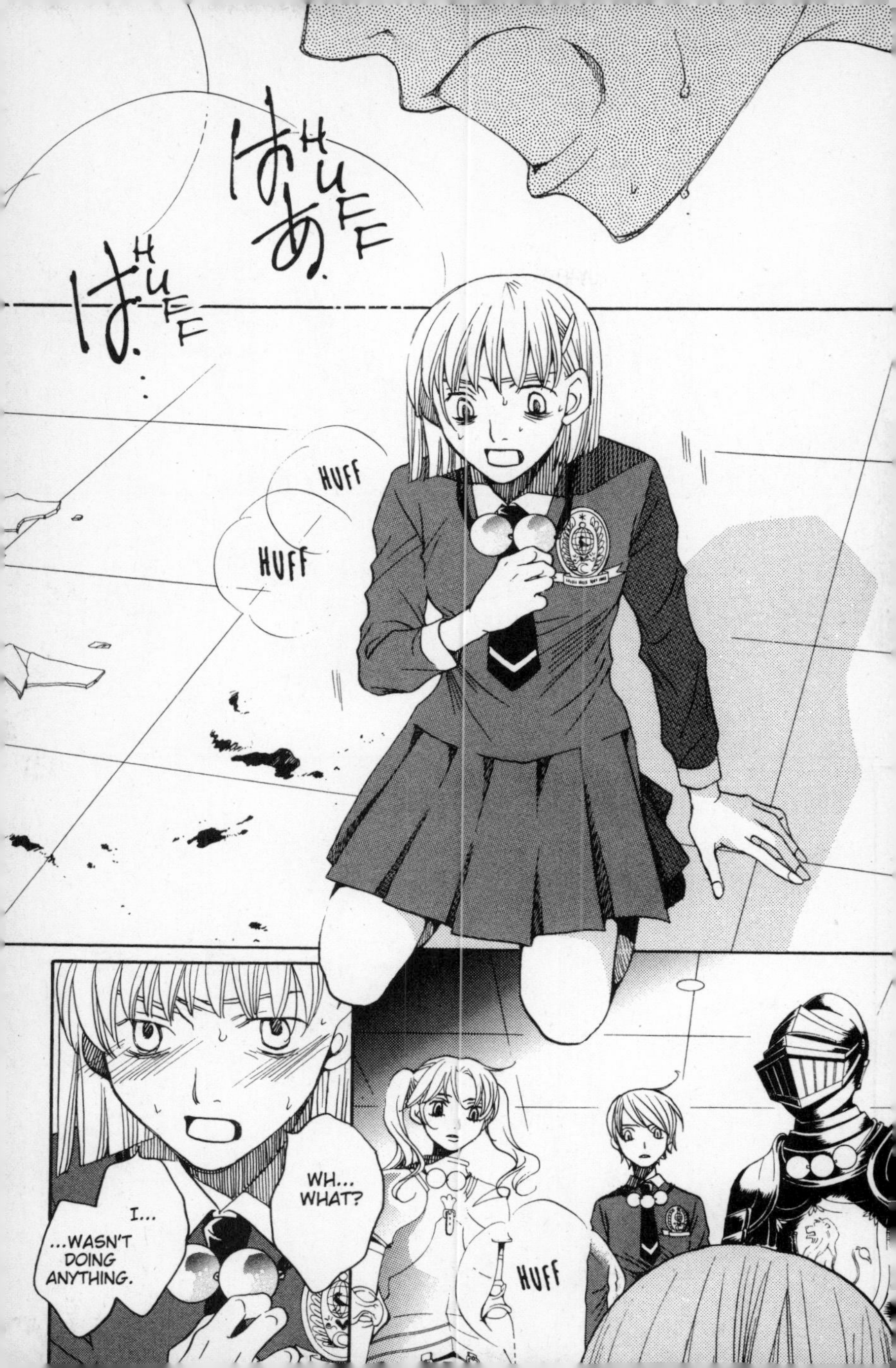
はあ HUFF
は HUFF
HUFF
HUFF
WH... WHAT?
HUFF
I...
...WASN'T DOING ANYTHING.

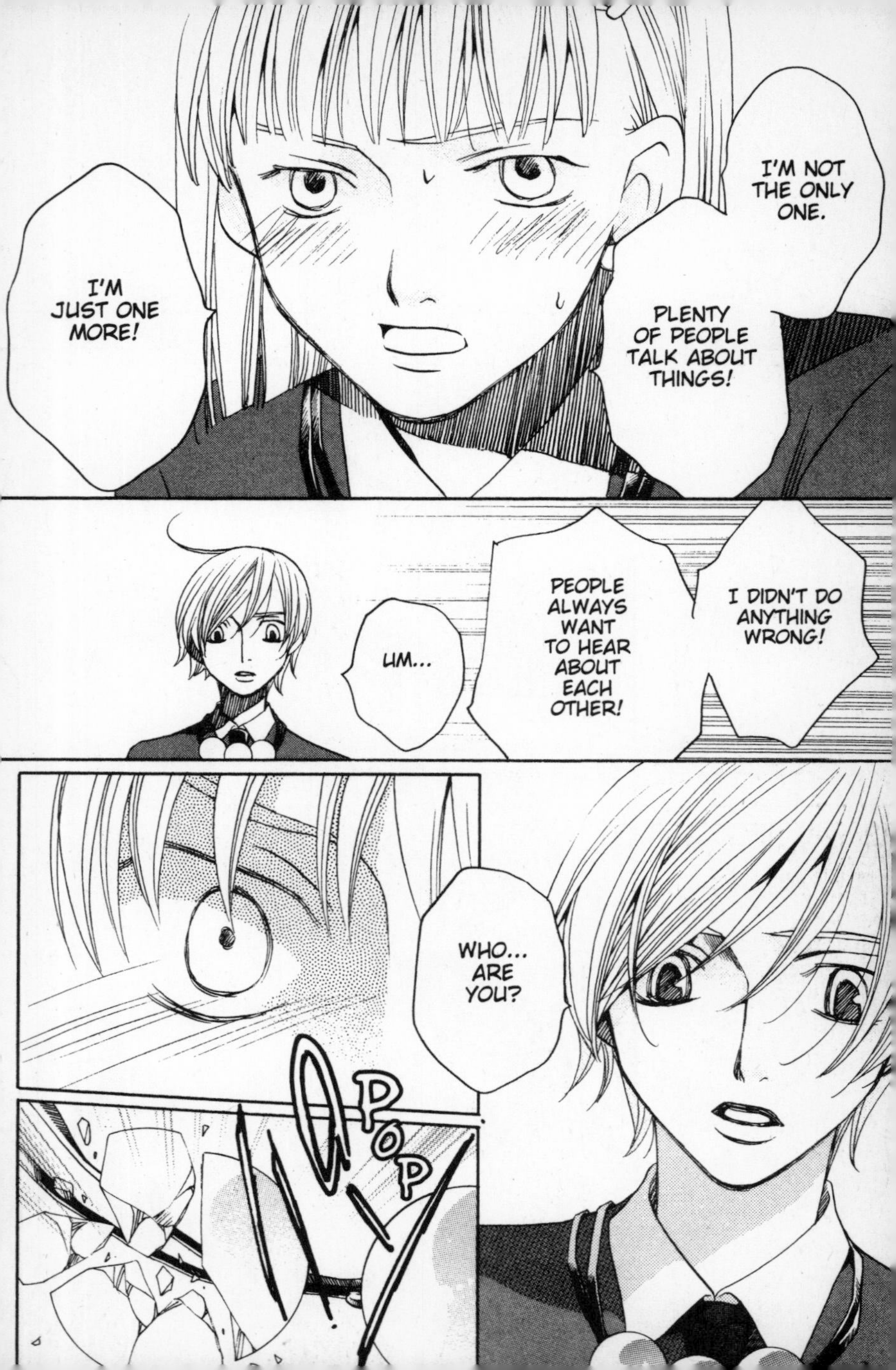
I'M NOT THE ONLY ONE.
PLENTY OF PEOPLE TALK ABOUT THINGS!
I'M JUST ONE MORE!
I DIDN'T DO ANYTHING WRONG!
PEOPLE ALWAYS WANT TO HEAR ABOUT EACH OTHER!
UM...
WHO... ARE YOU?
POP

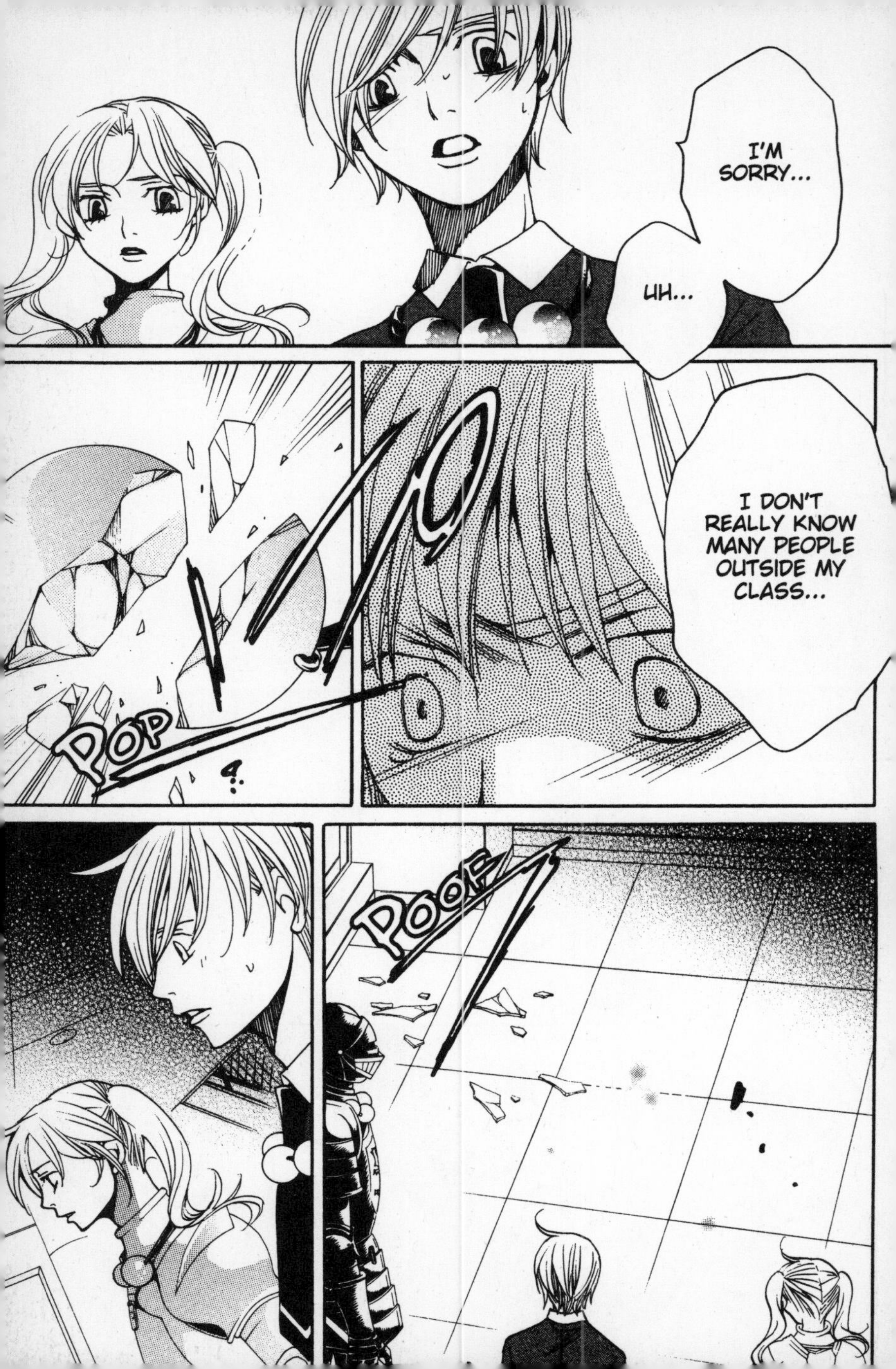
I'M SORRY...
UH...
I DON'T REALLY KNOW MANY PEOPLE OUTSIDE MY CLASS...
POP
POOF

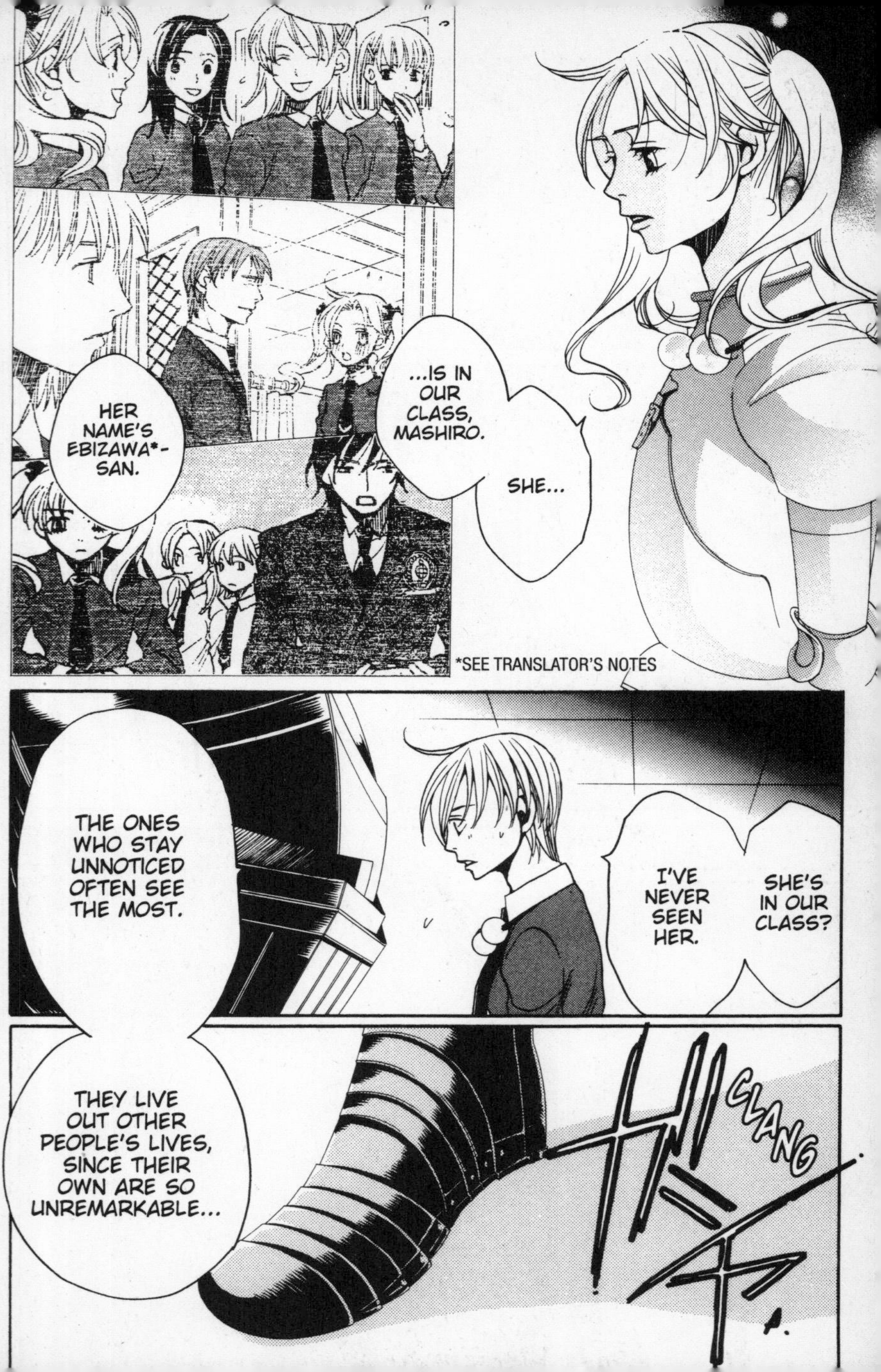
SHE...
...IS IN OUR CLASS, MASHIRO.
HER NAME'S EBIZAWA*-SAN.
*SEE TRANSLATOR'S NOTES
SHE'S IN OUR CLASS?
I'VE NEVER SEEN HER.
THE ONES WHO STAY UNNOTICED OFTEN SEE THE MOST.
CLANG
THEY LIVE OUT OTHER PEOPLE'S LIVES, SINCE THEIR OWN ARE SO UNREMARKABLE...

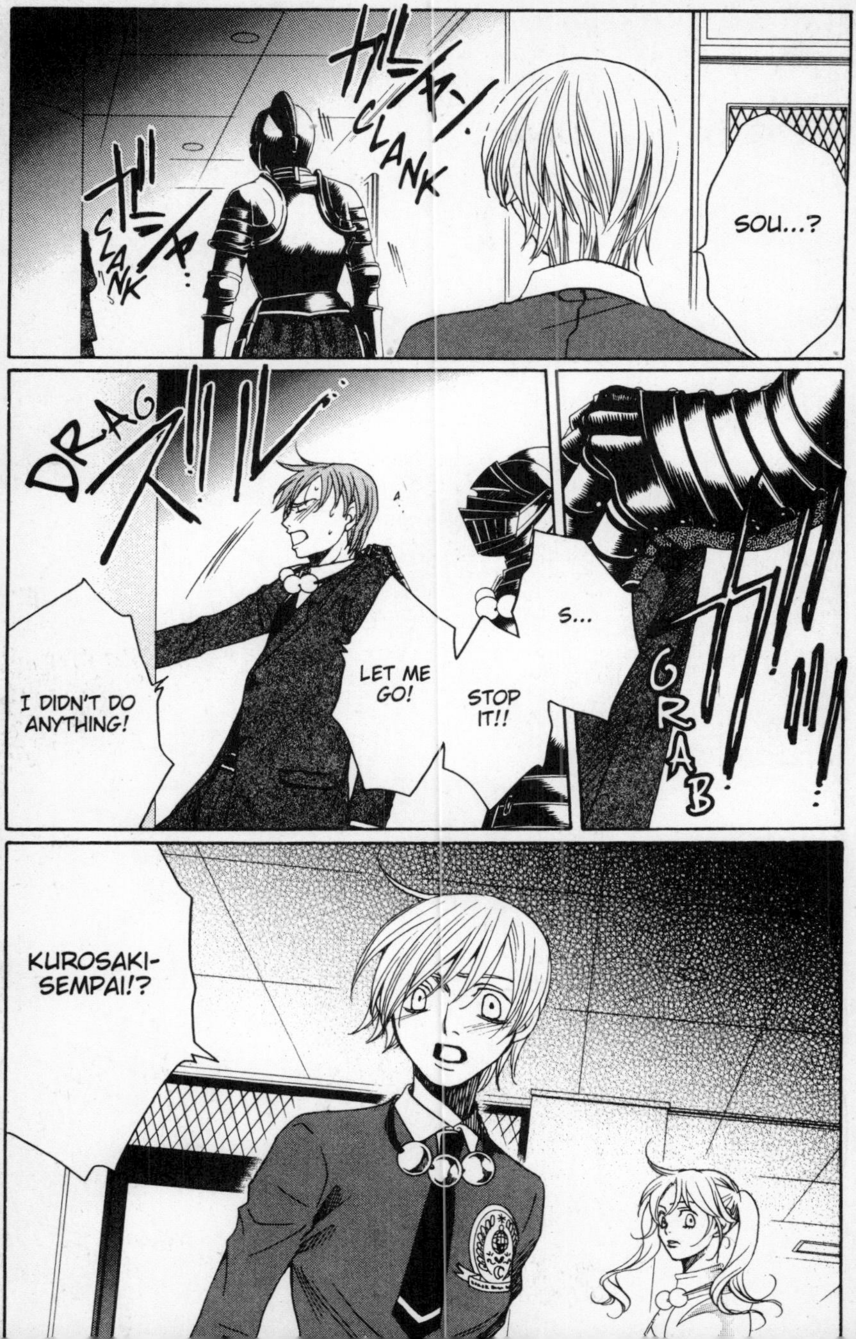
SOU...?
CLANK
CLANK
GRAB
S...
STOP IT!!
LET ME GO!
I DIDN'T DO ANYTHING!
DRAG
KUROSAKI-SEMPAI!?

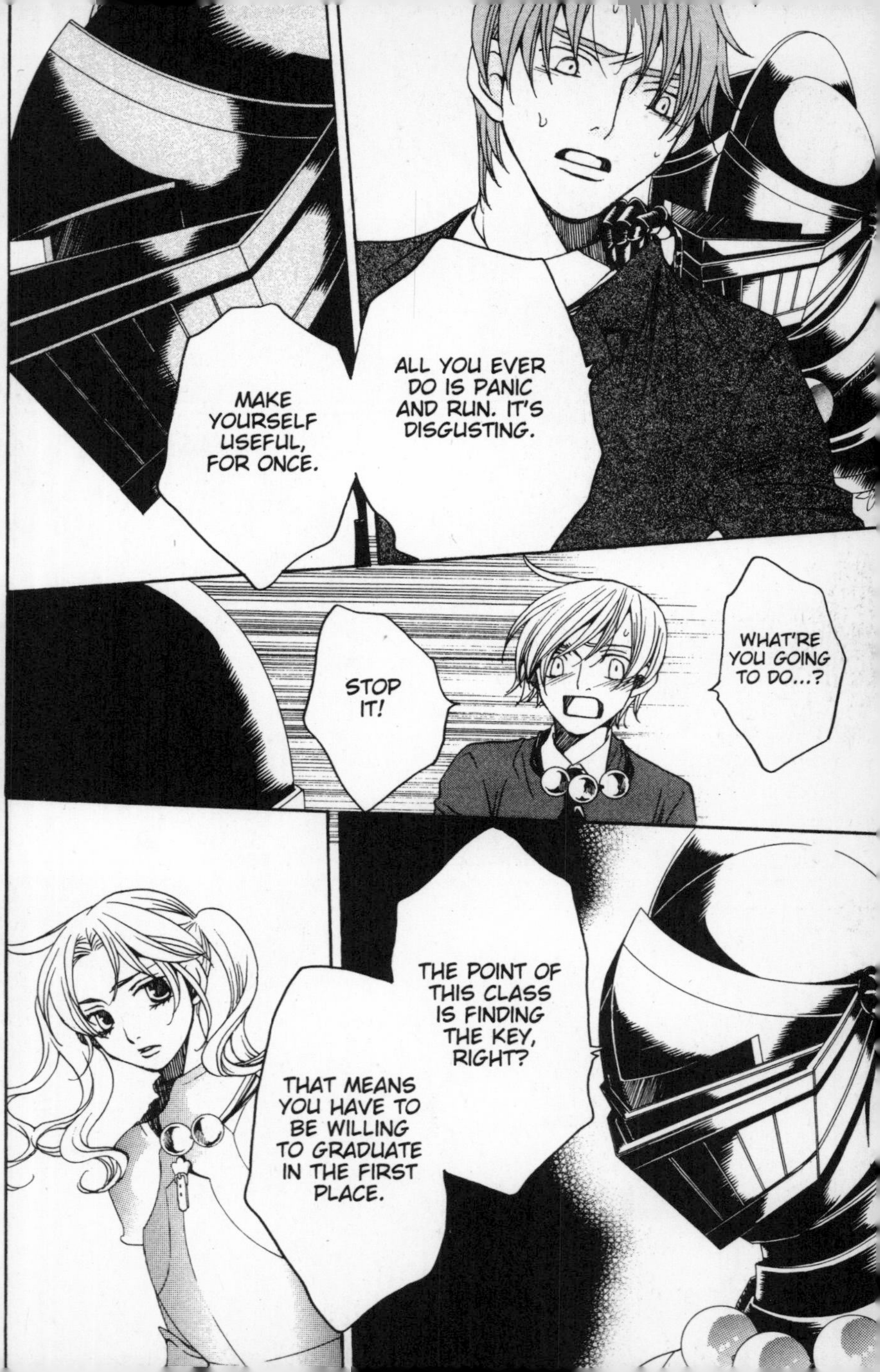
ALL YOU EVER DO IS PANIC AND RUN. IT'S DISGUSTING.
MAKE YOURSELF USEFUL, FOR ONCE.
WHAT'RE YOU GOING TO DO...?
STOP IT!
THE POINT OF THIS CLASS IS FINDING THE KEY, RIGHT?
THAT MEANS YOU HAVE TO BE WILLING TO GRADUATE IN THE FIRST PLACE.

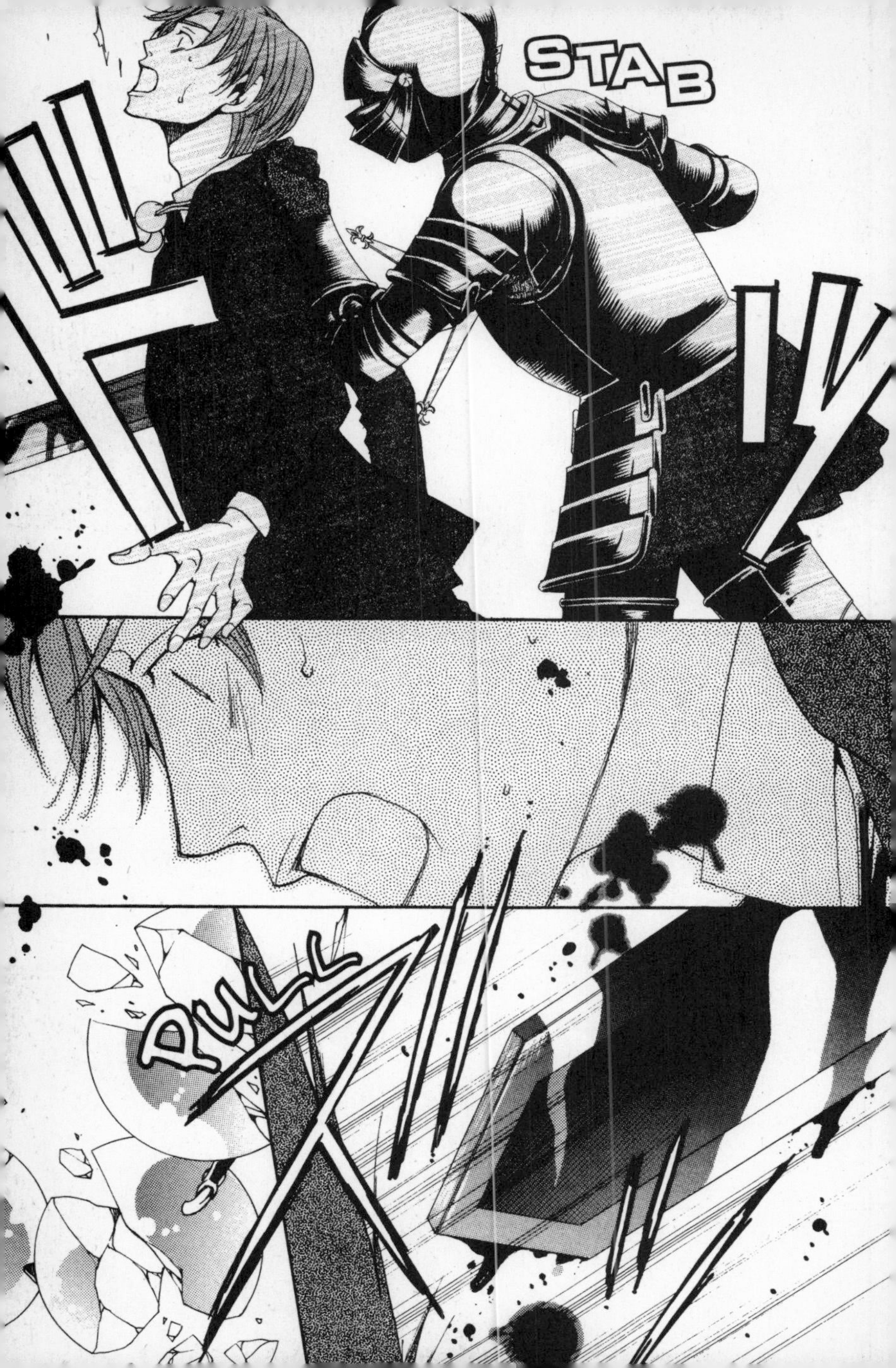
STAB
PULL

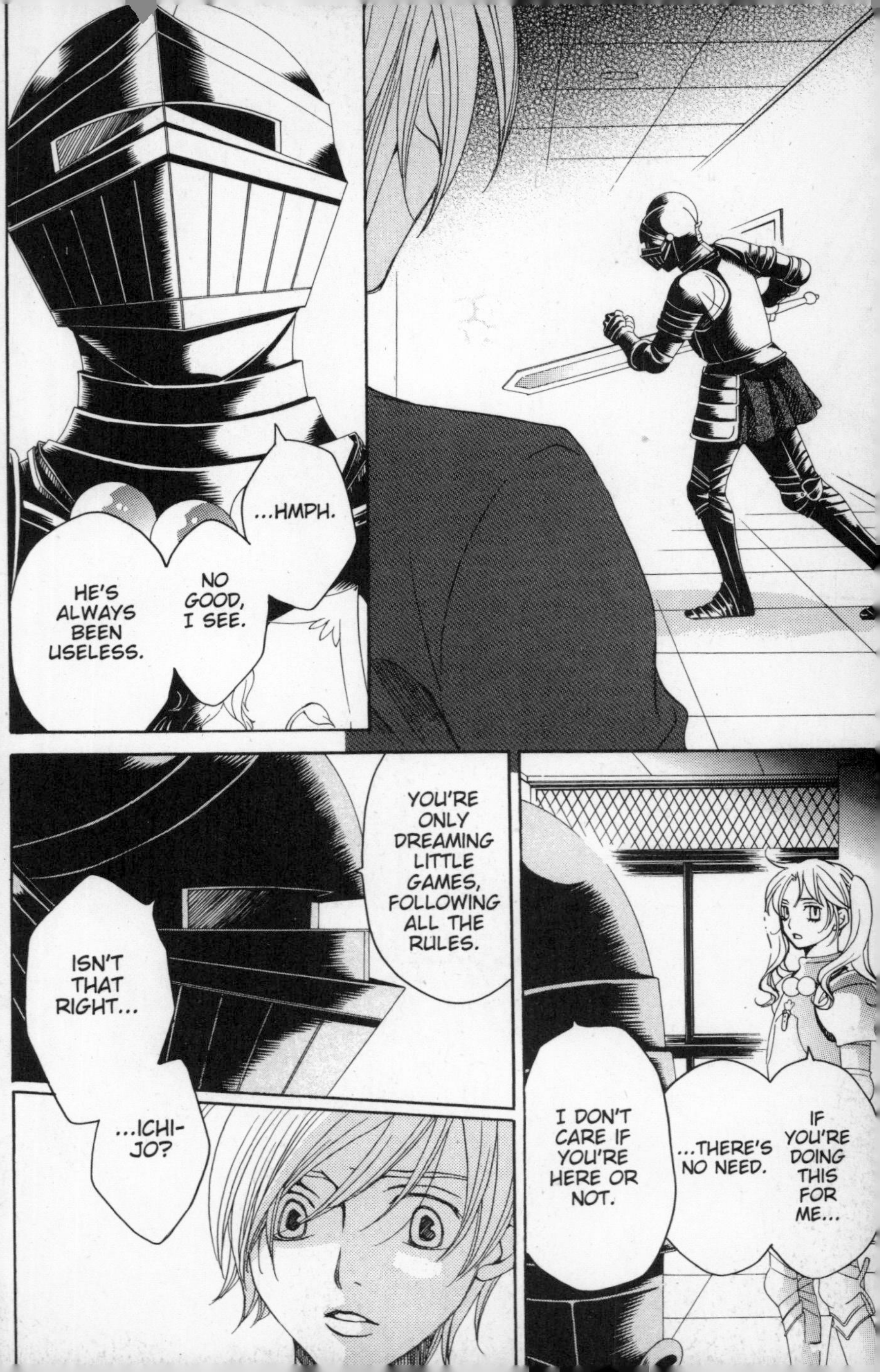
...HMPH.
NO GOOD, I SEE.
HE'S ALWAYS BEEN USELESS.
IF YOU'RE DOING THIS FOR ME...
...THERE'S NO NEED.
I DON'T CARE IF YOU'RE HERE OR NOT.
YOU'RE ONLY DREAMING LITTLE GAMES, FOLLOWING ALL THE RULES.
ISN'T THAT RIGHT...
...ICHI-JO?

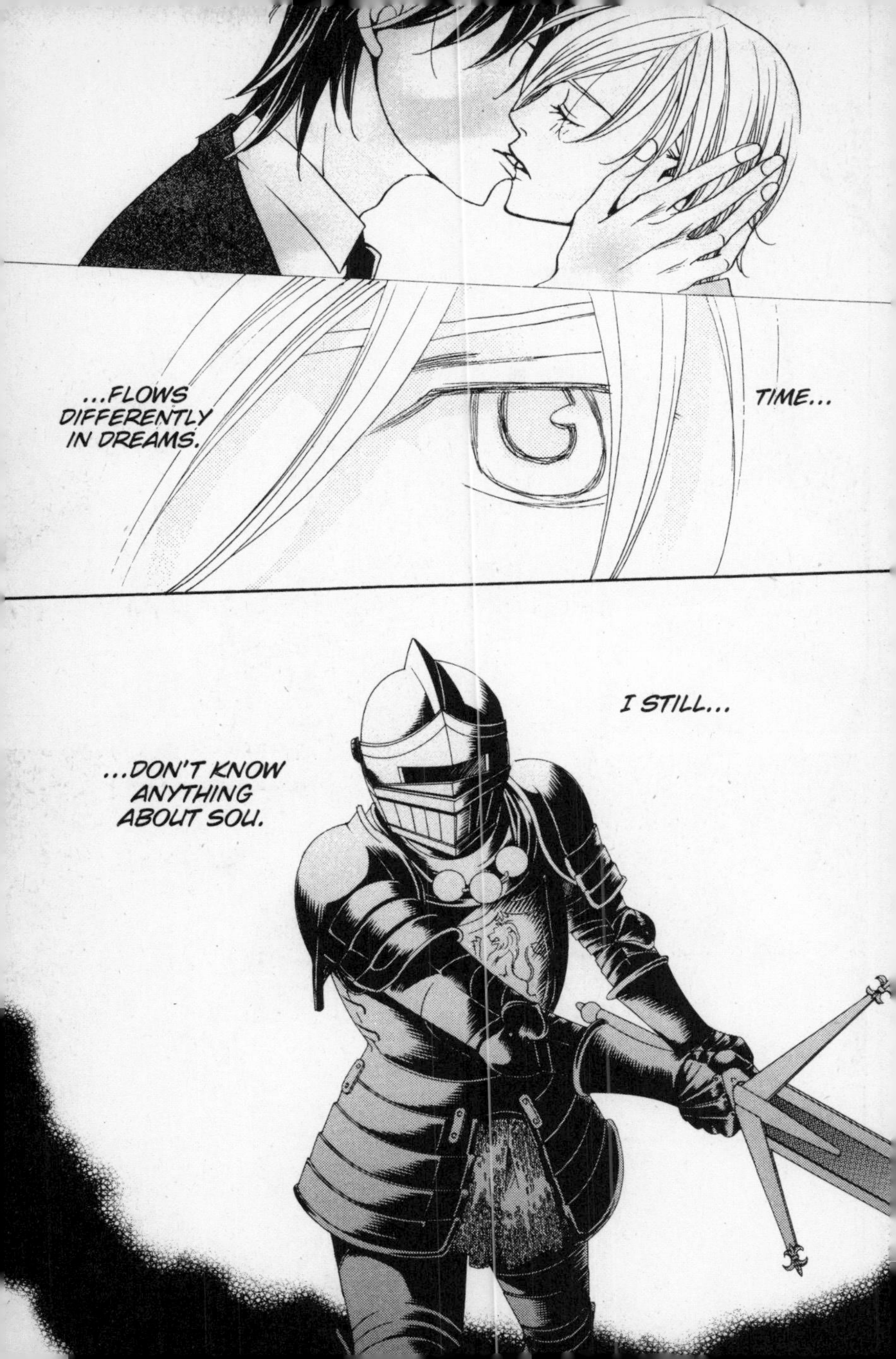
TIME...
...FLOWS DIFFERENTLY IN DREAMS.
I STILL...
...DON'T KNOW ANYTHING ABOUT SOU.

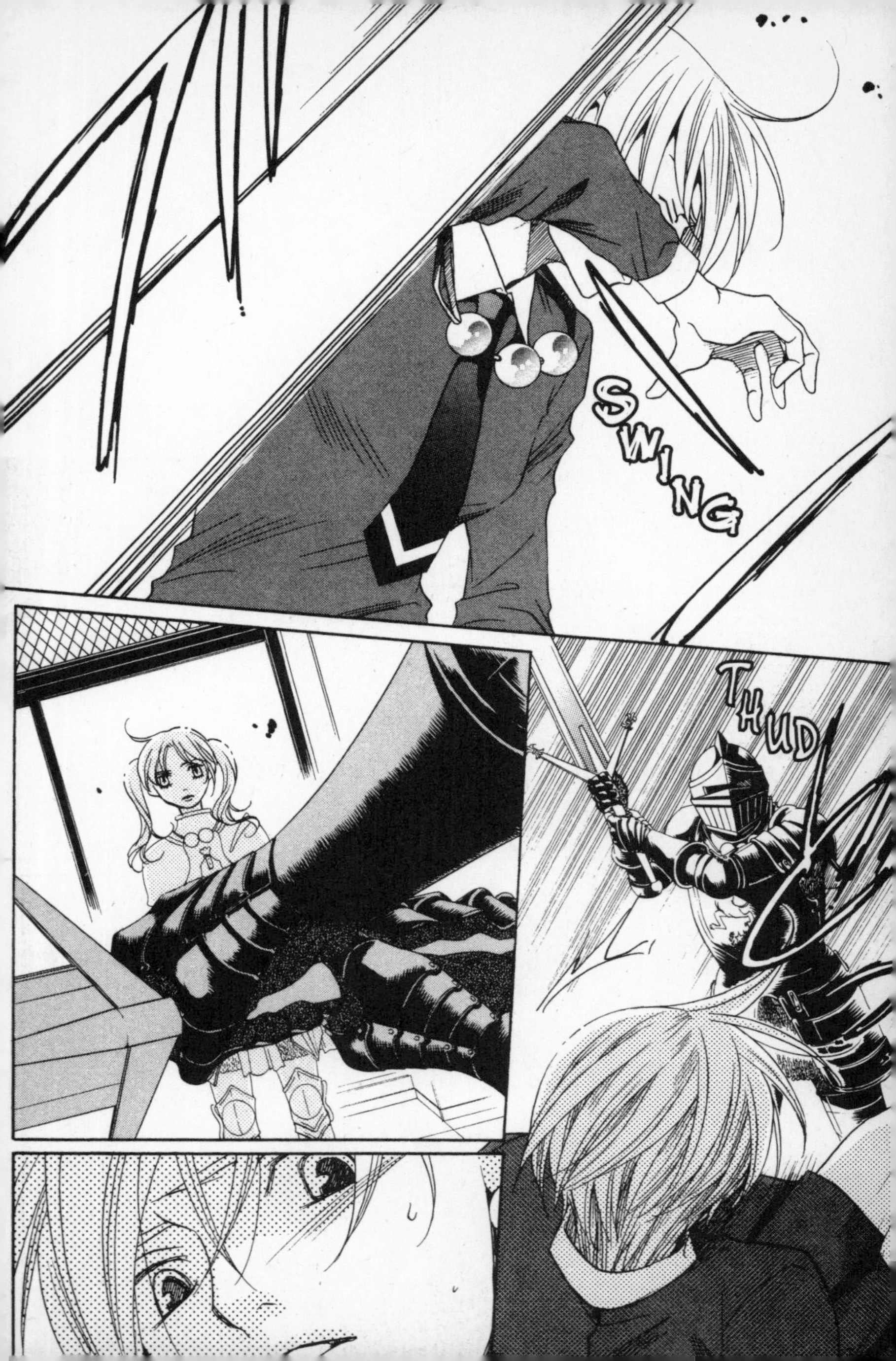
SWING
THUD

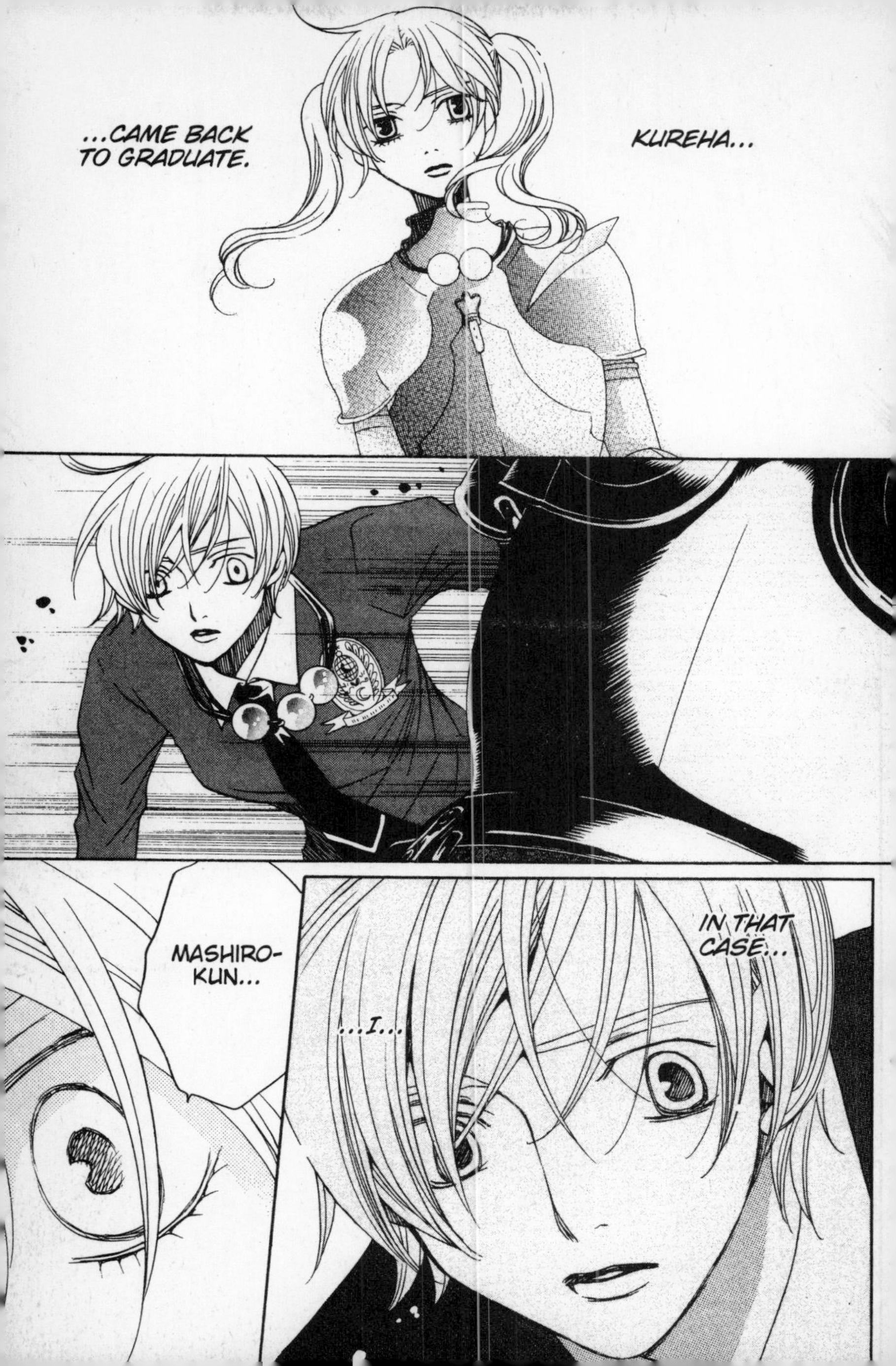
KUREHA...
...CAME BACK TO GRADUATE.
IN THAT CASE...
...I...
MASHIRO-KUN...

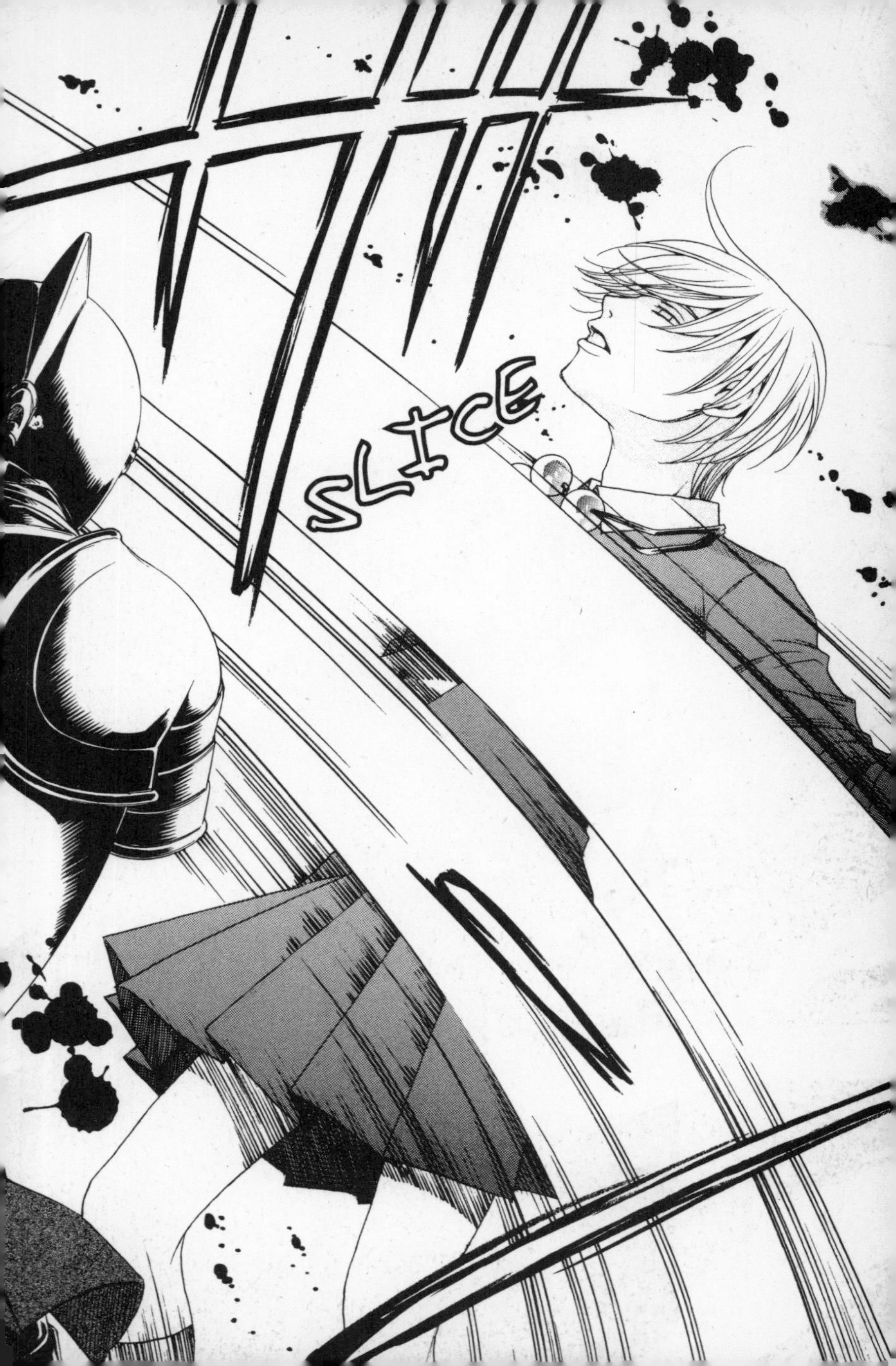
SLICE

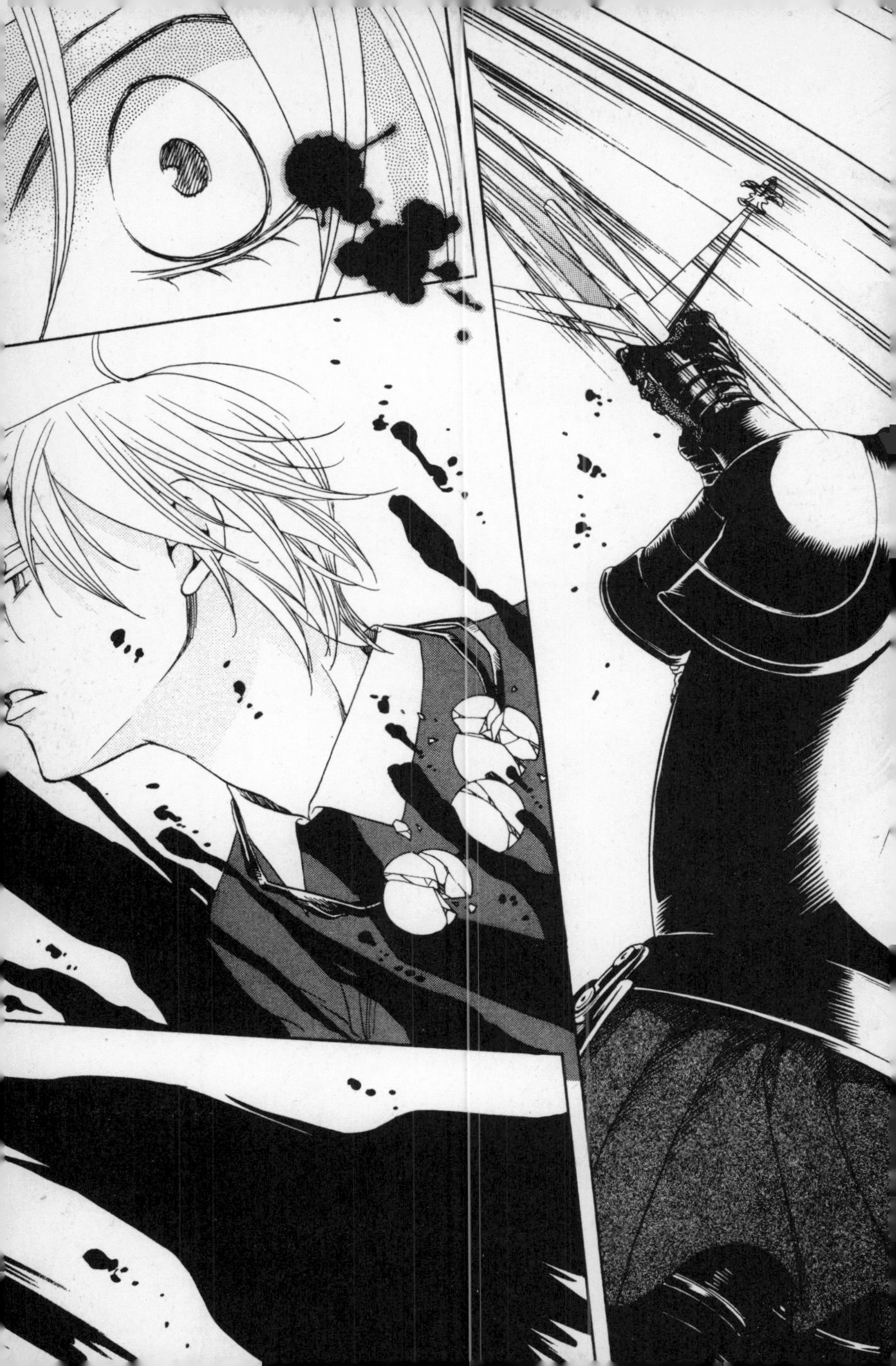

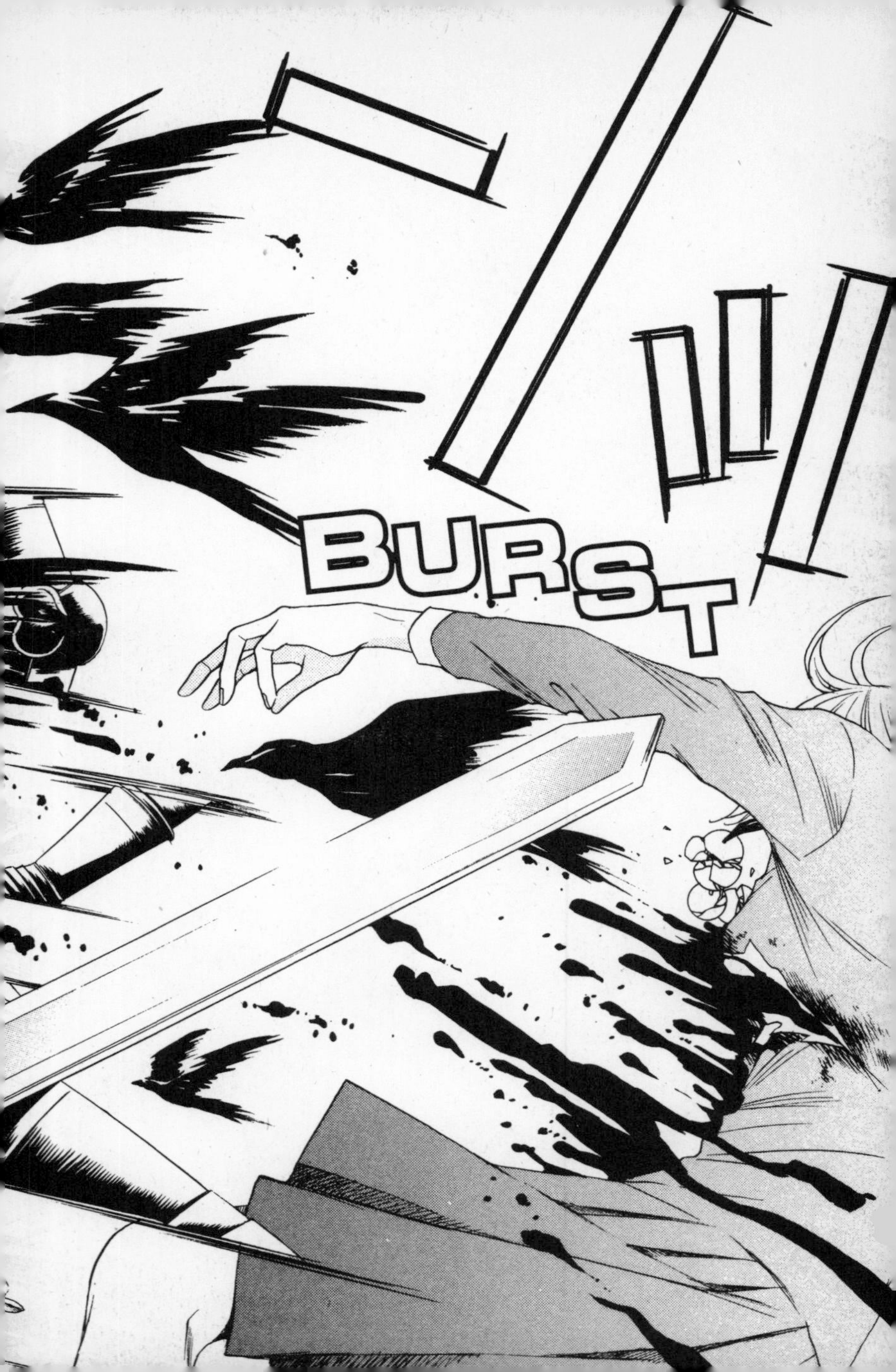
BURST

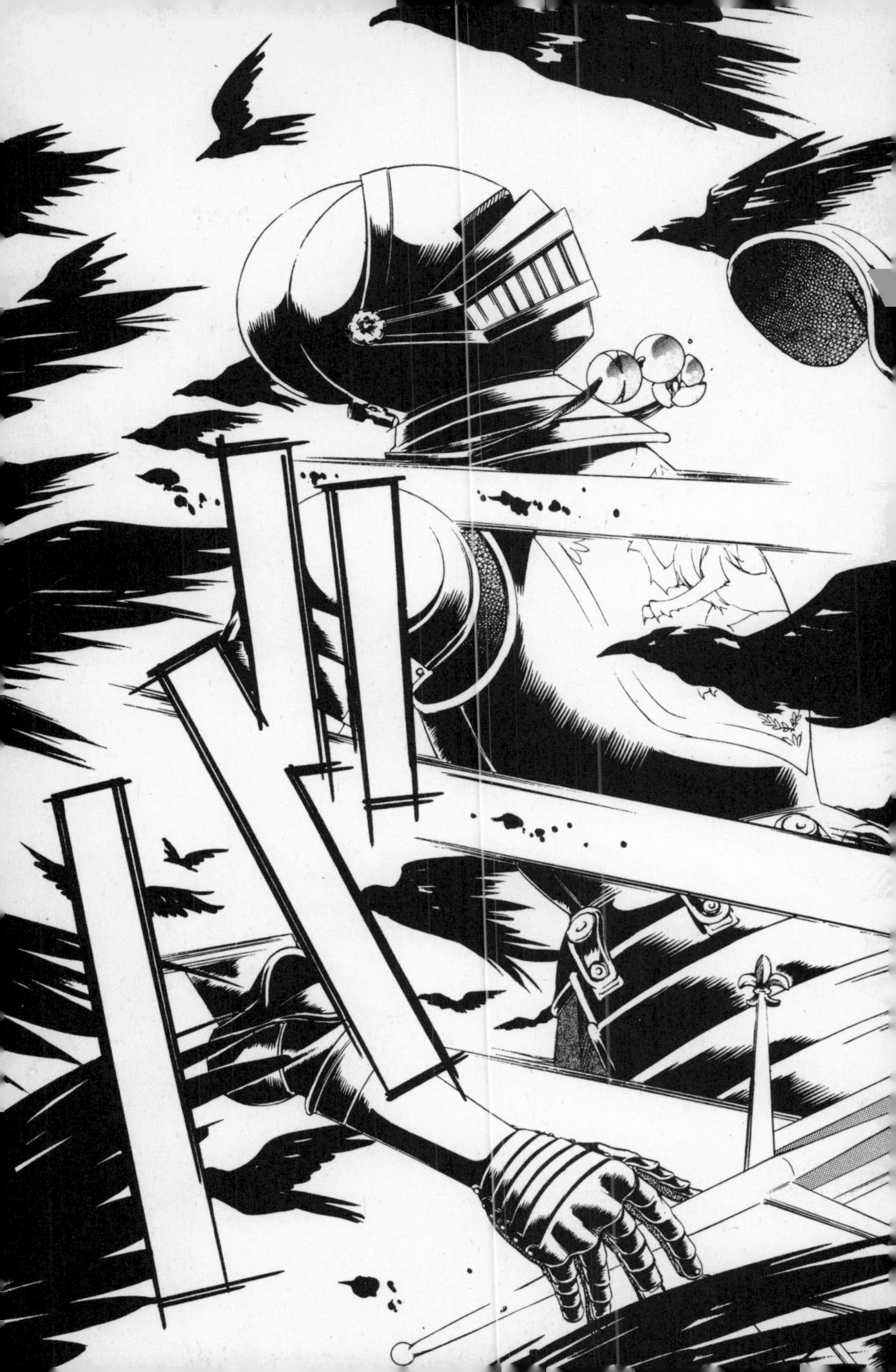

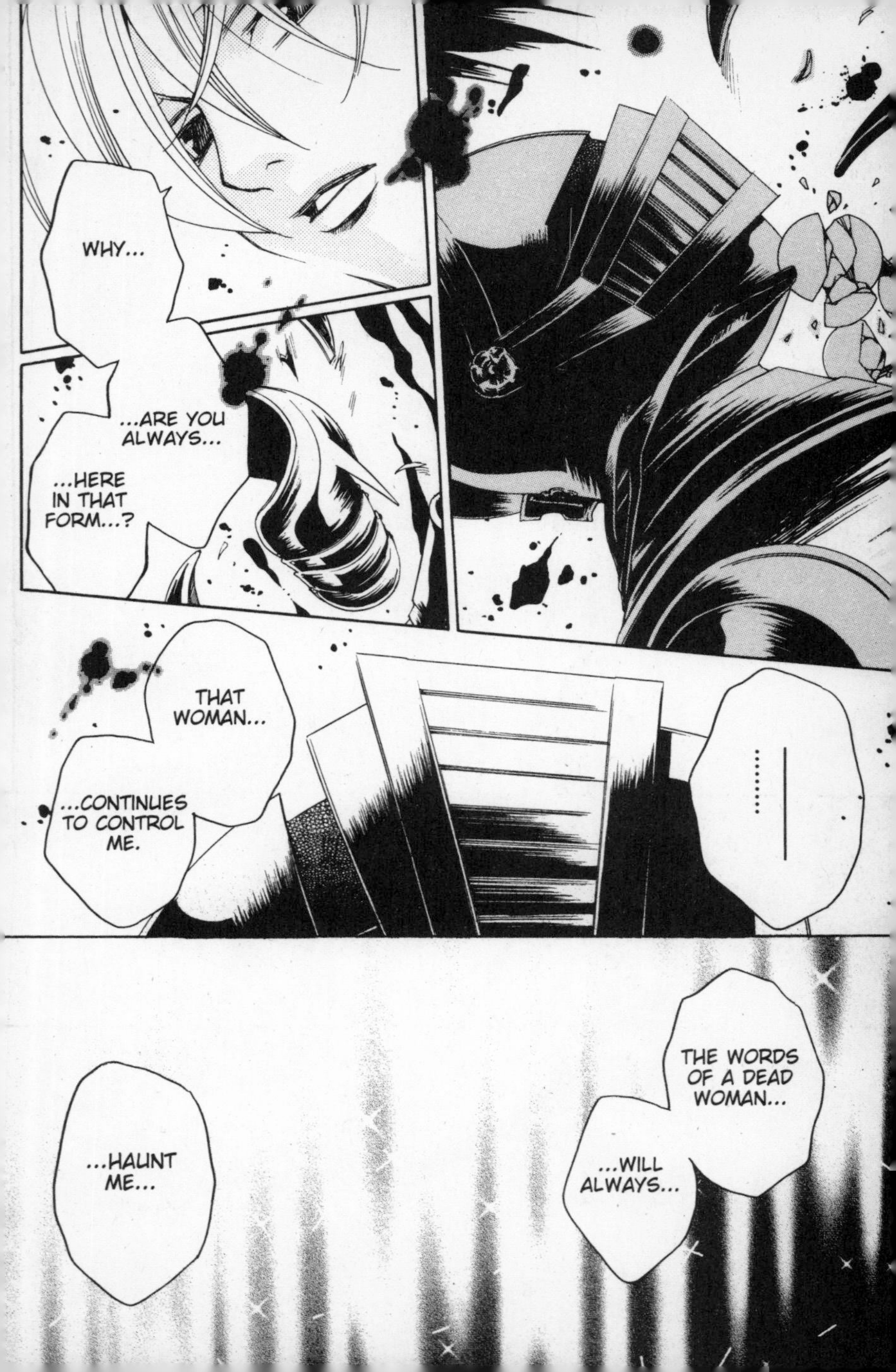
WHY...
...ARE YOU ALWAYS...
...HERE IN THAT FORM...?
THAT WOMAN...
...CONTINUES TO CONTROL ME.
......—
THE WORDS OF A DEAD WOMAN...
...WILL ALWAYS...
...HAUNT ME...

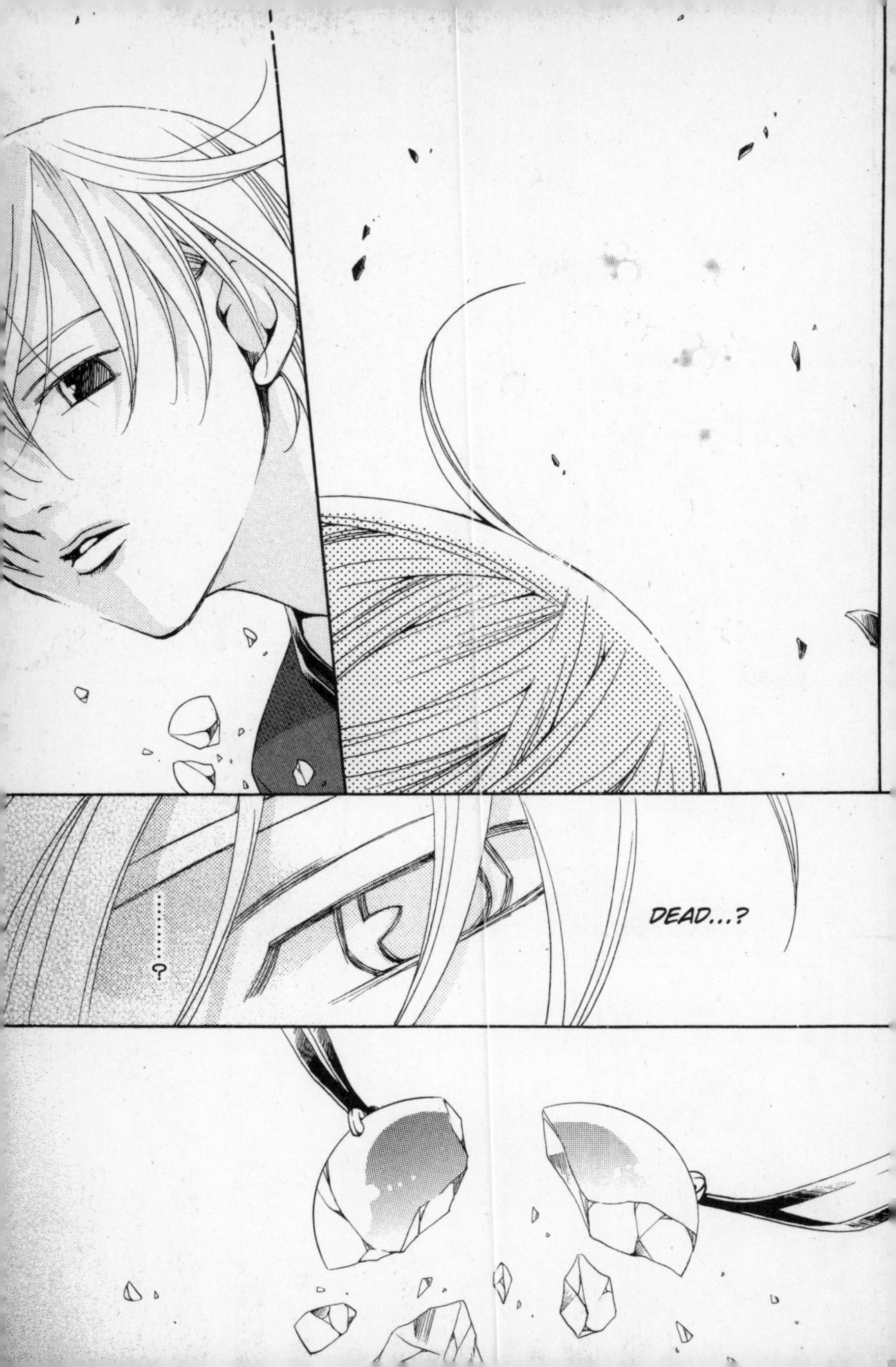
DEAD...?
......?

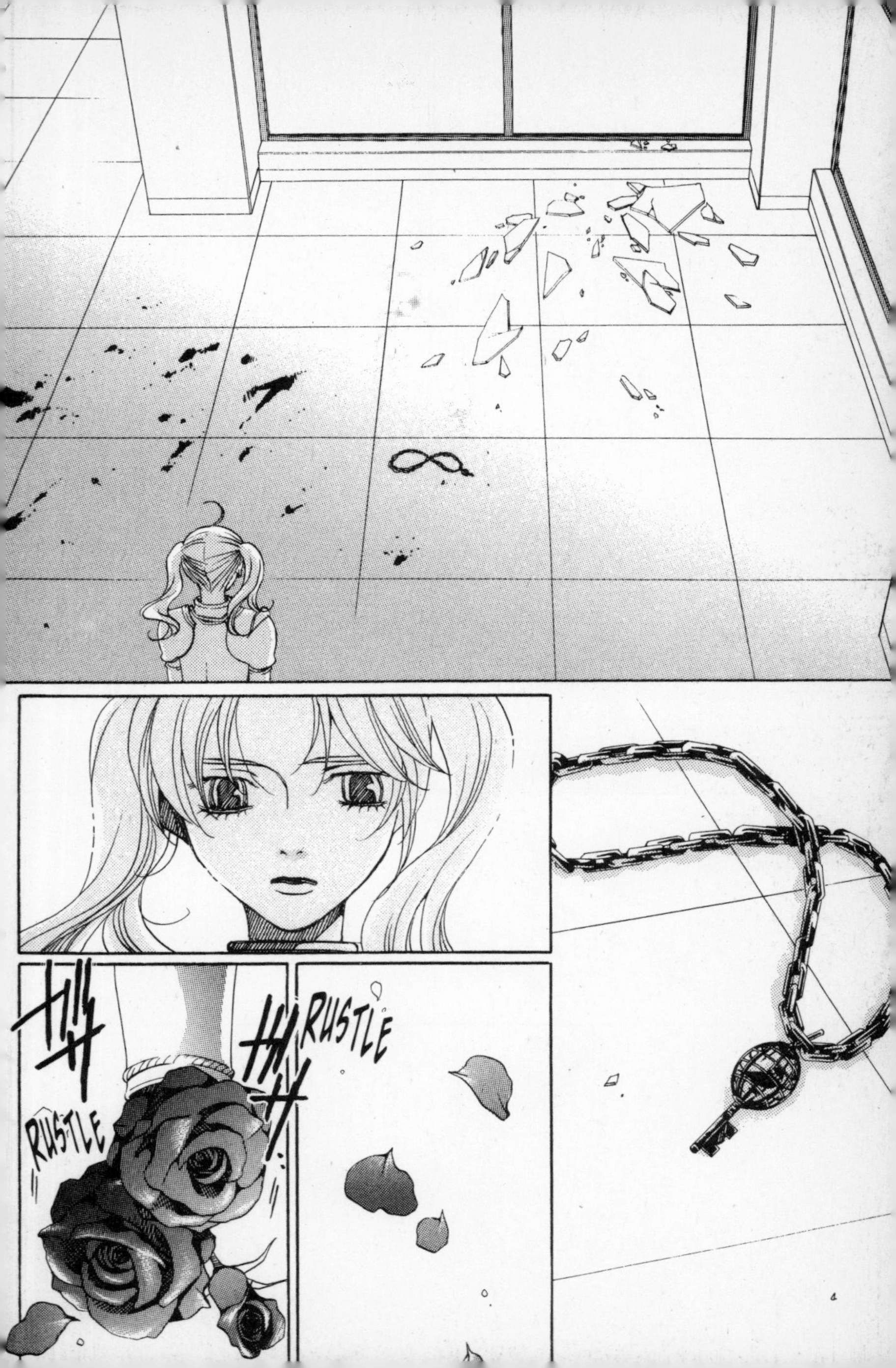
RUSTLE
RUSTLE

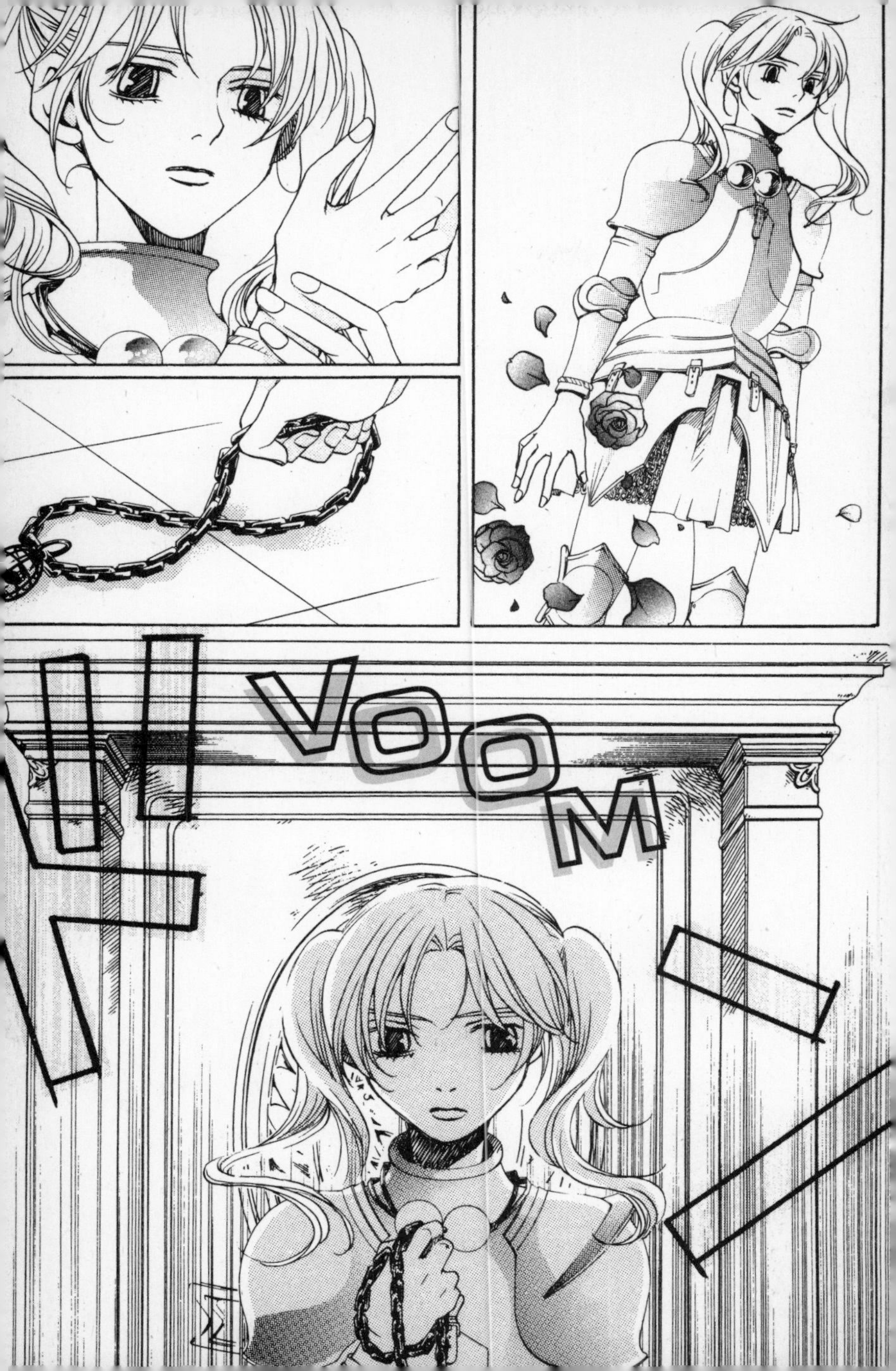
VOOM

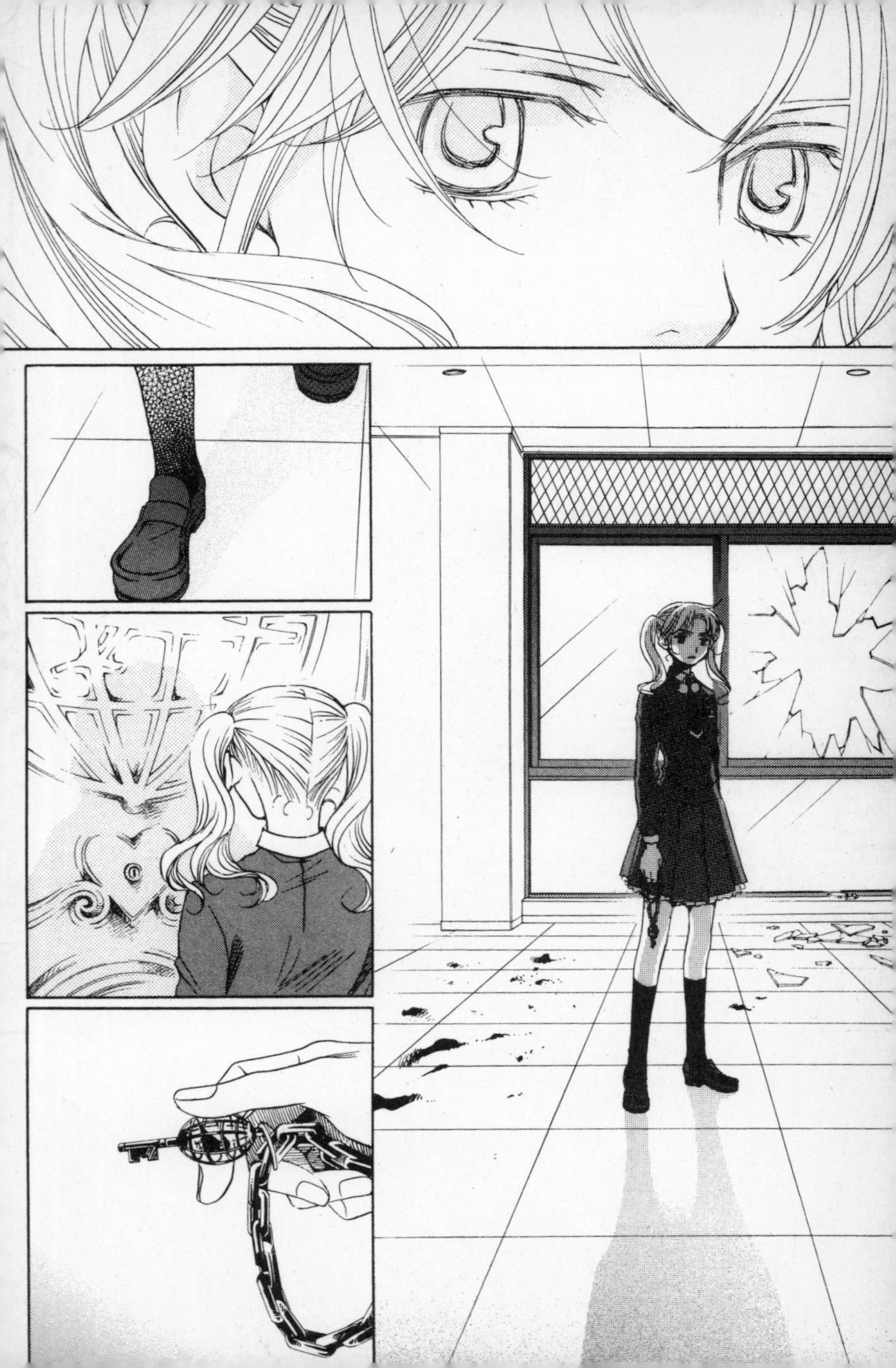

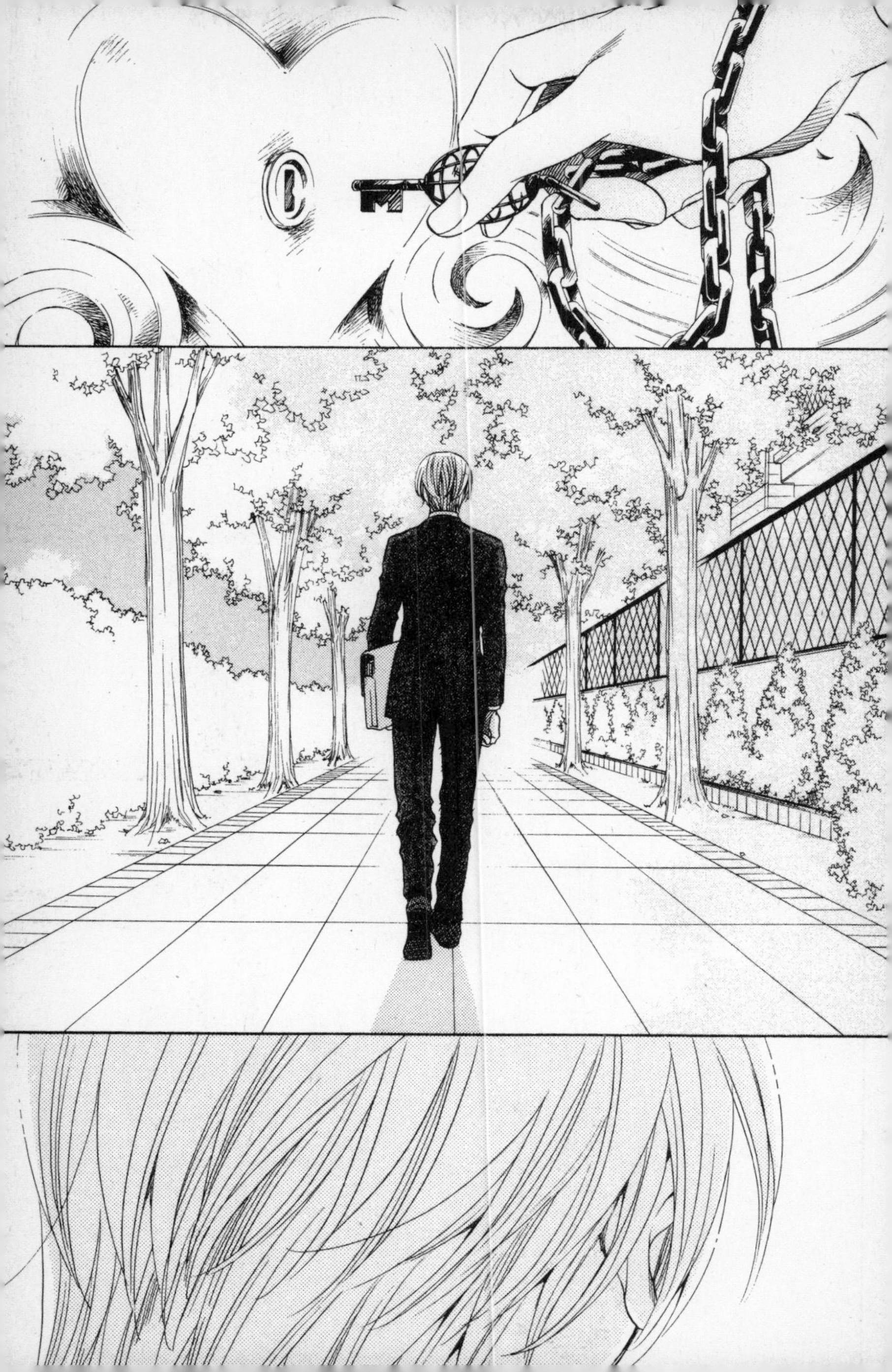

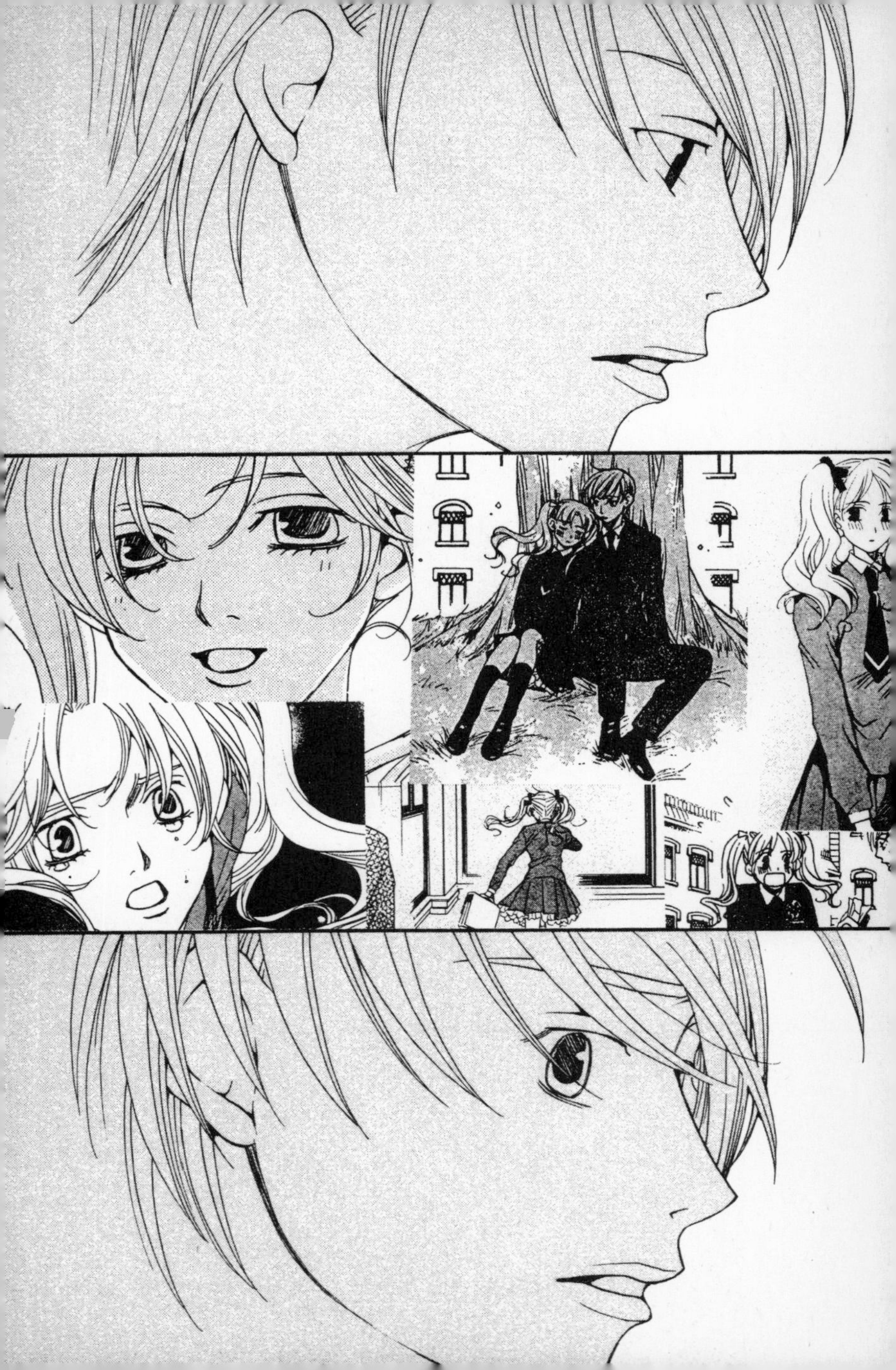

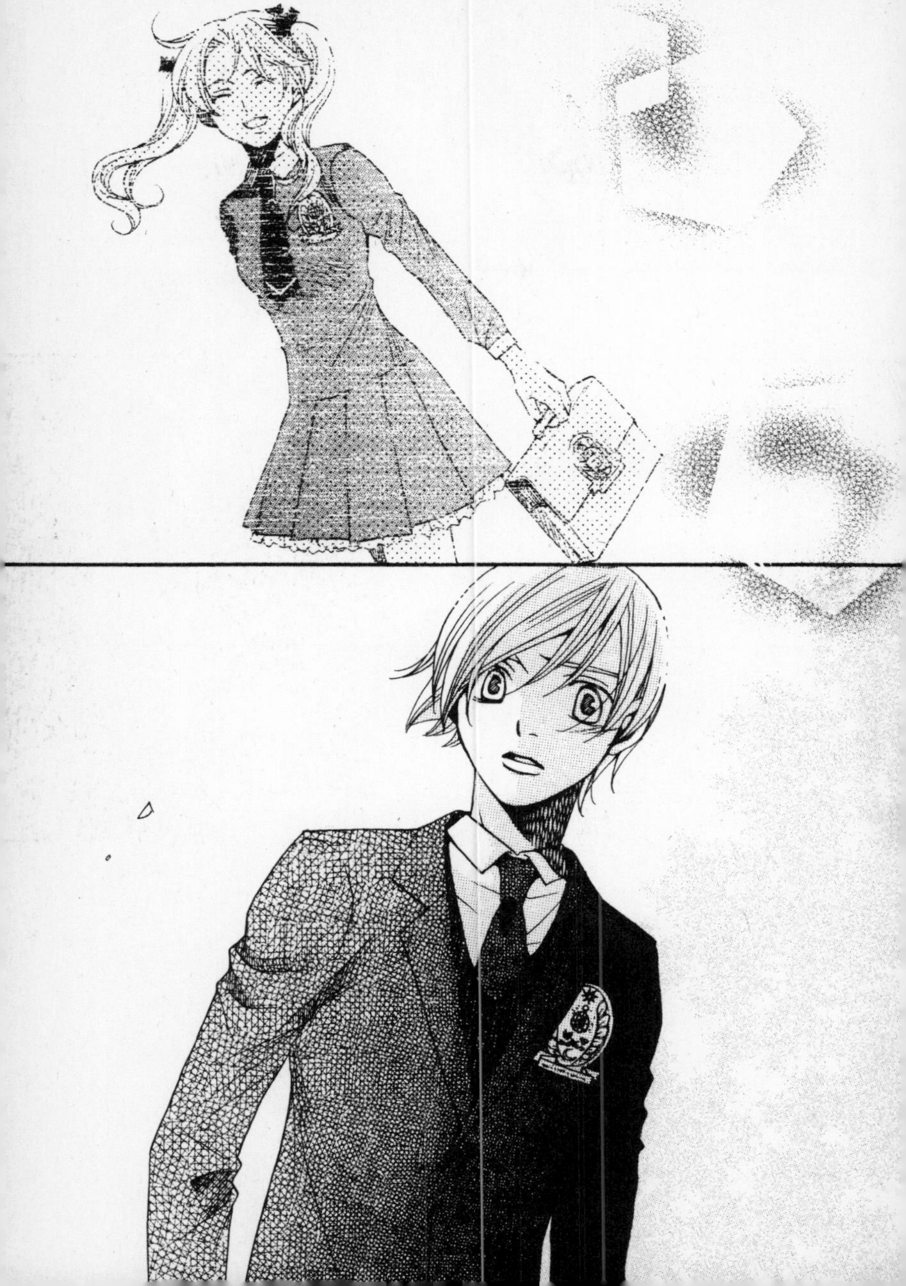

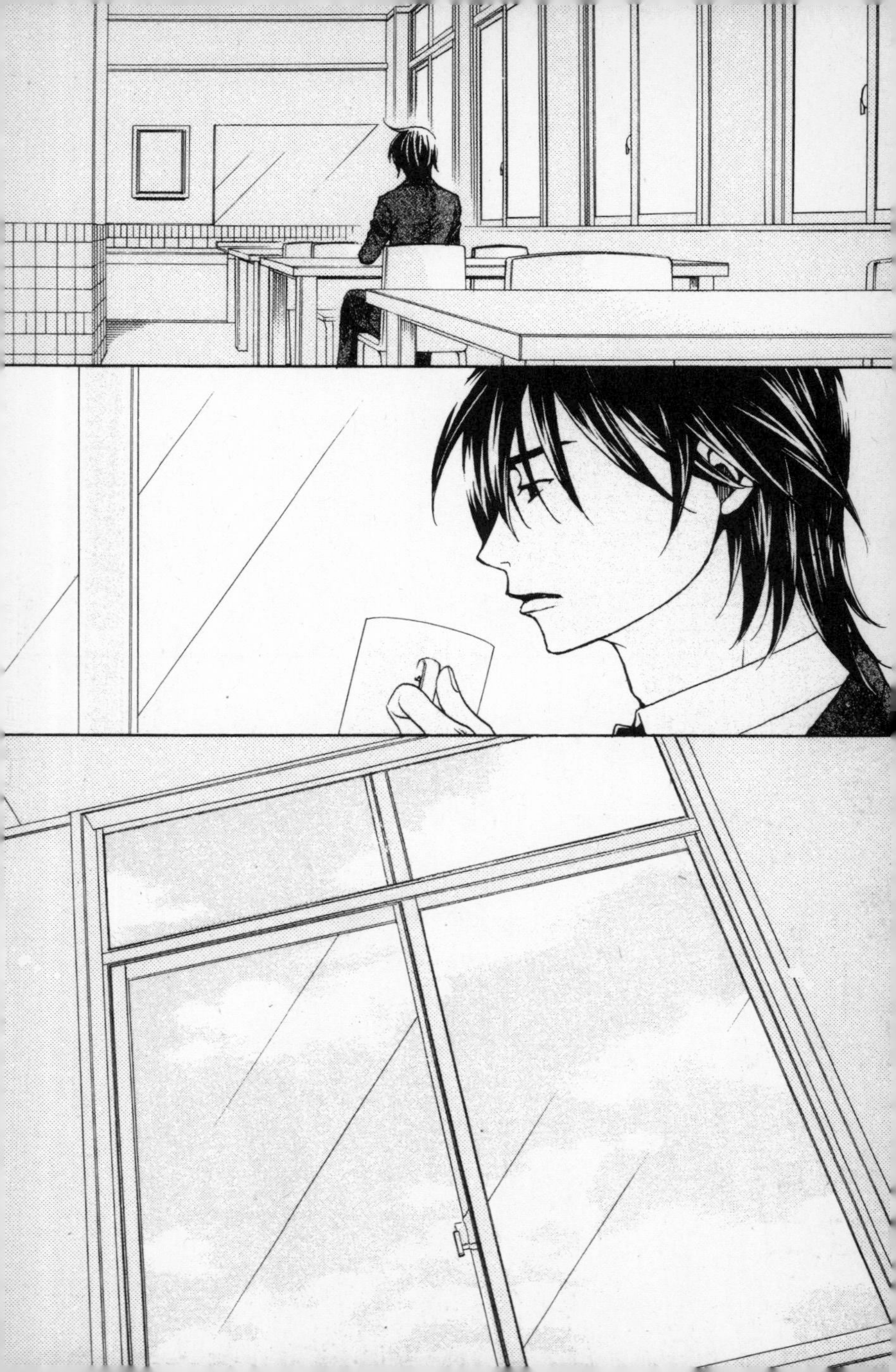

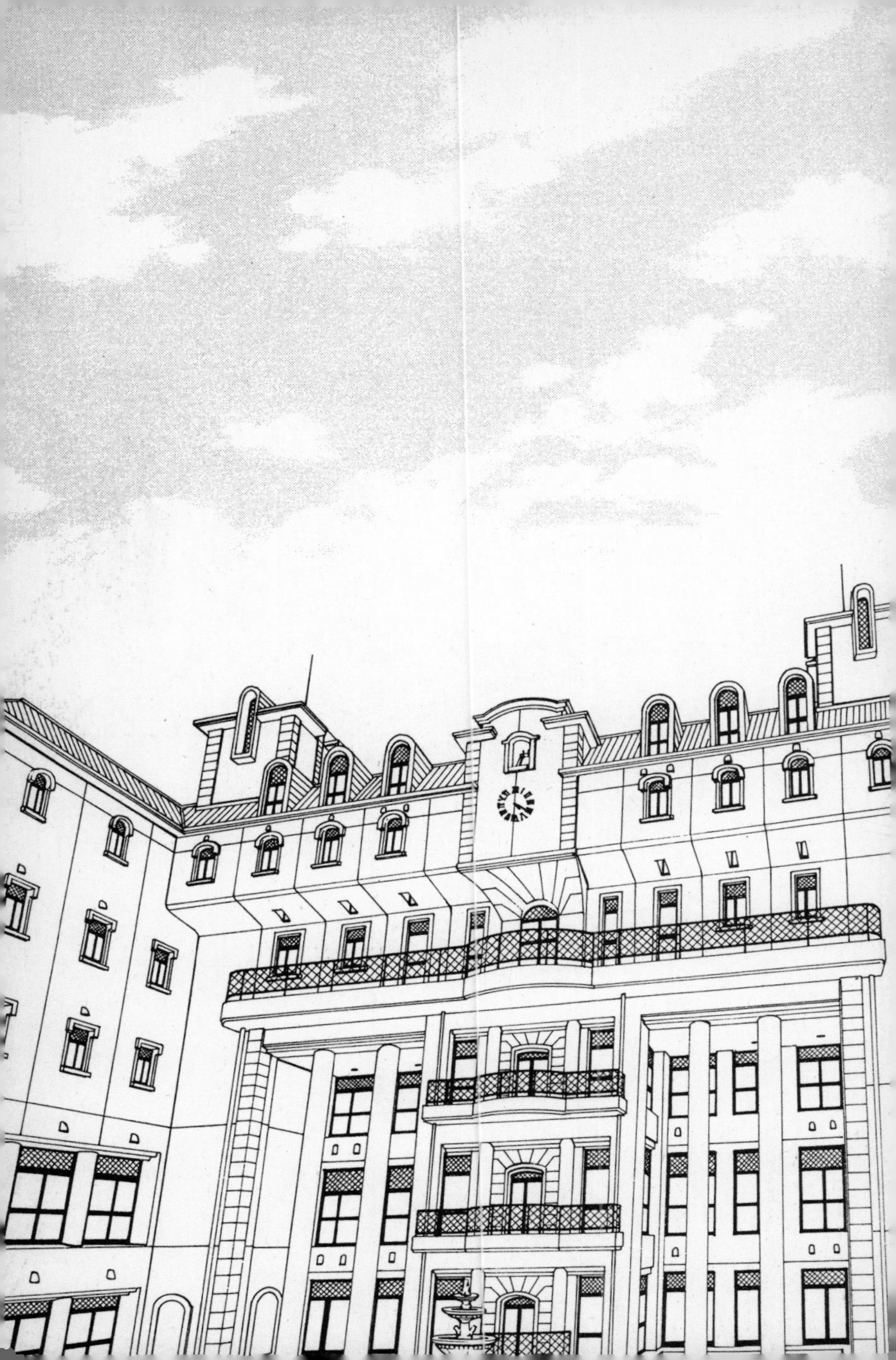

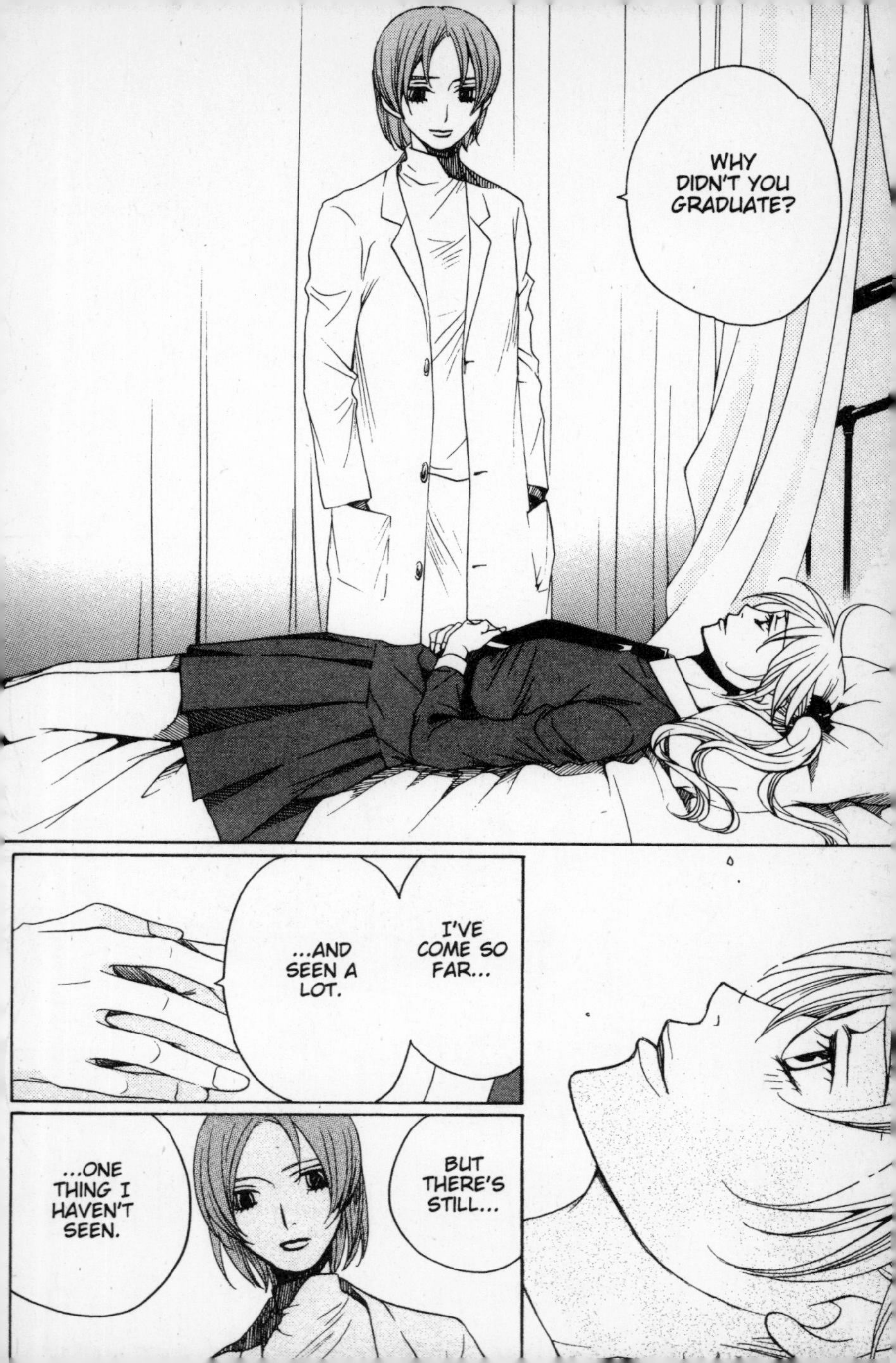
WHY DIDN'T YOU GRADUATE?
I'VE COME SO FAR...
...AND SEEN A LOT.
BUT THERE'S STILL...
...ONE THING I HAVEN'T SEEN.

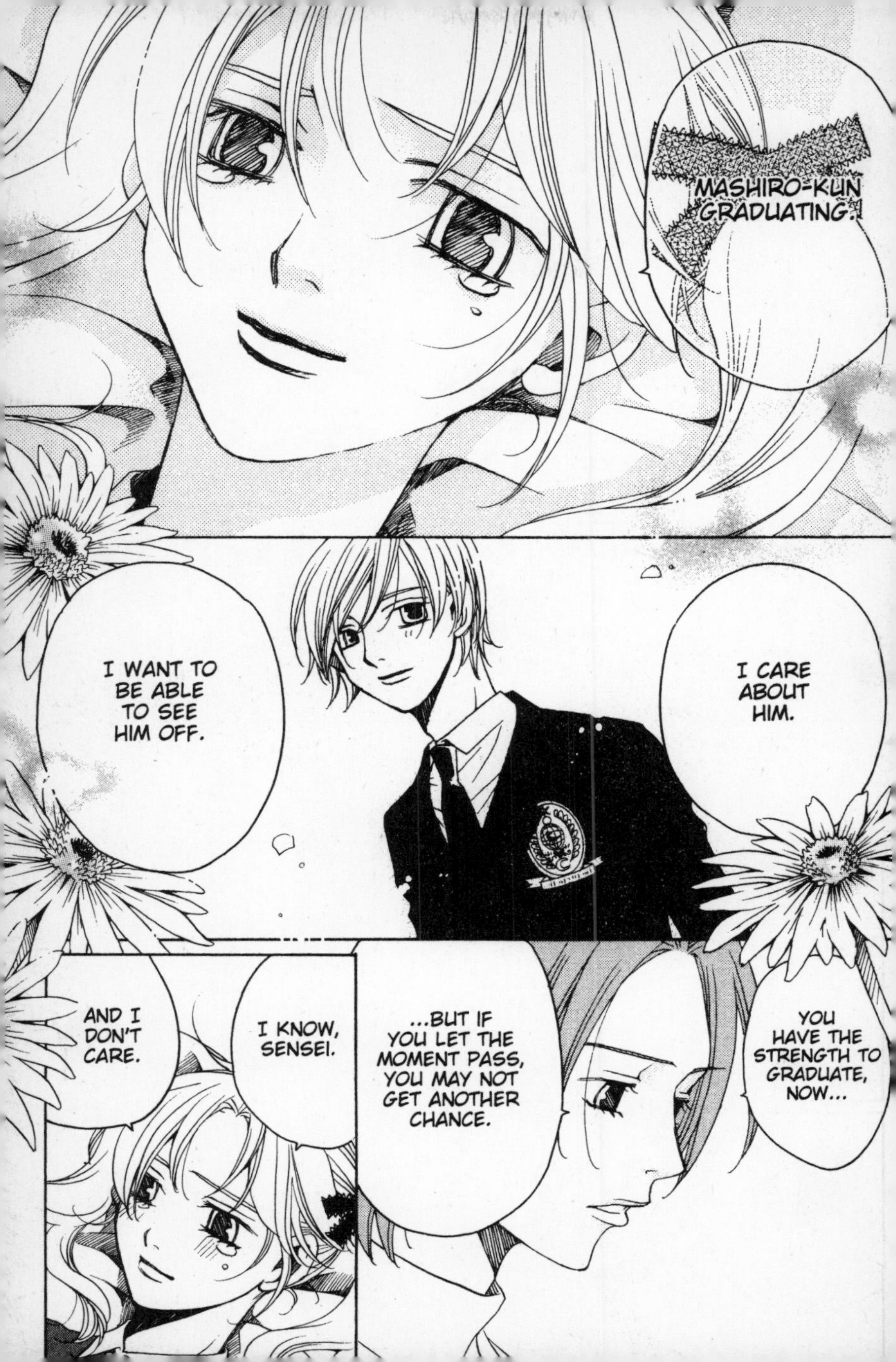

MASHIRO-KUN GRADUATING.
I CARE ABOUT HIM.
I WANT TO BE ABLE TO SEE HIM OFF.
YOU HAVE THE STRENGTH TO GRADUATE, NOW...
...BUT IF YOU LET THE MOMENT PASS, YOU MAY NOT GET ANOTHER CHANCE.
I KNOW, SENSEI.
AND I DON'T CARE.

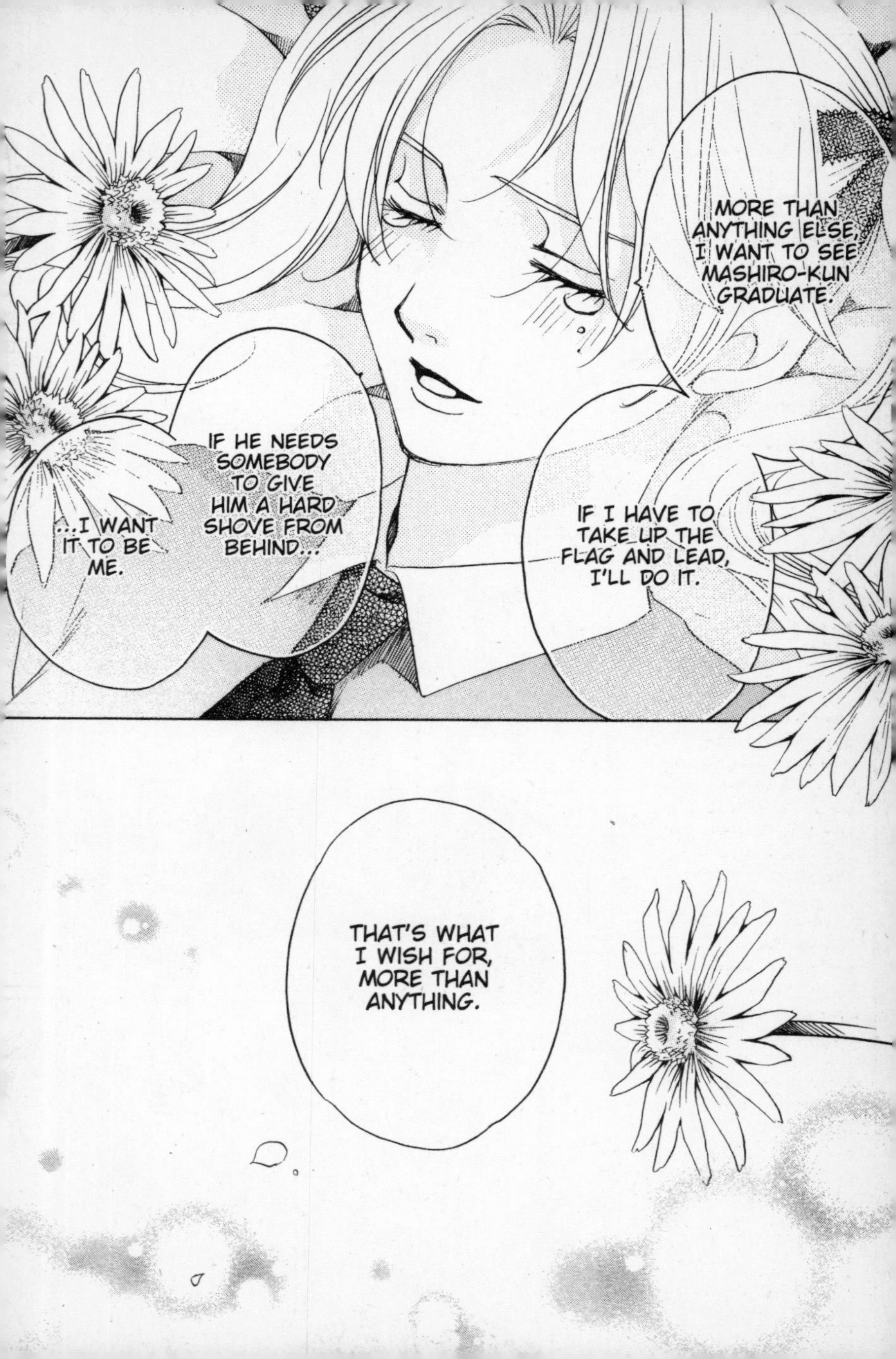
MORE THAN ANYTHING ELSE, I WANT TO SEE MASHIRO-KUN GRADUATE.
IF I HAVE TO TAKE UP THE FLAG AND LEAD, I'LL DO IT.
IF HE NEEDS SOMEBODY TO GIVE HIM A HARD SHOVE FROM BEHIND...
...I WANT IT TO BE ME.
THAT'S WHAT I WISH FOR, MORE THAN ANYTHING.

Extra ASN Talk ①

■Message:
ASN is finally nearing its end. When I look back at the plot that it had before it was even serialized (when the world view, character stats, and whatnot had already been established), I feel like the story's almost completely followed through as planned, and I've drawn it consistently for the most part. But the one thing that did change was some characters' names and order of appearance.

■Shinbashi —> "Aoyagi"
When I was in elementary school, there was a boy in my class with glasses named Aoyagi-kun, so that's where I stole the name from. Since there are lots of blue-oriented names like "Sou" and "Ai," I was supposed to change it. But "Shinbashi" also fits the blue pattern, now doesn't it? D'oh!

■Shinonome —> "Kikawada"
Since he's a giraffe, I thought it might be going too far to have his name have the character for "yellow" in it. Then, I went and used it for another character's name anyway. Ha!
Then, when I first established him, he was going to be a classmate in the dream world who was there from the start. He'd be the navigation guide for Mashiro, who'd tell him how the dream world worked, in exchange for one bead. He'd seem like a nice guy at first, but he'd be a character who liked making deals from the very get-go!

As for why I changed my mind about him being an initial member to having a later appearance, well...

Continue to ②

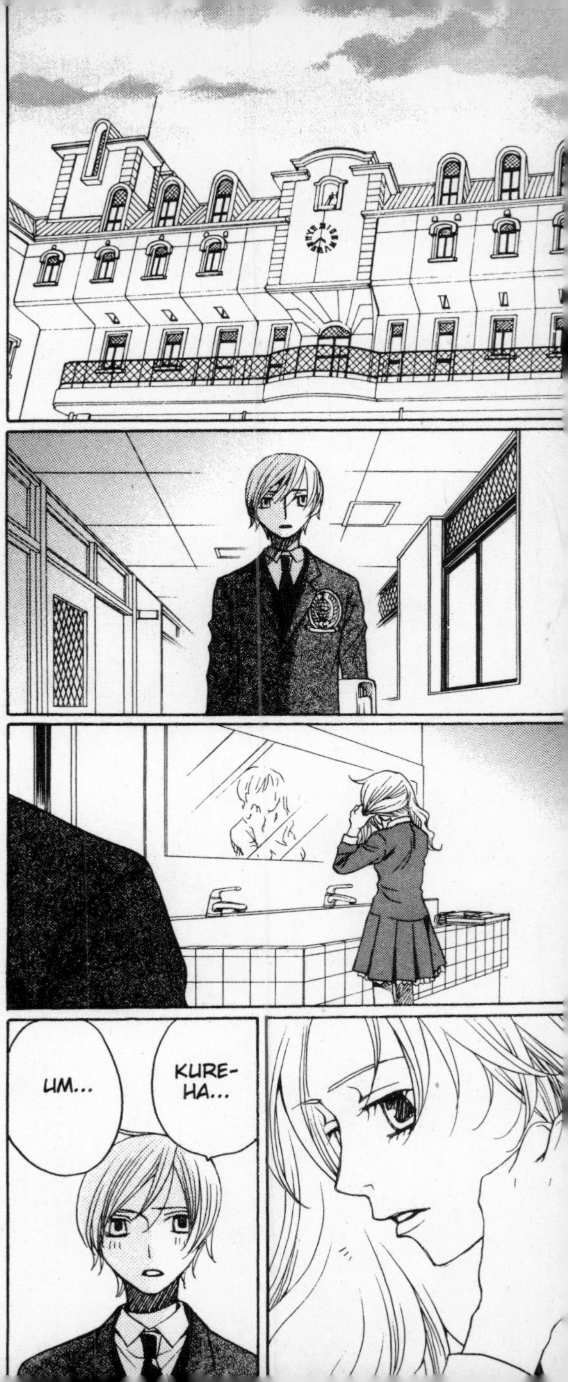
KURE-HA...
UM...

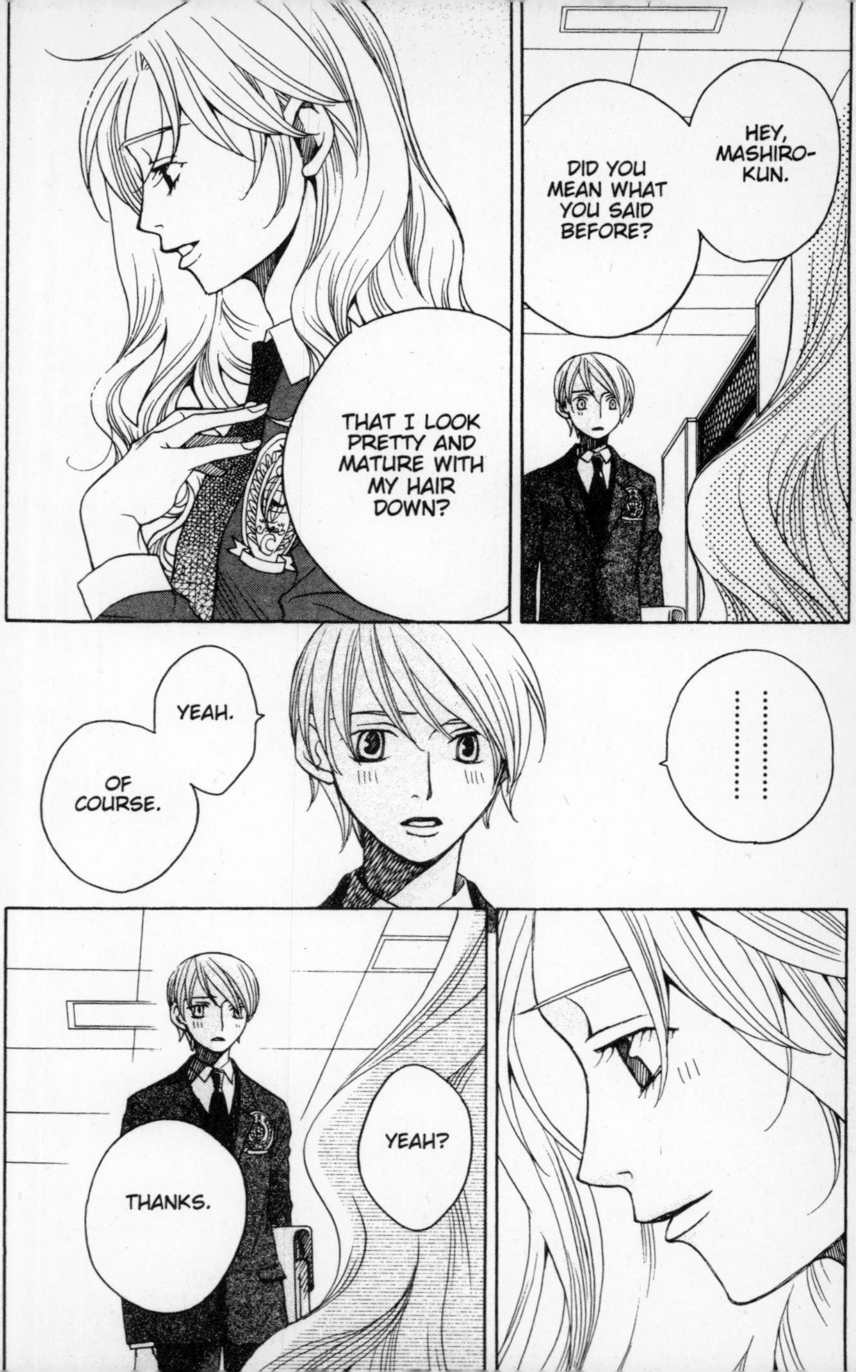
HEY, MASHIRO-KUN.
DID YOU MEAN WHAT YOU SAID BEFORE?
THAT I LOOK PRETTY AND MATURE WITH MY HAIR DOWN?
......
YEAH.
OF COURSE.
YEAH?
THANKS.

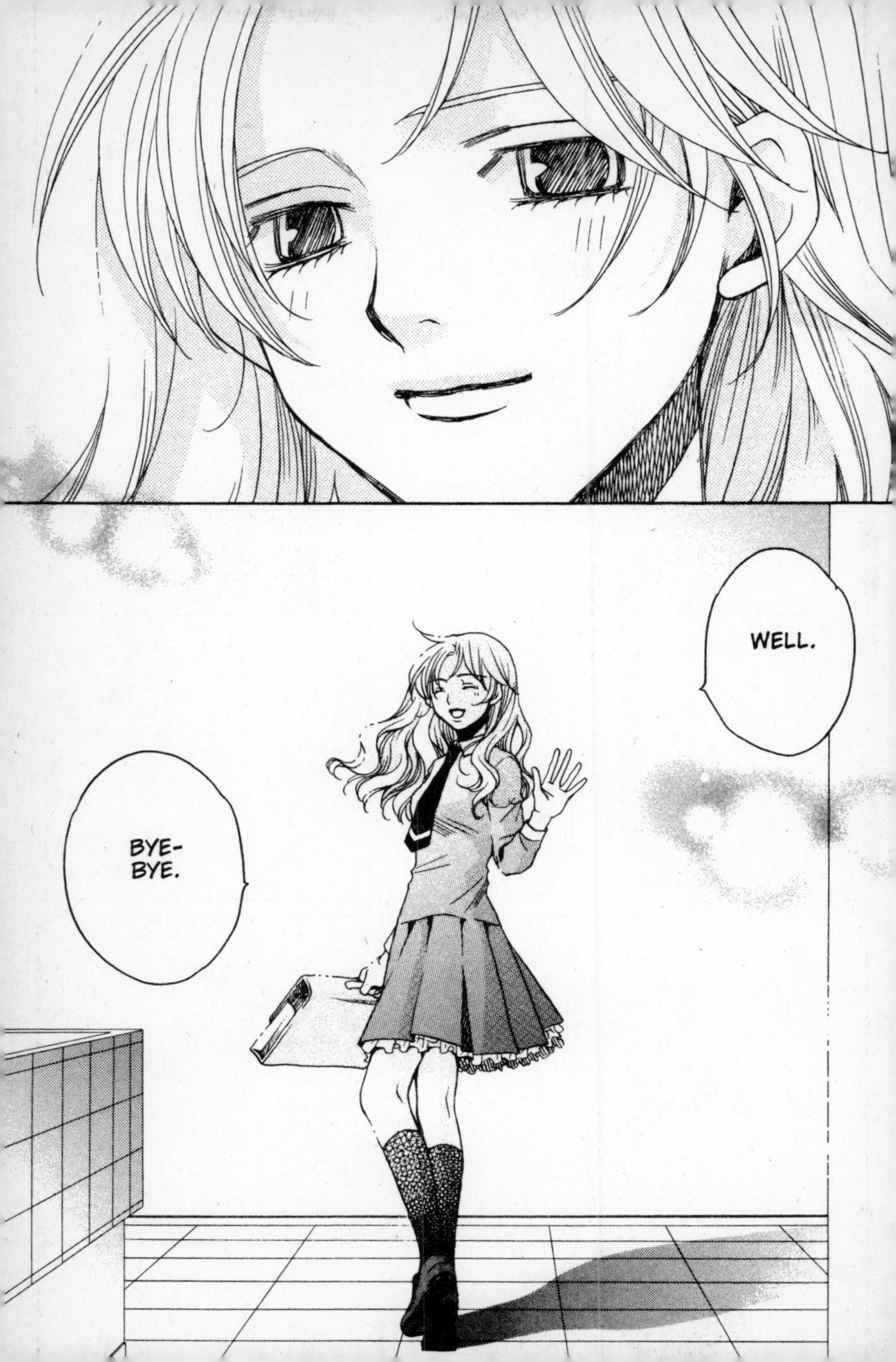
WELL.
BYE-BYE.

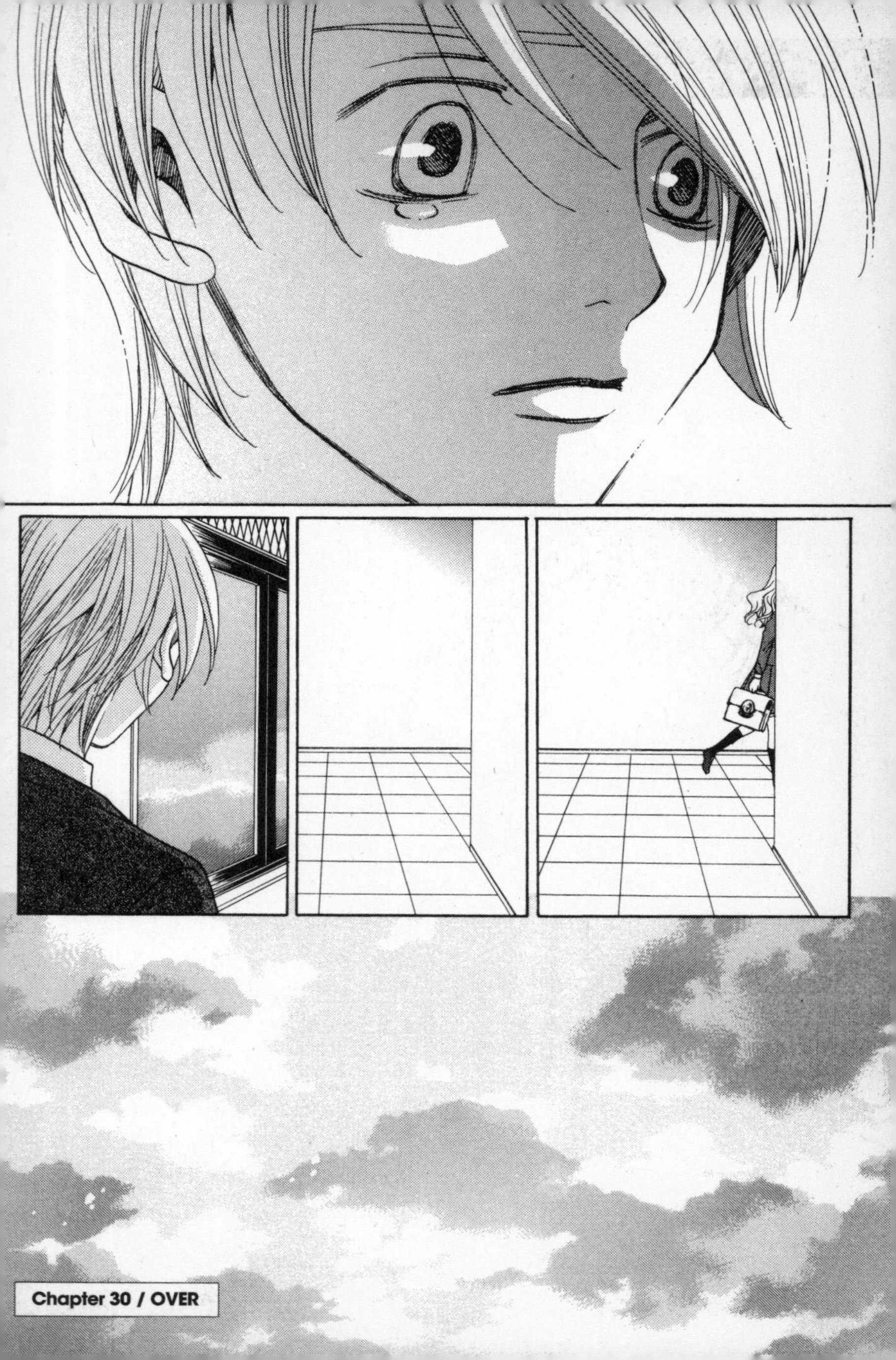
Chapter 30 / OVER

AFTER SCHOOL NIGHTMARE Chapter 31

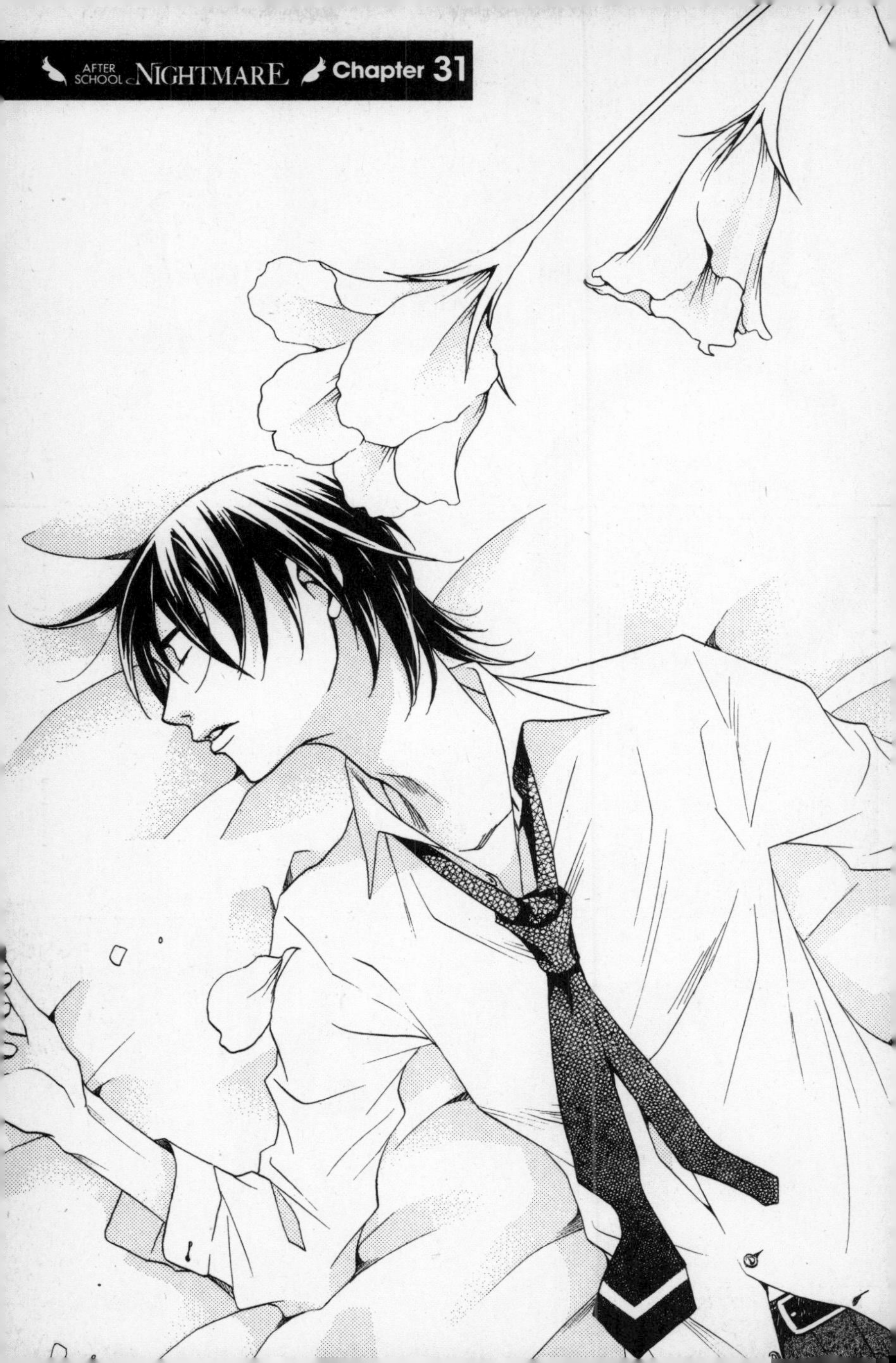

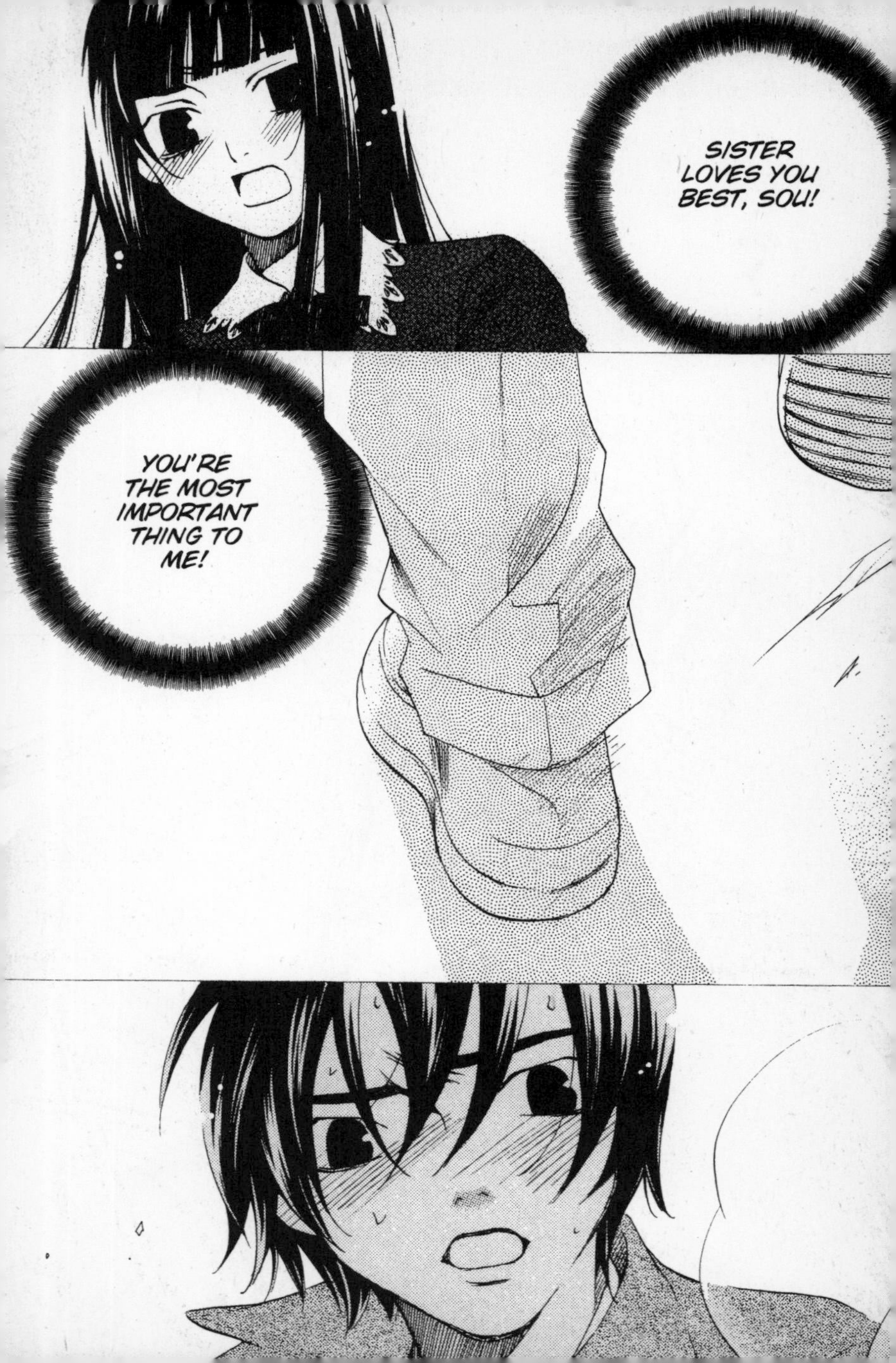
SISTER LOVES YOU BEST, SOU!
YOU'RE THE MOST IMPORTANT THING TO ME!

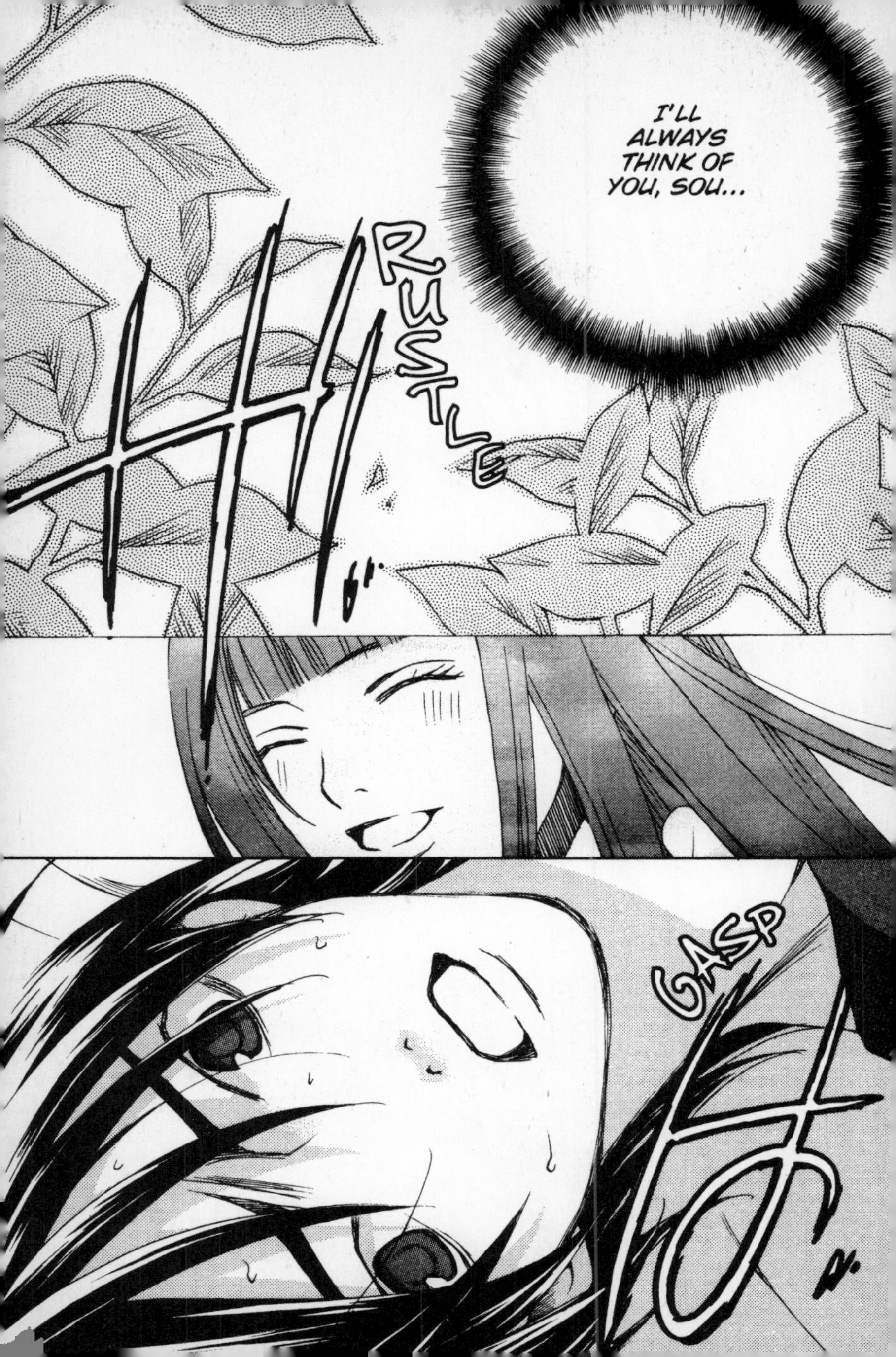
I'LL ALWAYS THINK OF YOU, SOU...
RUSTLE
GASP

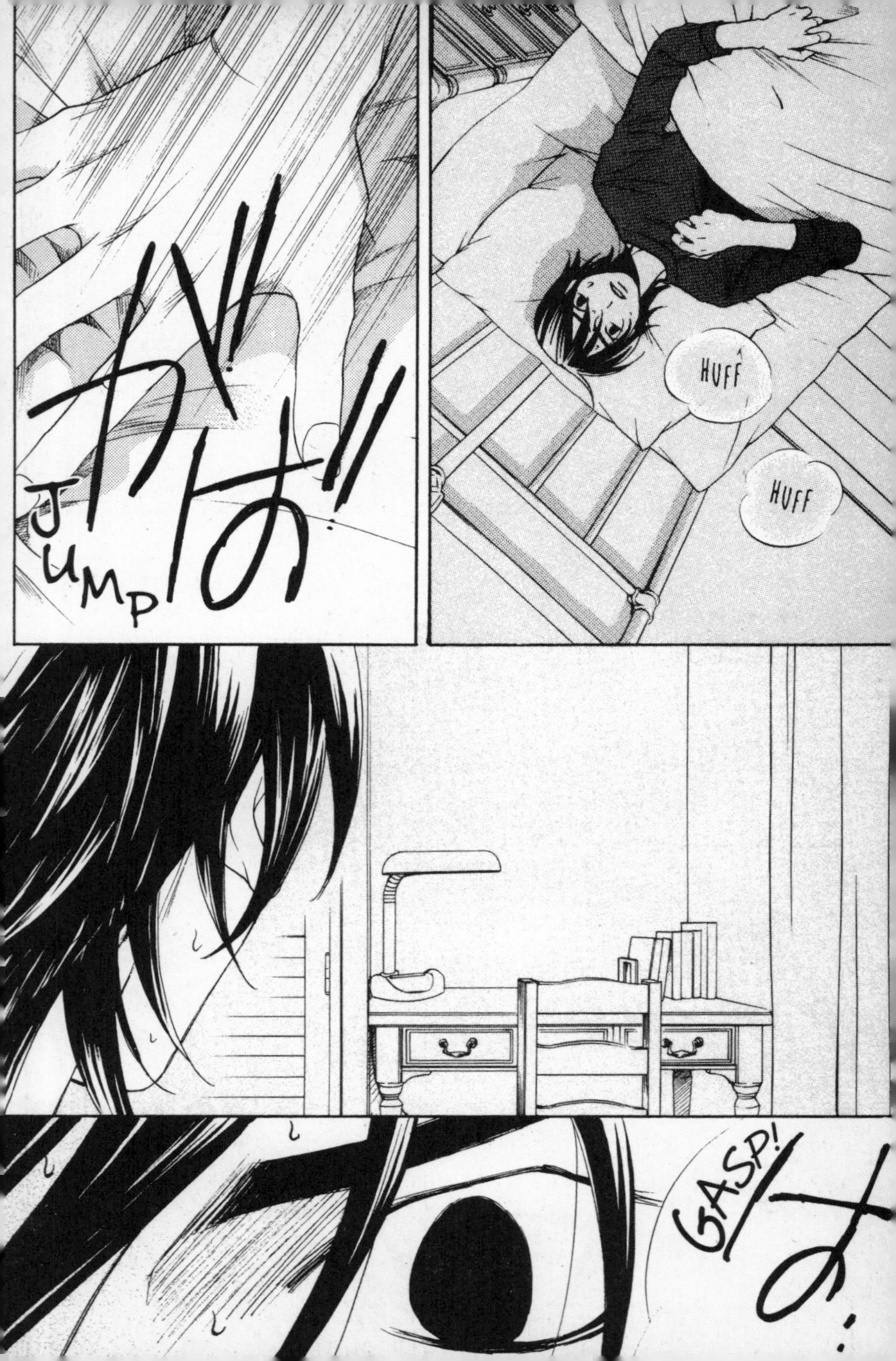
HUFF
HUFF
JUMP
GASP!

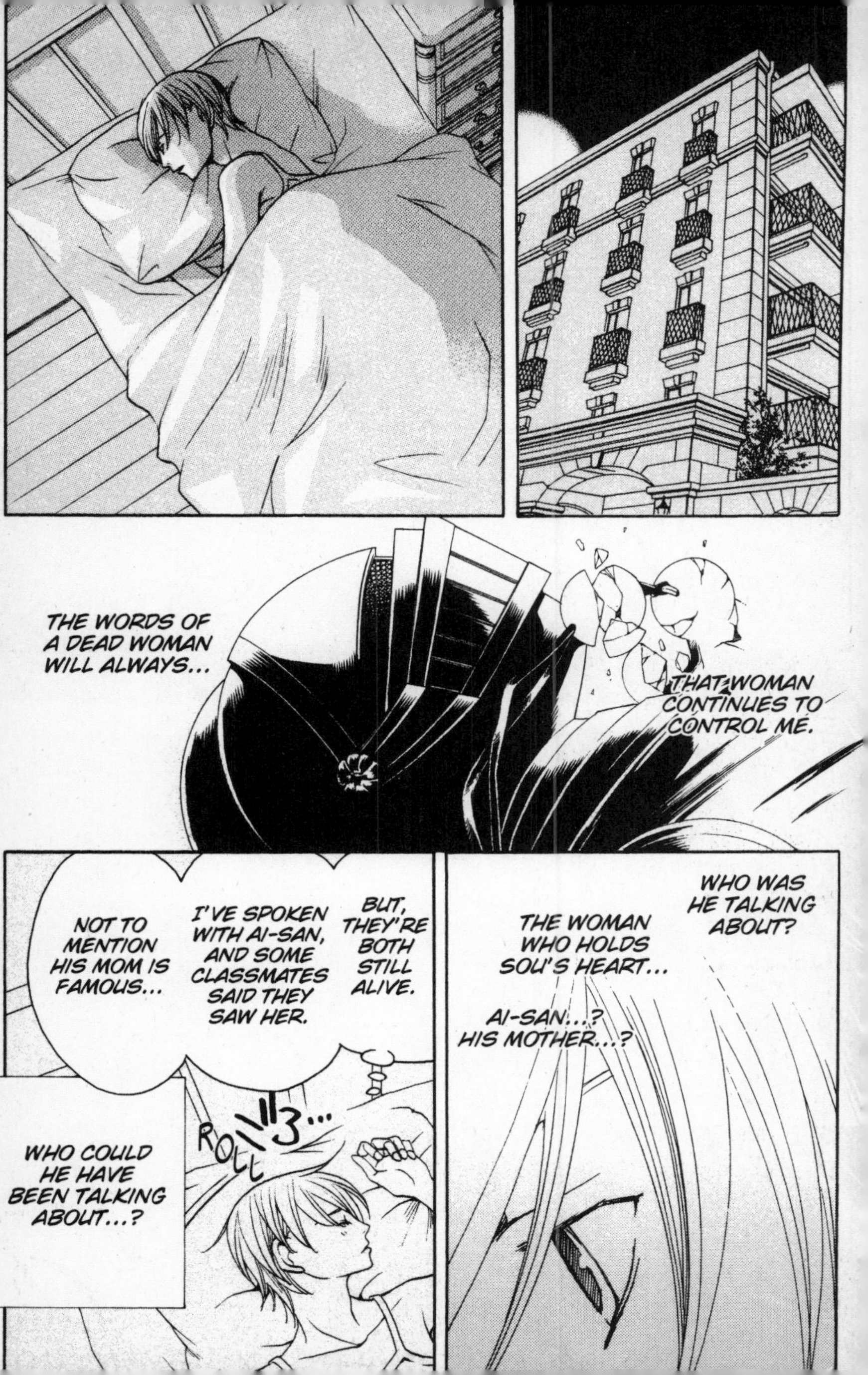
THE WORDS OF A DEAD WOMAN WILL ALWAYS...
THAT WOMAN CONTINUES TO CONTROL ME.
WHO WAS HE TALKING ABOUT?
THE WOMAN WHO HOLDS SOU'S HEART...
AI-SAN...? HIS MOTHER...?
NOT TO MENTION HIS MOM IS FAMOUS...
I'VE SPOKEN WITH AI-SAN, AND SOME CLASSMATES SAID THEY SAW HER.
BUT, THEY'RE BOTH STILL ALIVE.
ROLL
WHO COULD HE HAVE BEEN TALKING ABOUT...?

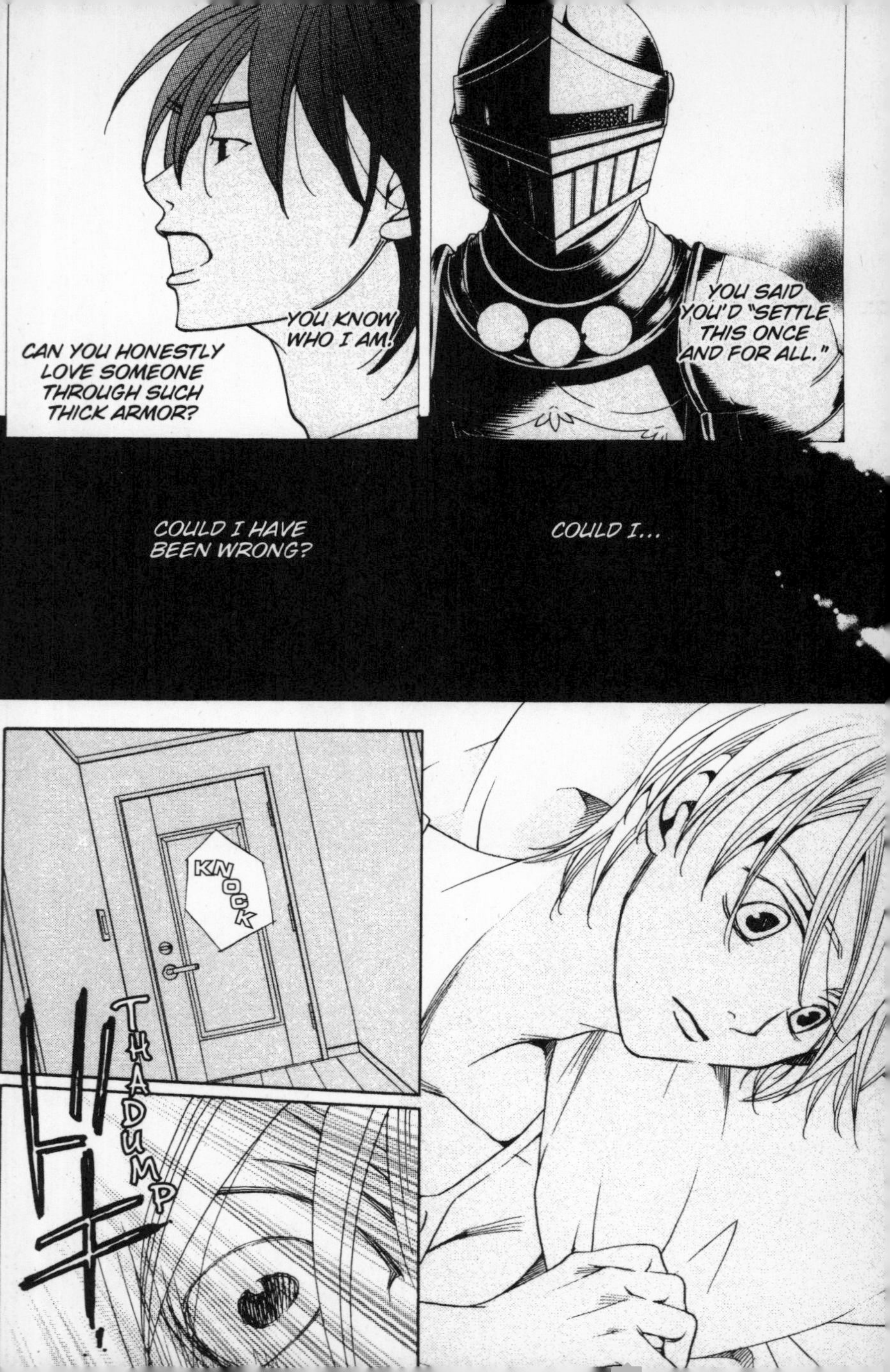
YOU SAID YOU'D "SETTLE THIS ONCE AND FOR ALL."
YOU KNOW WHO I AM!
CAN YOU HONESTLY LOVE SOMEONE THROUGH SUCH THICK ARMOR?
COULD I...
COULD I HAVE BEEN WRONG?
KNOCK
THADUMP

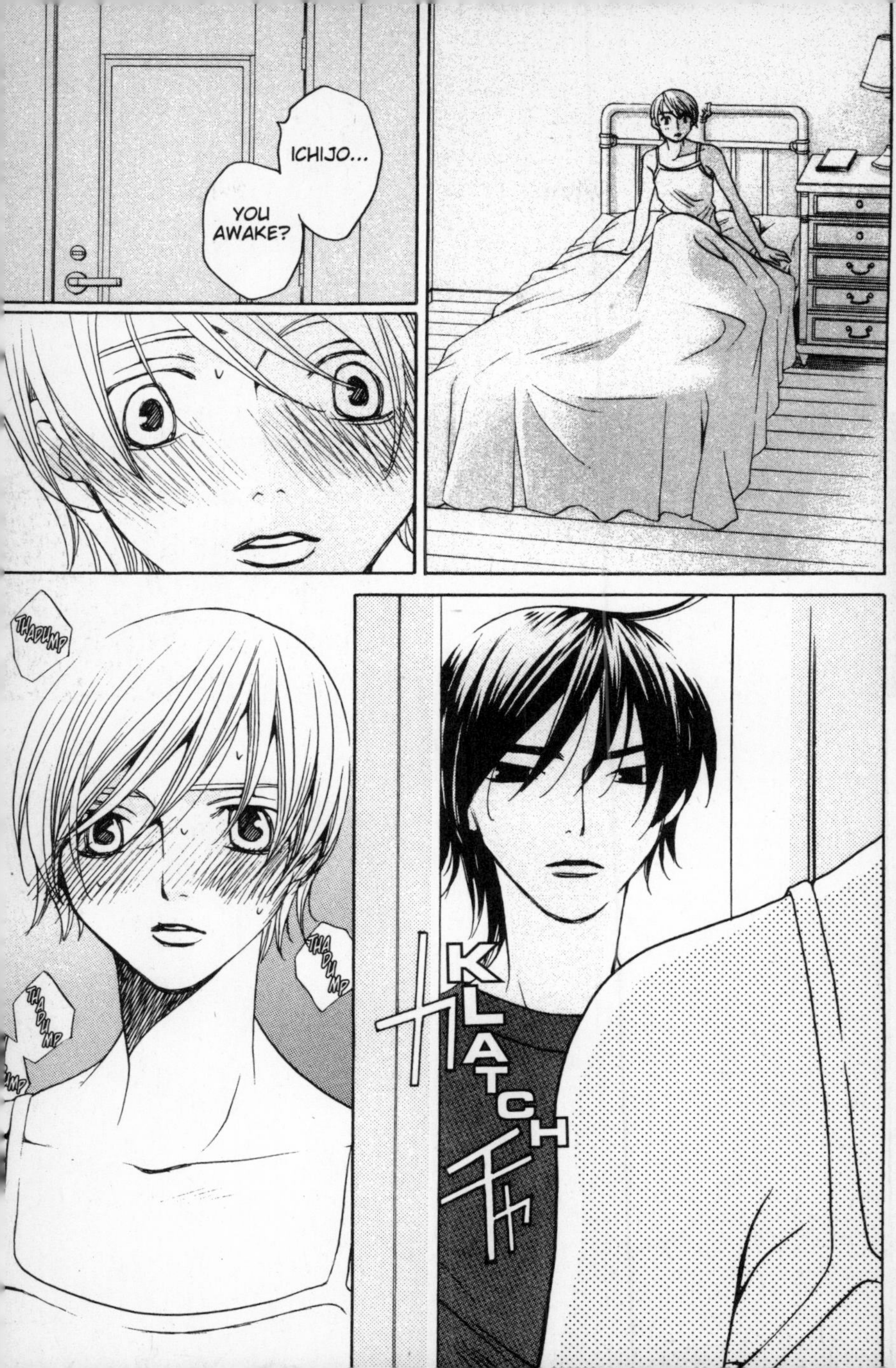
ICHIJO...
YOU AWAKE?
KLATCH
THADUMP
THADUMP
THADUMP

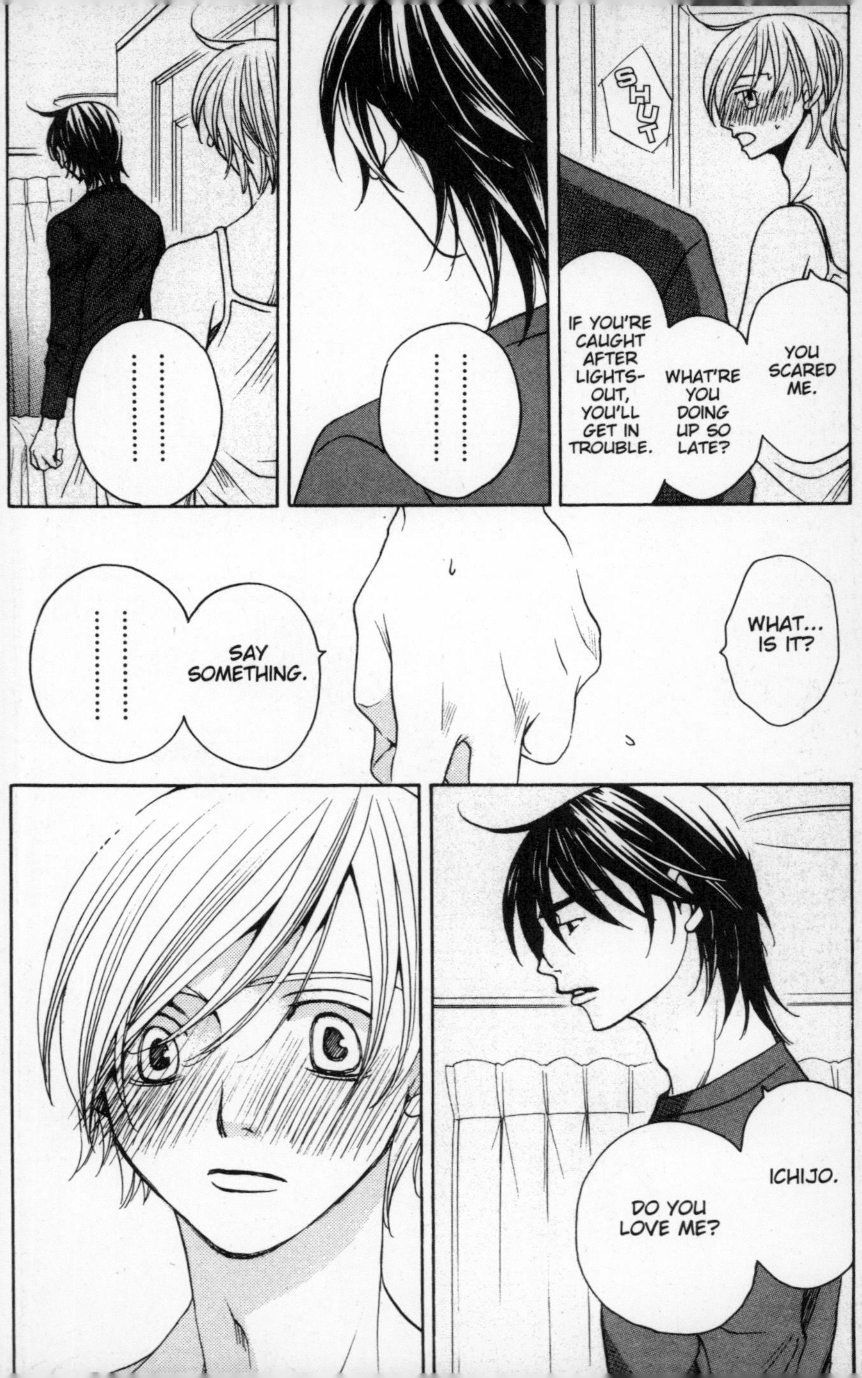
SHUT
YOU SCARED ME.
WHAT'RE YOU DOING UP SO LATE?
IF YOU'RE CAUGHT AFTER LIGHTS-OUT, YOU'LL GET IN TROUBLE.
……
……
WHAT… IS IT?
SAY SOMETHING.
……
ICHIJO.
DO YOU LOVE ME?

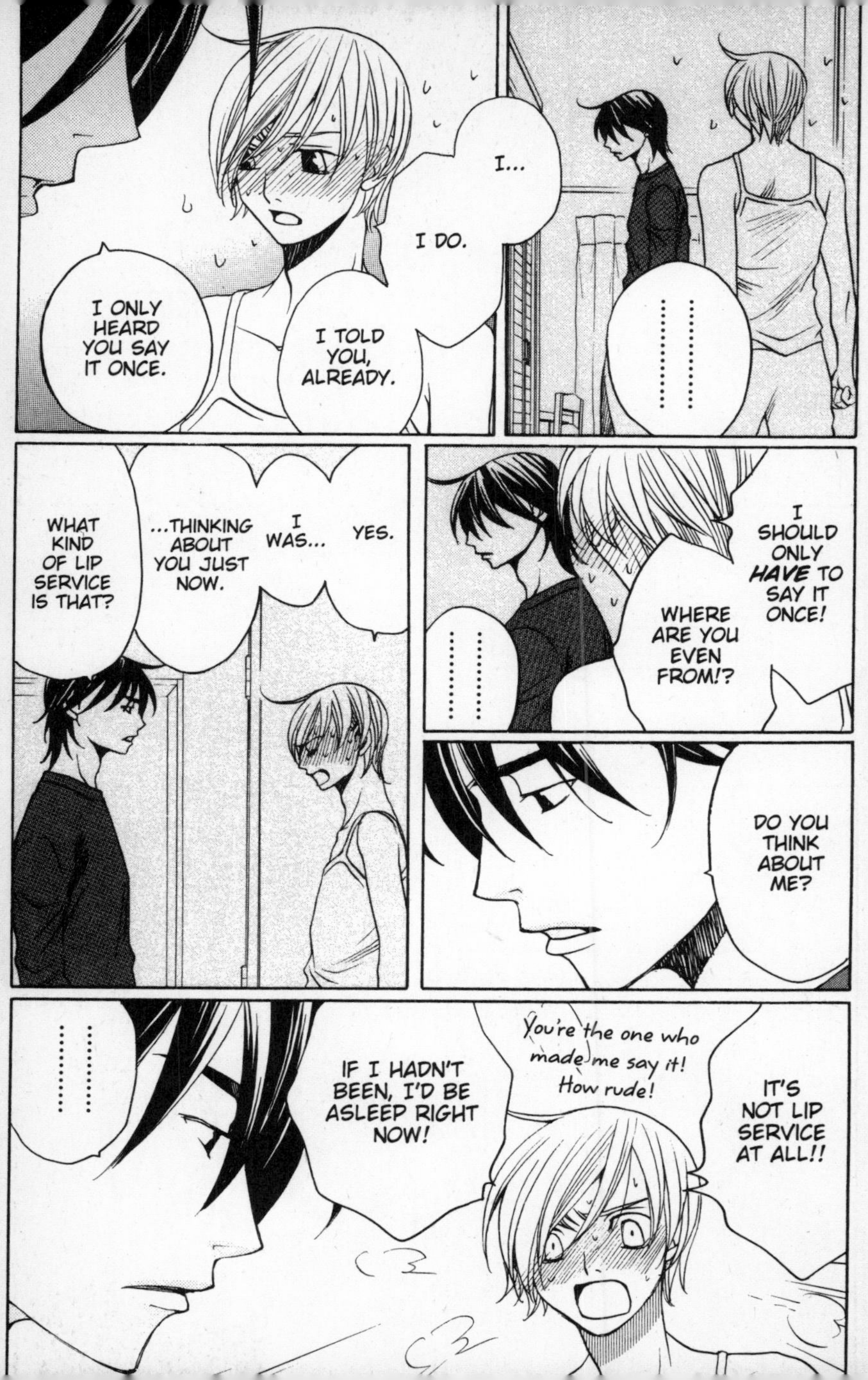
......
I...
I DO.
I TOLD YOU, ALREADY.
I ONLY HEARD YOU SAY IT ONCE.
I SHOULD ONLY *HAVE* TO SAY IT ONCE!
WHERE ARE YOU EVEN FROM!?
......
DO YOU THINK ABOUT ME?
YES.
I WAS...
...THINKING ABOUT YOU JUST NOW.
WHAT KIND OF LIP SERVICE IS THAT?
IT'S NOT LIP SERVICE AT ALL!!
You're the one who made me say it! How rude!
IF I HADN'T BEEN, I'D BE ASLEEP RIGHT NOW!
......

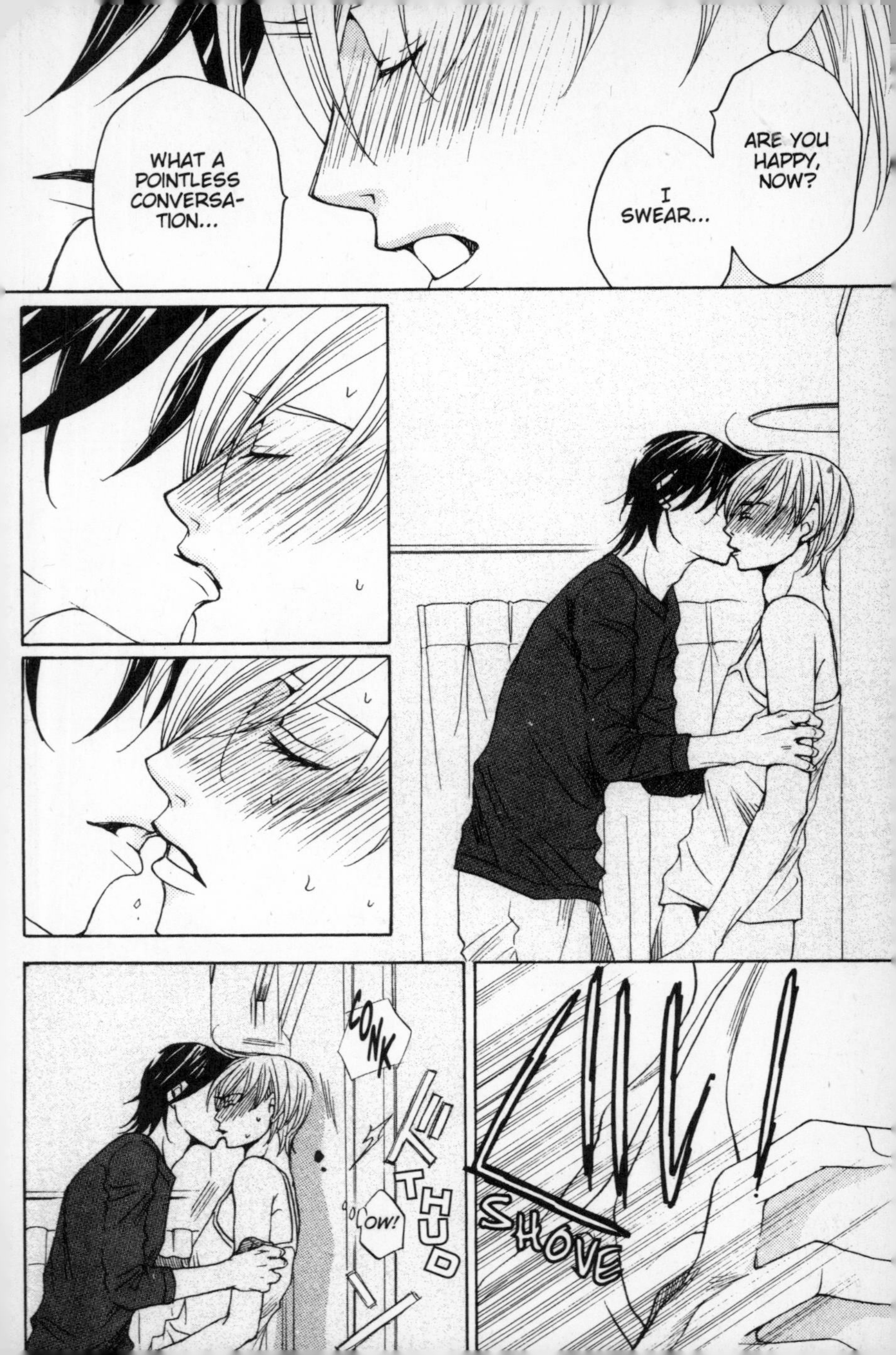
ARE YOU HAPPY, NOW?
I SWEAR...
WHAT A POINTLESS CONVERSA-TION...
SHOVE
CONK
THUD
OW!

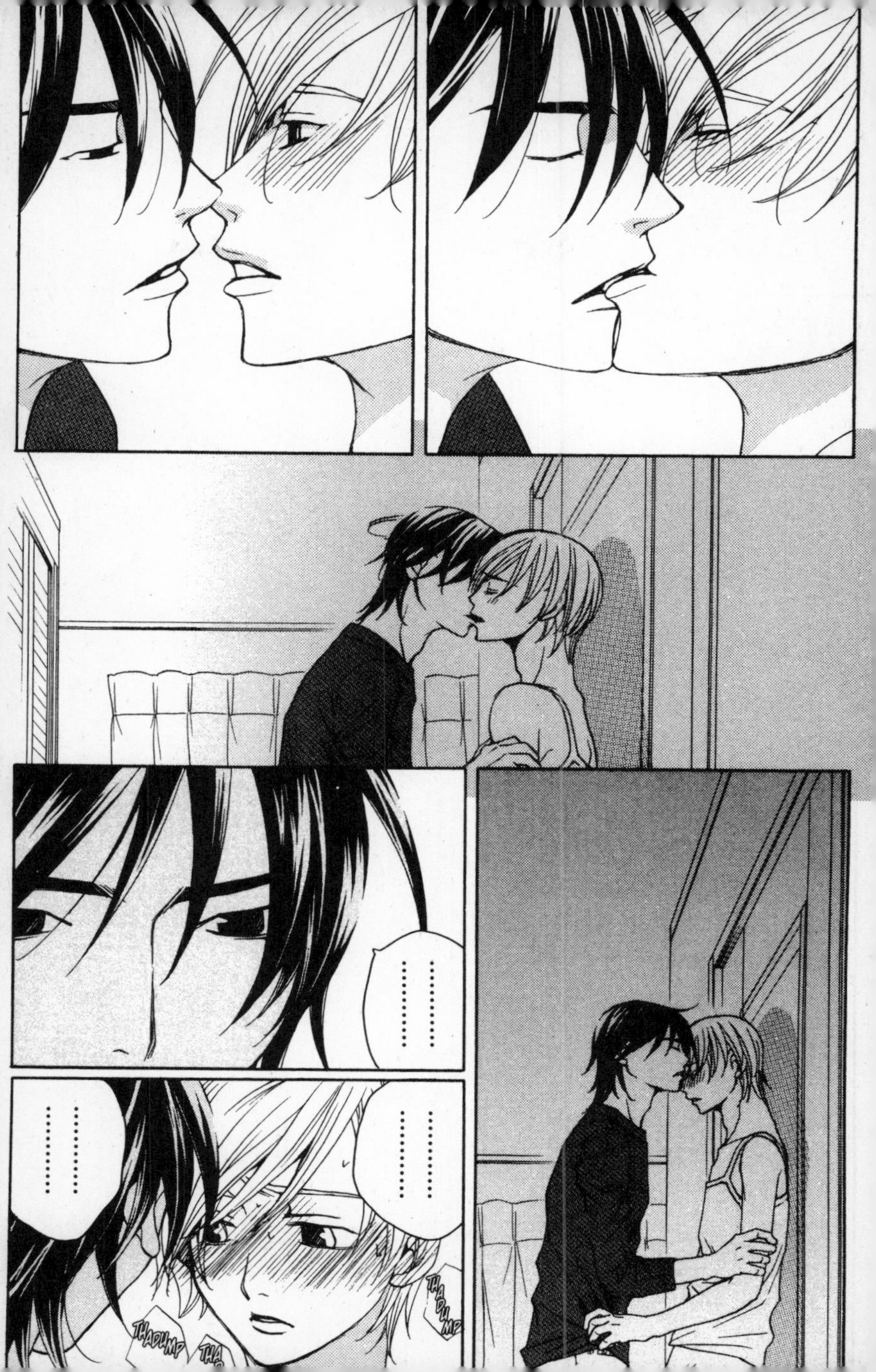
......
......
......
THADUMP
THADUMP

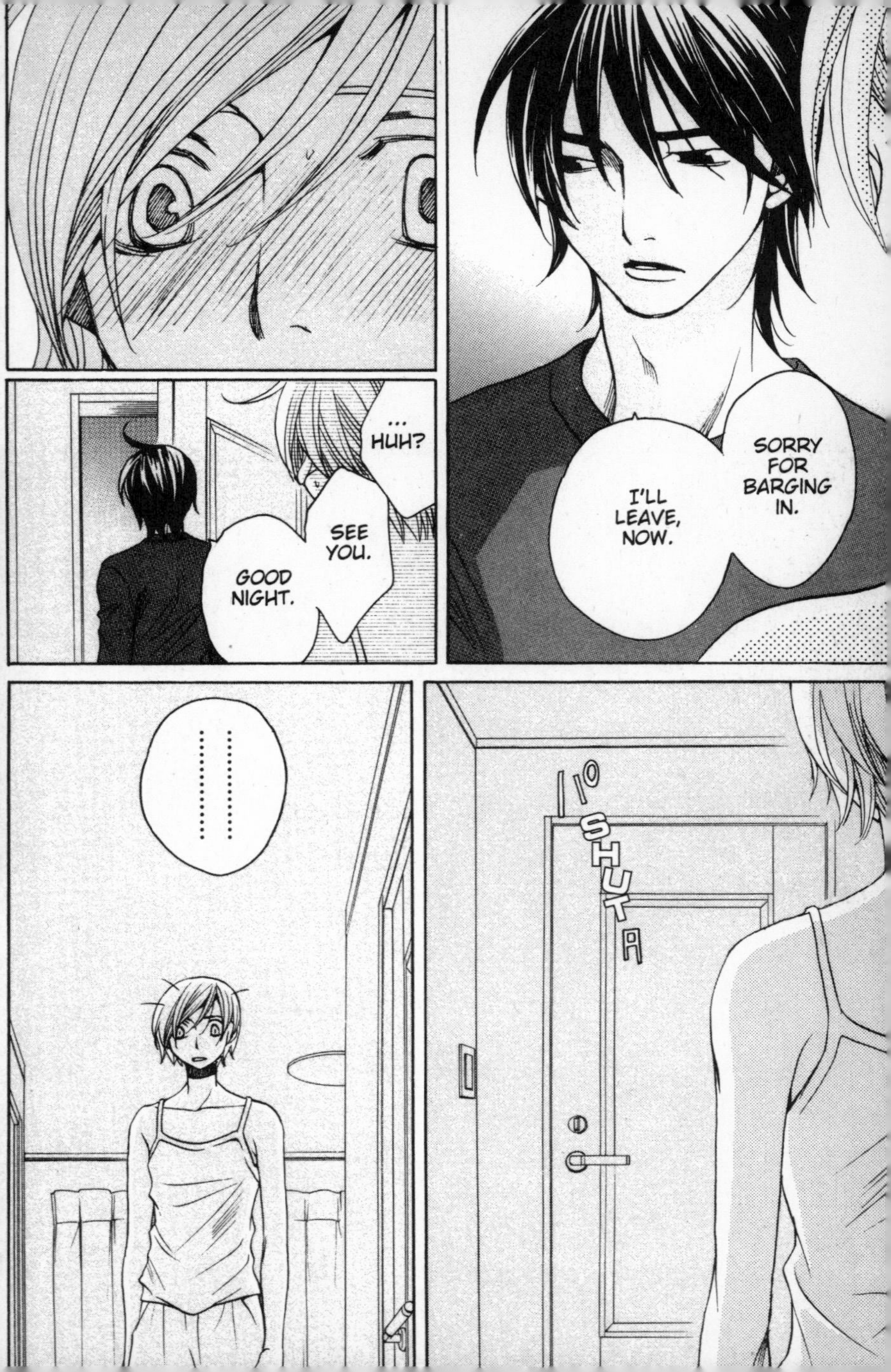
SORRY FOR BARGING IN.
I'LL LEAVE, NOW.
... HUH?
SEE YOU.
GOOD NIGHT.
SHUTA
......

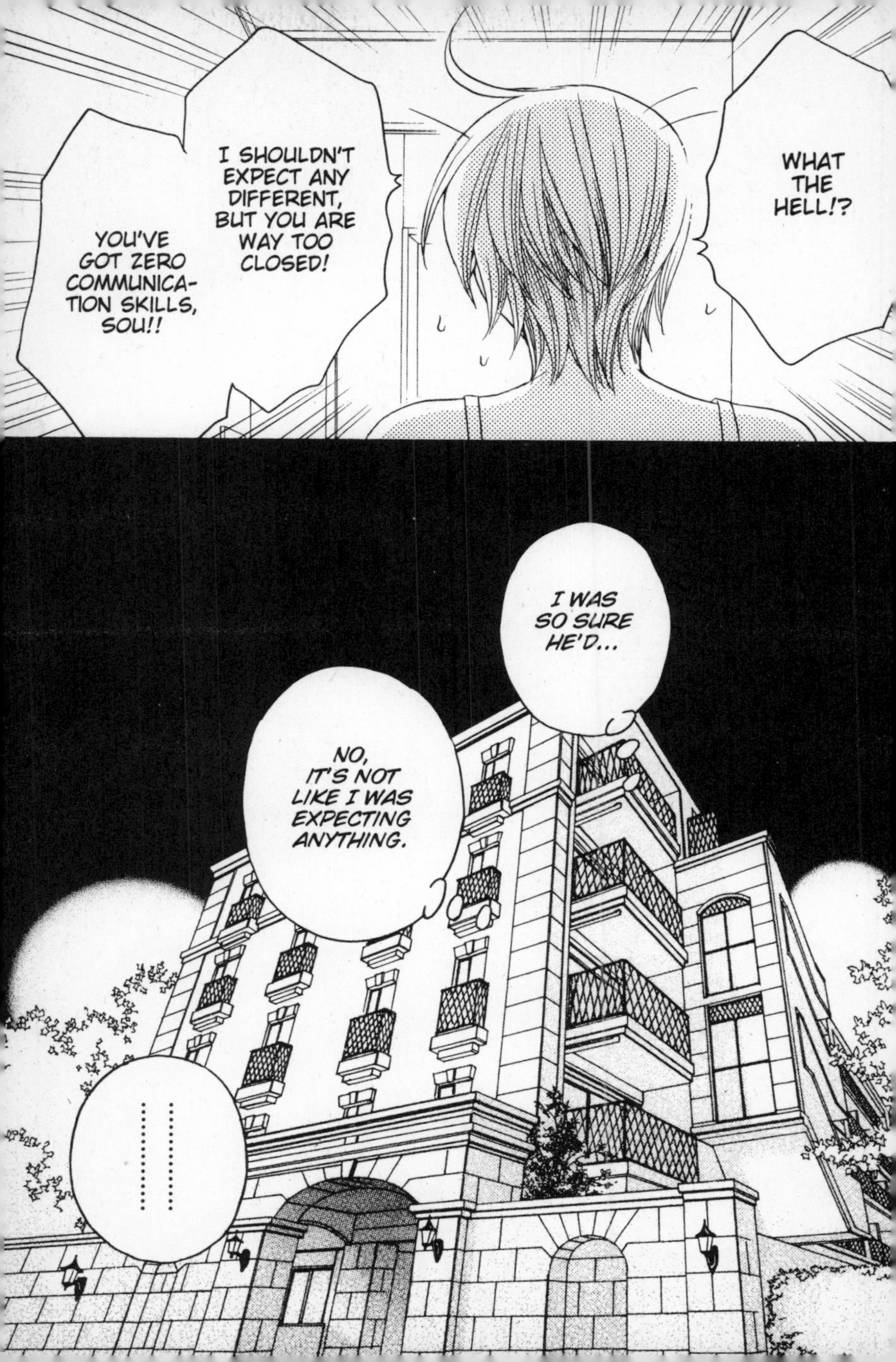
WHAT THE HELL!?
I SHOULDN'T EXPECT ANY DIFFERENT, BUT YOU ARE WAY TOO CLOSED!
YOU'VE GOT ZERO COMMUNICA-TION SKILLS, SOU!!
I WAS SO SURE HE'D...
NO, IT'S NOT LIKE I WAS EXPECTING ANYTHING.
......

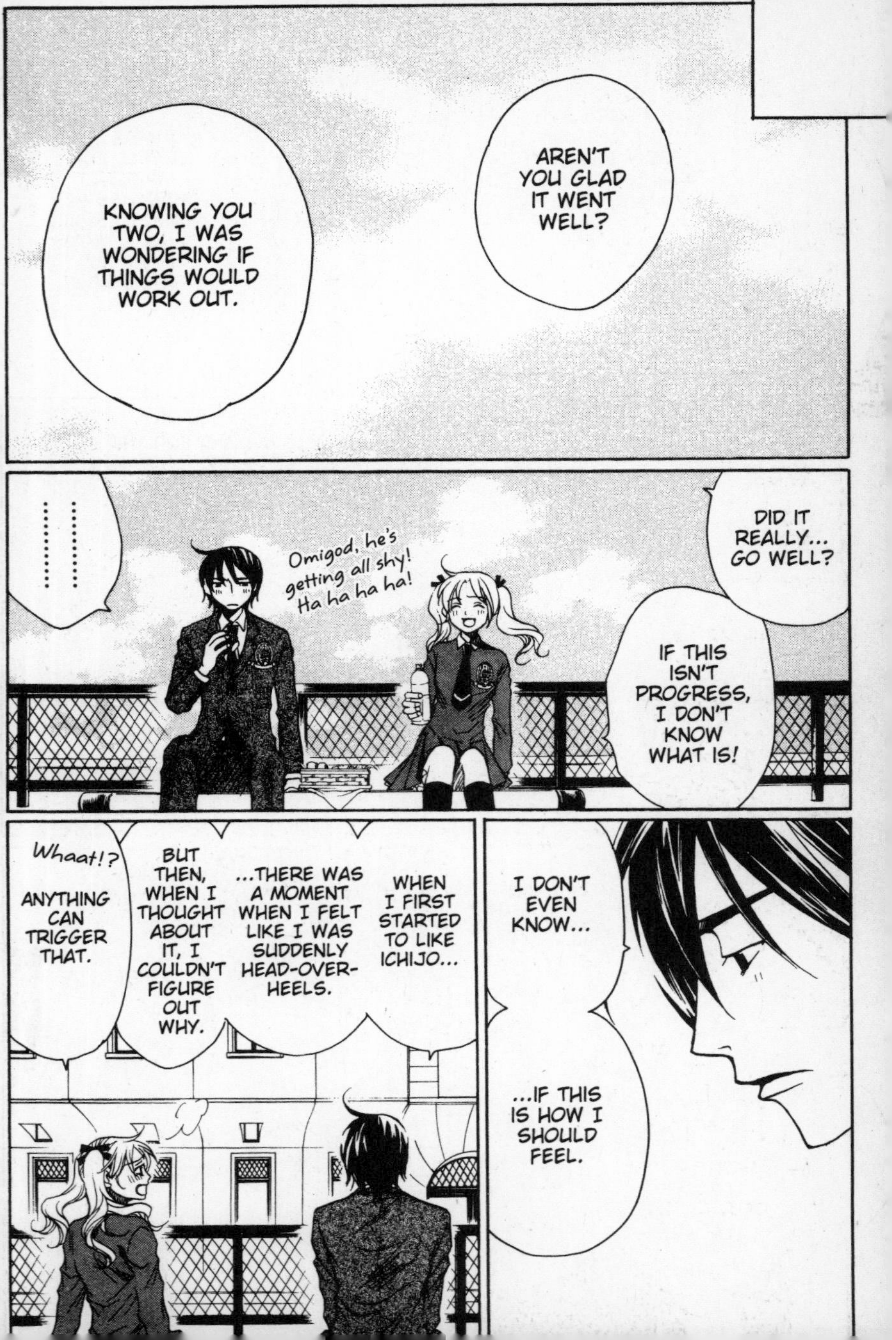
AREN'T YOU GLAD IT WENT WELL?
KNOWING YOU TWO, I WAS WONDERING IF THINGS WOULD WORK OUT.
DID IT REALLY... GO WELL?
IF THIS ISN'T PROGRESS, I DON'T KNOW WHAT IS!
Omigod, he's getting all shy! Ha ha ha ha!
......
I DON'T EVEN KNOW...
...IF THIS IS HOW I SHOULD FEEL.
WHEN I FIRST STARTED TO LIKE ICHIJO...
...THERE WAS A MOMENT WHEN I FELT LIKE I WAS SUDDENLY HEAD-OVER-HEELS.
BUT THEN, WHEN I THOUGHT ABOUT IT, I COULDN'T FIGURE OUT WHY.
Whaat!?
ANYTHING CAN TRIGGER THAT.

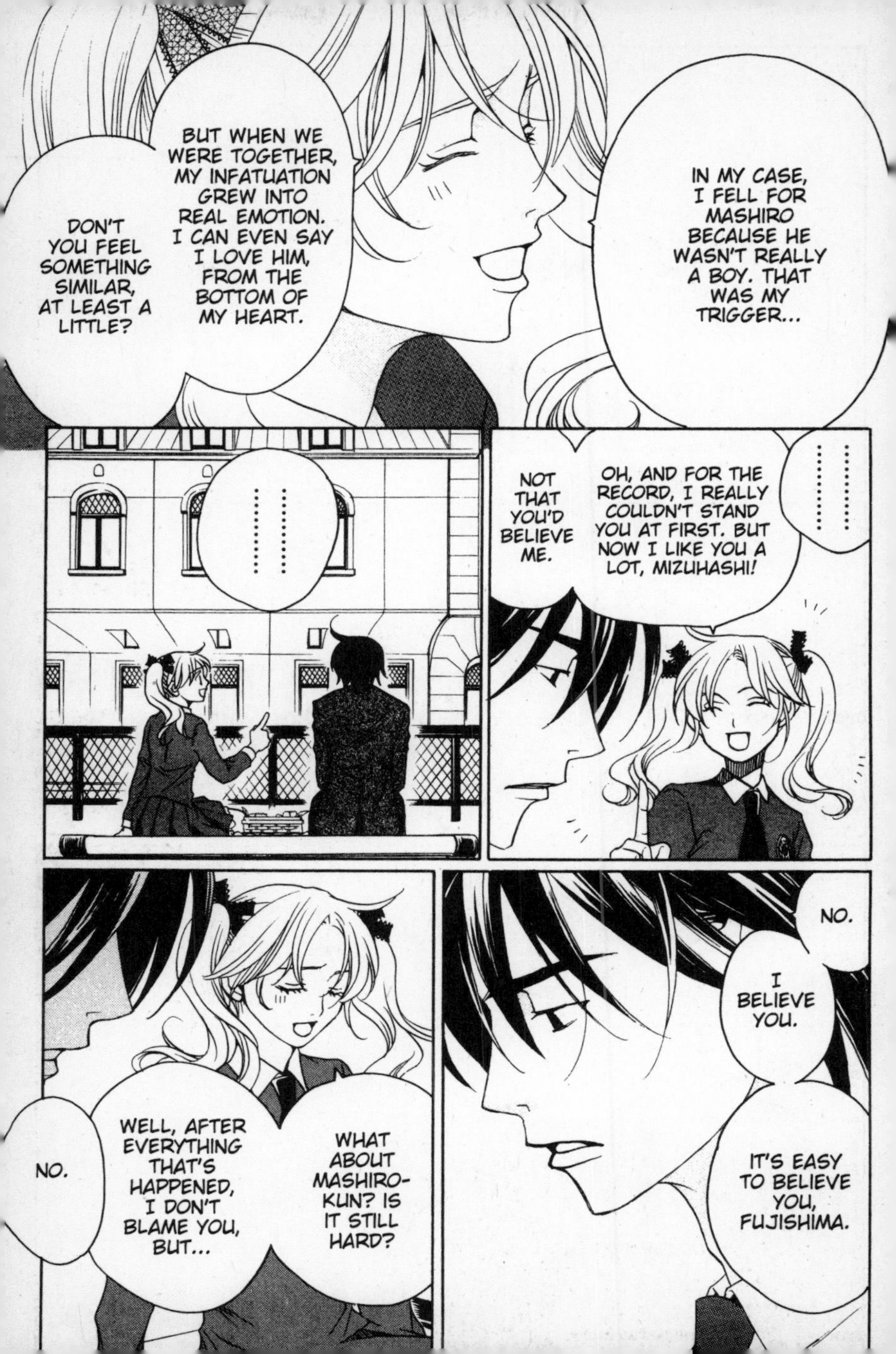
IN MY CASE, I FELL FOR MASHIRO BECAUSE HE WASN'T REALLY A BOY. THAT WAS MY TRIGGER...
BUT WHEN WE WERE TOGETHER, MY INFATUATION GREW INTO REAL EMOTION. I CAN EVEN SAY I LOVE HIM, FROM THE BOTTOM OF MY HEART.
DON'T YOU FEEL SOMETHING SIMILAR, AT LEAST A LITTLE?
......
OH, AND FOR THE RECORD, I REALLY COULDN'T STAND YOU AT FIRST. BUT NOW I LIKE YOU A LOT, MIZUHASHI!
NOT THAT YOU'D BELIEVE ME.
......
NO.
I BELIEVE YOU.
IT'S EASY TO BELIEVE YOU, FUJISHIMA.
WHAT ABOUT MASHIRO-KUN? IS IT STILL HARD?
WELL, AFTER EVERYTHING THAT'S HAPPENED, I DON'T BLAME YOU, BUT...
NO.

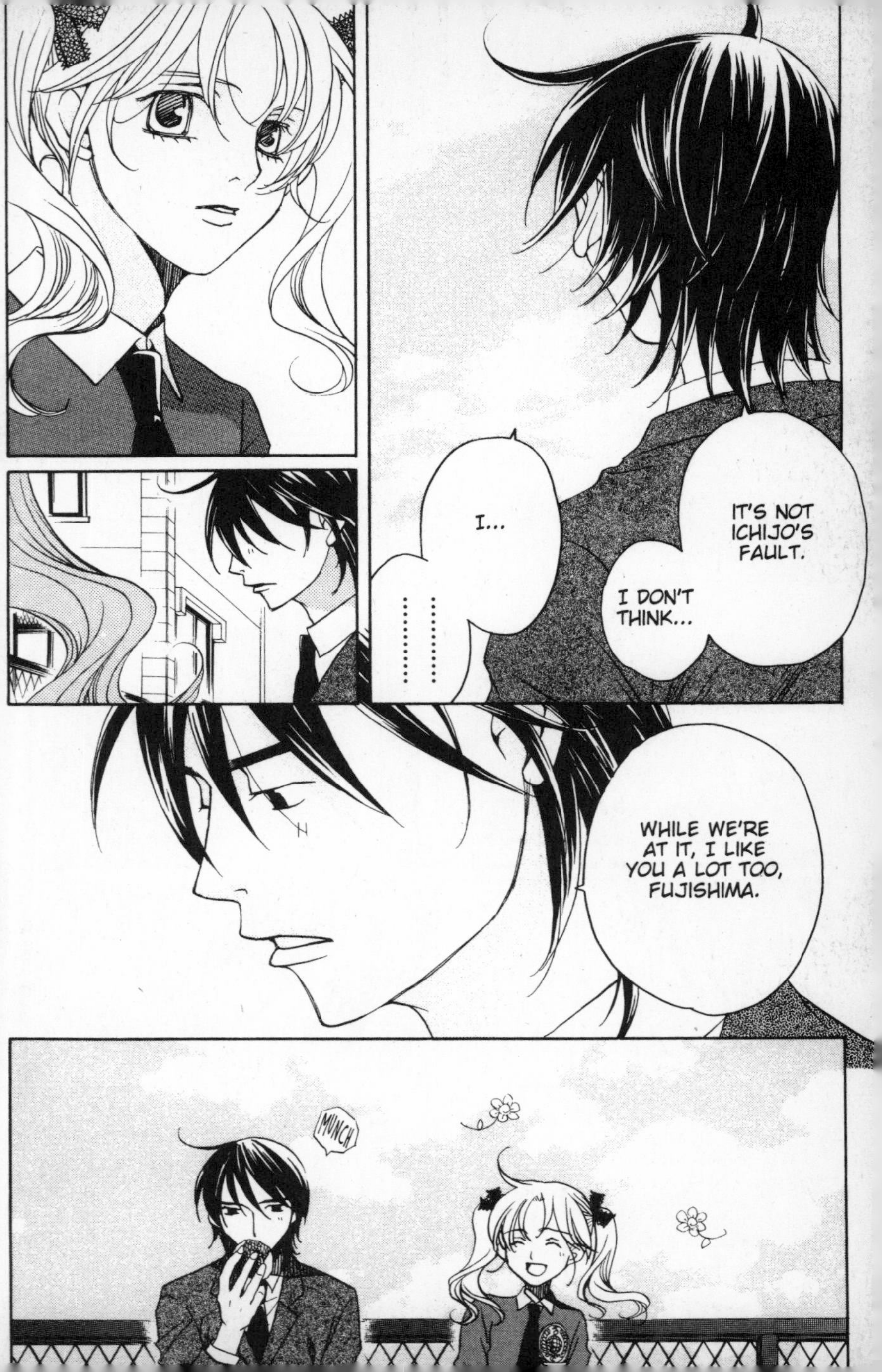
IT'S NOT ICHIJO'S FAULT.
I DON'T THINK...
I...
......
WHILE WE'RE AT IT, I LIKE YOU A LOT TOO, FUJISHIMA.
MUNCH

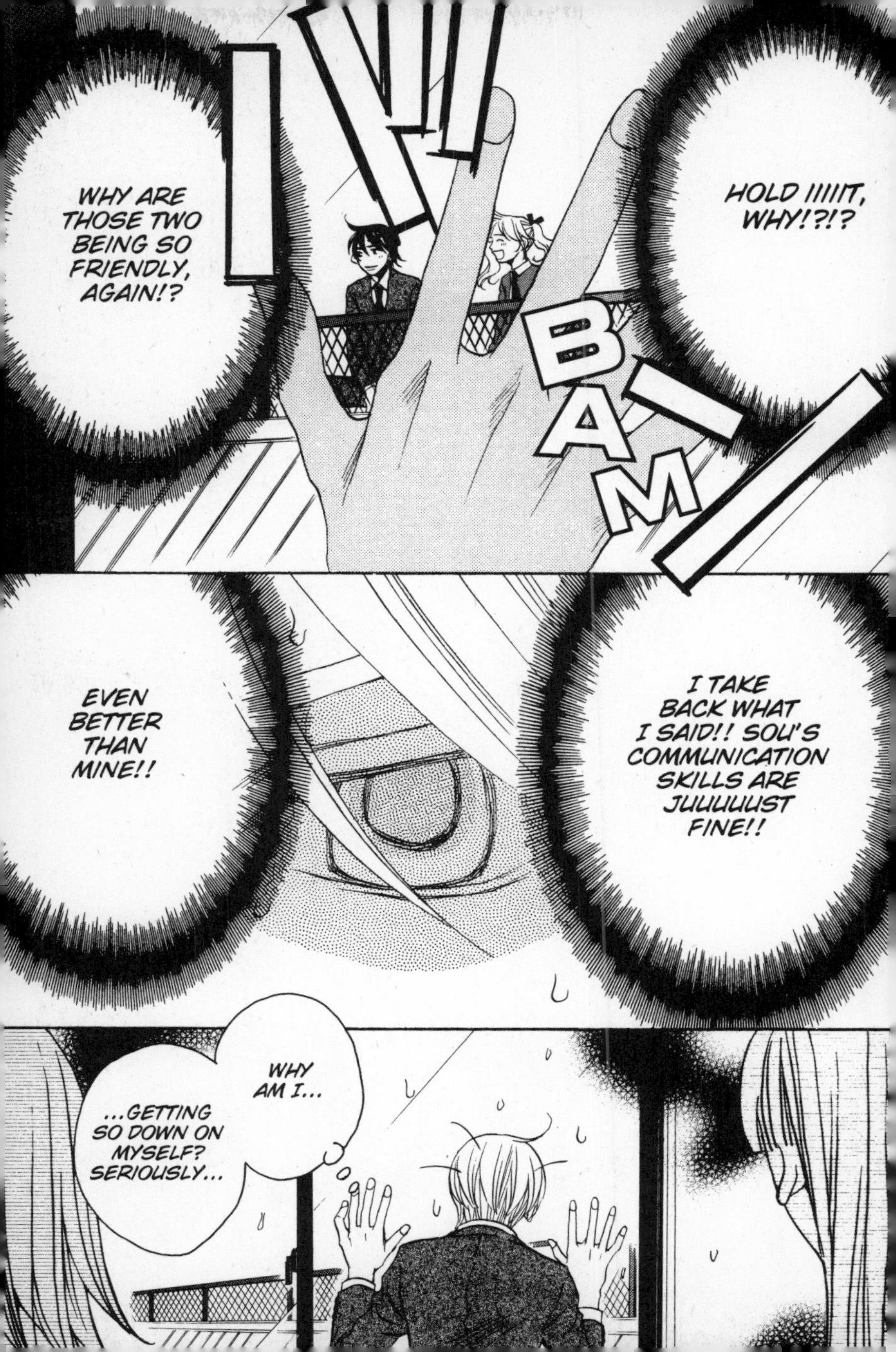
HOLD IIIIIT, WHY!?!?
BAM
WHY ARE THOSE TWO BEING SO FRIENDLY, AGAIN!?
I TAKE BACK WHAT I SAID!! SOU'S COMMUNICATION SKILLS ARE JUUUUUST FINE!!
EVEN BETTER THAN MINE!!
WHY AM I...
...GETTING SO DOWN ON MYSELF? SERIOUSLY...

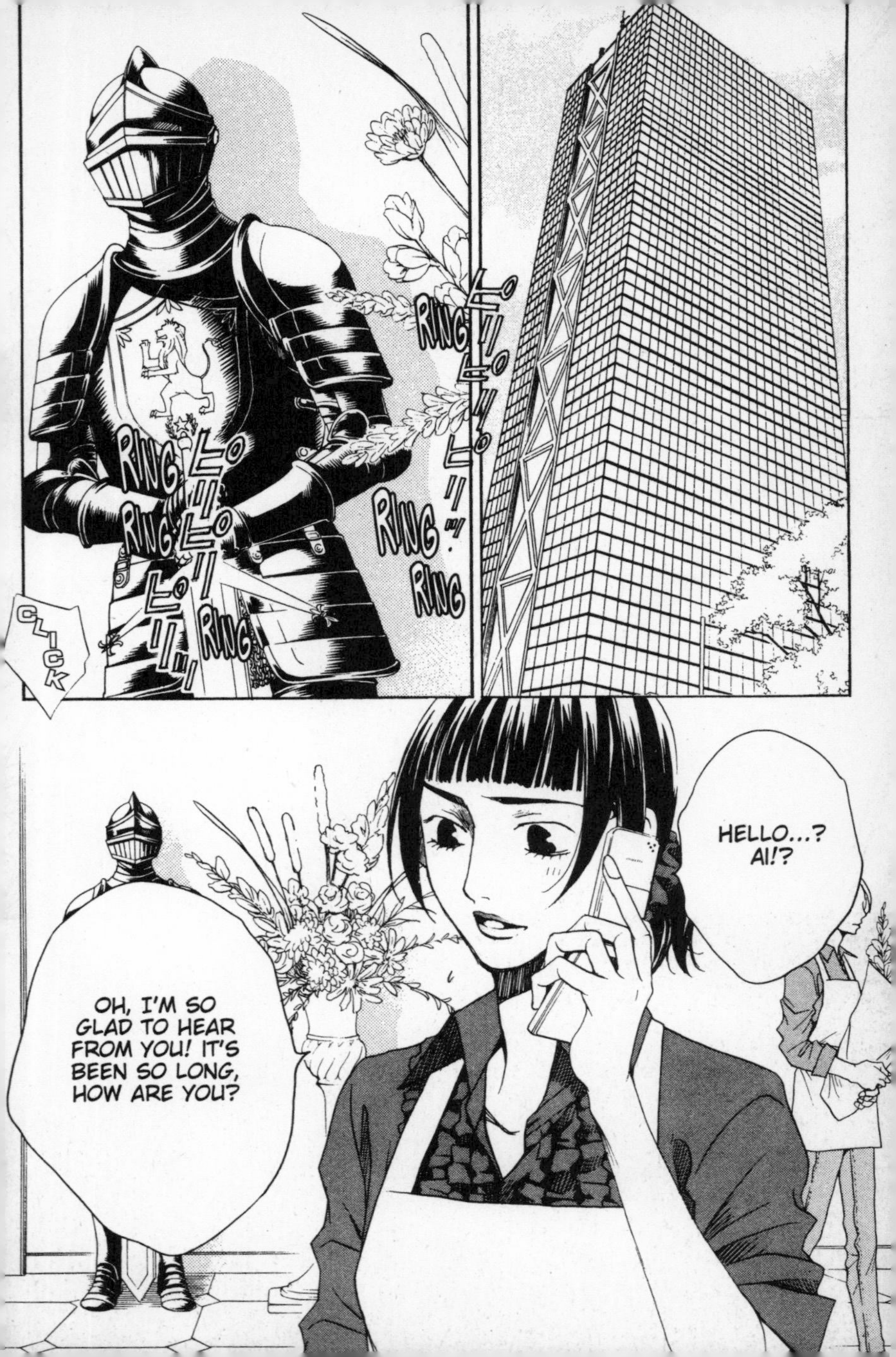
RING
RING RING
RING RING RING
CLICK
HELLO...? AI!?
OH, I'M SO GLAD TO HEAR FROM YOU! IT'S BEEN SO LONG, HOW ARE YOU?

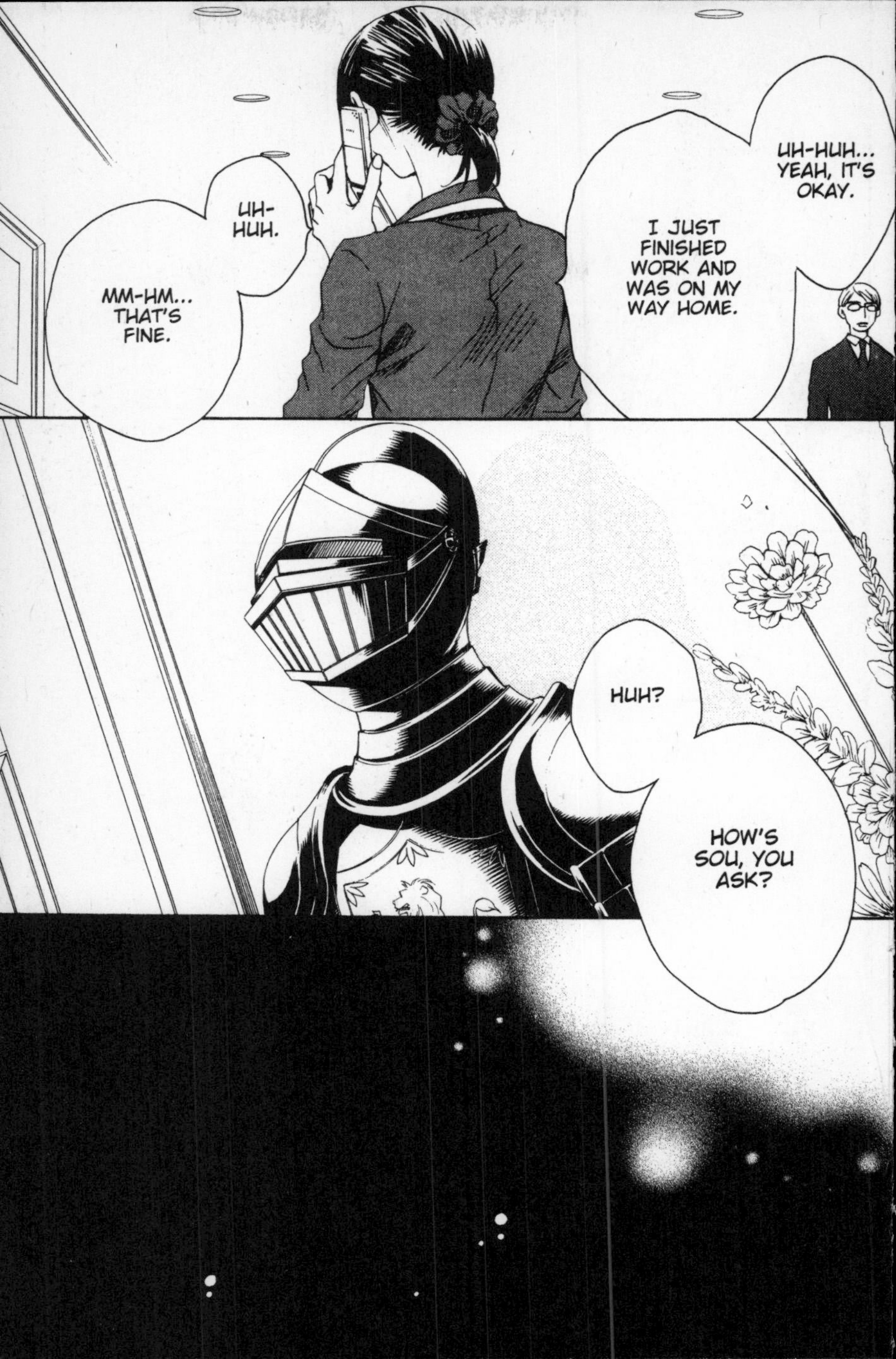
UH-HUH... YEAH, IT'S OKAY.
I JUST FINISHED WORK AND WAS ON MY WAY HOME.
UH-HUH.
MM-HM... THAT'S FINE.
HUH?
HOW'S SOU, YOU ASK?

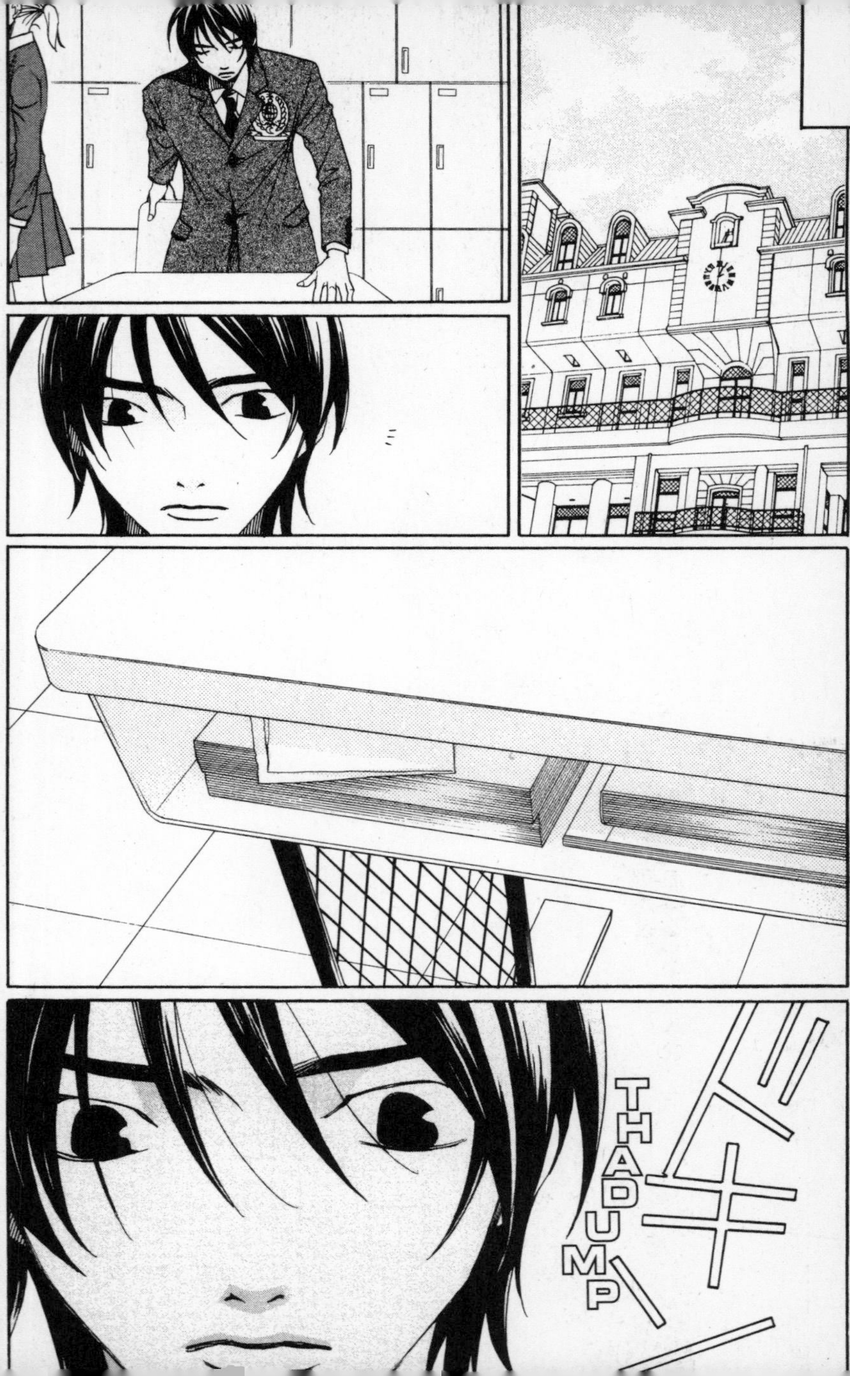
THADUMP

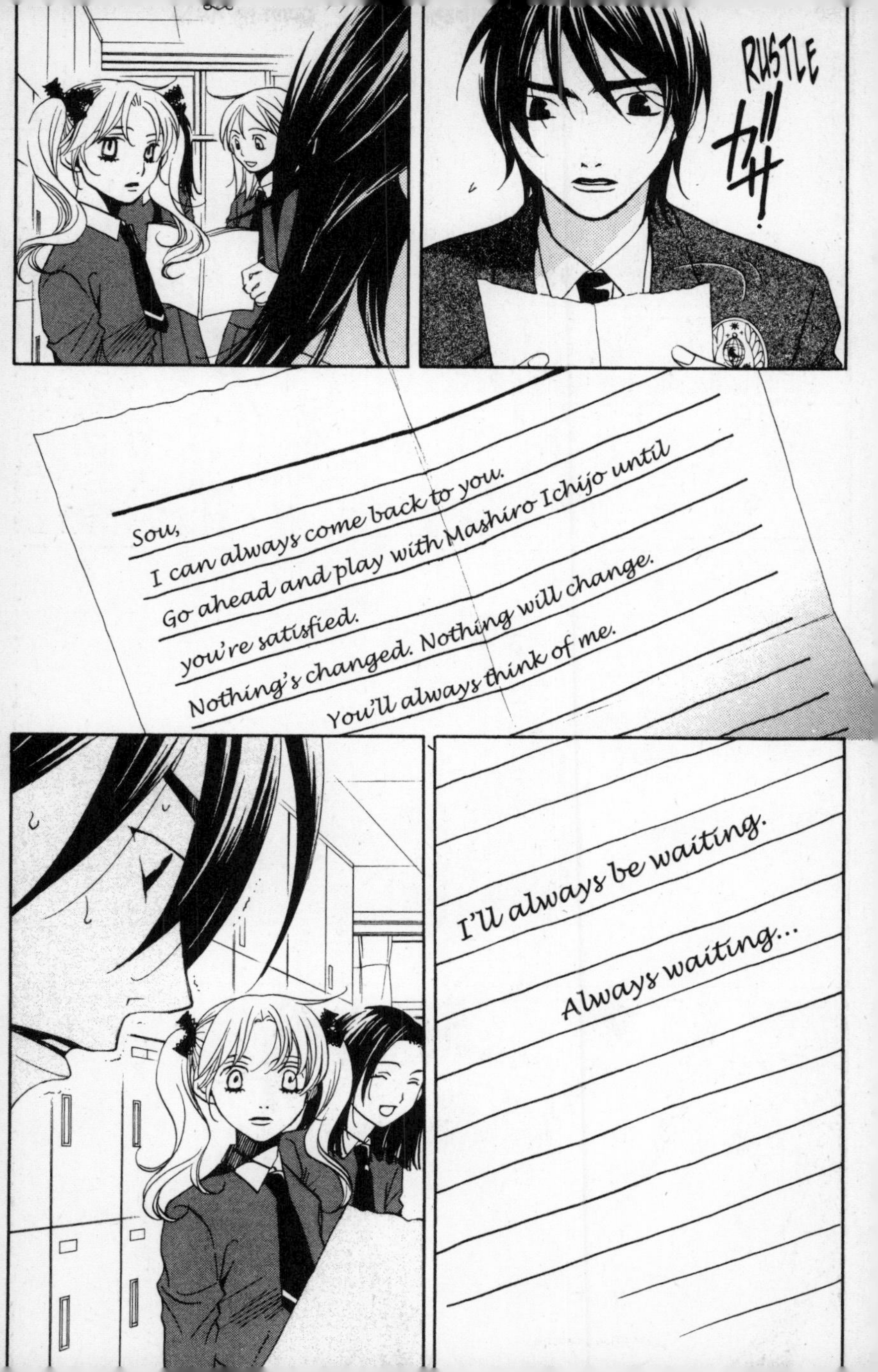
RUSTLE
Sou,
I can always come back to you.
Go ahead and play with Mashiro Ichijo until
you're satisfied.
Nothing's changed. Nothing will change.
You'll always think of me.
I'll always be waiting.
Always waiting...

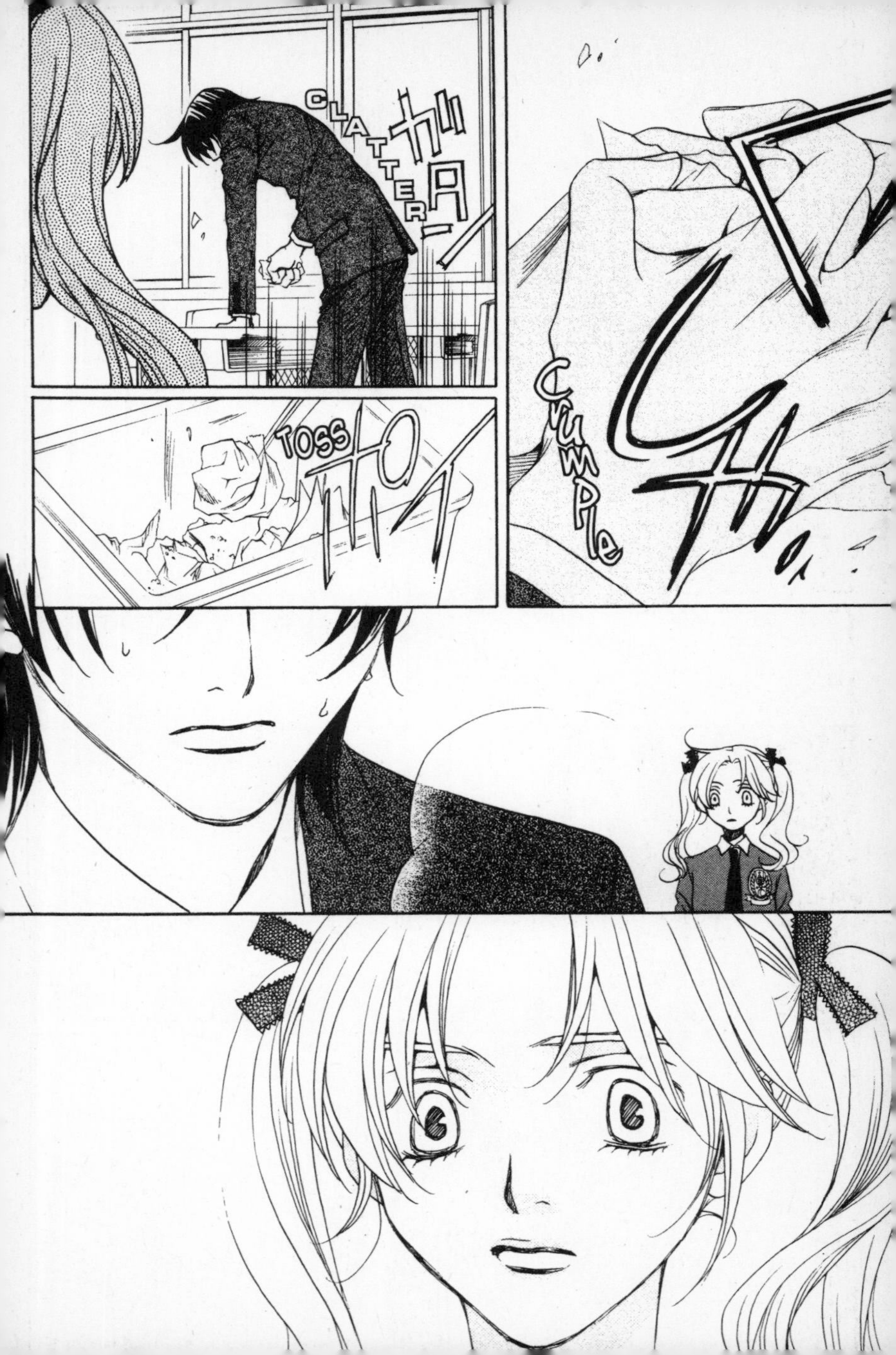
Crumple
CLATTER
TOSS

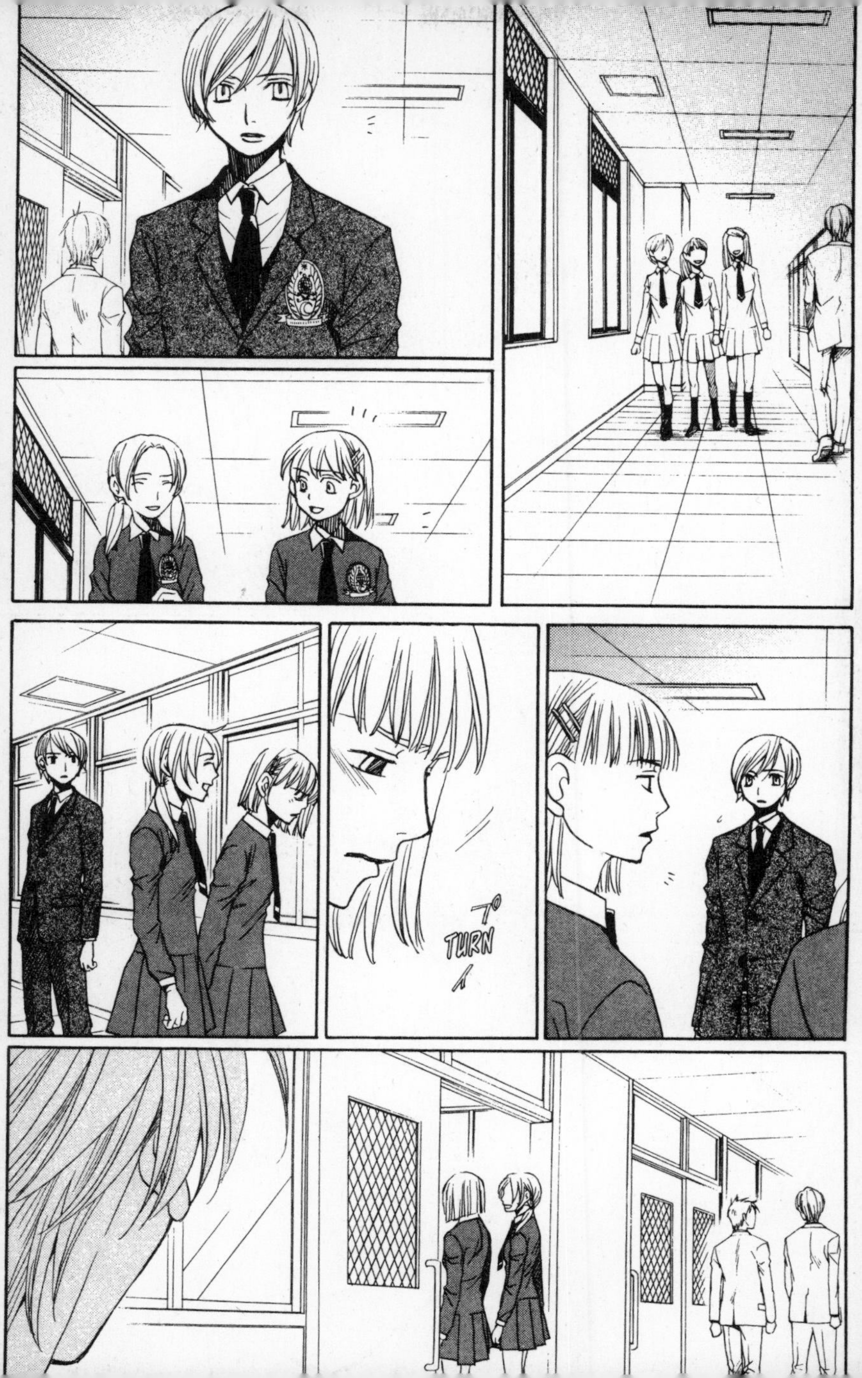
プイ
TURN

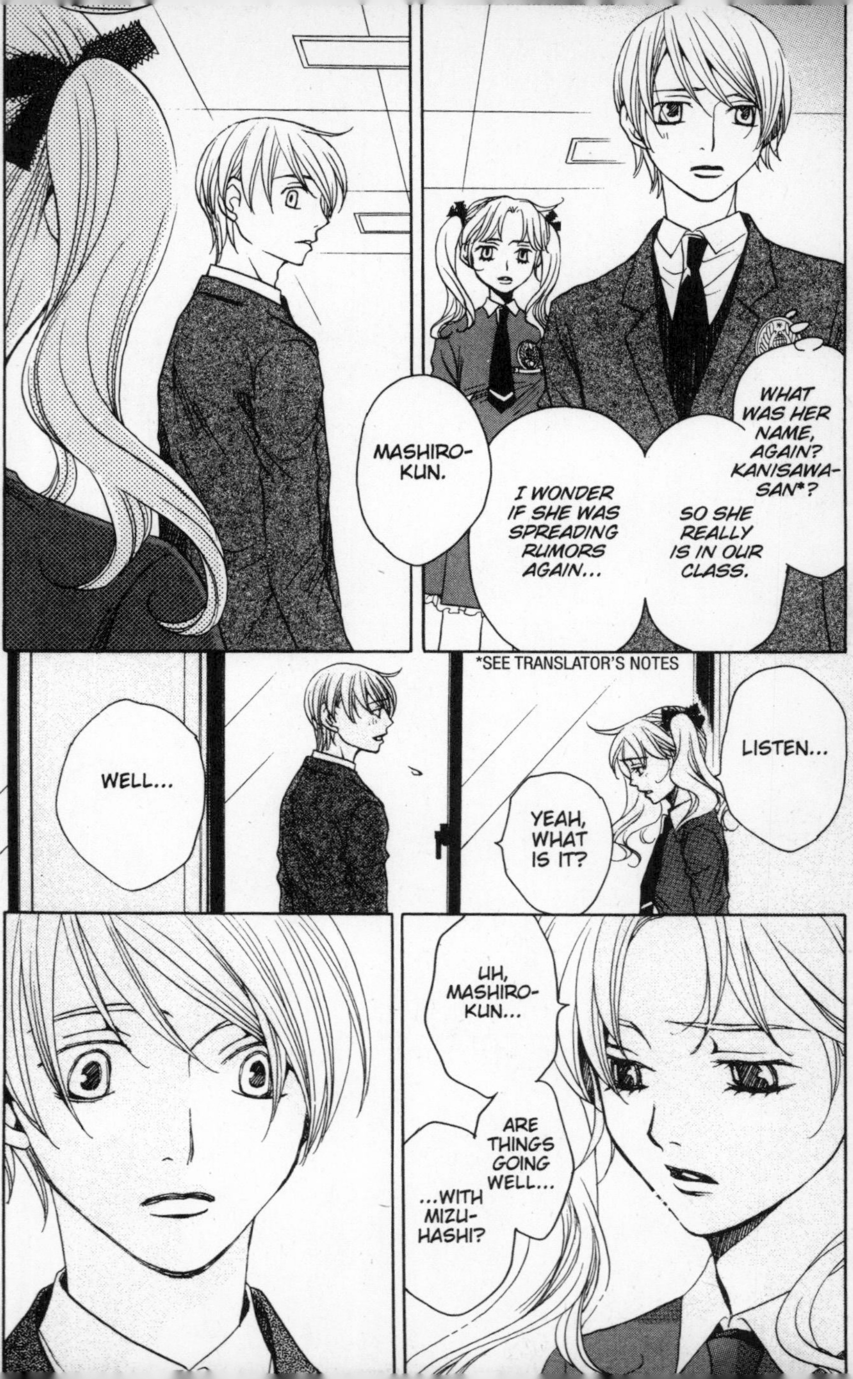
WHAT WAS HER NAME, AGAIN? KANISAWA-SAN*?
SO SHE REALLY IS IN OUR CLASS.
I WONDER IF SHE WAS SPREADING RUMORS AGAIN...
MASHIRO-KUN.
LISTEN...
YEAH, WHAT IS IT?
WELL...
UH, MASHIRO-KUN...
ARE THINGS GOING WELL...
...WITH MIZU-HASHI?

*SEE TRANSLATOR'S NOTES

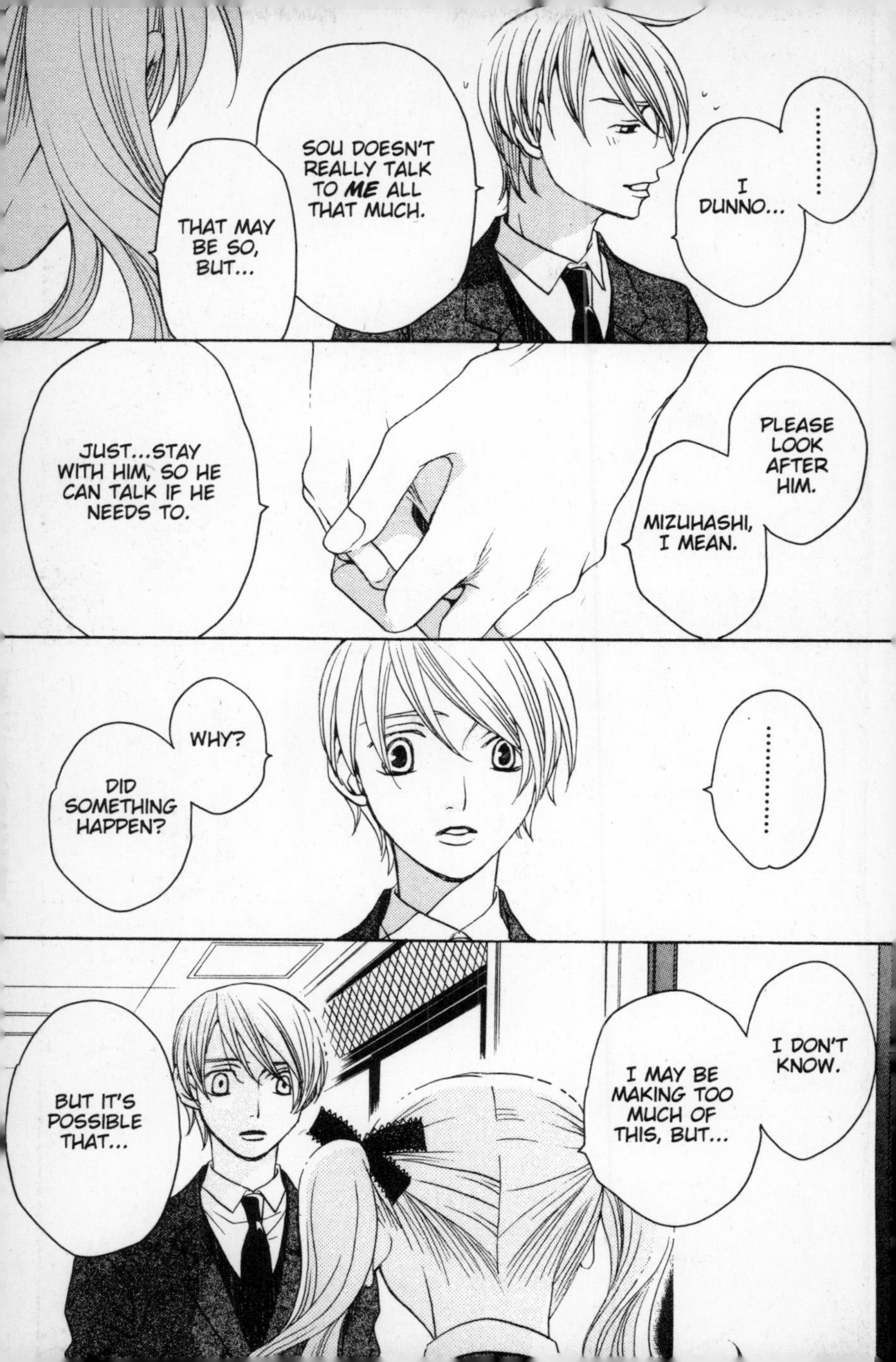
....
I DUNNO...
SOU DOESN'T REALLY TALK TO *ME* ALL THAT MUCH.
THAT MAY BE SO, BUT...
PLEASE LOOK AFTER HIM.
MIZUHASHI, I MEAN.
JUST...STAY WITH HIM, SO HE CAN TALK IF HE NEEDS TO.
....
WHY?
DID SOMETHING HAPPEN?
I DON'T KNOW.
I MAY BE MAKING TOO MUCH OF THIS, BUT...
BUT IT'S POSSIBLE THAT...

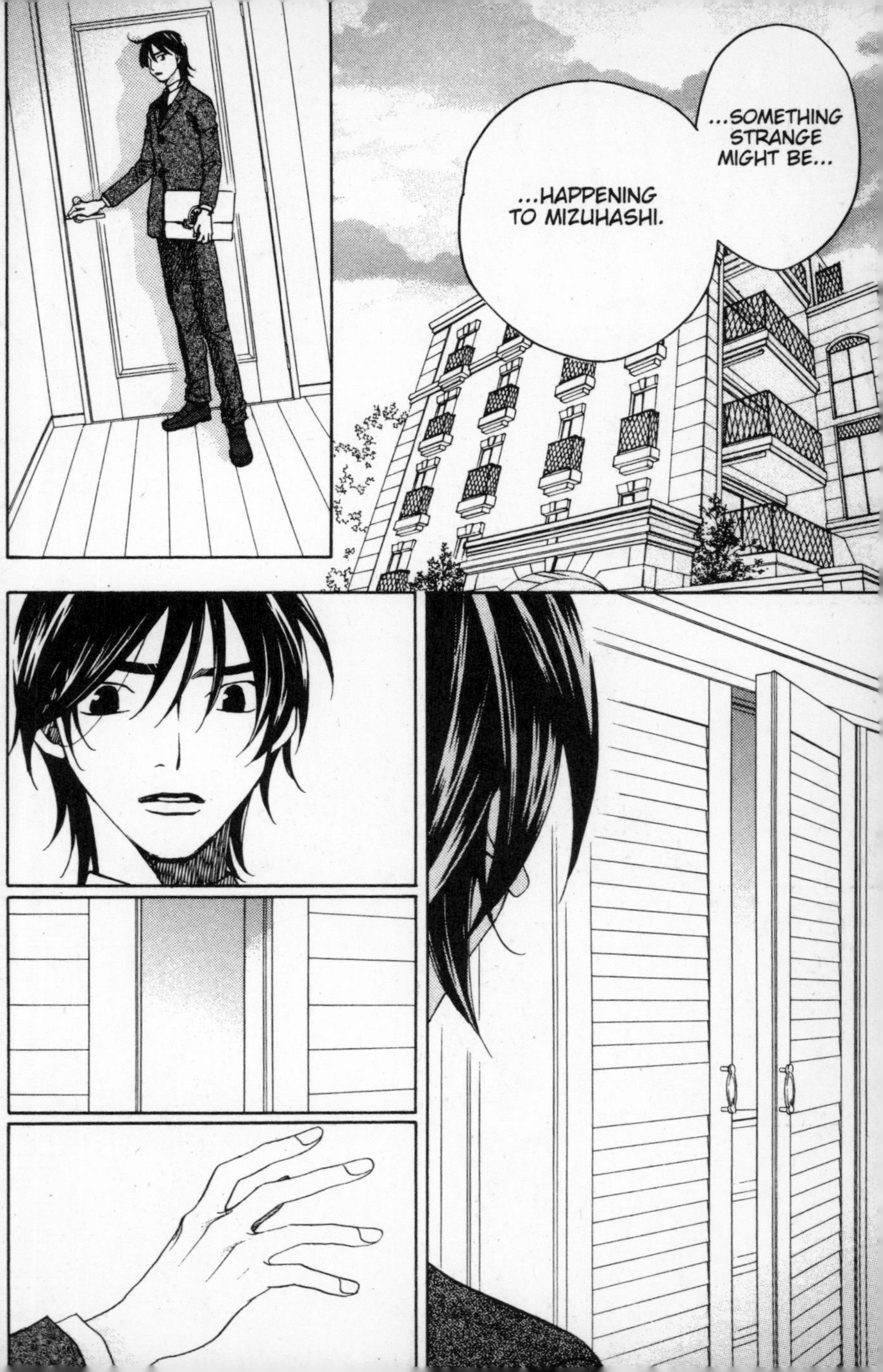
...SOMETHING STRANGE MIGHT BE...
...HAPPENING TO MIZUHASHI.

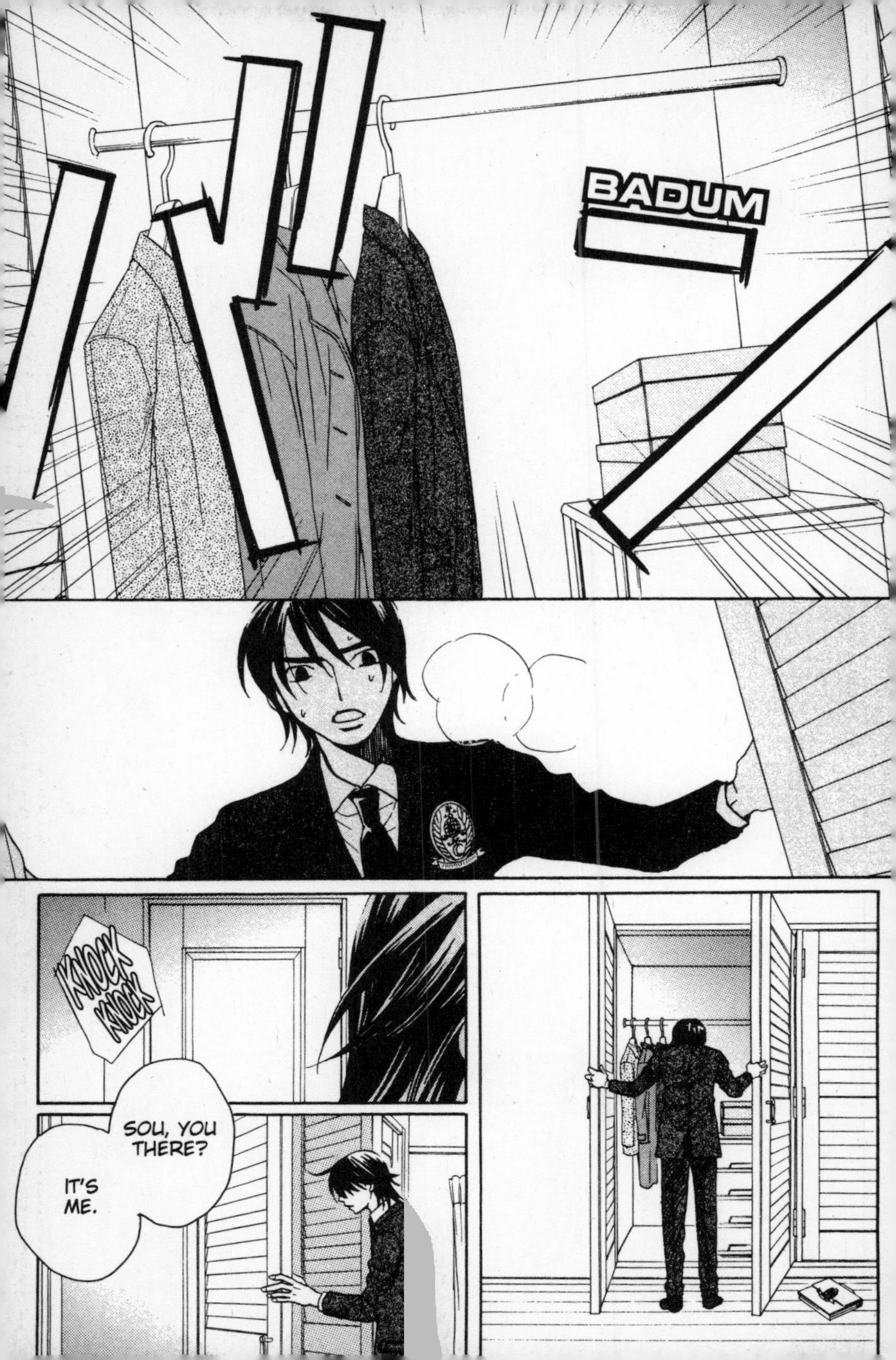
BADUM
KNOCK KNOCK
SOU, YOU THERE? IT'S ME.

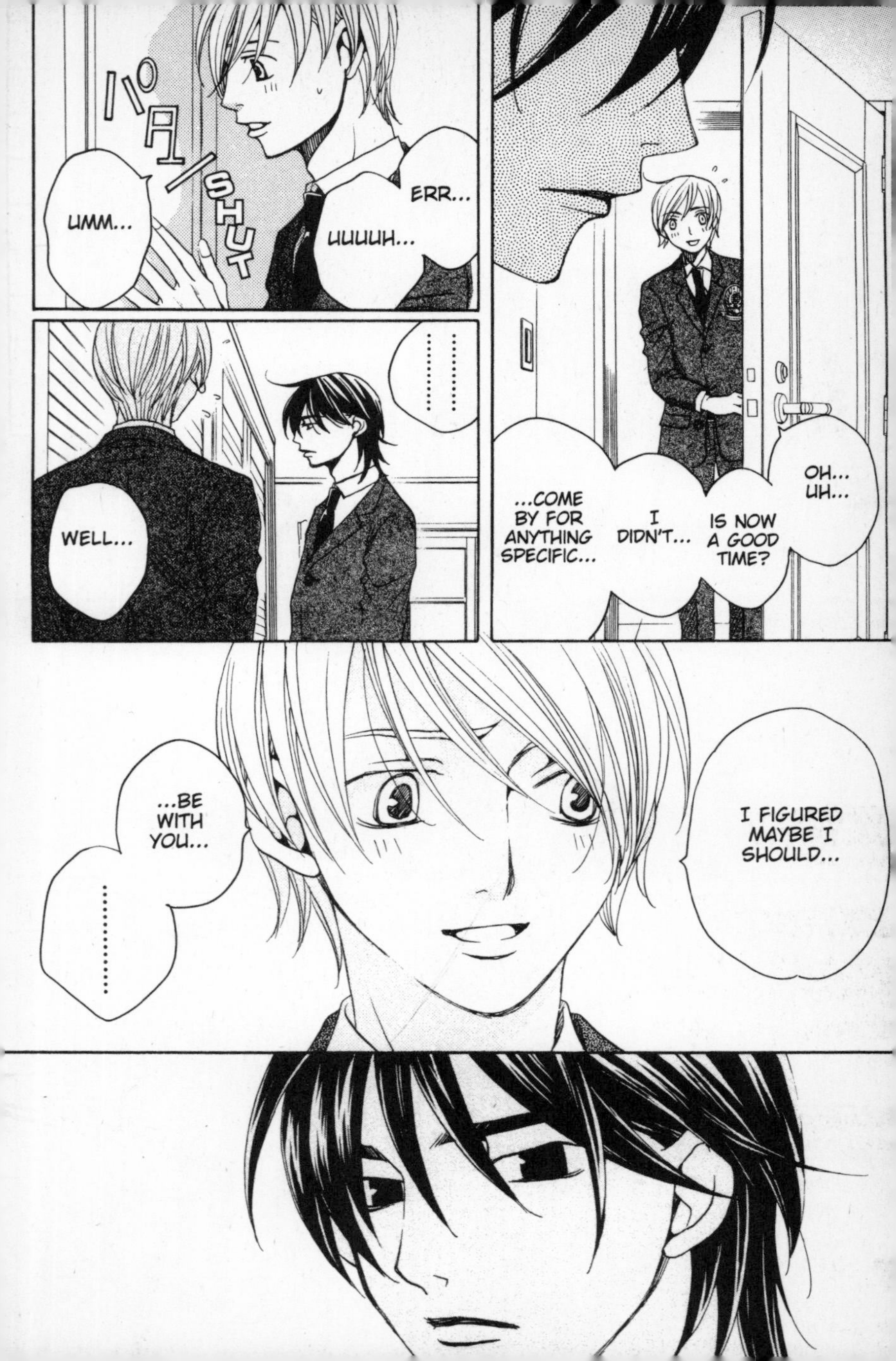
OH... UH...
IS NOW A GOOD TIME?
I DIDN'T...
...COME BY FOR ANYTHING SPECIFIC...
ERR...
UUUUH...
パタ/SHUT
UMM...
......
WELL...
I FIGURED MAYBE I SHOULD...
...BE WITH YOU...
......

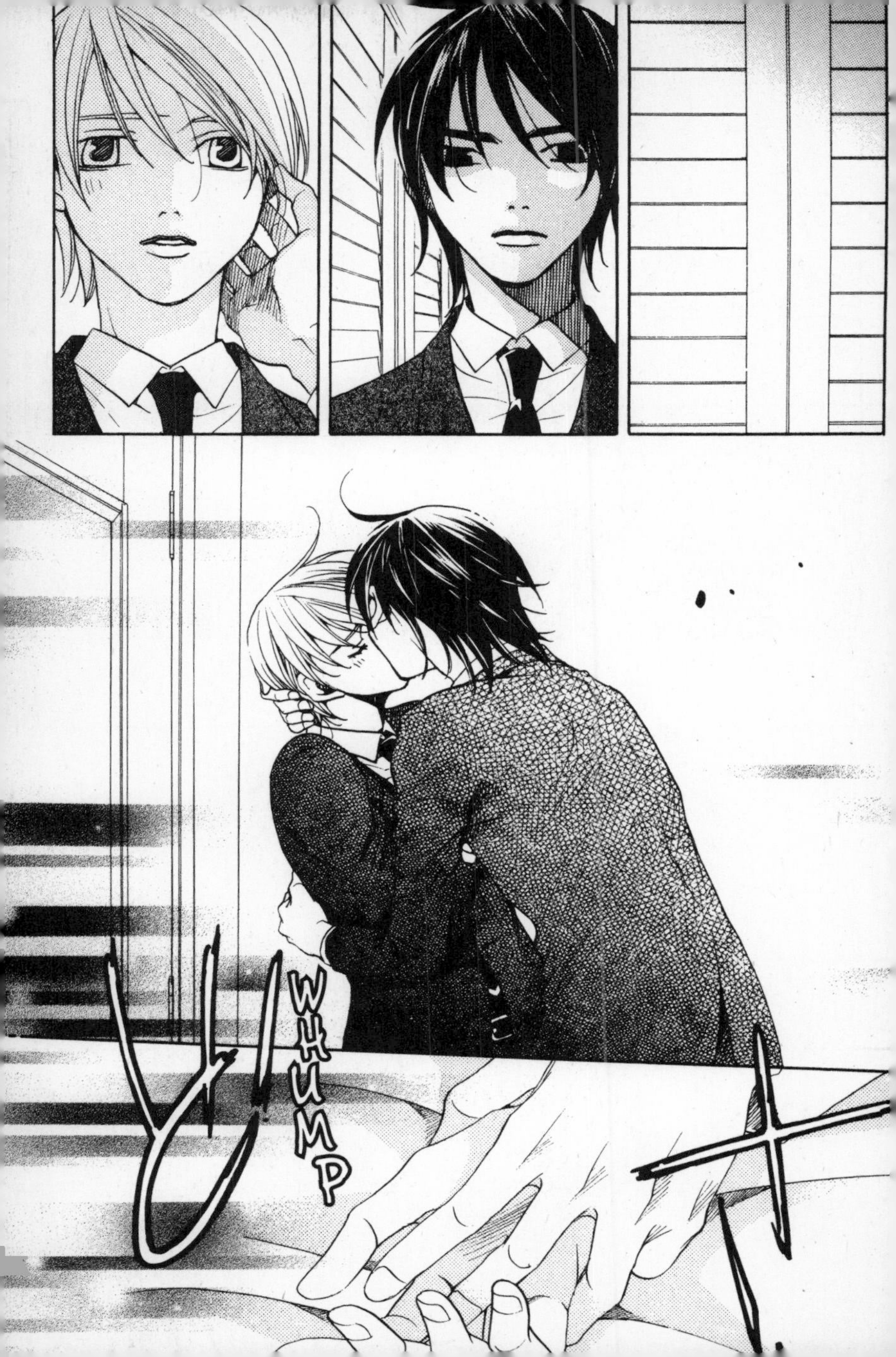
WHUMP

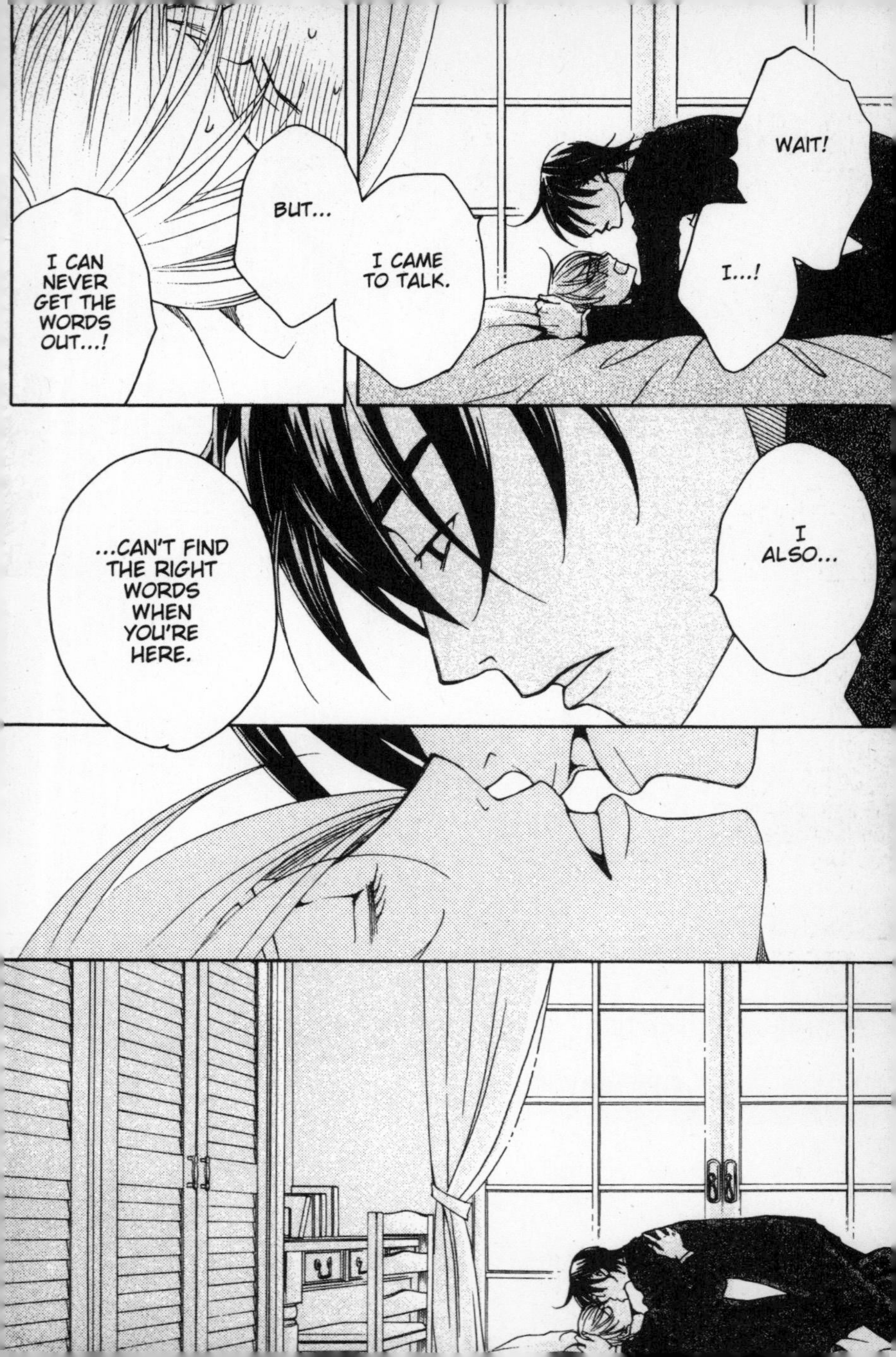
WAIT!
I...!
BUT...
I CAME TO TALK.
I CAN NEVER GET THE WORDS OUT...!
I ALSO...
...CAN'T FIND THE RIGHT WORDS WHEN YOU'RE HERE.

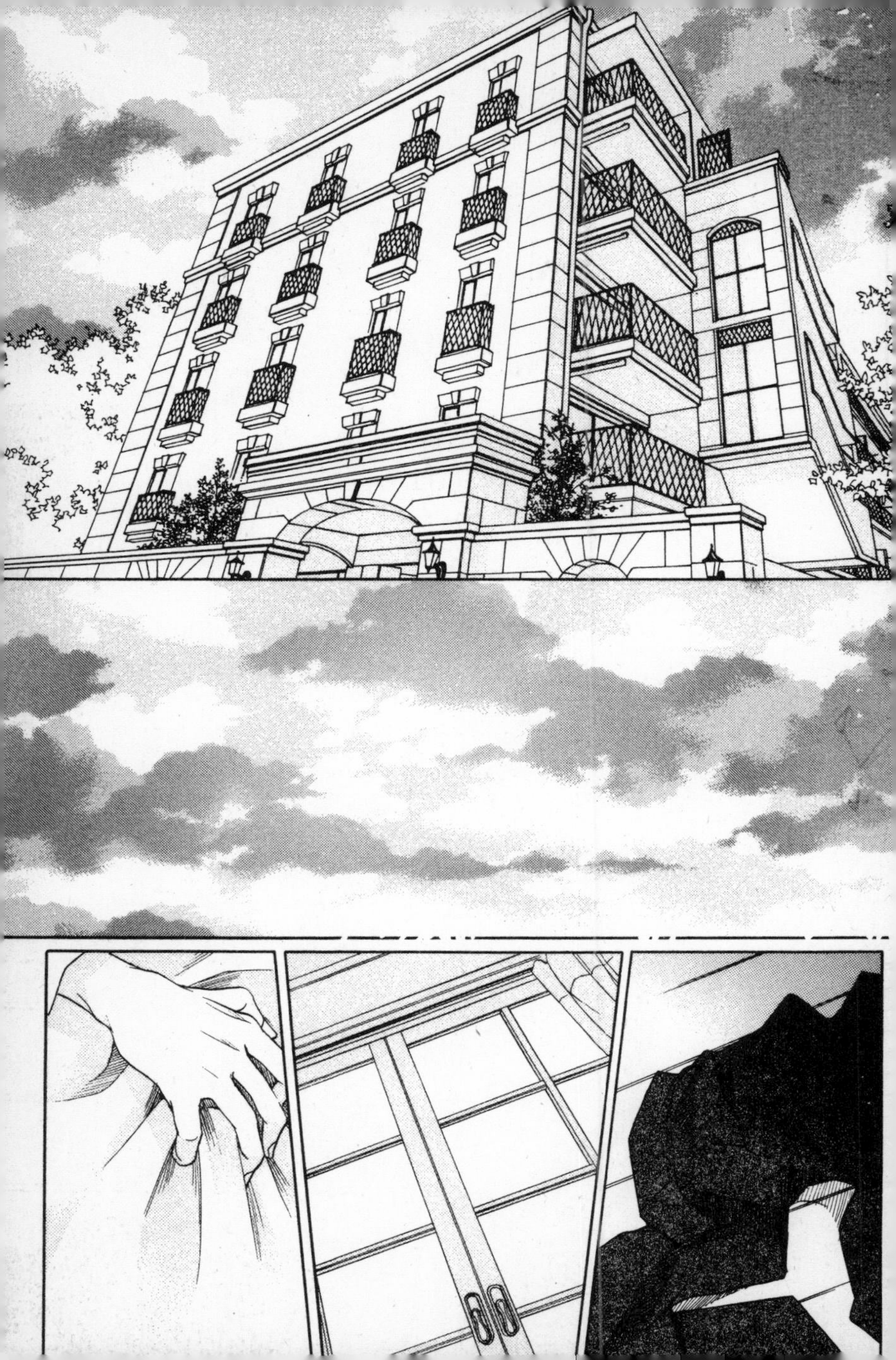

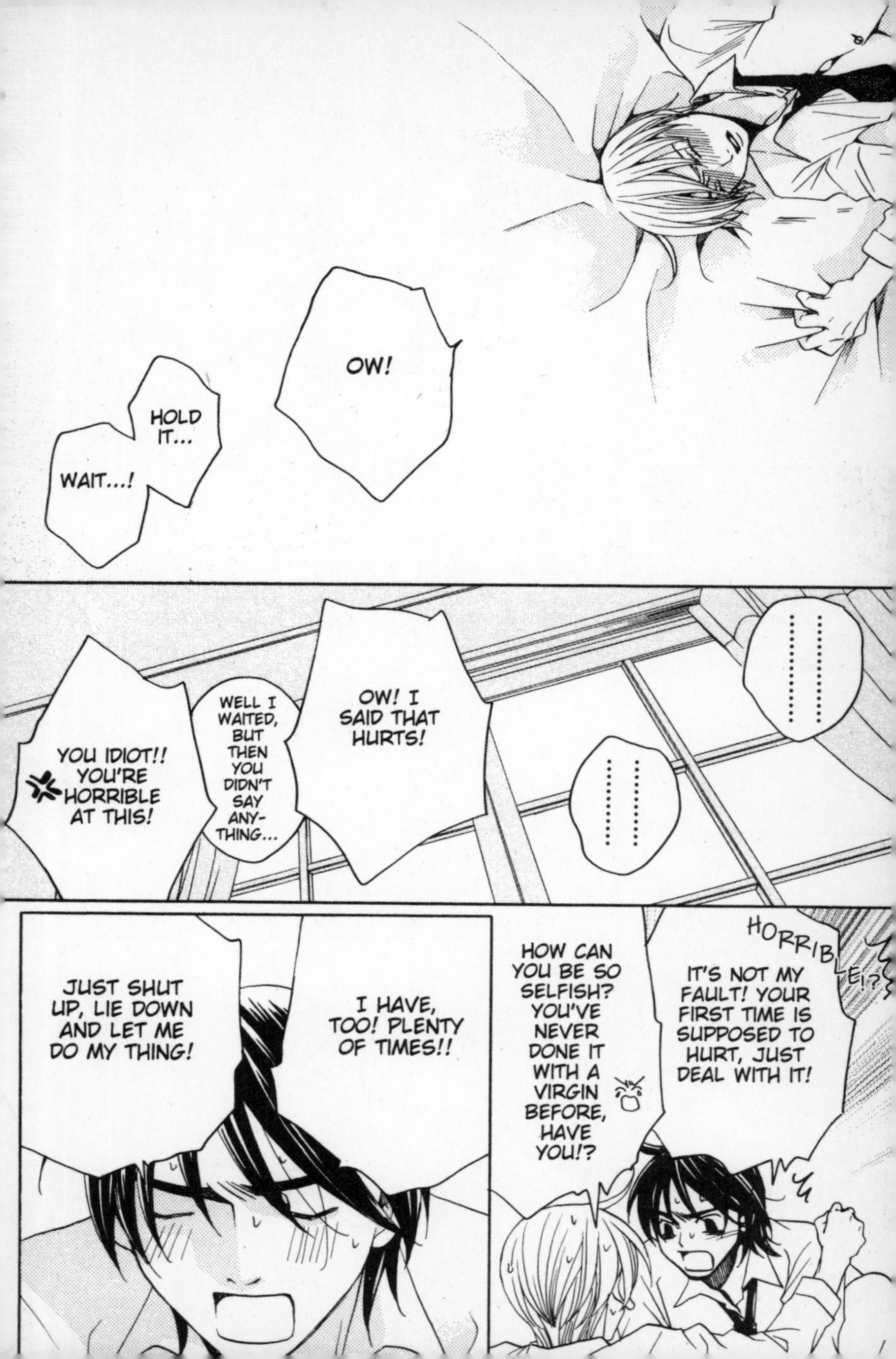
OW!
HOLD IT...
WAIT...!
......
......
OW! I SAID THAT HURTS!
WELL I WAITED, BUT THEN YOU DIDN'T SAY ANYTHING...
YOU IDIOT!! YOU'RE HORRIBLE AT THIS!
HORRIBLE!?
IT'S NOT MY FAULT! YOUR FIRST TIME IS SUPPOSED TO HURT, JUST DEAL WITH IT!
HOW CAN YOU BE SO SELFISH? YOU'VE NEVER DONE IT WITH A VIRGIN BEFORE, HAVE YOU!?
I HAVE, TOO! PLENTY OF TIMES!!
JUST SHUT UP, LIE DOWN AND LET ME DO MY THING!

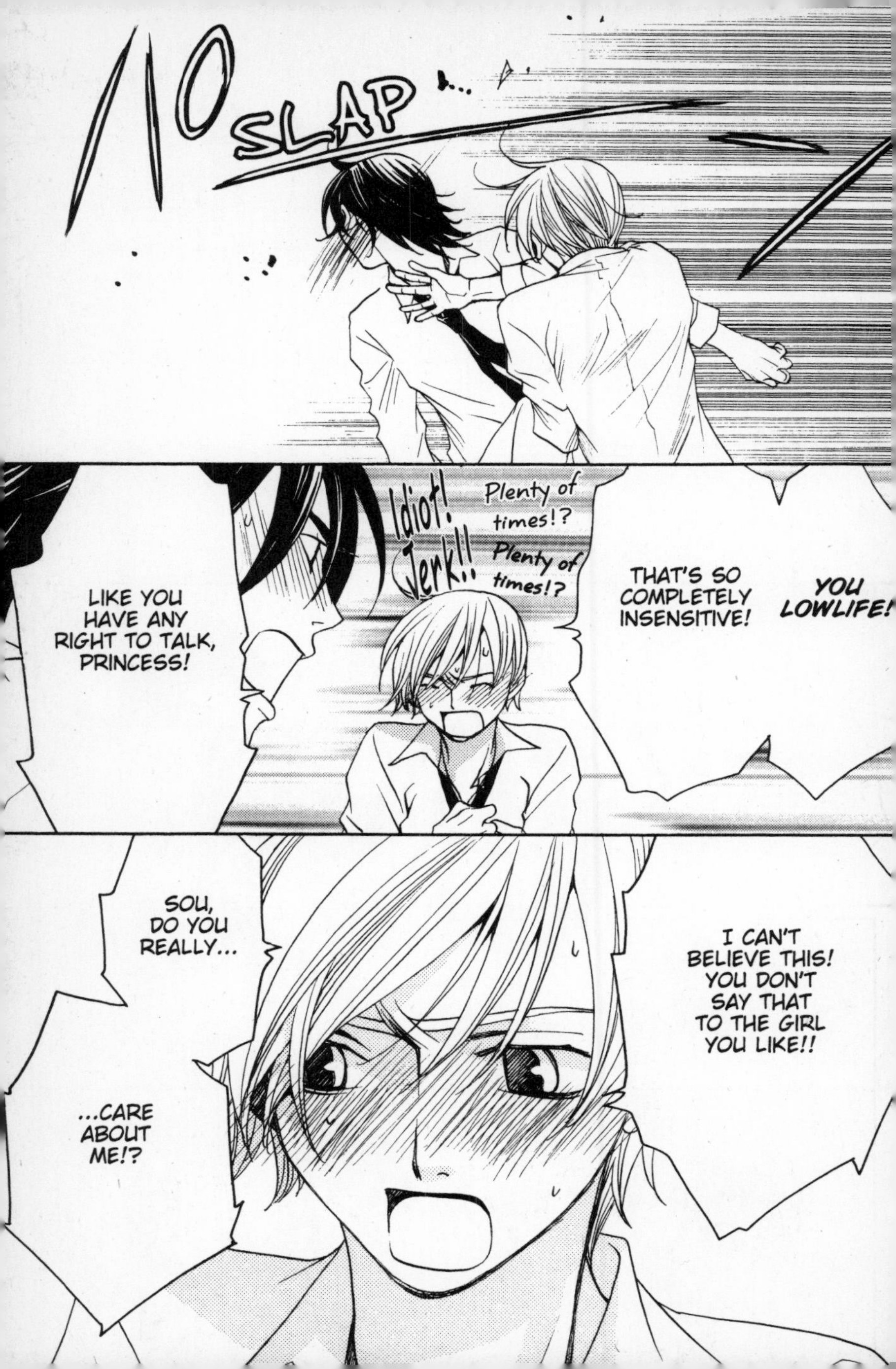
SLAP
YOU LOWLIFE!
THAT'S SO COMPLETELY INSENSITIVE!
Plenty of times!? Plenty of times!?
Idiot! Jerk!!
LIKE YOU HAVE ANY RIGHT TO TALK, PRINCESS!
I CAN'T BELIEVE THIS! YOU DON'T SAY THAT TO THE GIRL YOU LIKE!!
SOU, DO YOU REALLY...
...CARE ABOUT ME!?

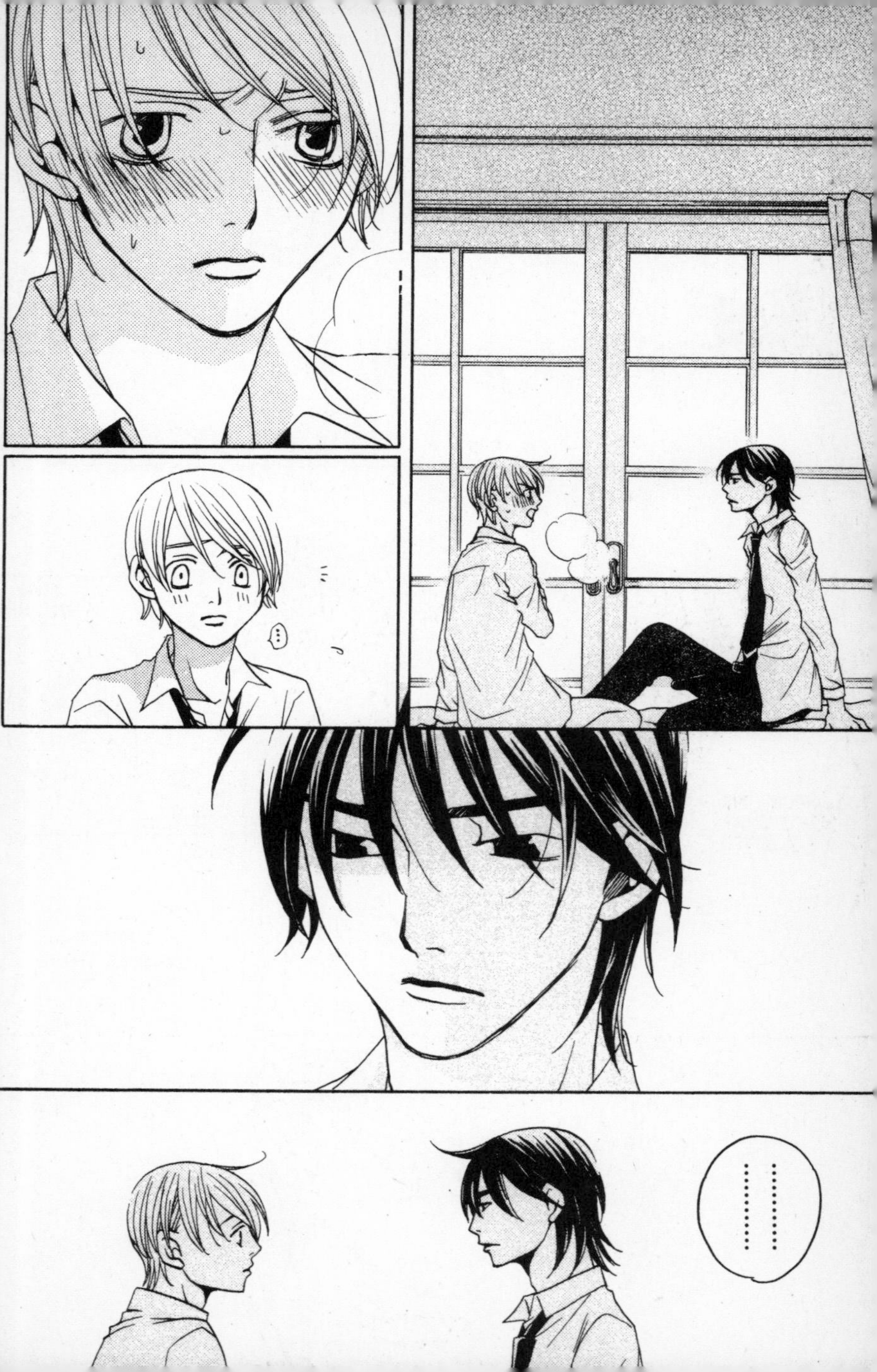
…
……

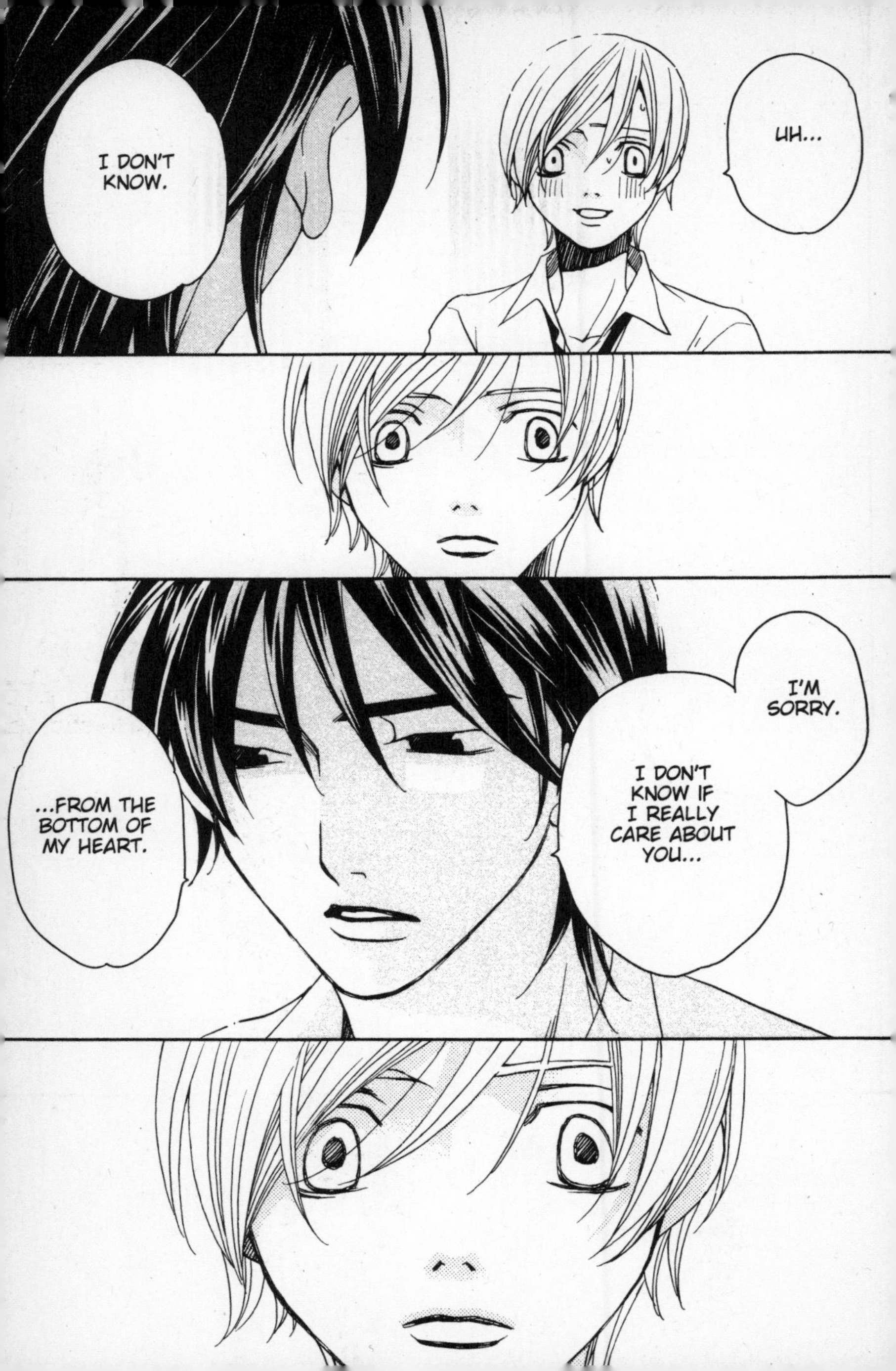
UH...
I DON'T KNOW.
I'M SORRY.
I DON'T KNOW IF I REALLY CARE ABOUT YOU...
...FROM THE BOTTOM OF MY HEART.

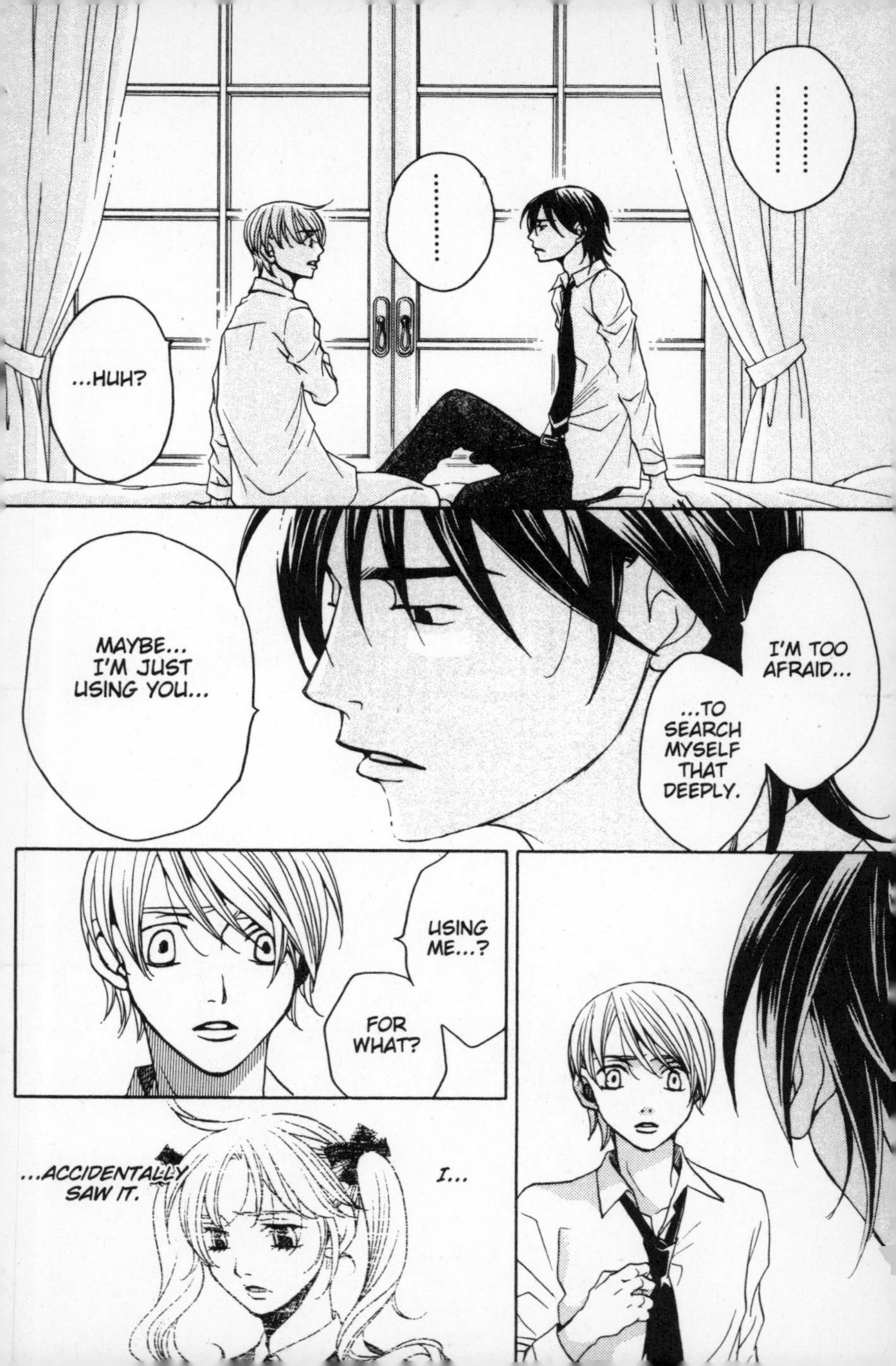

......
......
...HUH?
I'M TOO AFRAID...
...TO SEARCH MYSELF THAT DEEPLY.
MAYBE... I'M JUST USING YOU...
USING ME...?
FOR WHAT?
I...
...ACCIDENTALLY SAW IT.

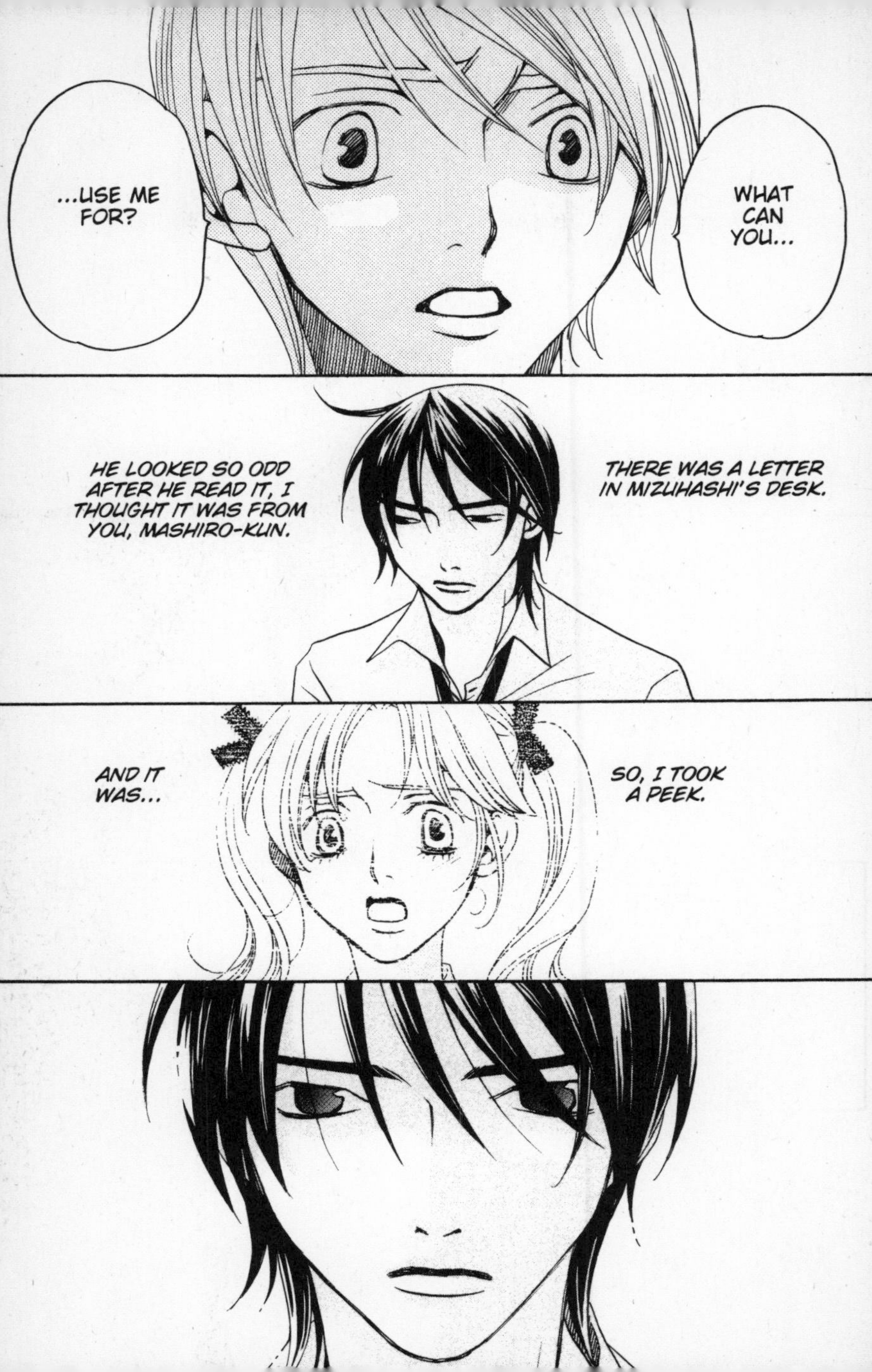
WHAT CAN YOU...
...USE ME FOR?
THERE WAS A LETTER IN MIZUHASHI'S DESK.
HE LOOKED SO ODD AFTER HE READ IT, I THOUGHT IT WAS FROM YOU, MASHIRO-KUN.
SO, I TOOK A PEEK.
AND IT WAS...

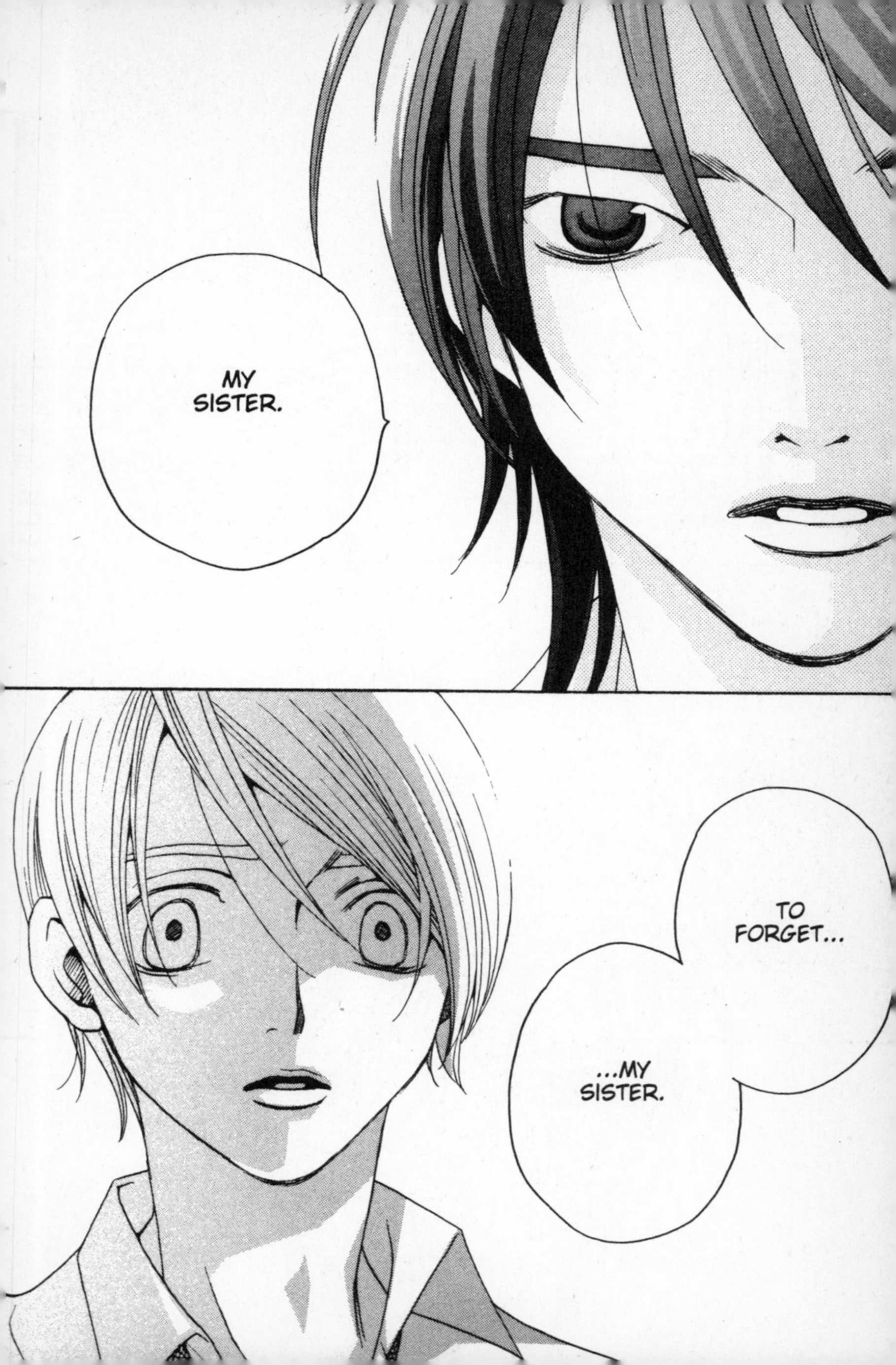
MY SISTER.
TO FORGET...
...MY SISTER.

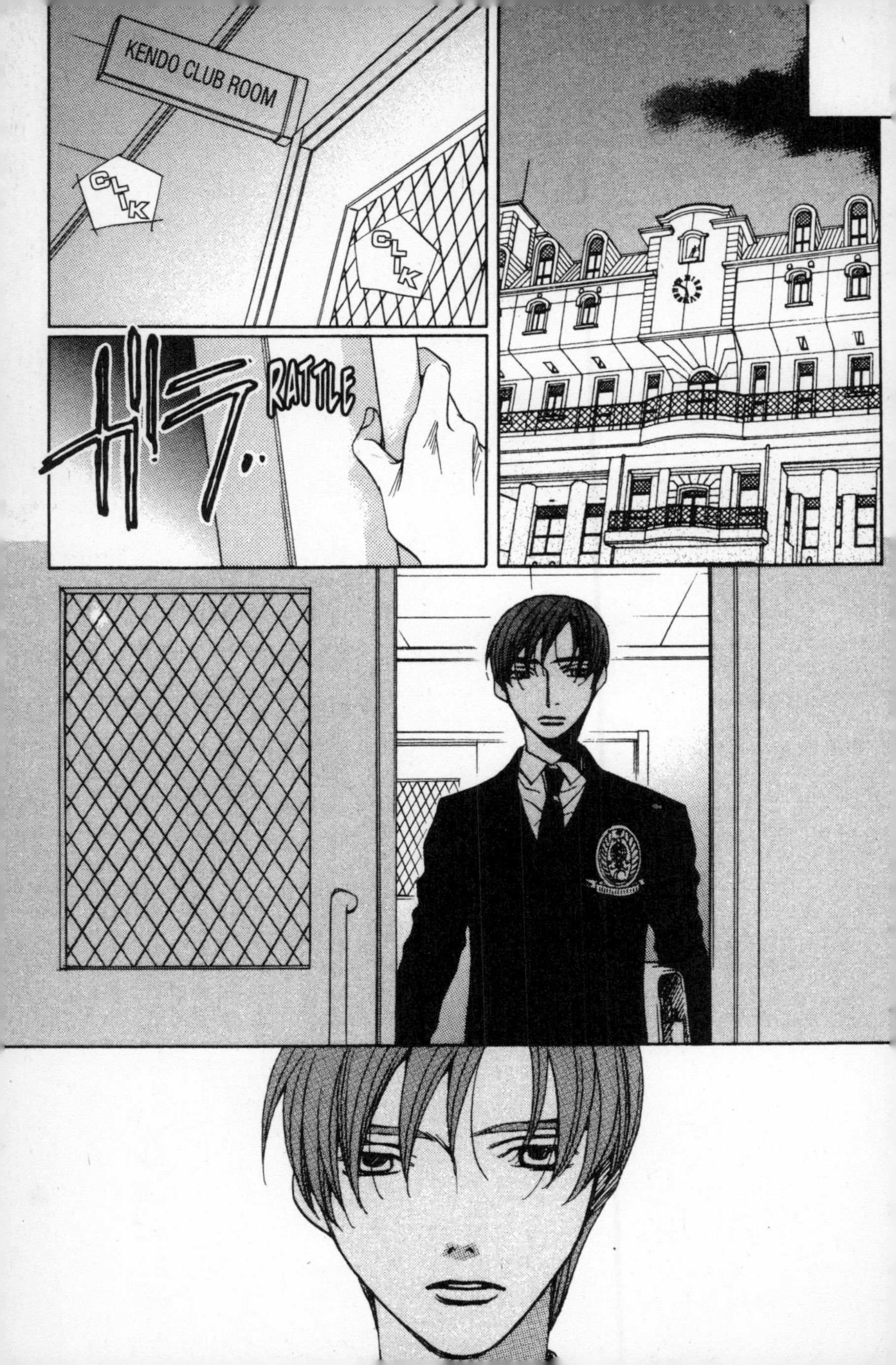
KENDO CLUB ROOM
CLIK
CLIK
RATTLE

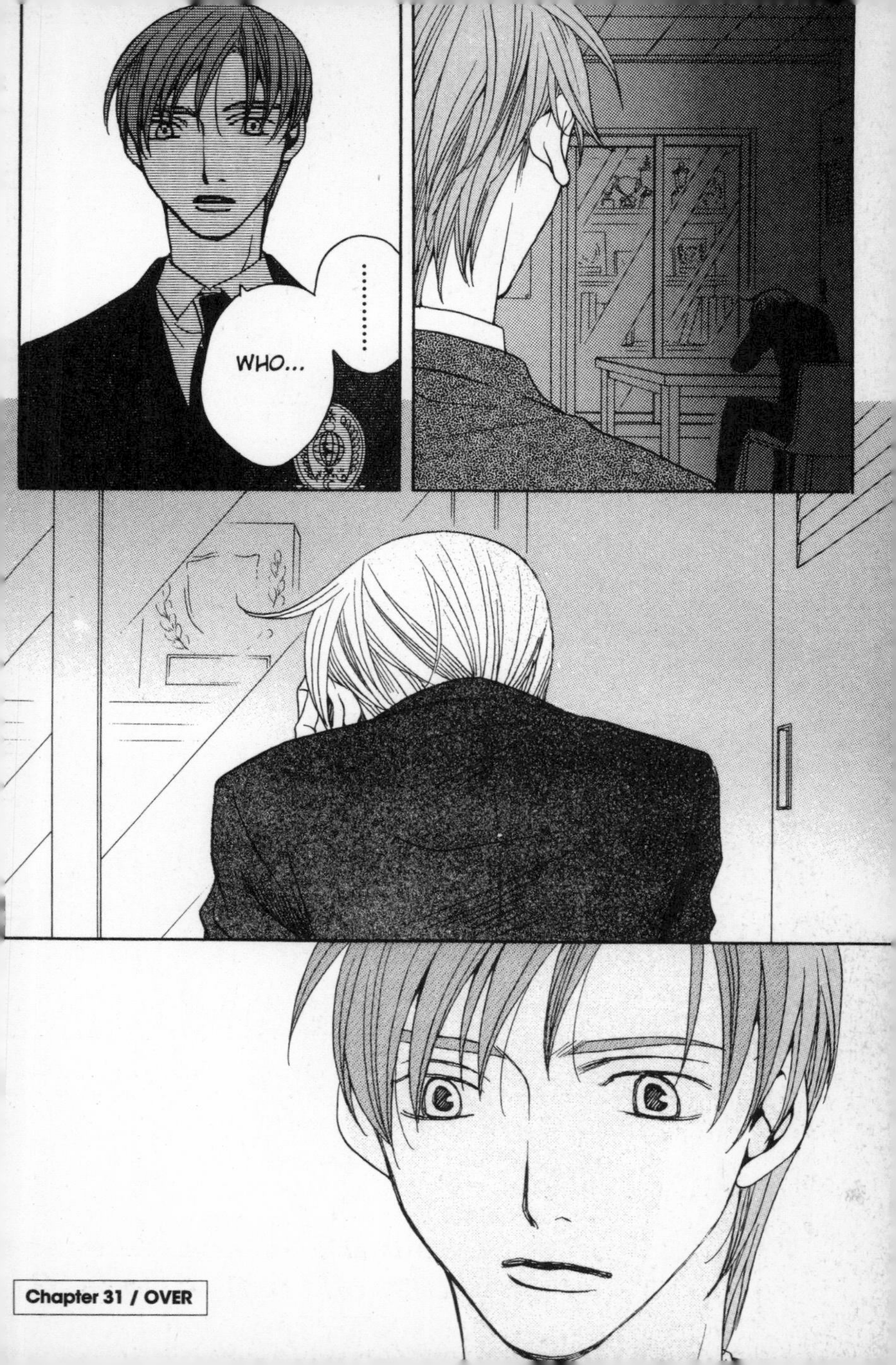
......
WHO...
Chapter 31 / OVER

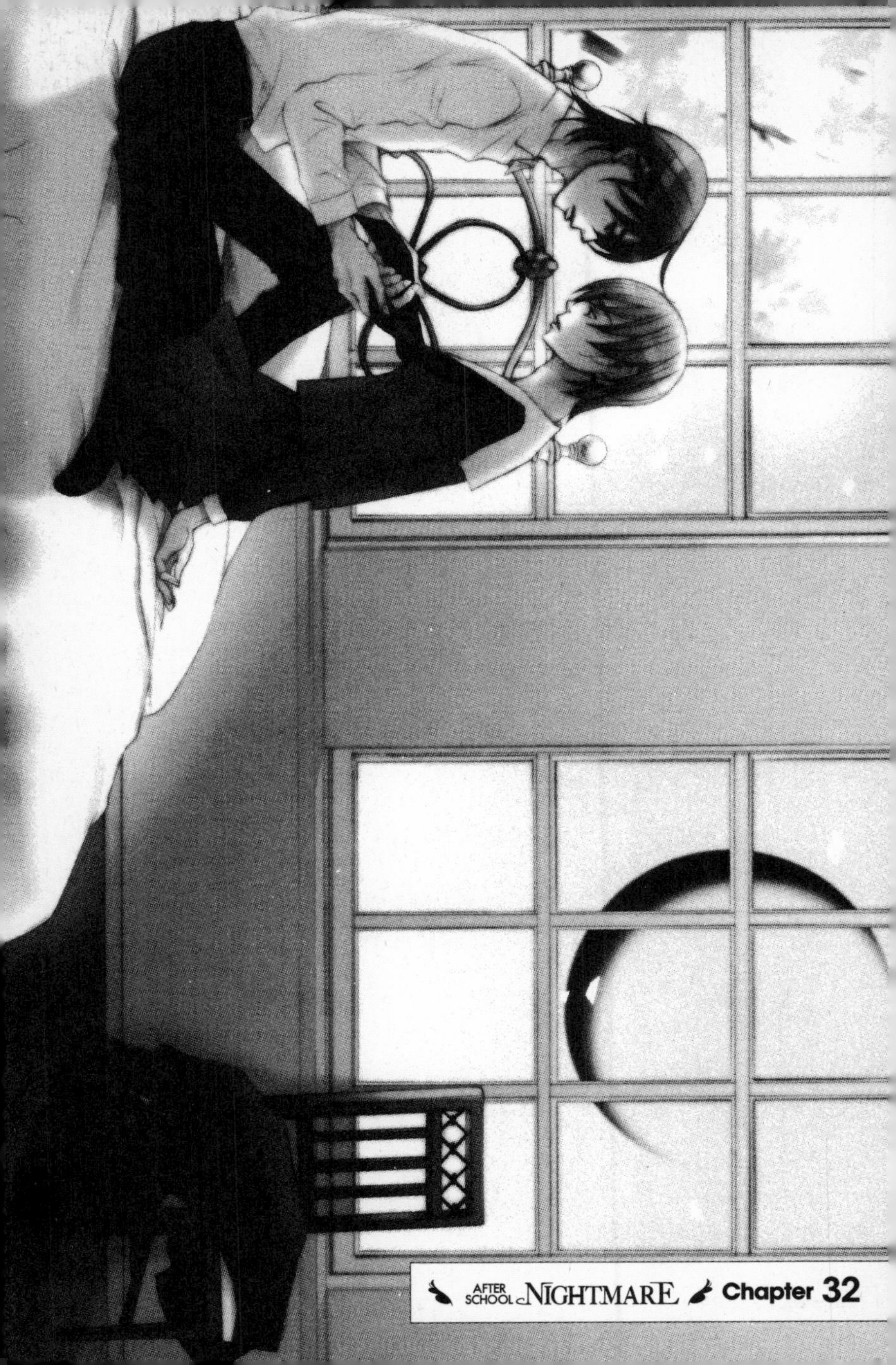
AFTER SCHOOL NIGHTMARE Chapter 32

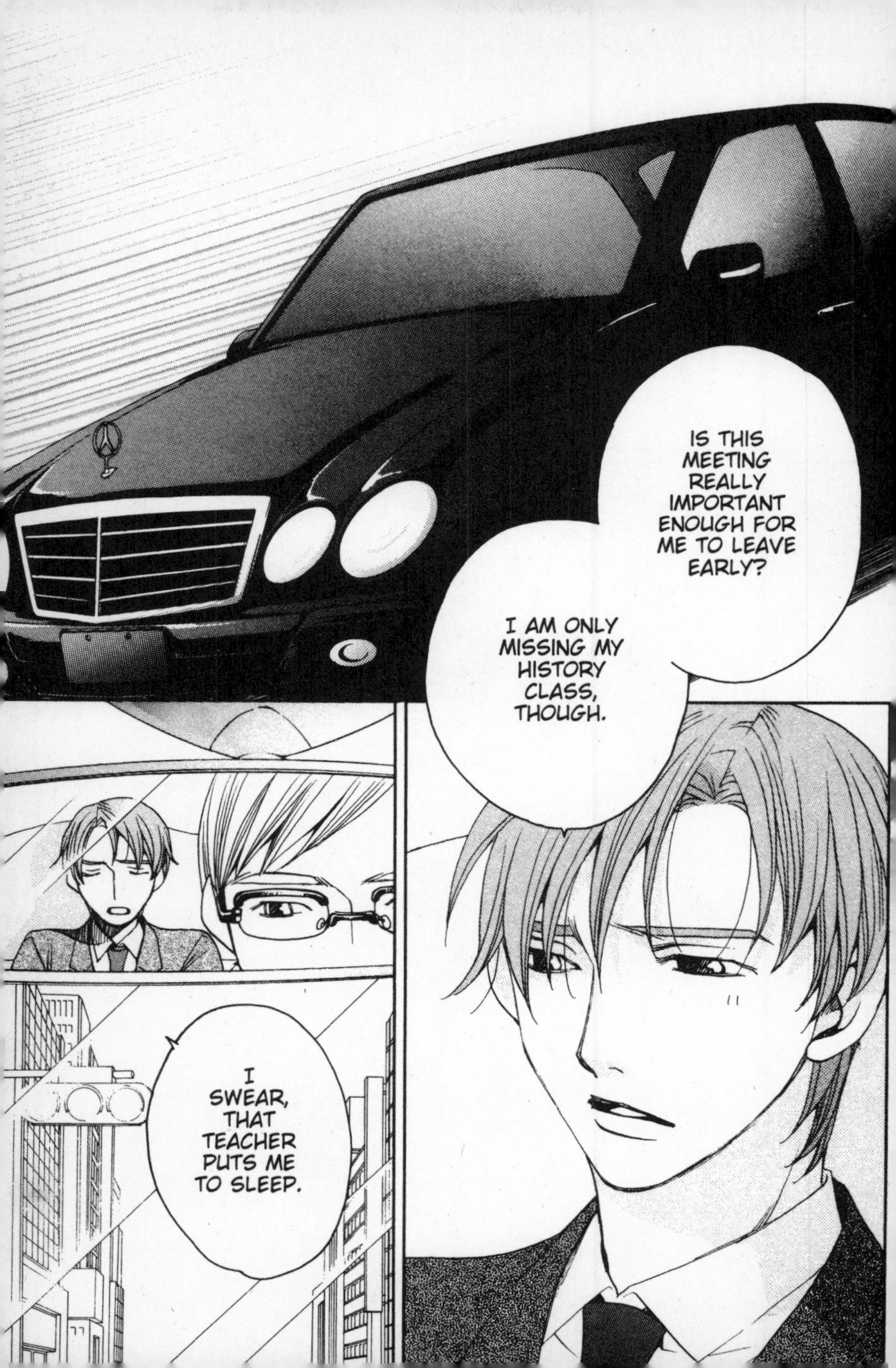
IS THIS MEETING REALLY IMPORTANT ENOUGH FOR ME TO LEAVE EARLY?
I AM ONLY MISSING MY HISTORY CLASS, THOUGH.
I SWEAR, THAT TEACHER PUTS ME TO SLEEP.

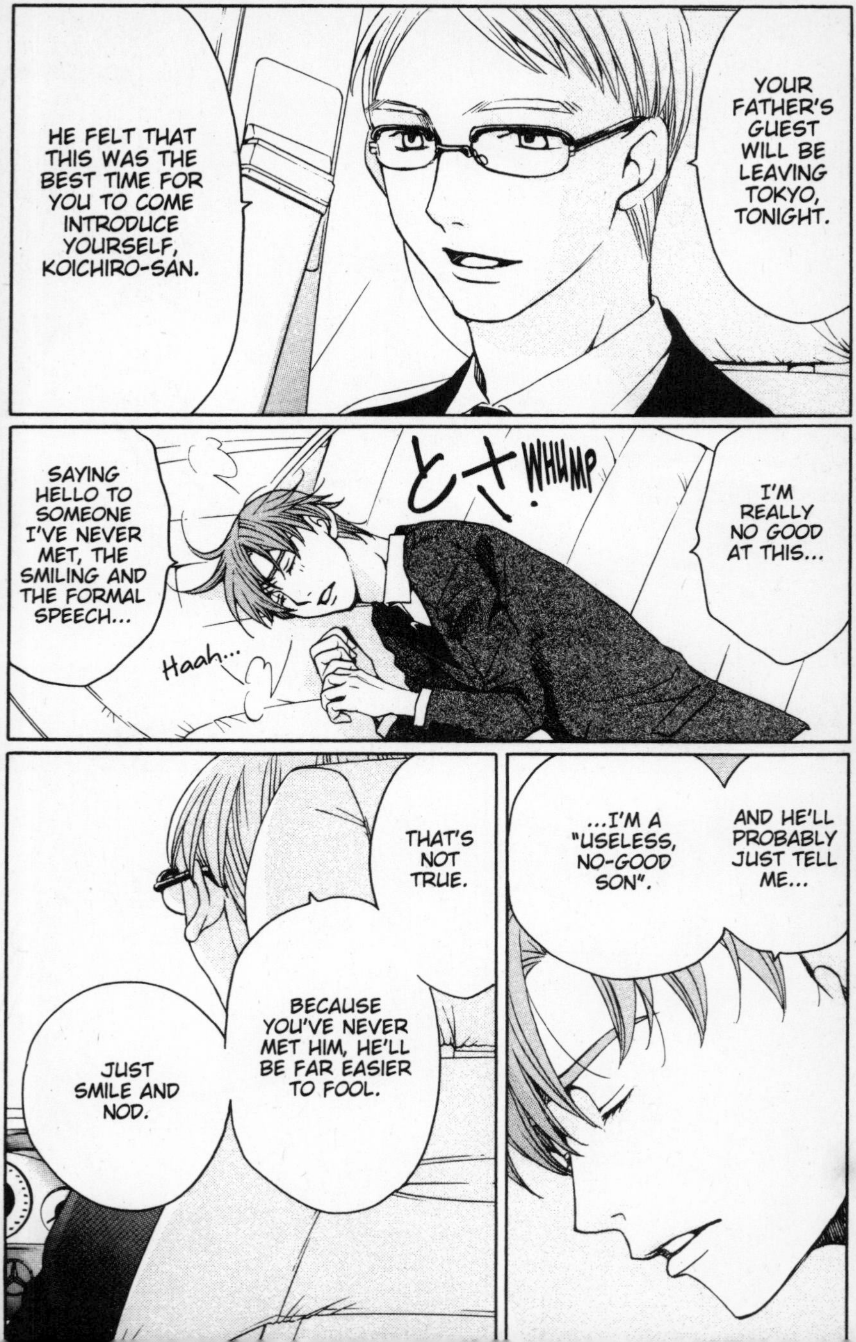

YOUR FATHER'S GUEST WILL BE LEAVING TOKYO, TONIGHT.
HE FELT THAT THIS WAS THE BEST TIME FOR YOU TO COME INTRODUCE YOURSELF, KOICHIRO-SAN.
I'M REALLY NO GOOD AT THIS...
とさ WHUMP
SAYING HELLO TO SOMEONE I'VE NEVER MET, THE SMILING AND THE FORMAL SPEECH...
Haah...
AND HE'LL PROBABLY JUST TELL ME...
...I'M A "USELESS, NO-GOOD SON".
THAT'S NOT TRUE.
BECAUSE YOU'VE NEVER MET HIM, HE'LL BE FAR EASIER TO FOOL.
JUST SMILE AND NOD.

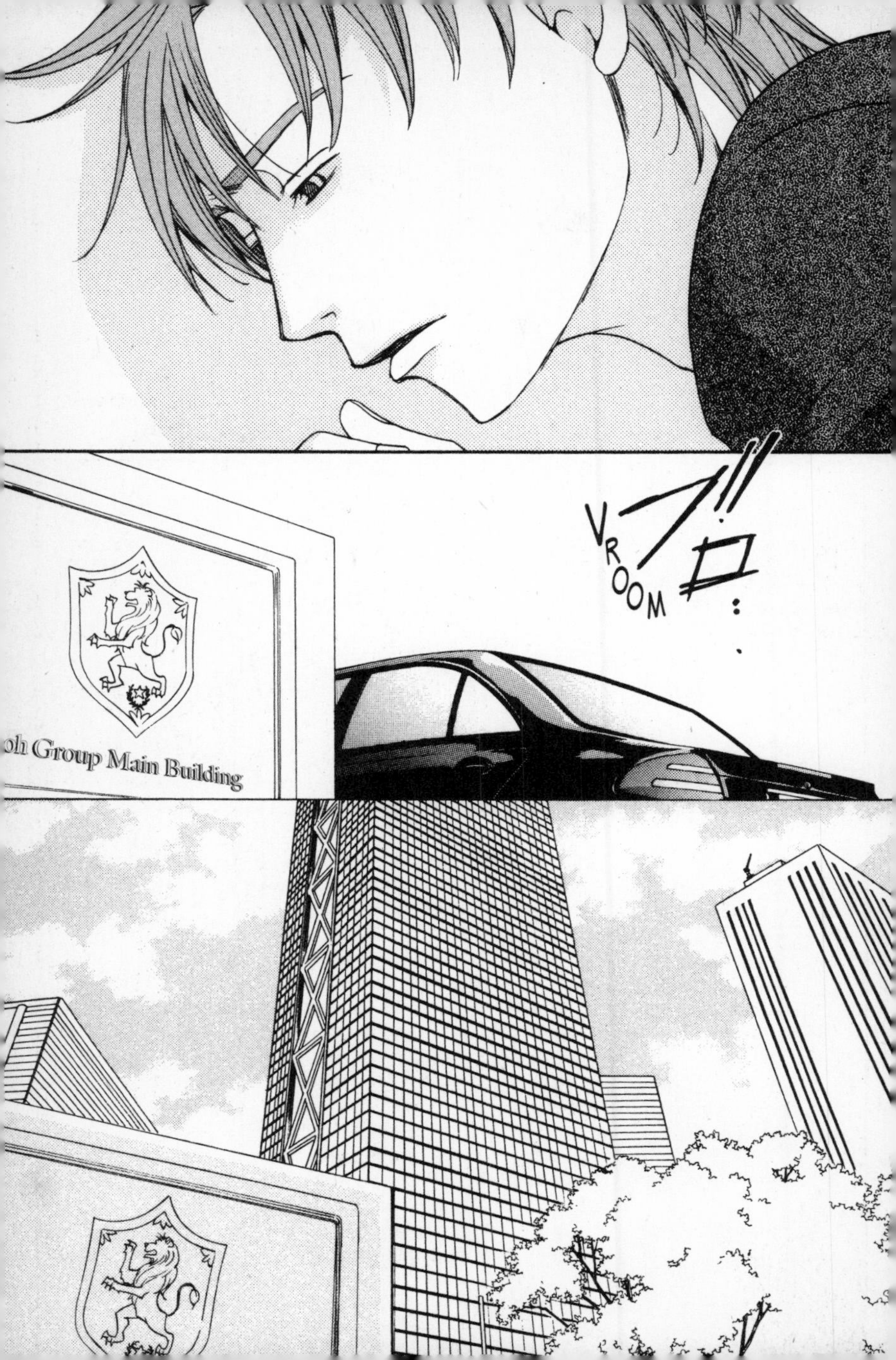
VROOM
oh Group Main Building

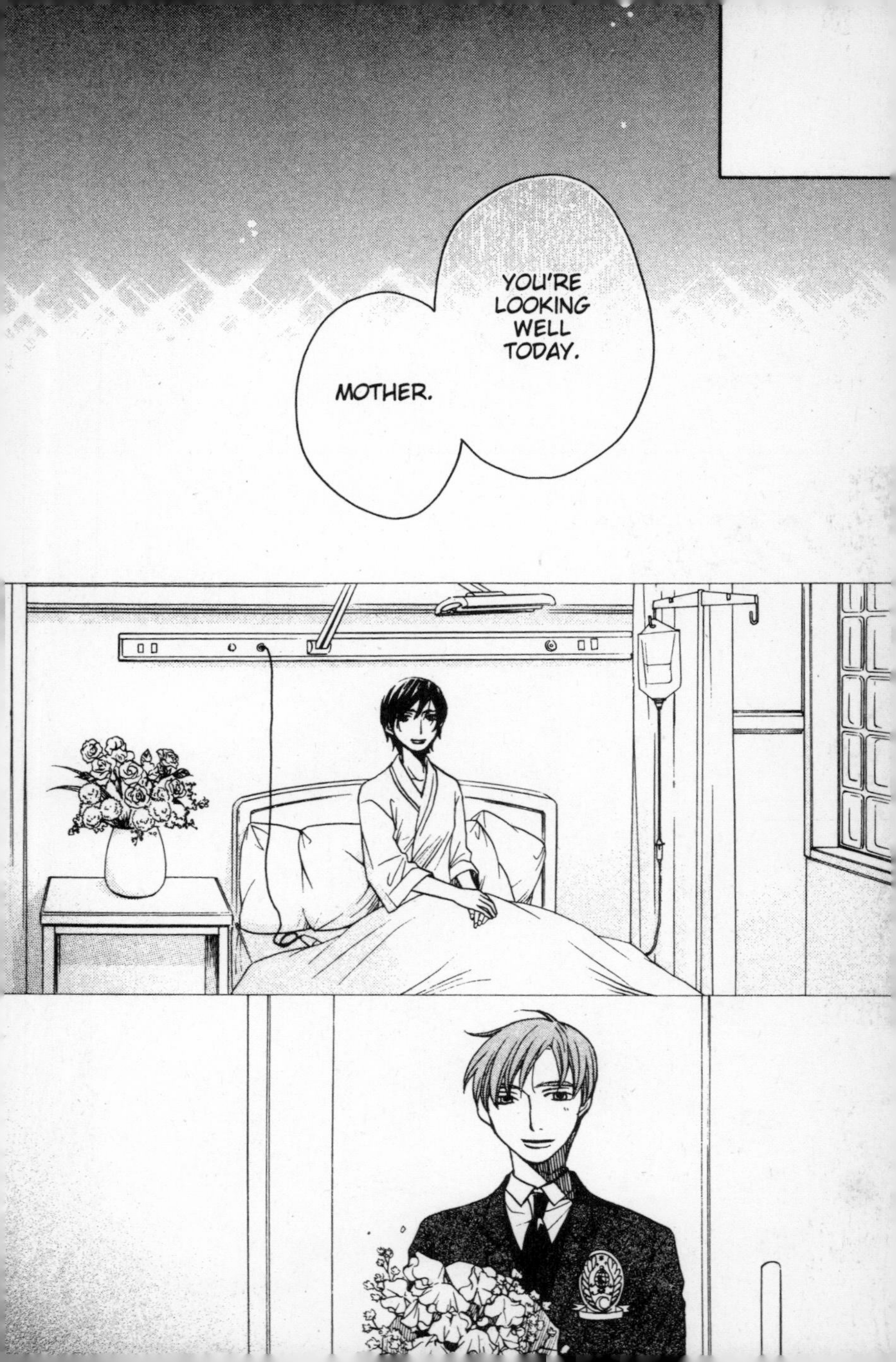
YOU'RE LOOKING WELL TODAY.
MOTHER.

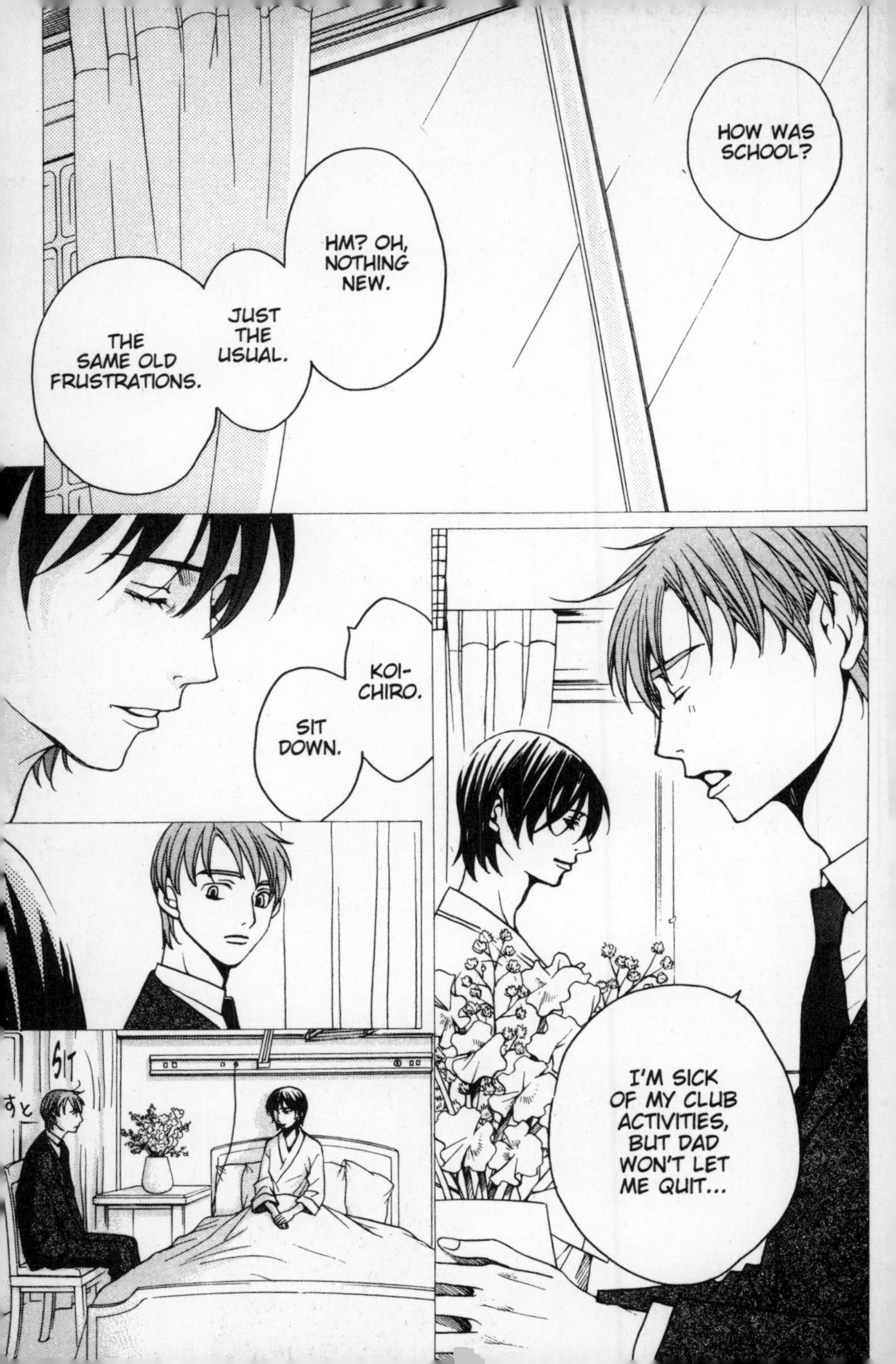
HOW WAS SCHOOL?
HM? OH, NOTHING NEW.
JUST THE USUAL.
THE SAME OLD FRUSTRATIONS.
I'M SICK OF MY CLUB ACTIVITIES, BUT DAD WON'T LET ME QUIT...
KOI-CHIRO.
SIT DOWN.
SIT
すと

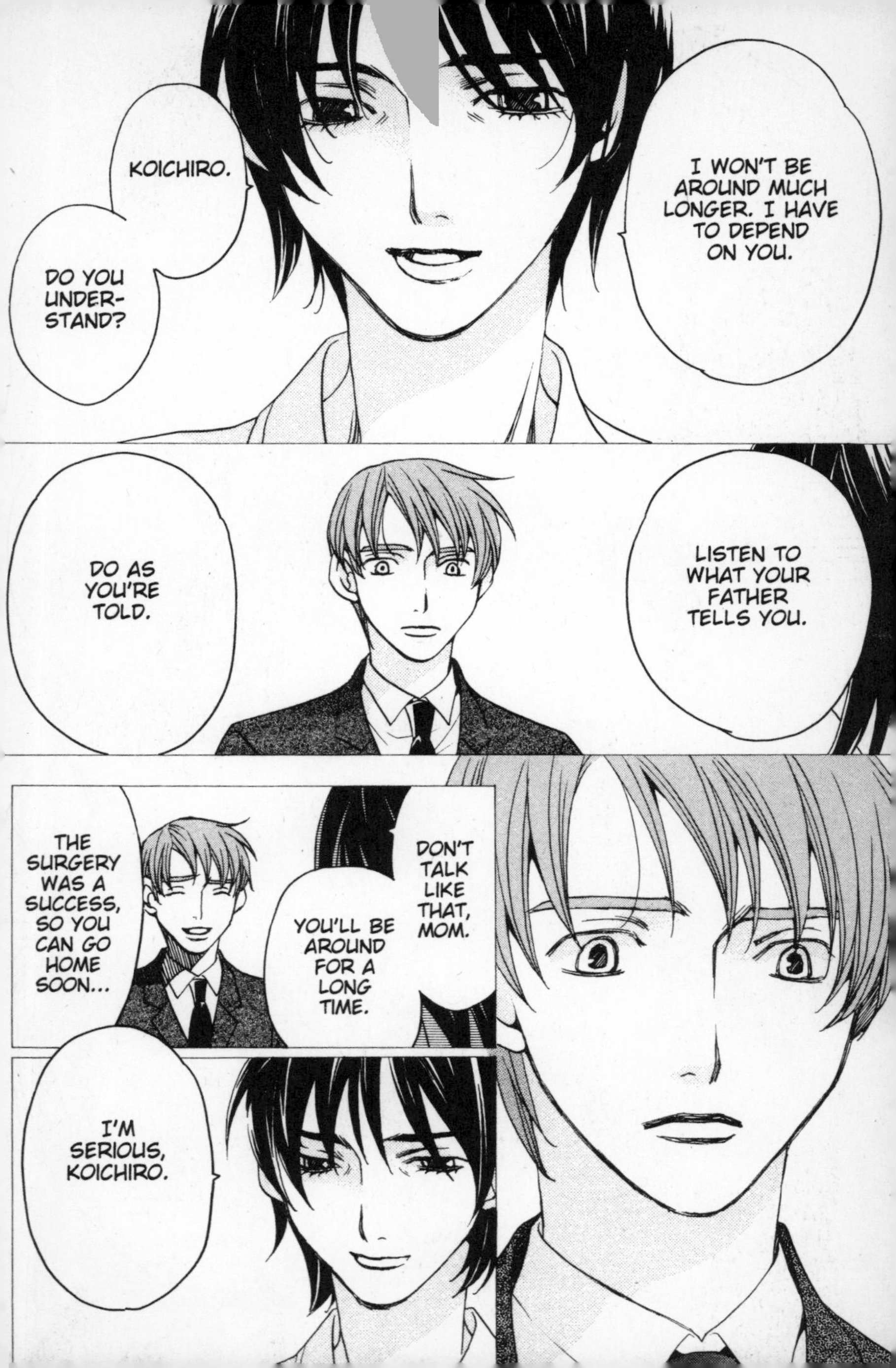
I WON'T BE AROUND MUCH LONGER. I HAVE TO DEPEND ON YOU.
KOICHIRO.
DO YOU UNDER-STAND?
LISTEN TO WHAT YOUR FATHER TELLS YOU.
DO AS YOU'RE TOLD.
DON'T TALK LIKE THAT, MOM.
YOU'LL BE AROUND FOR A LONG TIME.
THE SURGERY WAS A SUCCESS, SO YOU CAN GO HOME SOON...
I'M SERIOUS, KOICHIRO.

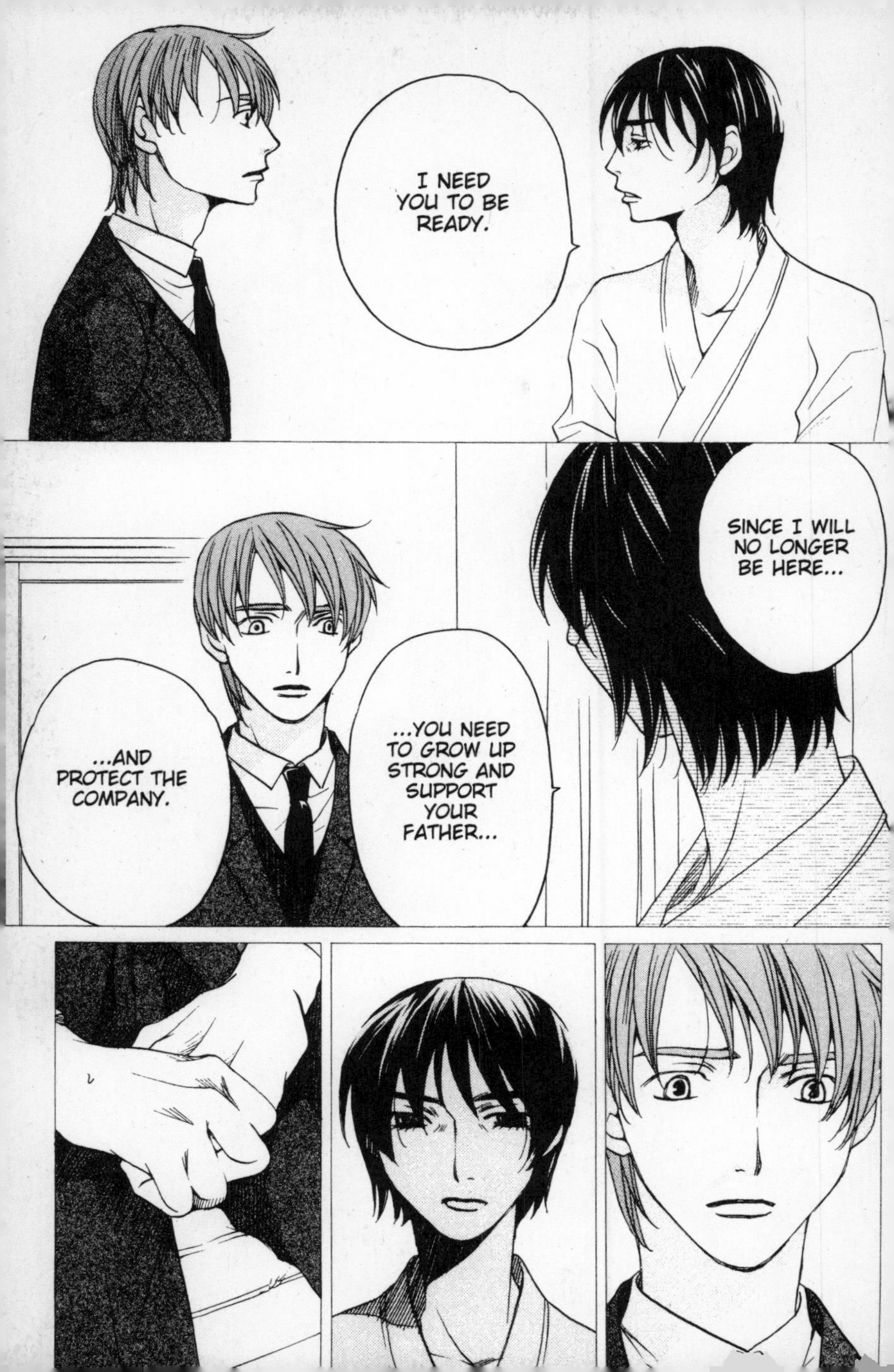
I NEED YOU TO BE READY.
SINCE I WILL NO LONGER BE HERE...
...YOU NEED TO GROW UP STRONG AND SUPPORT YOUR FATHER...
...AND PROTECT THE COMPANY.

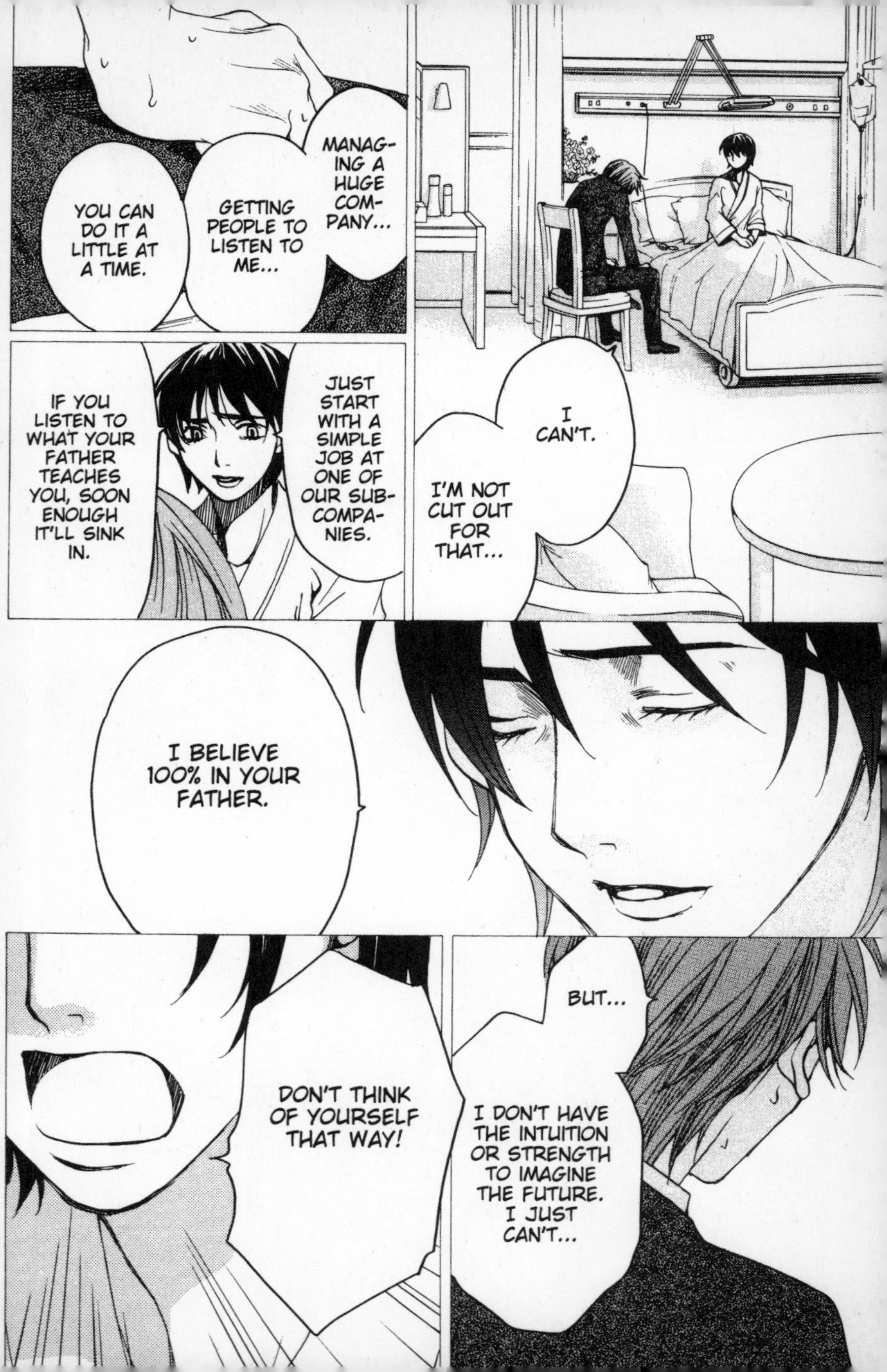
MANAGING A HUGE COMPANY...
GETTING PEOPLE TO LISTEN TO ME...
YOU CAN DO IT A LITTLE AT A TIME.
I CAN'T.
I'M NOT CUT OUT FOR THAT...
JUST START WITH A SIMPLE JOB AT ONE OF OUR SUB-COMPANIES.
IF YOU LISTEN TO WHAT YOUR FATHER TEACHES YOU, SOON ENOUGH IT'LL SINK IN.
I BELIEVE 100% IN YOUR FATHER.
BUT...
I DON'T HAVE THE INTUITION OR STRENGTH TO IMAGINE THE FUTURE. I JUST CAN'T...
DON'T THINK OF YOURSELF THAT WAY!

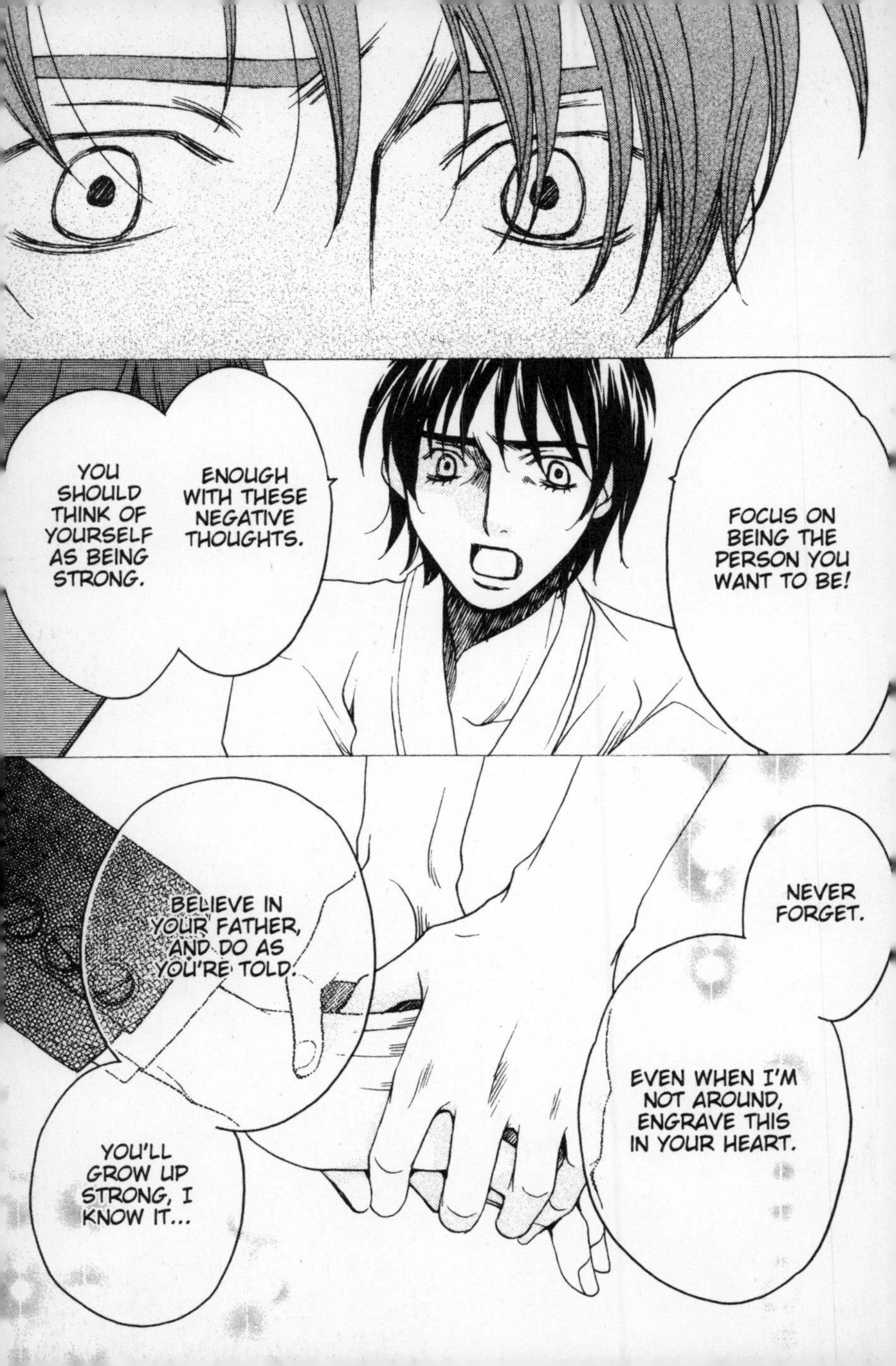
FOCUS ON BEING THE PERSON YOU WANT TO BE!
ENOUGH WITH THESE NEGATIVE THOUGHTS.
YOU SHOULD THINK OF YOURSELF AS BEING STRONG.
NEVER FORGET.
EVEN WHEN I'M NOT AROUND, ENGRAVE THIS IN YOUR HEART.
BELIEVE IN YOUR FATHER, AND DO AS YOU'RE TOLD.
YOU'LL GROW UP STRONG, I KNOW IT...

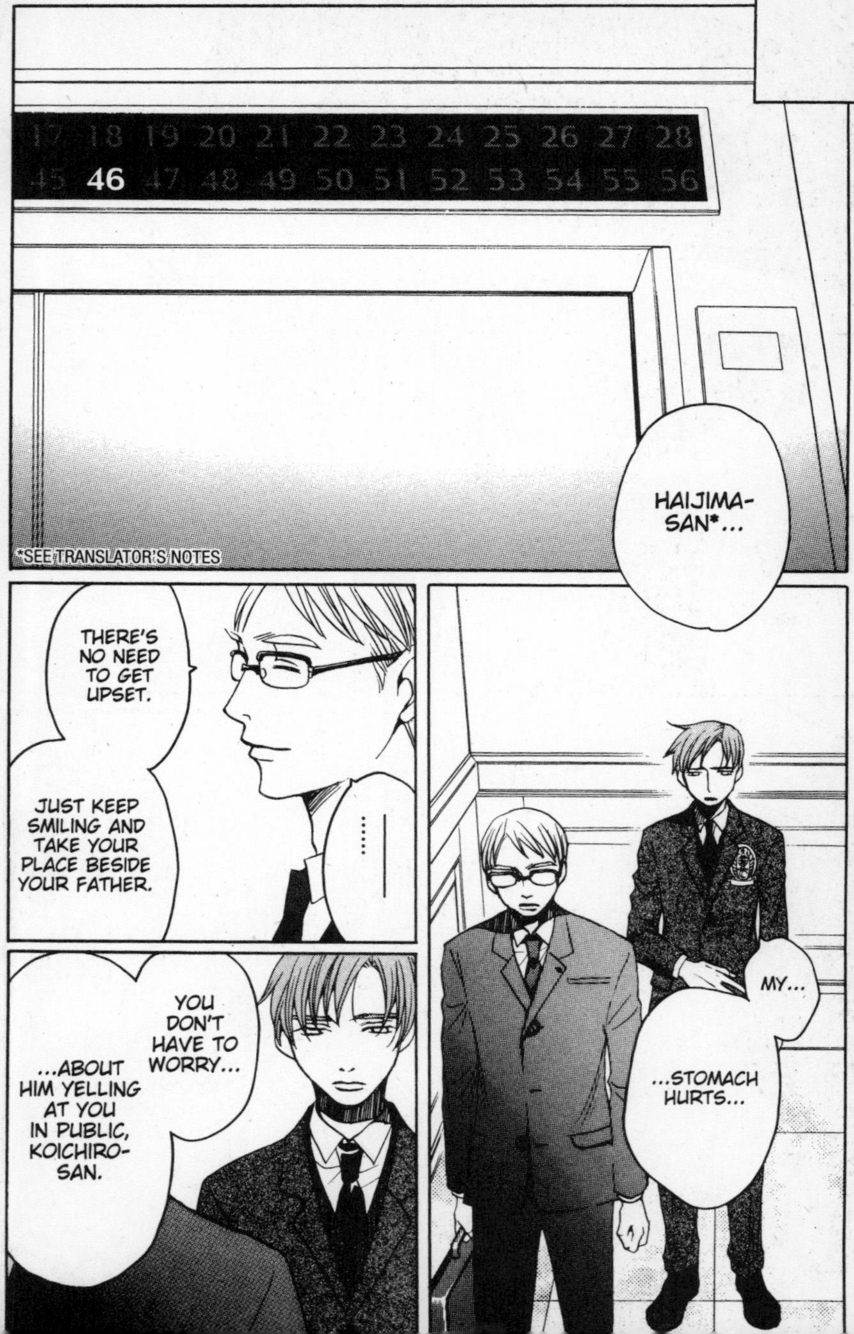
17 18 19 20 21 22 23 24 25 26 27 28
45 46 47 48 49 50 51 52 53 54 55 56
HAIJIMA-SAN*...
*SEE TRANSLATOR'S NOTES
MY...
...STOMACH HURTS...
THERE'S NO NEED TO GET UPSET.
......
JUST KEEP SMILING AND TAKE YOUR PLACE BESIDE YOUR FATHER.
YOU DON'T HAVE TO WORRY...
...ABOUT HIM YELLING AT YOU IN PUBLIC, KOICHIRO-SAN.

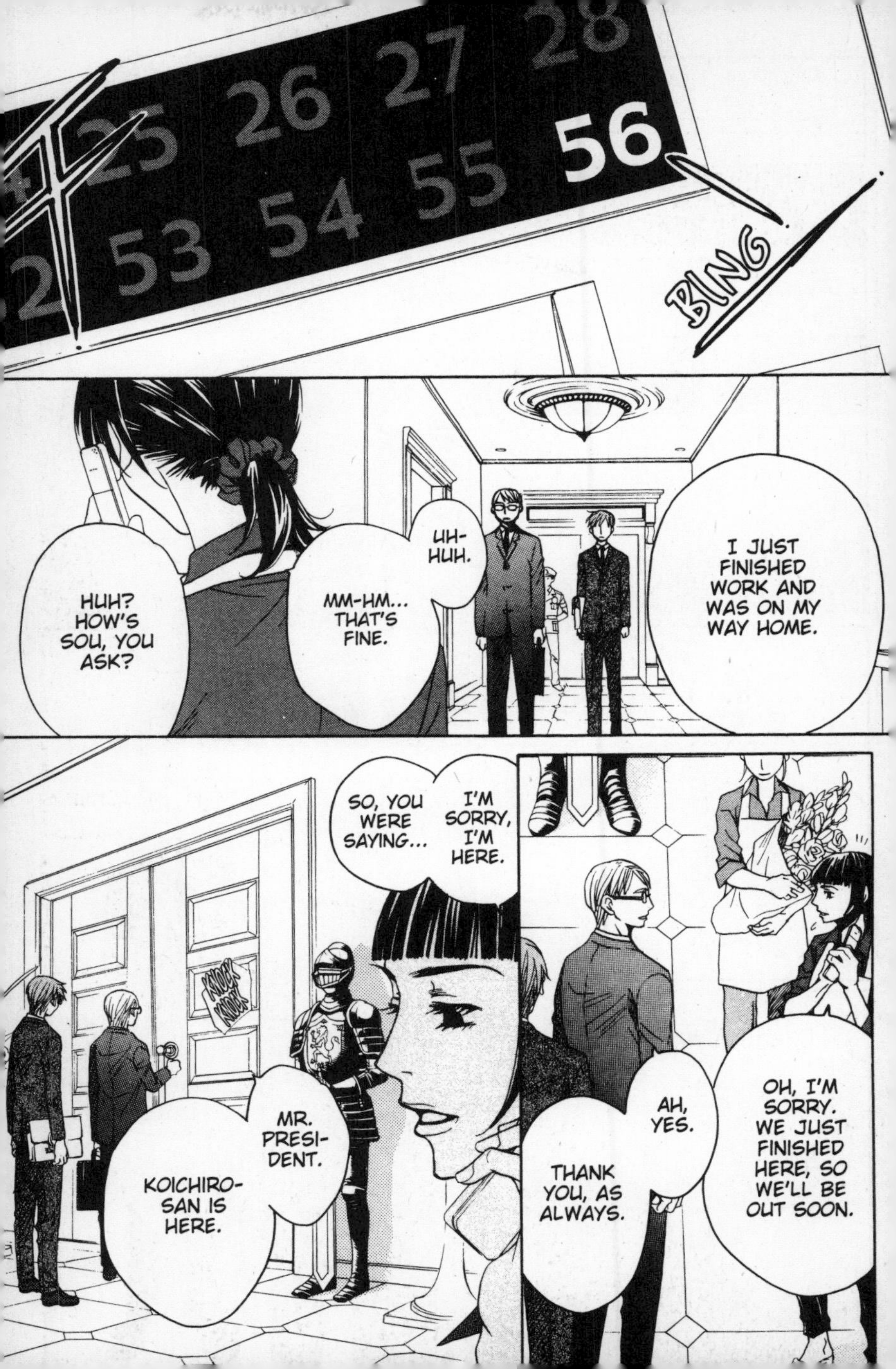
BING
I JUST FINISHED WORK AND WAS ON MY WAY HOME.
UH-HUH.
MM-HM... THAT'S FINE.
HUH? HOW'S SOU, YOU ASK?
OH, I'M SORRY. WE JUST FINISHED HERE, SO WE'LL BE OUT SOON.
AH, YES.
THANK YOU, AS ALWAYS.
I'M SORRY, I'M HERE.
SO, YOU WERE SAYING...
KNOCK KNOCK
MR. PRESIDENT.
KOICHIRO-SAN IS HERE.

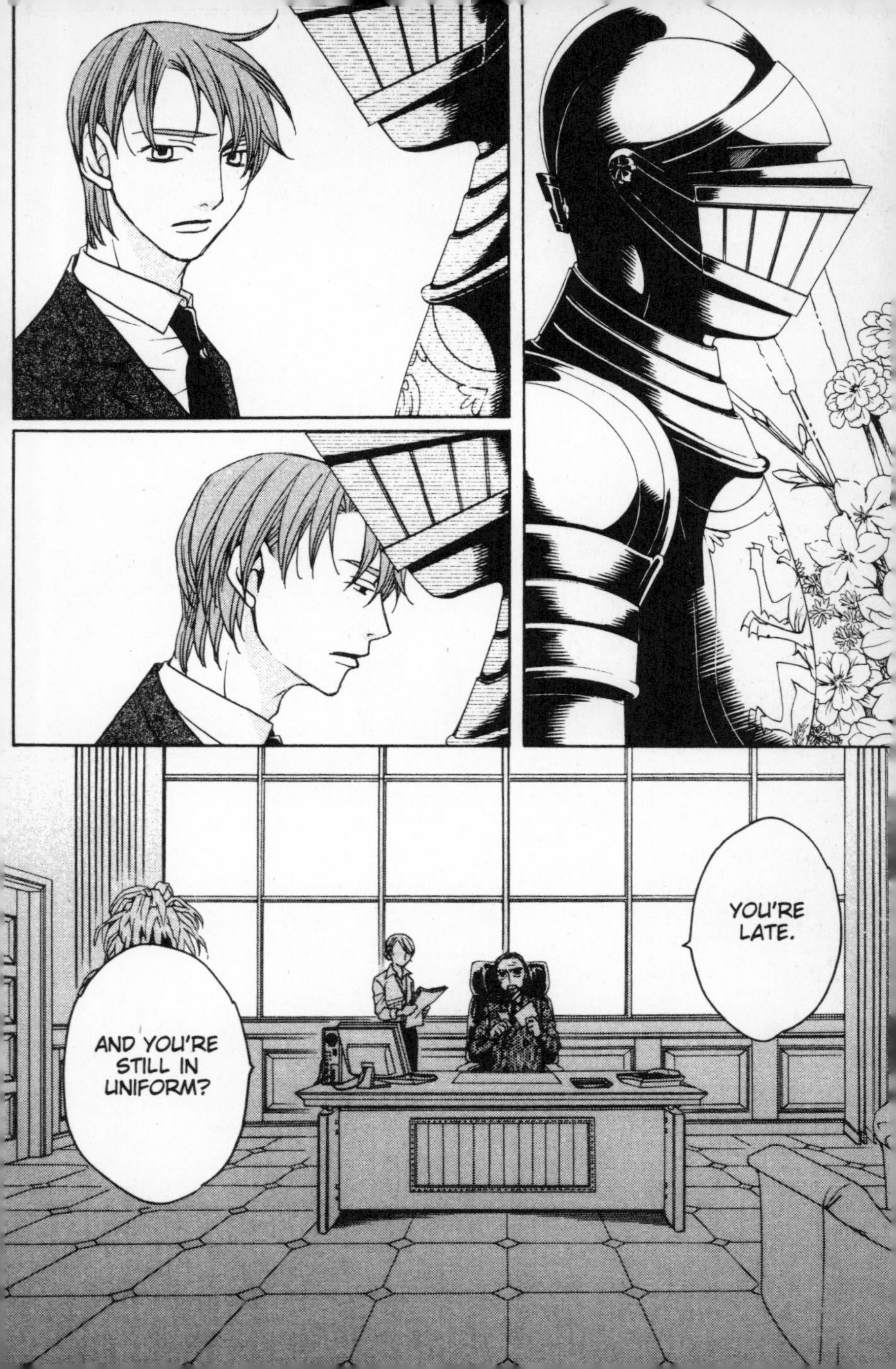
YOU'RE LATE.
AND YOU'RE STILL IN UNIFORM?

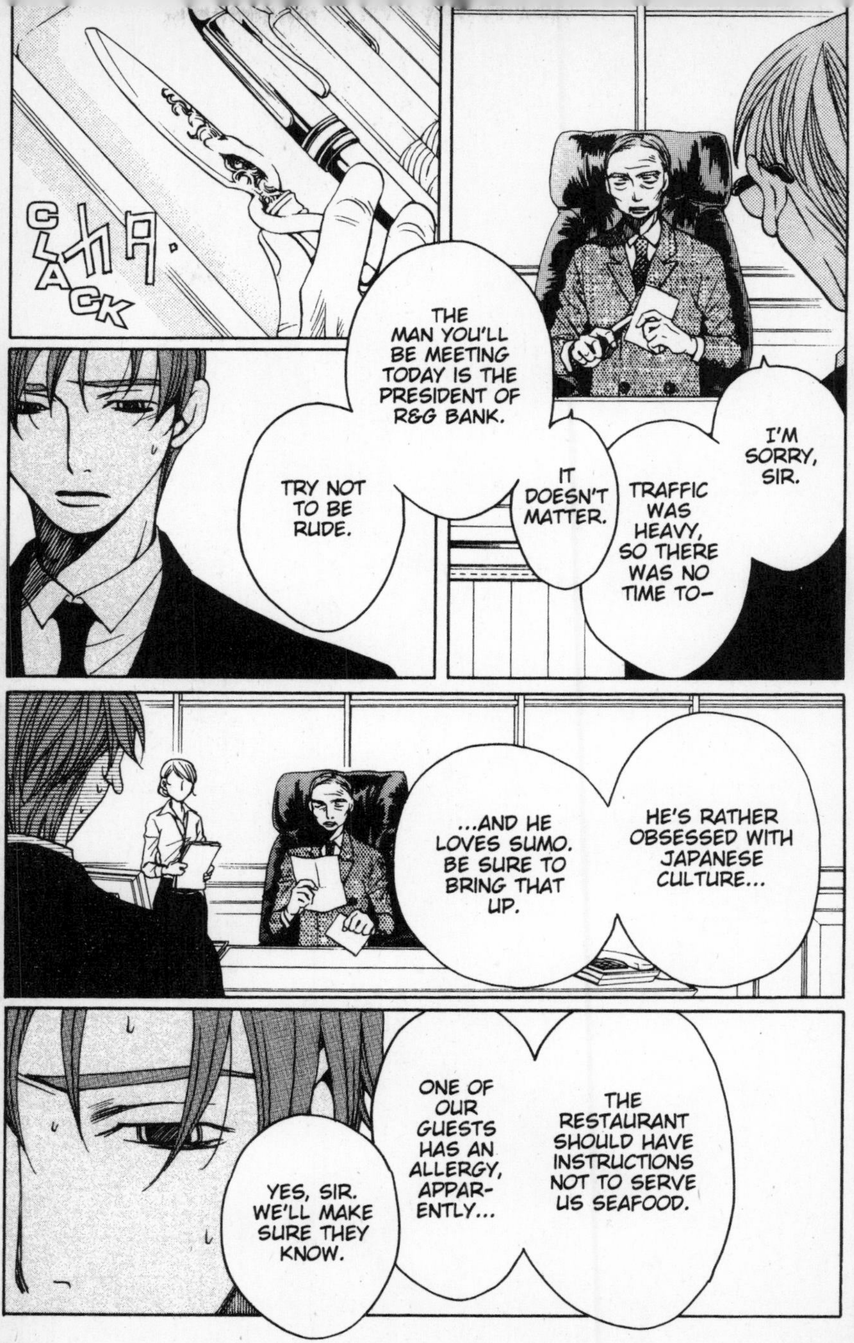
CLACK
I'M SORRY, SIR.
TRAFFIC WAS HEAVY, SO THERE WAS NO TIME TO–
IT DOESN'T MATTER.
THE MAN YOU'LL BE MEETING TODAY IS THE PRESIDENT OF R&G BANK.
TRY NOT TO BE RUDE.
HE'S RATHER OBSESSED WITH JAPANESE CULTURE...
...AND HE LOVES SUMO. BE SURE TO BRING THAT UP.
THE RESTAURANT SHOULD HAVE INSTRUCTIONS NOT TO SERVE US SEAFOOD.
ONE OF OUR GUESTS HAS AN ALLERGY, APPAR-ENTLY...
YES, SIR. WE'LL MAKE SURE THEY KNOW.

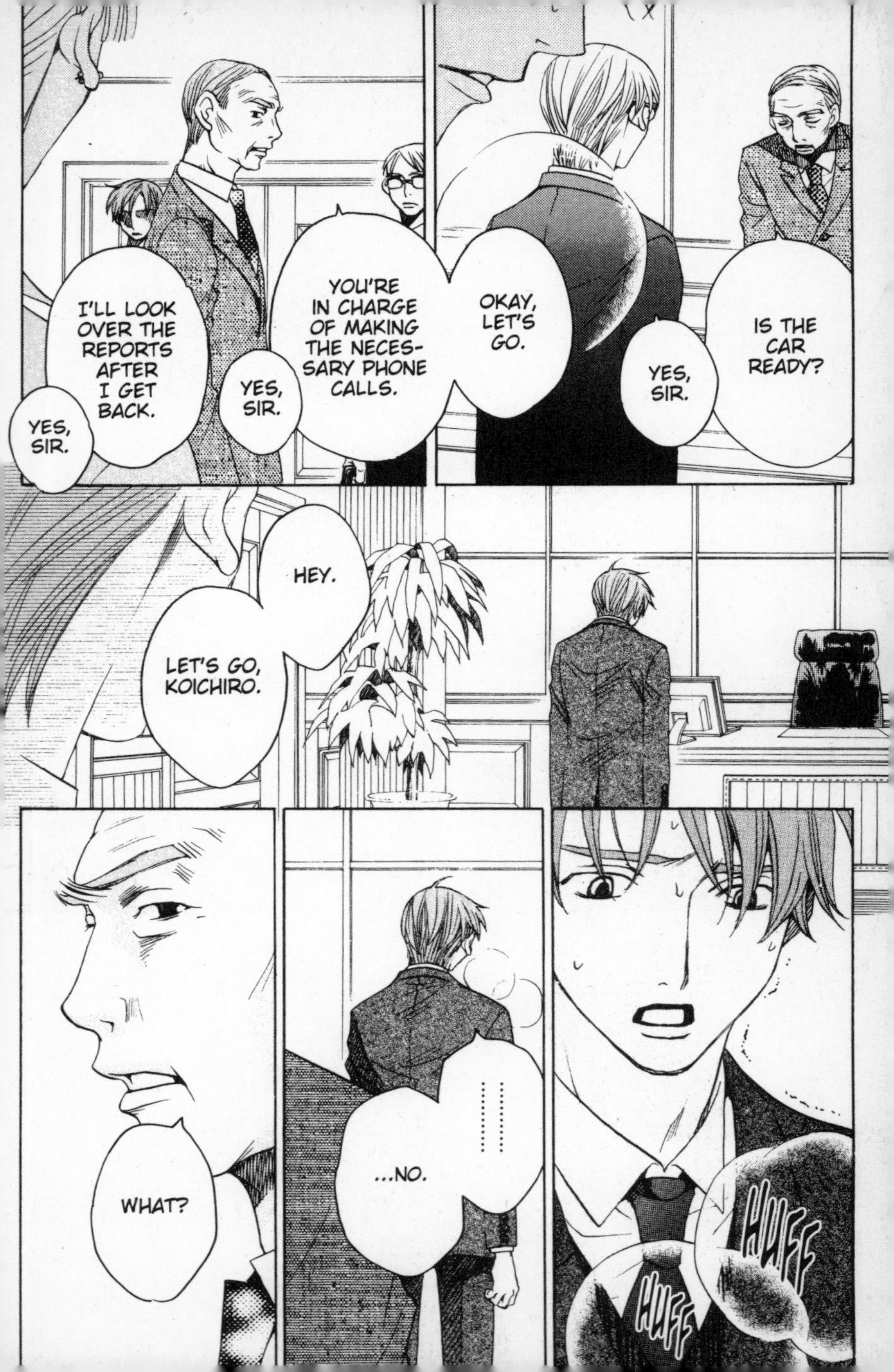
IS THE CAR READY?
YES, SIR.
OKAY, LET'S GO.
YOU'RE IN CHARGE OF MAKING THE NECESSARY PHONE CALLS.
YES, SIR.
I'LL LOOK OVER THE REPORTS AFTER I GET BACK.
YES, SIR.
HEY.
LET'S GO, KOICHIRO.
HUFF
HUFF
......
...NO.
WHAT?

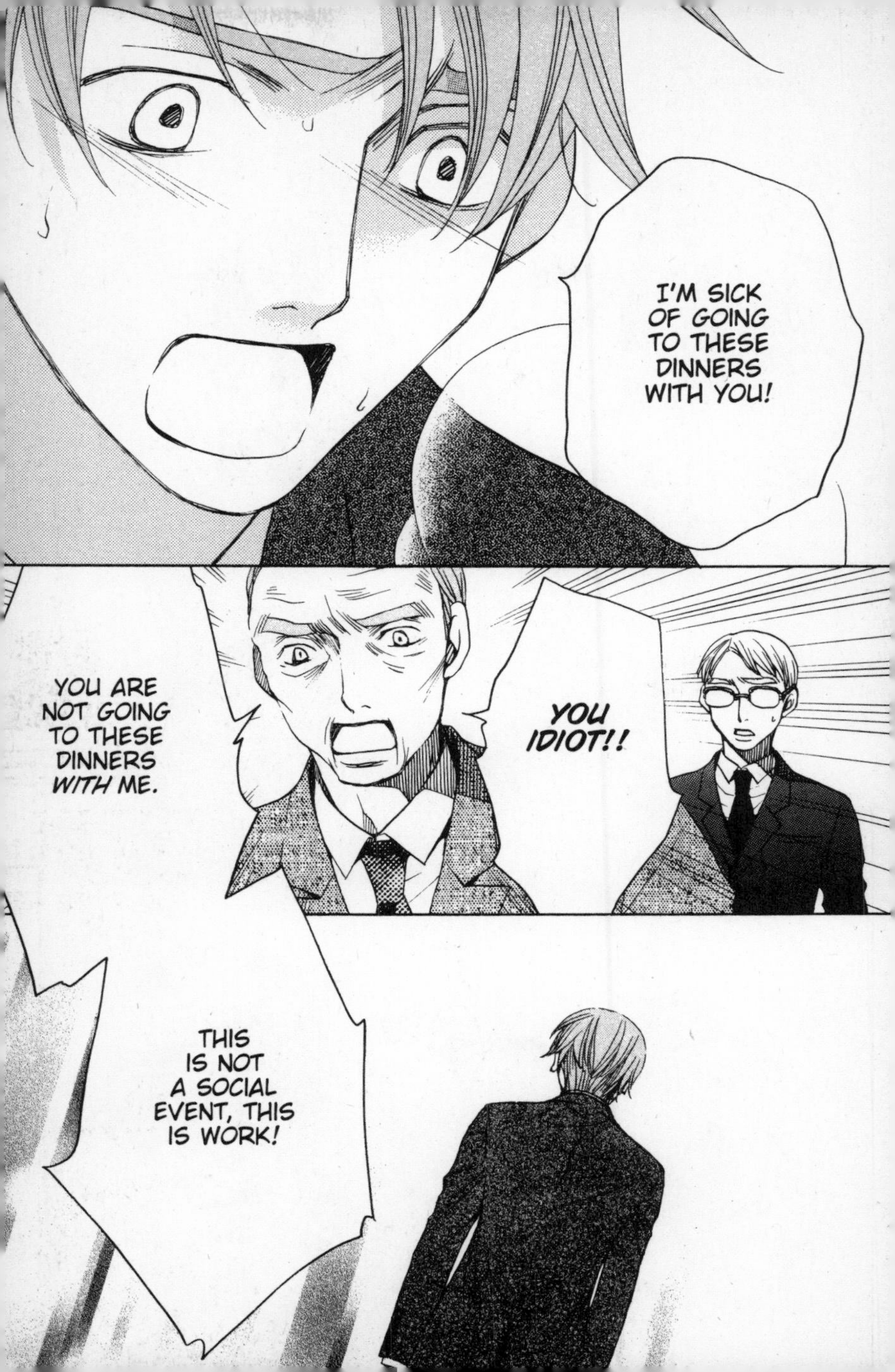
I'M SICK OF GOING TO THESE DINNERS WITH YOU!
YOU IDIOT!!
YOU ARE NOT GOING TO THESE DINNERS *WITH* ME.
THIS IS NOT A SOCIAL EVENT, THIS IS WORK!

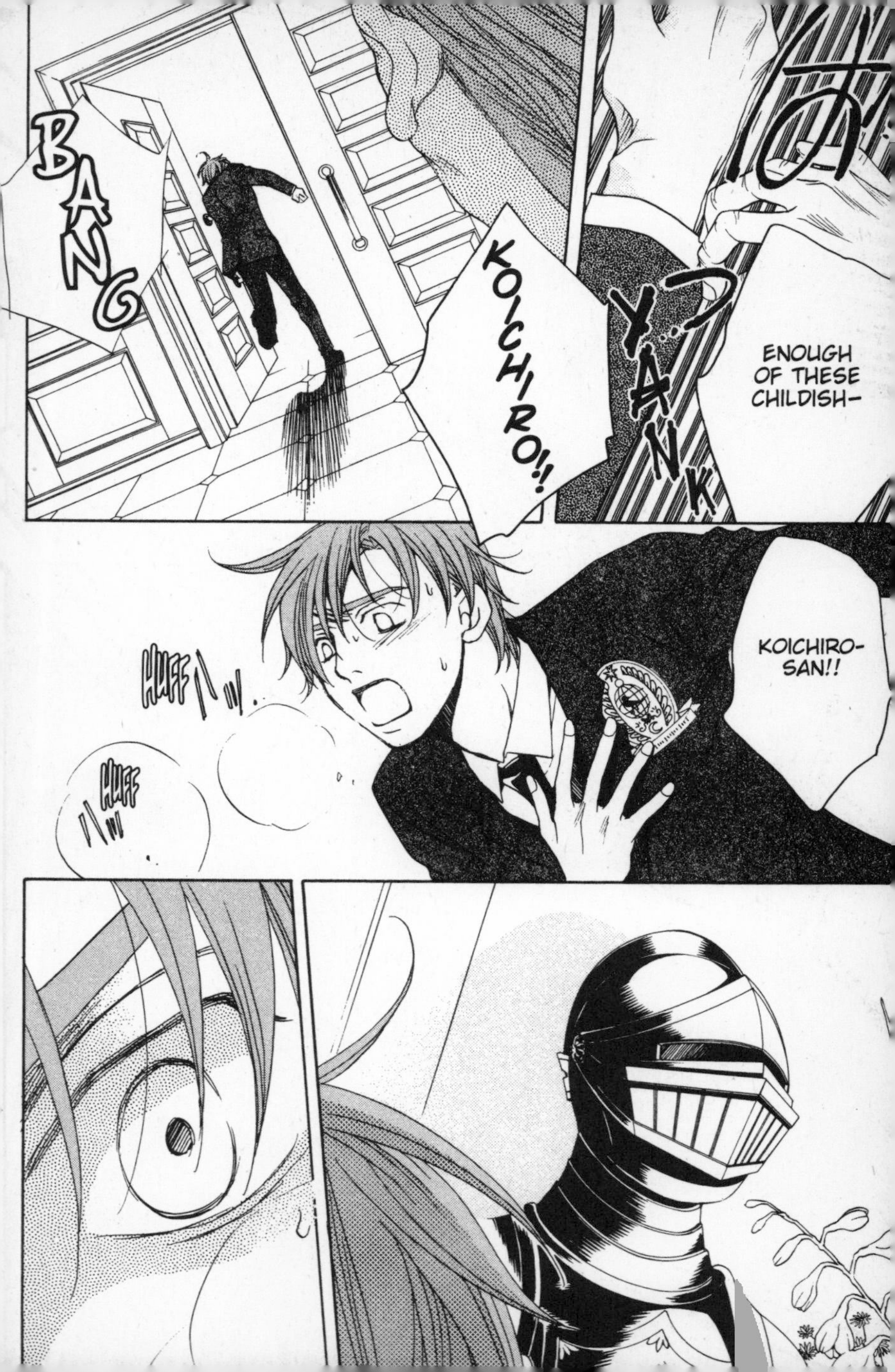

あ
YANK
つ
ENOUGH OF THESE CHILDISH-
KOICHIRO!!
BANG
KOICHIRO-SAN!!
HUFF
HUFF

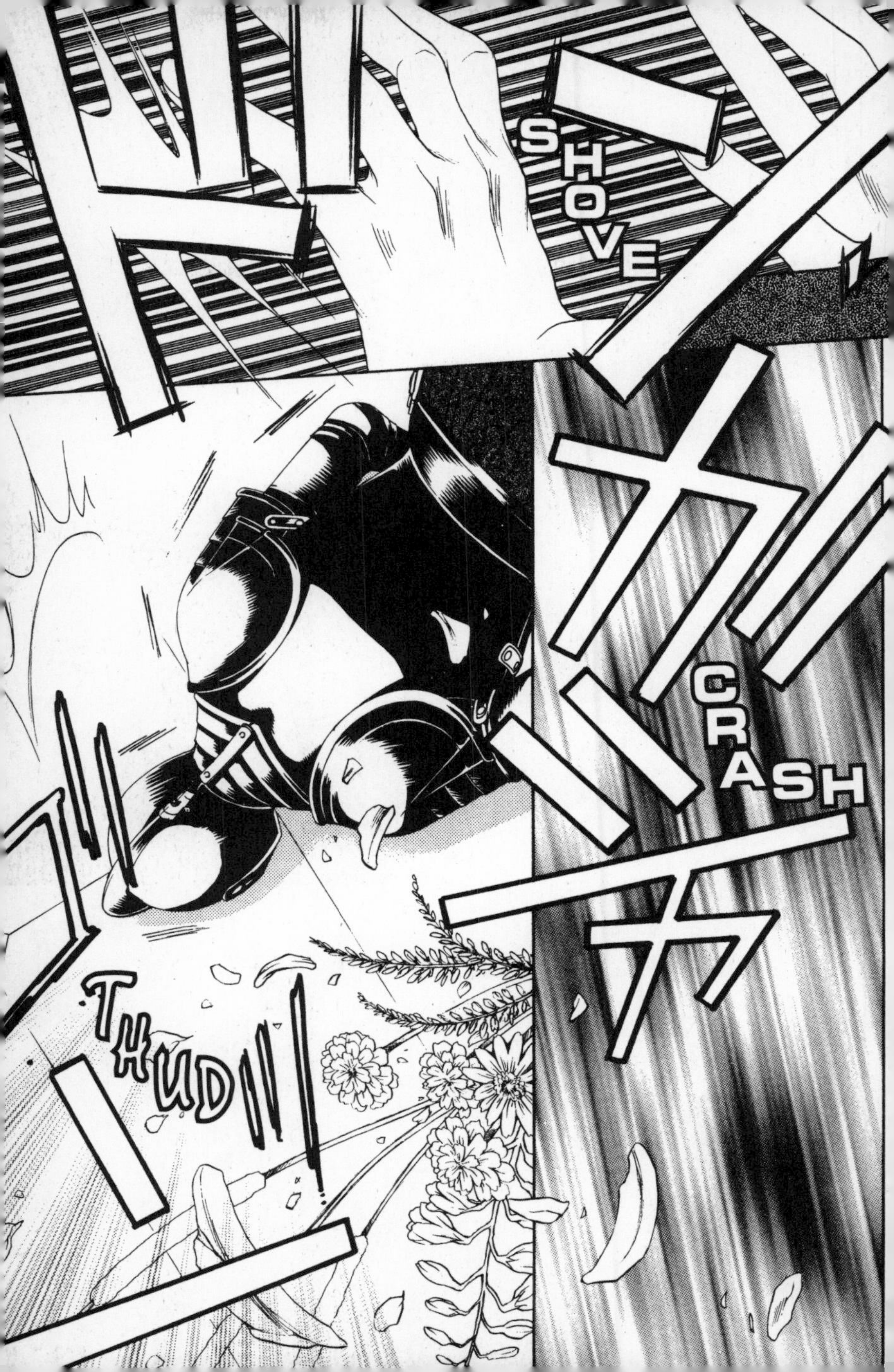
SHOVE
CRASH
THUD

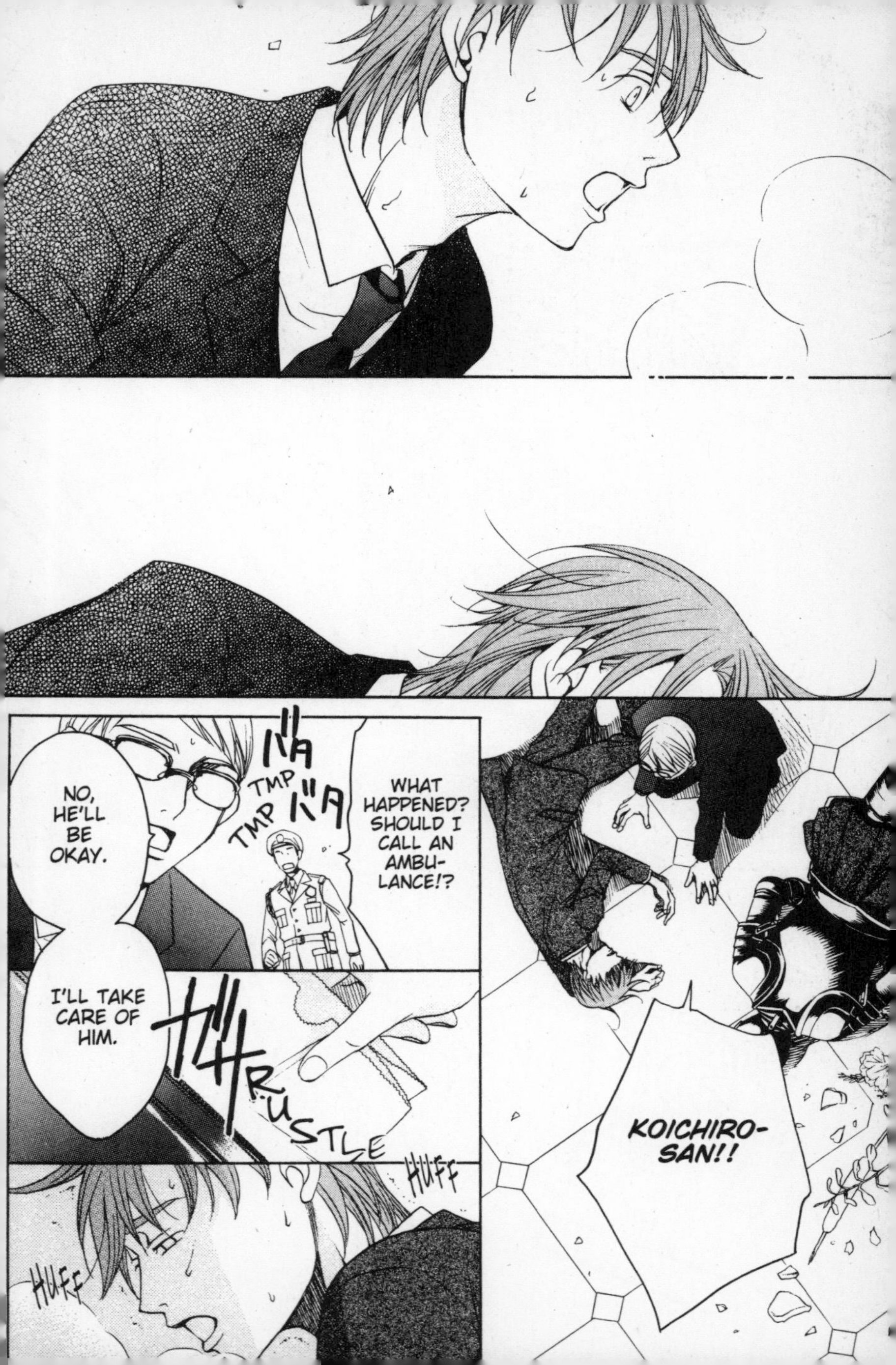
KOICHIRO-SAN!!
WHAT HAPPENED? SHOULD I CALL AN AMBU-LANCE!?
バタ TMP TMP バタ
NO, HE'LL BE OKAY.
I'LL TAKE CARE OF HIM.
RUSTLE
HUFF
HUFF

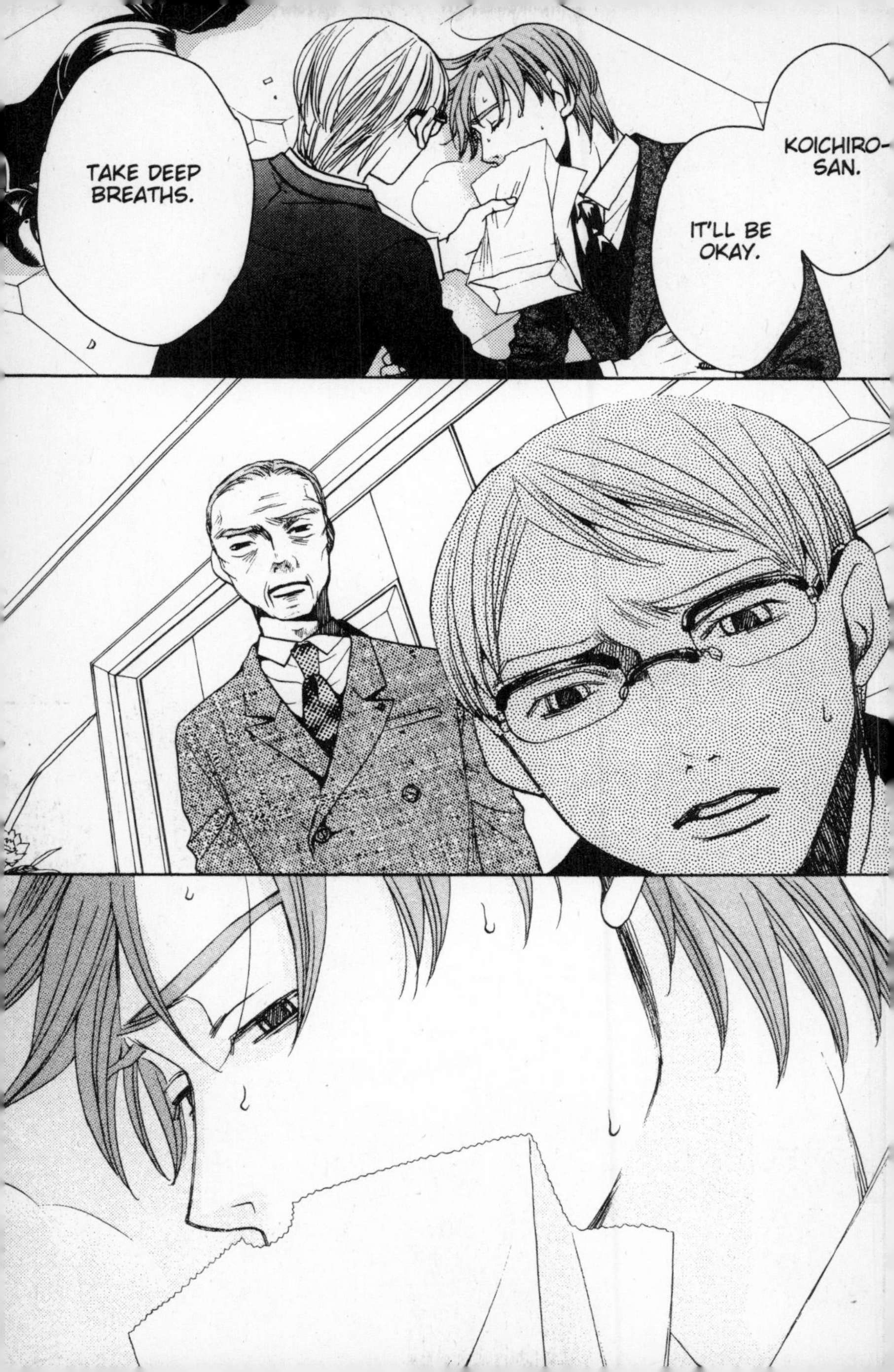
KOICHIRO-SAN.
IT'LL BE OKAY.
TAKE DEEP BREATHS.

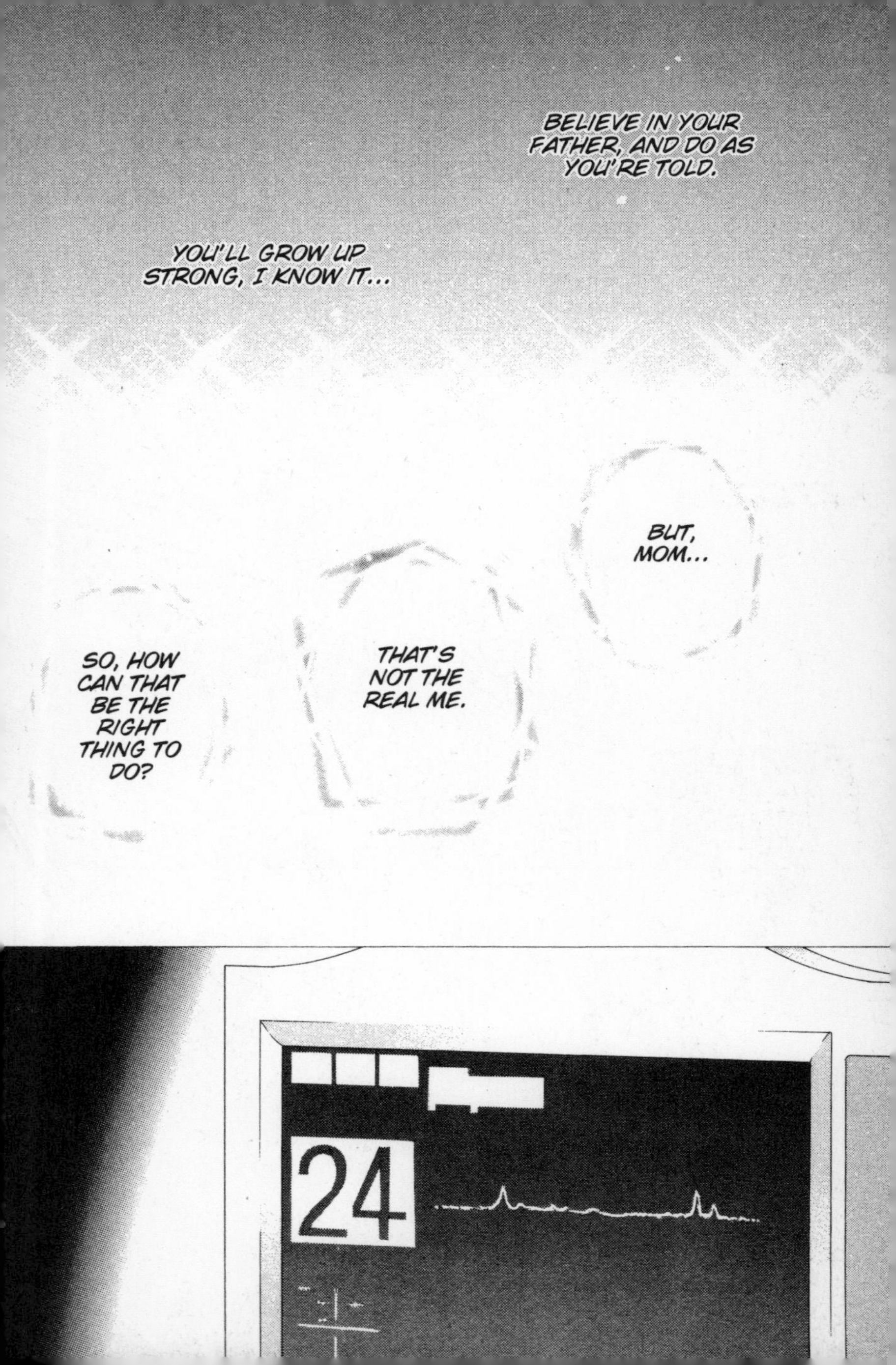
BELIEVE IN YOUR FATHER, AND DO AS YOU'RE TOLD.
YOU'LL GROW UP STRONG, I KNOW IT...
BUT, MOM...
THAT'S NOT THE REAL ME.
SO, HOW CAN THAT BE THE RIGHT THING TO DO?
24

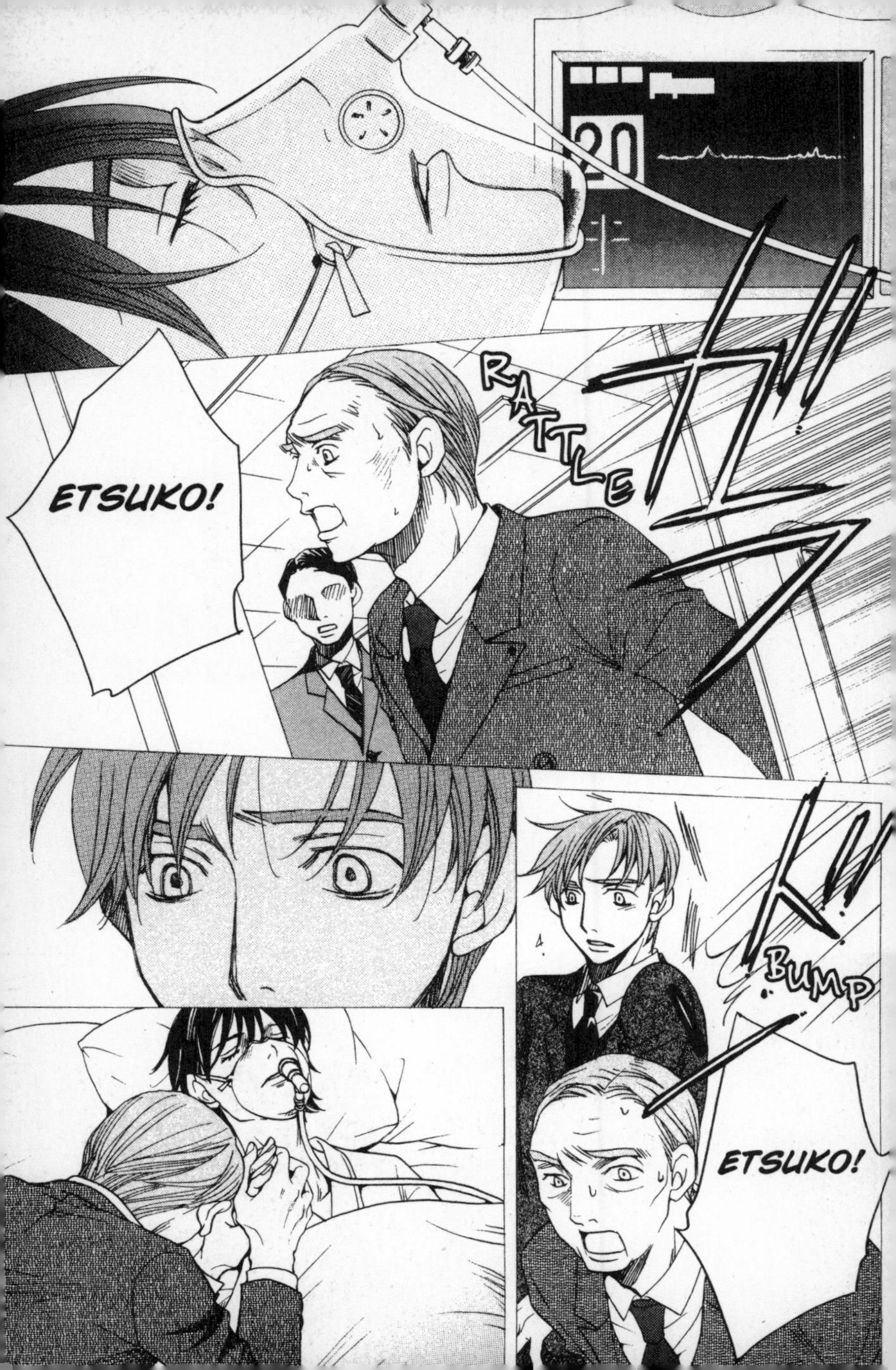
20
RATTLE
ETSUKO!
BUMP
ETSUKO!

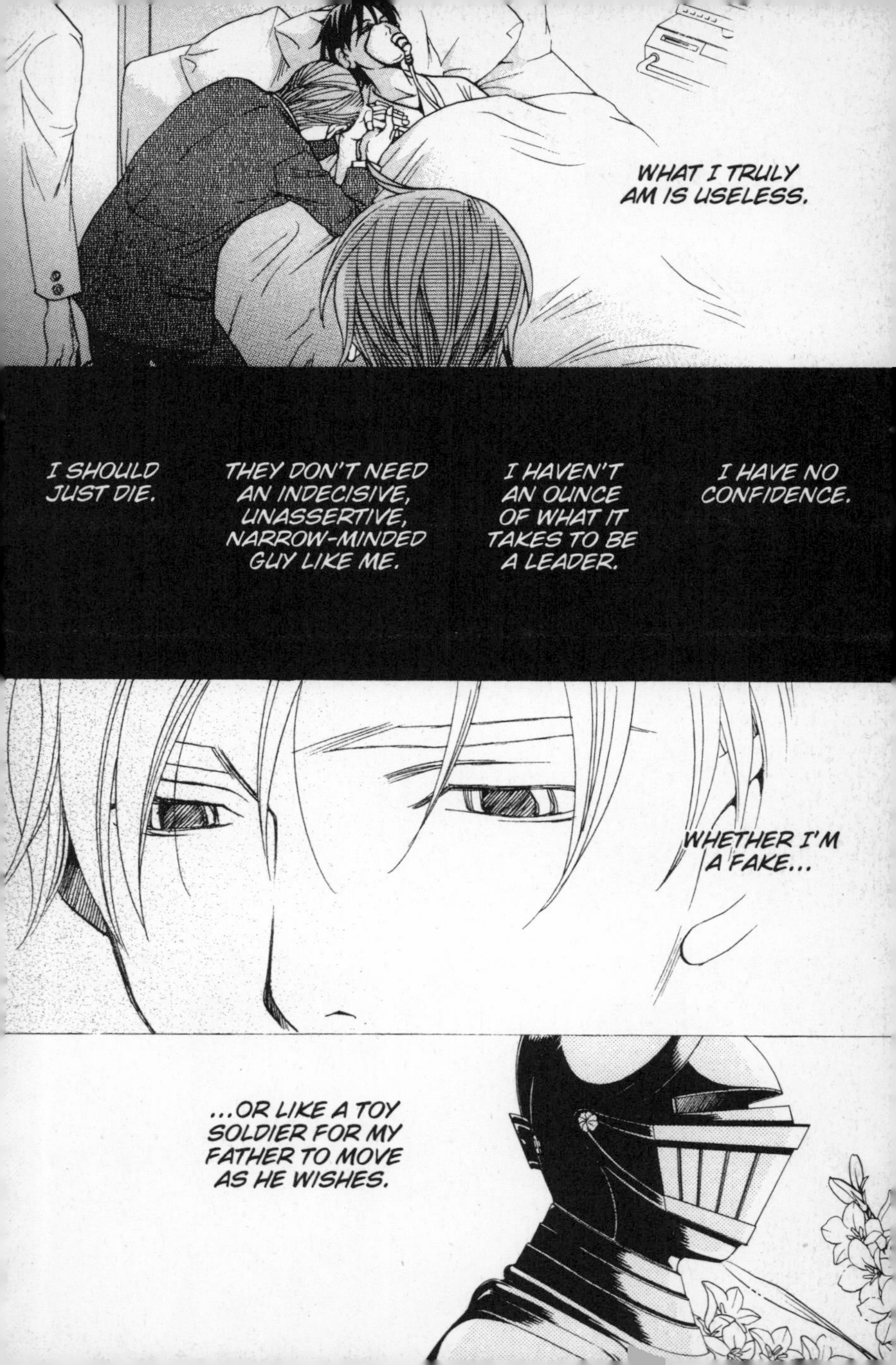
WHAT I TRULY AM IS USELESS.
I HAVE NO CONFIDENCE.
I HAVEN'T AN OUNCE OF WHAT IT TAKES TO BE A LEADER.
THEY DON'T NEED AN INDECISIVE, UNASSERTIVE, NARROW-MINDED GUY LIKE ME.
I SHOULD JUST DIE.
WHETHER I'M A FAKE...
...OR LIKE A TOY SOLDIER FOR MY FATHER TO MOVE AS HE WISHES.

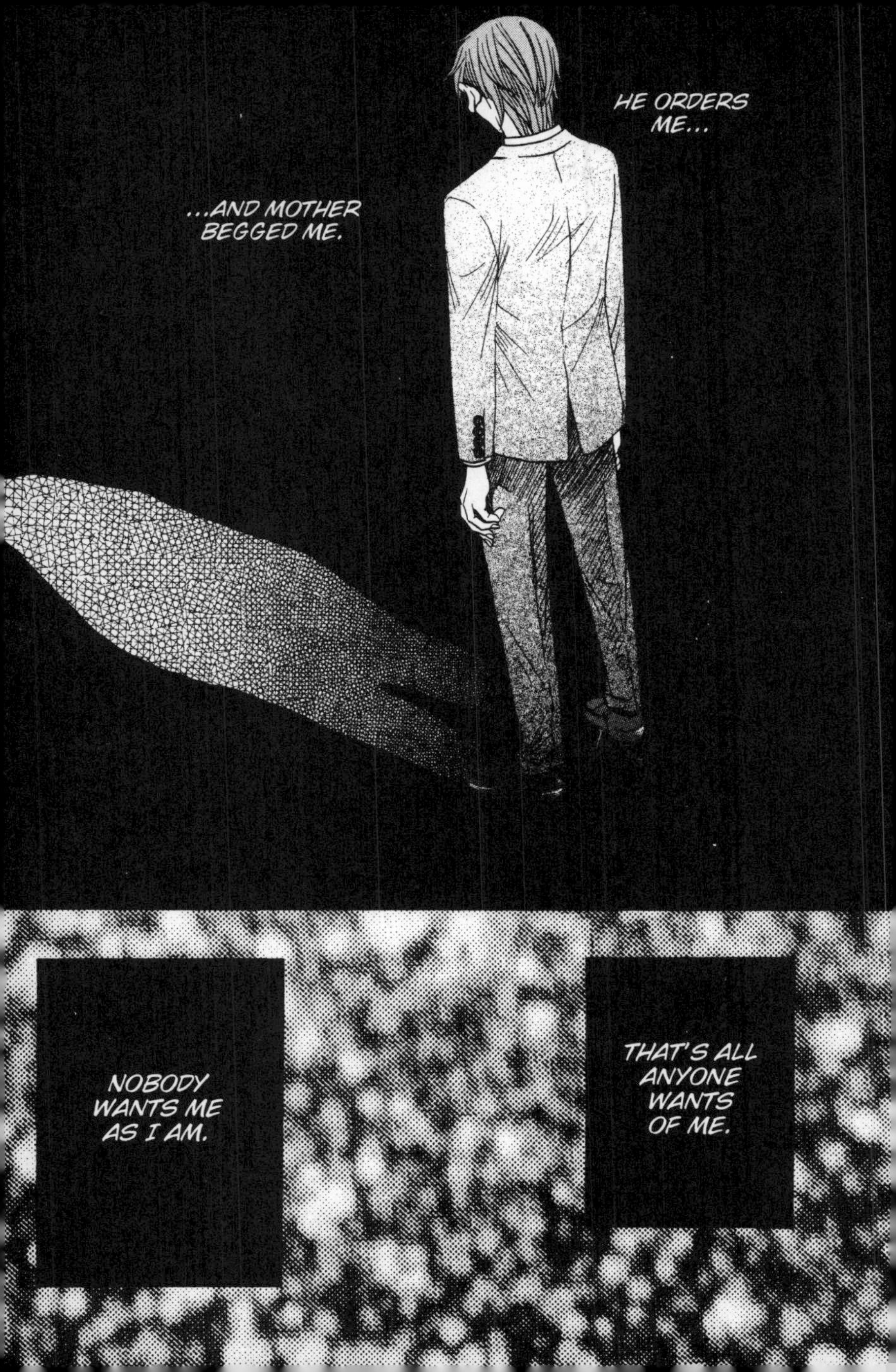
HE ORDERS ME...
...AND MOTHER BEGGED ME.
THAT'S ALL ANYONE WANTS OF ME.
NOBODY WANTS ME AS I AM.

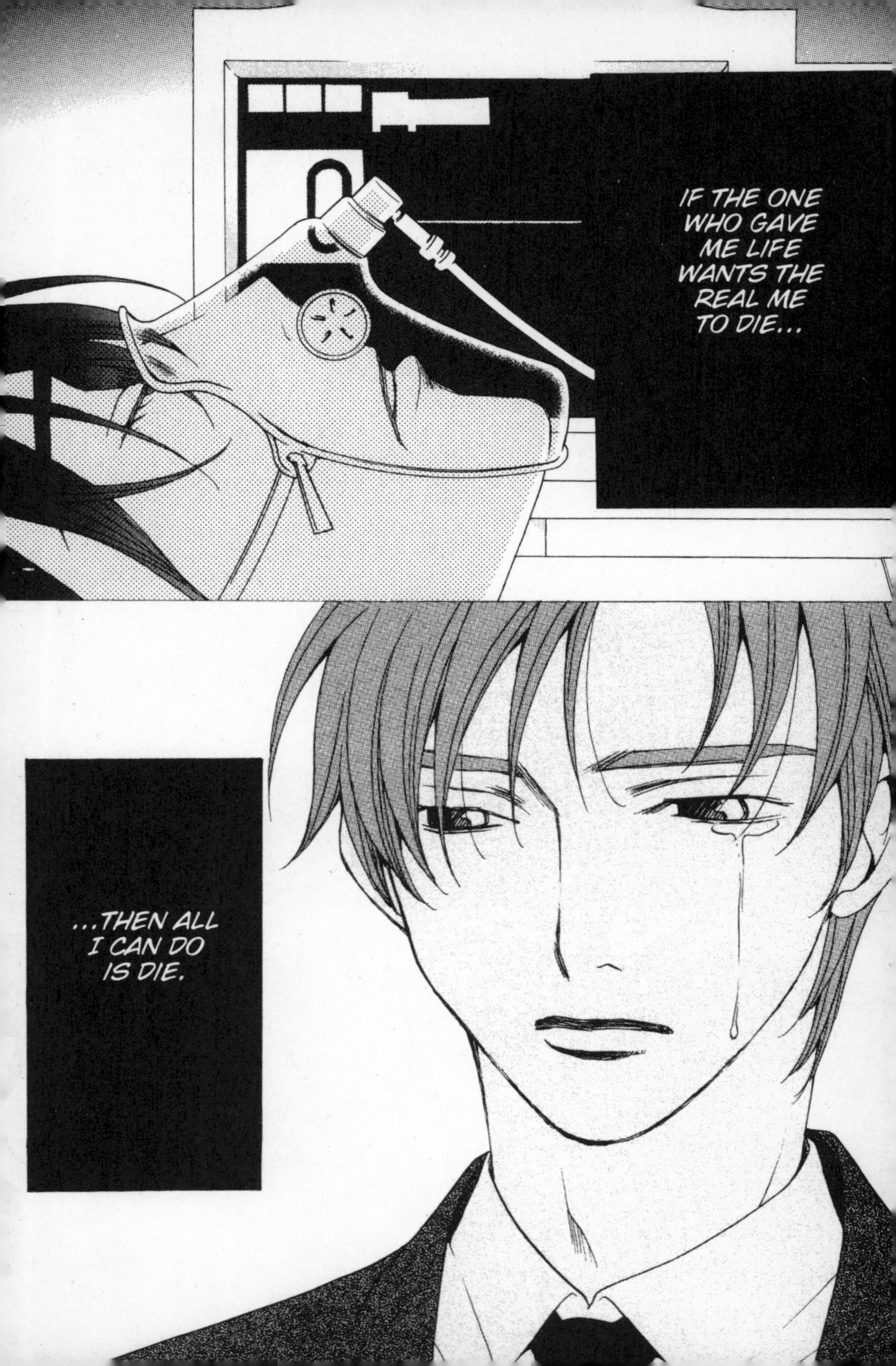
IF THE ONE WHO GAVE ME LIFE WANTS THE REAL ME TO DIE...
...THEN ALL I CAN DO IS DIE.

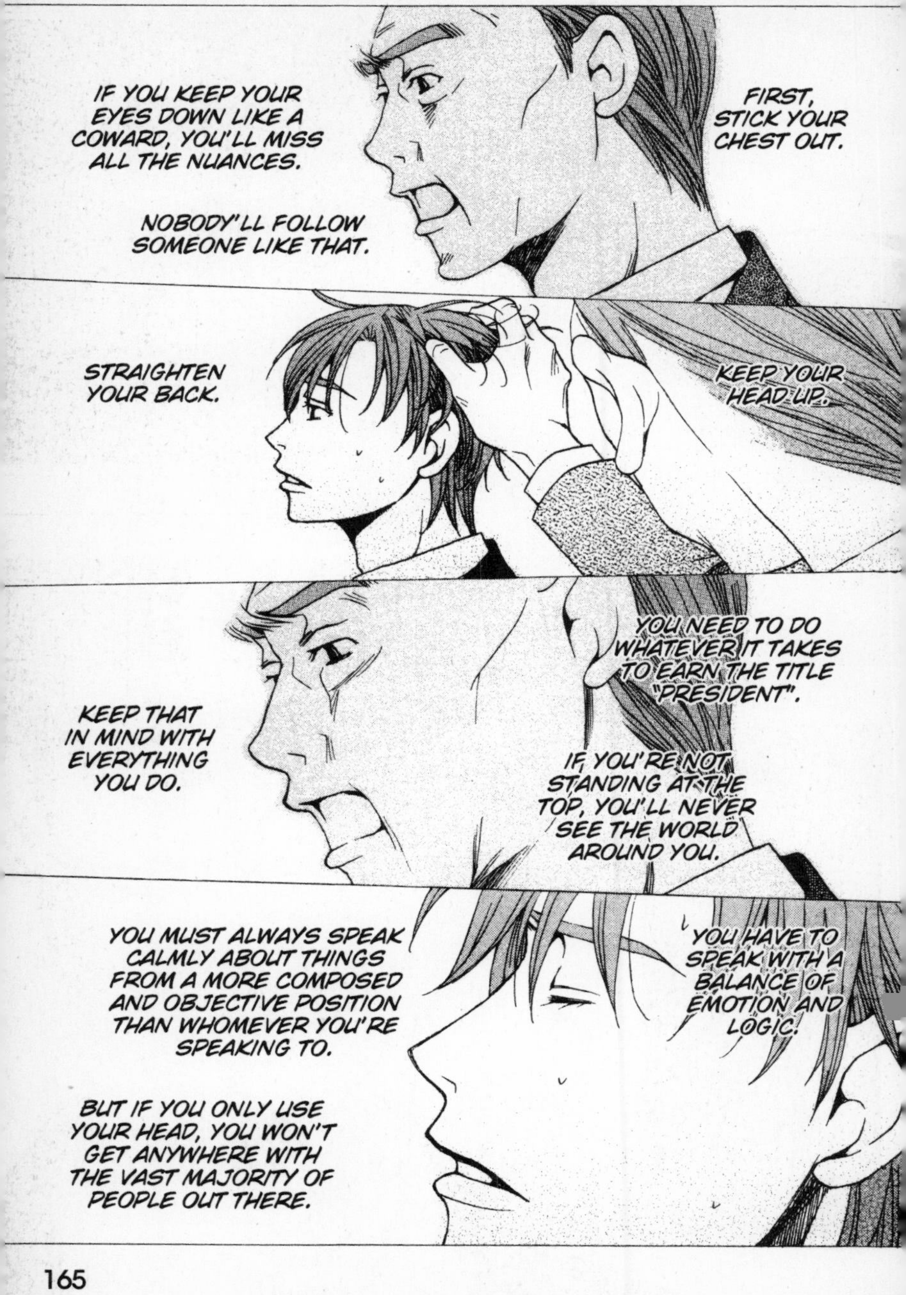
FIRST, STICK YOUR CHEST OUT.
IF YOU KEEP YOUR EYES DOWN LIKE A COWARD, YOU'LL MISS ALL THE NUANCES.
NOBODY'LL FOLLOW SOMEONE LIKE THAT.
KEEP YOUR HEAD UP.
STRAIGHTEN YOUR BACK.
YOU NEED TO DO WHATEVER IT TAKES TO EARN THE TITLE "PRESIDENT".
IF YOU'RE NOT STANDING AT THE TOP, YOU'LL NEVER SEE THE WORLD AROUND YOU.
KEEP THAT IN MIND WITH EVERYTHING YOU DO.
YOU HAVE TO SPEAK WITH A BALANCE OF EMOTION AND LOGIC.
YOU MUST ALWAYS SPEAK CALMLY ABOUT THINGS FROM A MORE COMPOSED AND OBJECTIVE POSITION THAN WHOMEVER YOU'RE SPEAKING TO.
BUT IF YOU ONLY USE YOUR HEAD, YOU WON'T GET ANYWHERE WITH THE VAST MAJORITY OF PEOPLE OUT THERE.

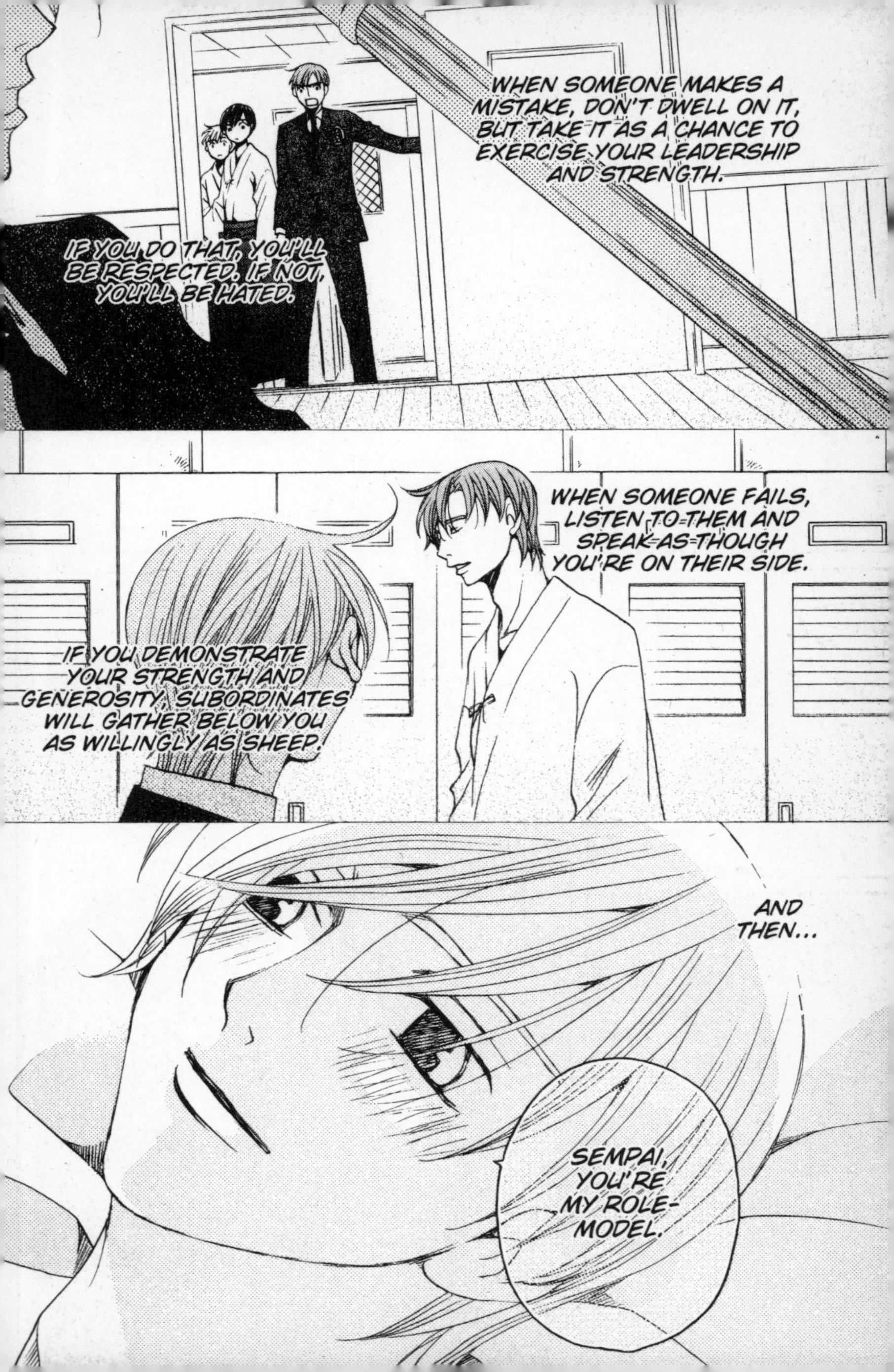
WHEN SOMEONE MAKES A MISTAKE, DON'T DWELL ON IT, BUT TAKE IT AS A CHANCE TO EXERCISE YOUR LEADERSHIP AND STRENGTH.
IF YOU DO THAT, YOU'LL BE RESPECTED. IF NOT, YOU'LL BE HATED.
WHEN SOMEONE FAILS, LISTEN TO THEM AND SPEAK AS THOUGH YOU'RE ON THEIR SIDE.
IF YOU DEMONSTRATE YOUR STRENGTH AND GENEROSITY, SUBORDINATES WILL GATHER BELOW YOU AS WILLINGLY AS SHEEP.
AND THEN...
SEMPAI, YOU'RE MY ROLE-MODEL.

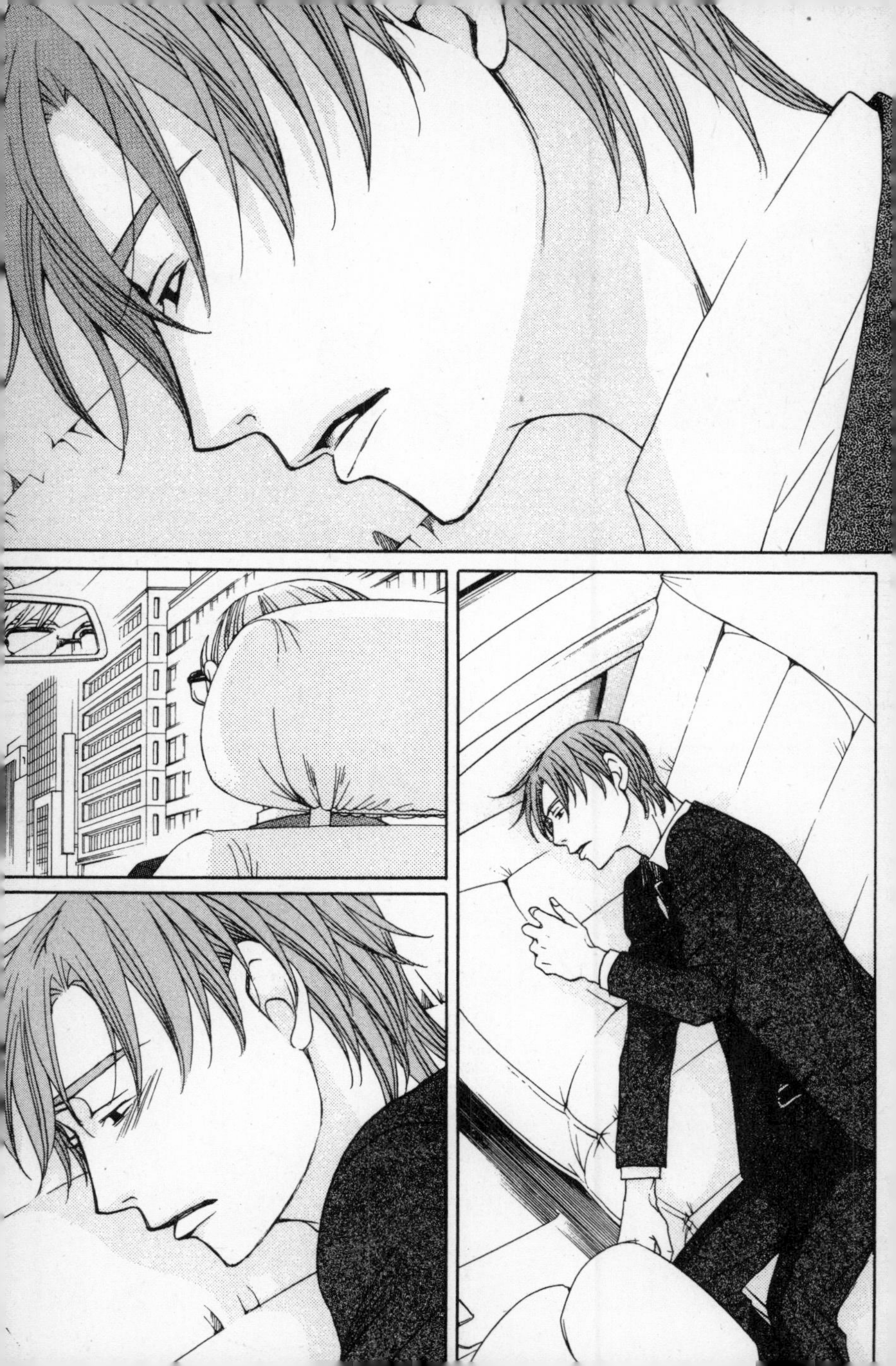

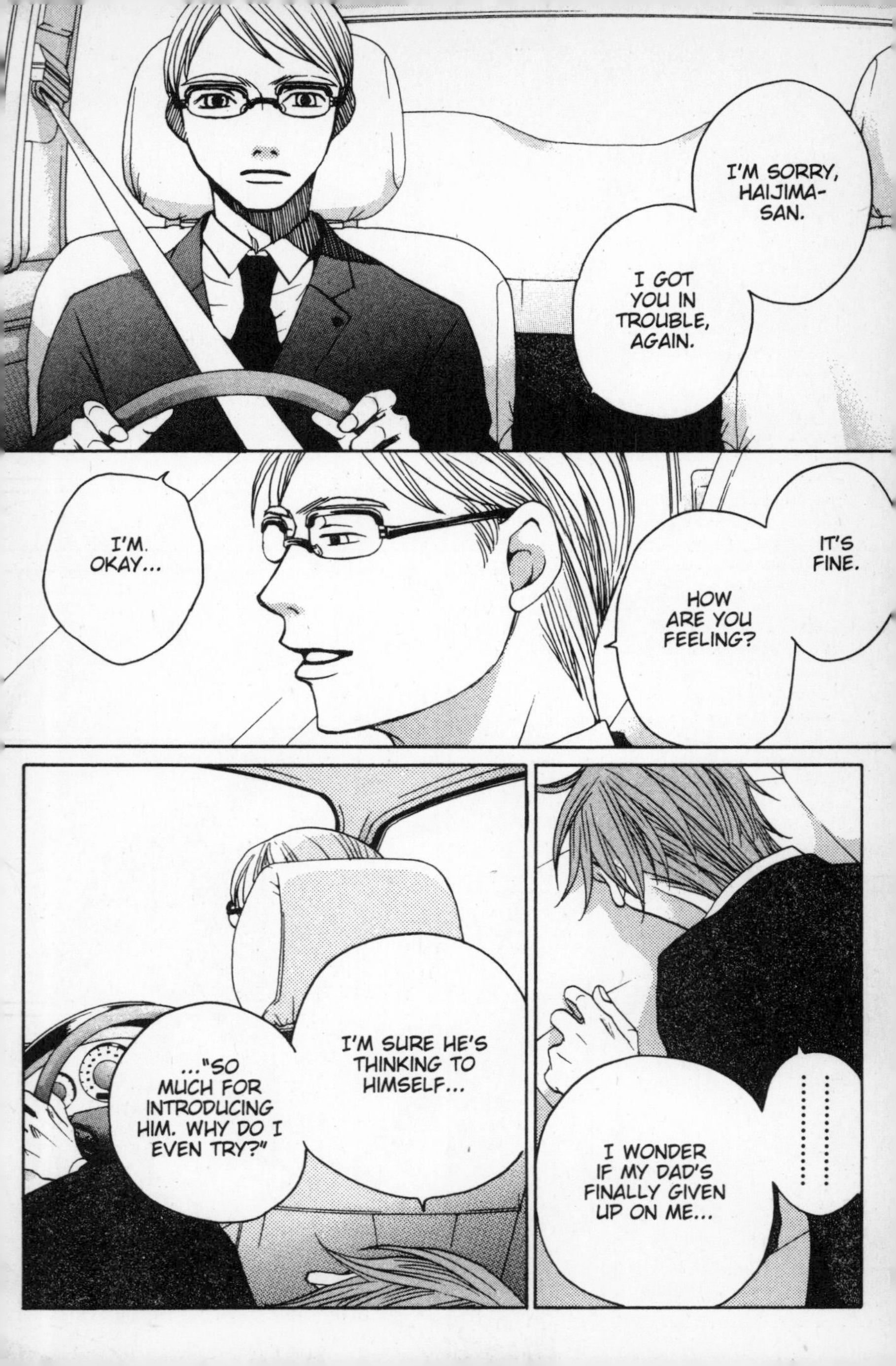
I'M SORRY, HAIJIMA-SAN.
I GOT YOU IN TROUBLE, AGAIN.
IT'S FINE.
HOW ARE YOU FEELING?
I'M. OKAY...
......
I WONDER IF MY DAD'S FINALLY GIVEN UP ON ME...
I'M SURE HE'S THINKING TO HIMSELF...
..."SO MUCH FOR INTRODUCING HIM. WHY DO I EVEN TRY?"

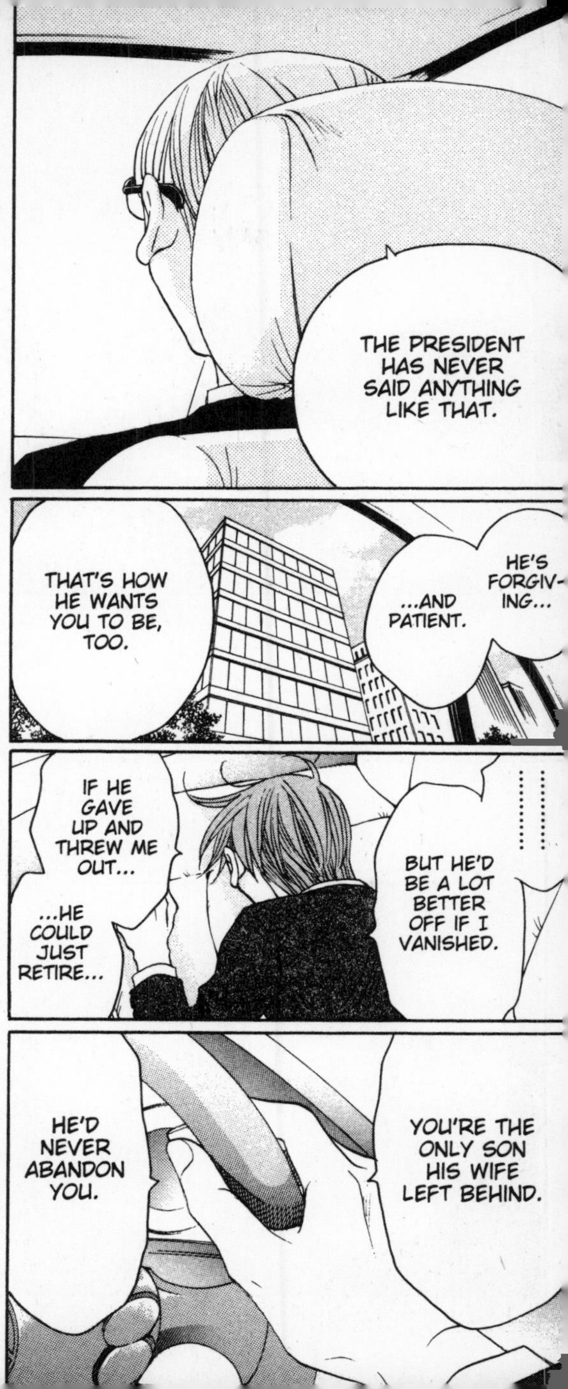
THE PRESIDENT HAS NEVER SAID ANYTHING LIKE THAT.
HE'S FORGIV-ING...
...AND PATIENT.
THAT'S HOW HE WANTS YOU TO BE, TOO.
......
BUT HE'D BE A LOT BETTER OFF IF I VANISHED.
IF HE GAVE UP AND THREW ME OUT...
...HE COULD JUST RETIRE...
YOU'RE THE ONLY SON HIS WIFE LEFT BEHIND.
HE'D NEVER ABANDON YOU.

Extra ASN Talk ②

■(Continued from ①)
In the magazine issue that had the preview page for ASN before it was even serialized, there was a strong tagline that went "A hair-raising horror...!" That got me thinking "Oh, that's right. This is supposed to be a horror manga, so I'd better draw it that way." And so in haste, I planted the idea of horror in my head and drew the uniform image of the initial dream world members with more horror-like qualities. As a result, those giraffe eyes that always give off a warm and fuzzy feeling were saved for later. That's why the mermaid, and her more fairytale-like(?) air also came far later. Incidentally, that line about the series being a "hair-raising horror" never made it to the final cut (ha).

■Asuka Suo —> Yukari
Much like the giraffe I spoke about, she was also saved for later and had a name that sounded more mature in her initial development. But I felt that she could use a stronger sounding name and changed it. I really like fairy tale elements so I wanted to draw the mermaid princess right away. Keeping that in mind, I actually wrote the story to introduce her sooner, but just before the final cut she disappeared—poof—like a bubble (ha).

When I finally gave drawing the mermaid a stab, I realized it was hard to draw all her jewelry and scales all the time...(ha)

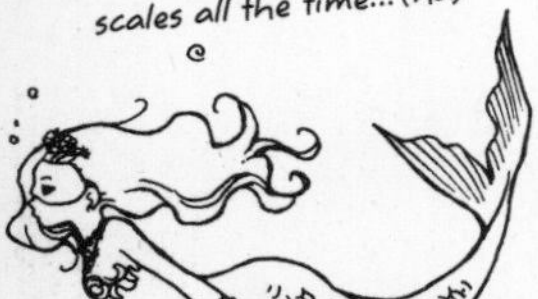

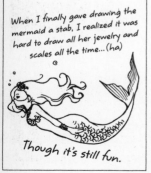

Though it's still fun.

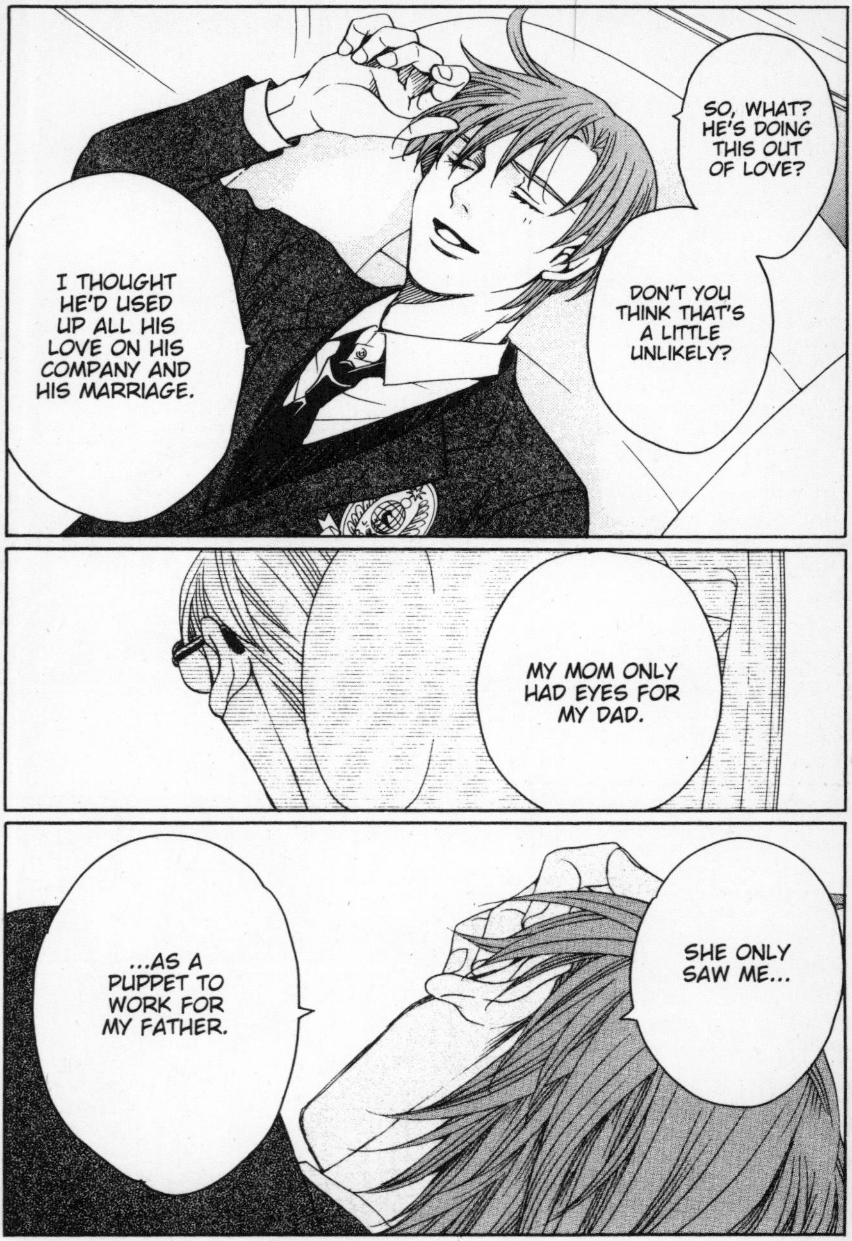
SO, WHAT? HE'S DOING THIS OUT OF LOVE?
DON'T YOU THINK THAT'S A LITTLE UNLIKELY?
I THOUGHT HE'D USED UP ALL HIS LOVE ON HIS COMPANY AND HIS MARRIAGE.
MY MOM ONLY HAD EYES FOR MY DAD.
SHE ONLY SAW ME...
...AS A PUPPET TO WORK FOR MY FATHER.

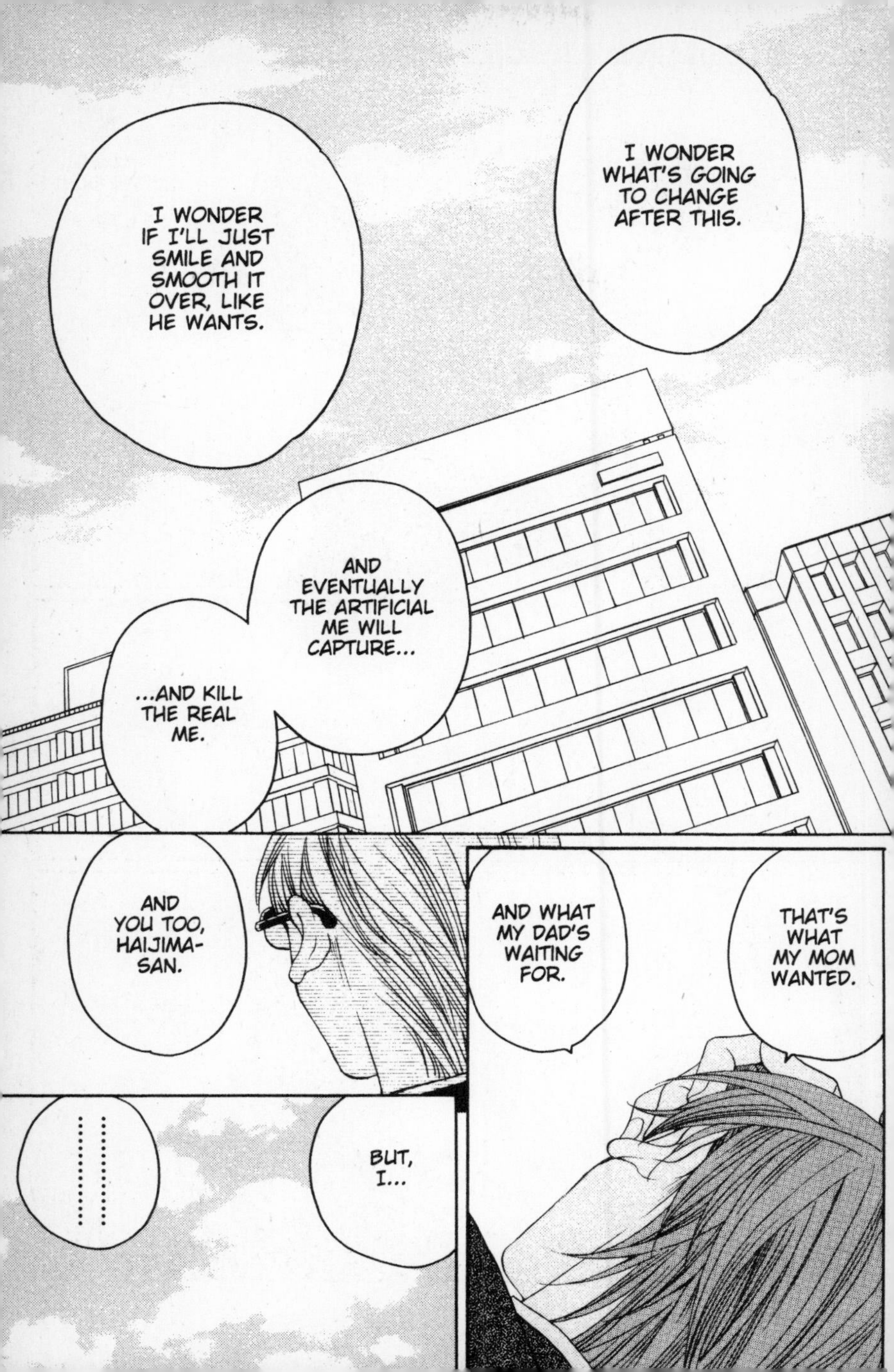
I WONDER WHAT'S GOING TO CHANGE AFTER THIS.
I WONDER IF I'LL JUST SMILE AND SMOOTH IT OVER, LIKE HE WANTS.
AND EVENTUALLY THE ARTIFICIAL ME WILL CAPTURE...
...AND KILL THE REAL ME.
THAT'S WHAT MY MOM WANTED.
AND WHAT MY DAD'S WAITING FOR.
AND YOU TOO, HAIJIMA-SAN.
BUT, I...
......

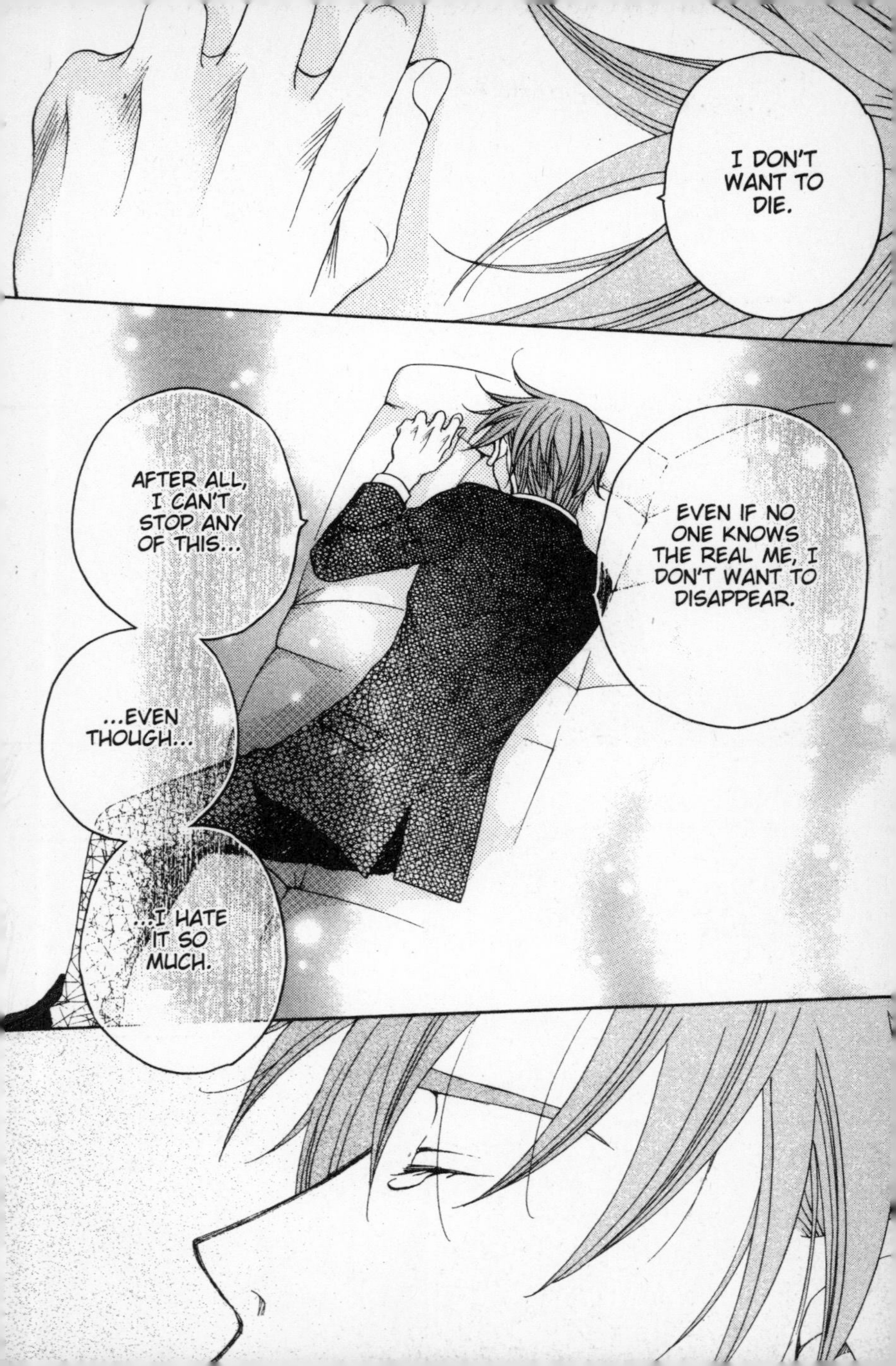
I DON'T WANT TO DIE.
EVEN IF NO ONE KNOWS THE REAL ME, I DON'T WANT TO DISAPPEAR.
AFTER ALL, I CAN'T STOP ANY OF THIS...
...EVEN THOUGH...
...I HATE IT SO MUCH.

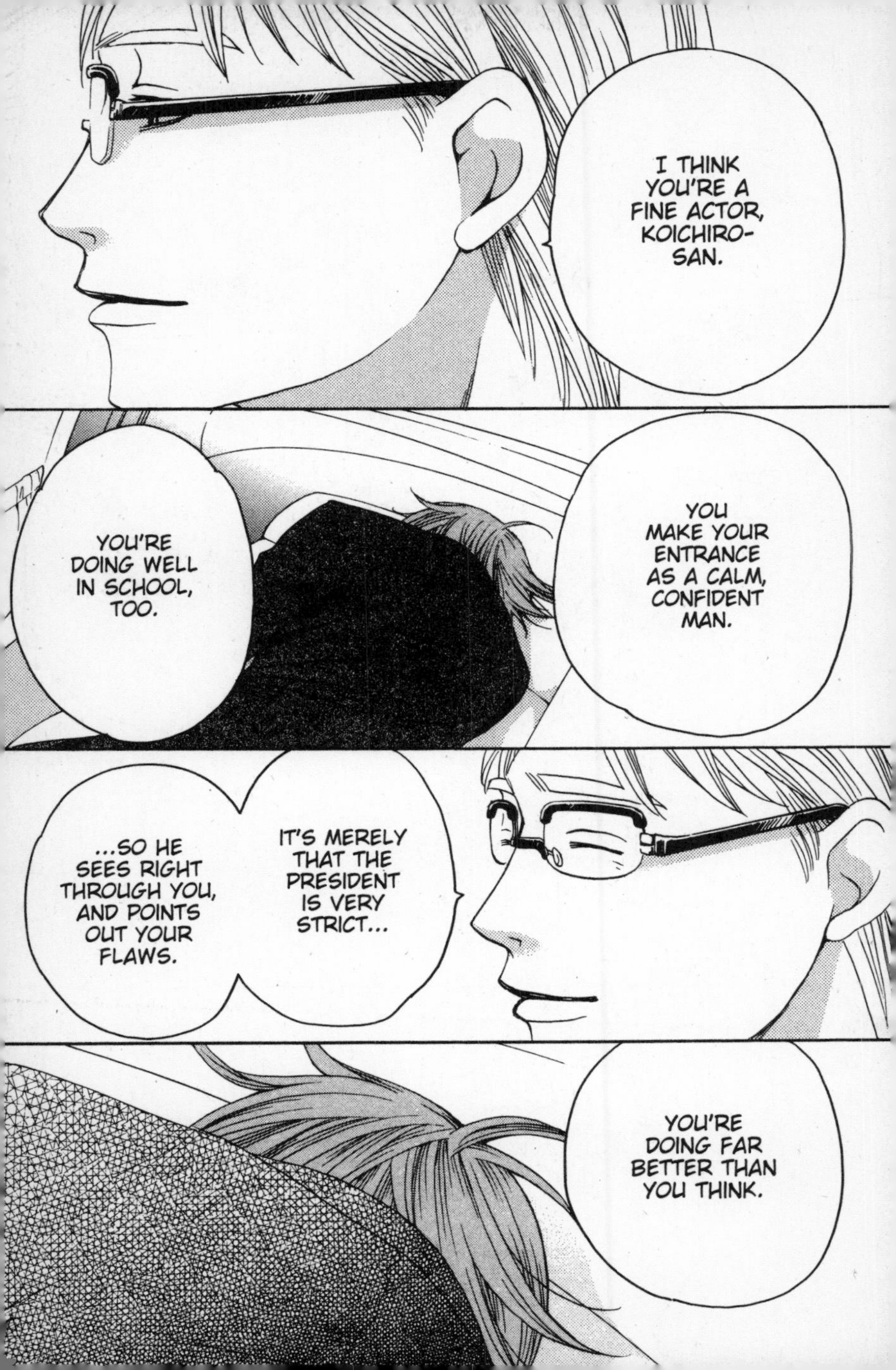
I THINK YOU'RE A FINE ACTOR, KOICHIRO-SAN.
YOU MAKE YOUR ENTRANCE AS A CALM, CONFIDENT MAN.
YOU'RE DOING WELL IN SCHOOL, TOO.
IT'S MERELY THAT THE PRESIDENT IS VERY STRICT...
...SO HE SEES RIGHT THROUGH YOU, AND POINTS OUT YOUR FLAWS.
YOU'RE DOING FAR BETTER THAN YOU THINK.

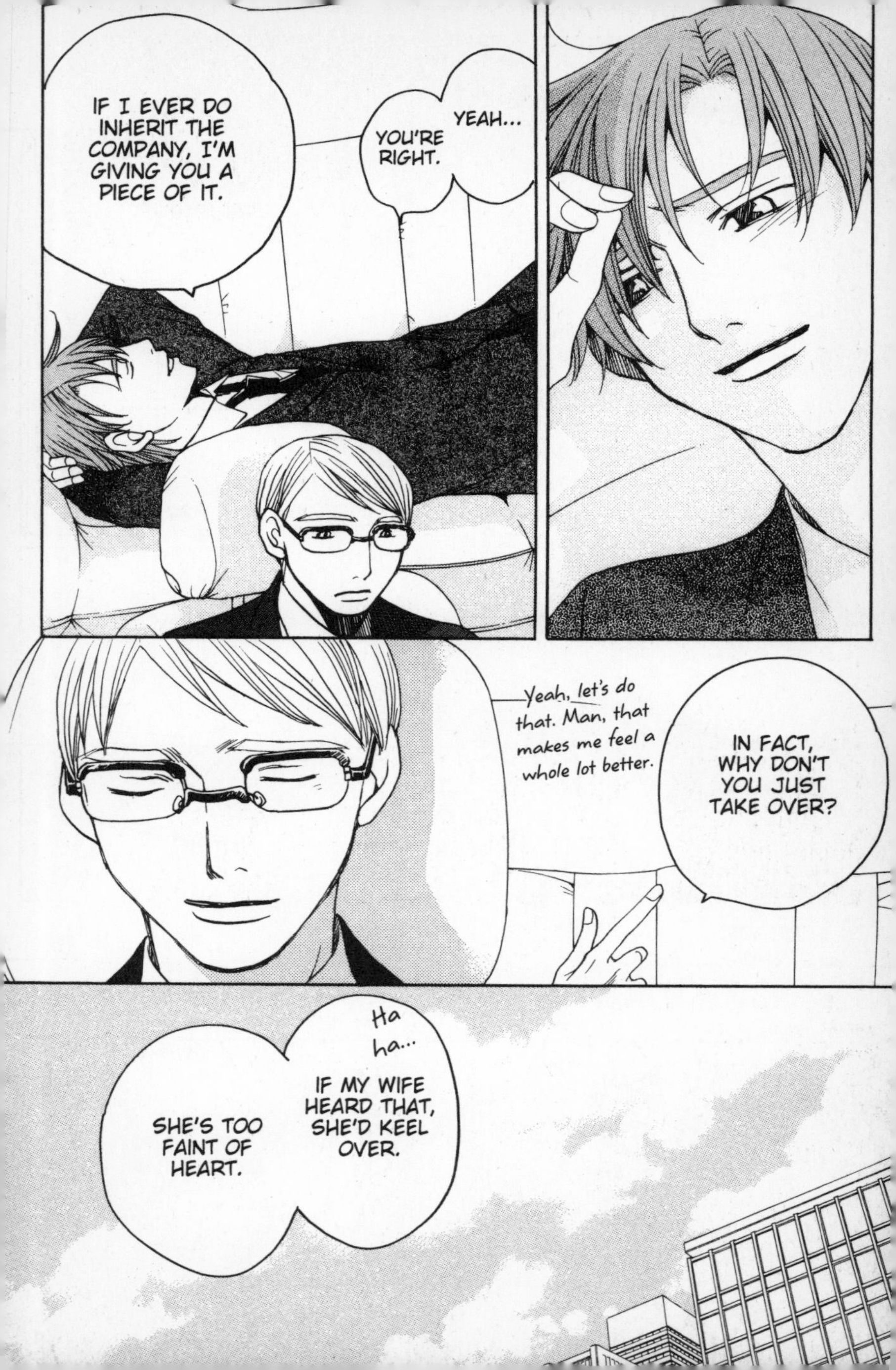
YEAH... YOU'RE RIGHT.
IF I EVER DO INHERIT THE COMPANY, I'M GIVING YOU A PIECE OF IT.
Yeah, let's do that. Man, that makes me feel a whole lot better.
IN FACT, WHY DON'T YOU JUST TAKE OVER?
Ha ha...
IF MY WIFE HEARD THAT, SHE'D KEEL OVER.
SHE'S TOO FAINT OF HEART.

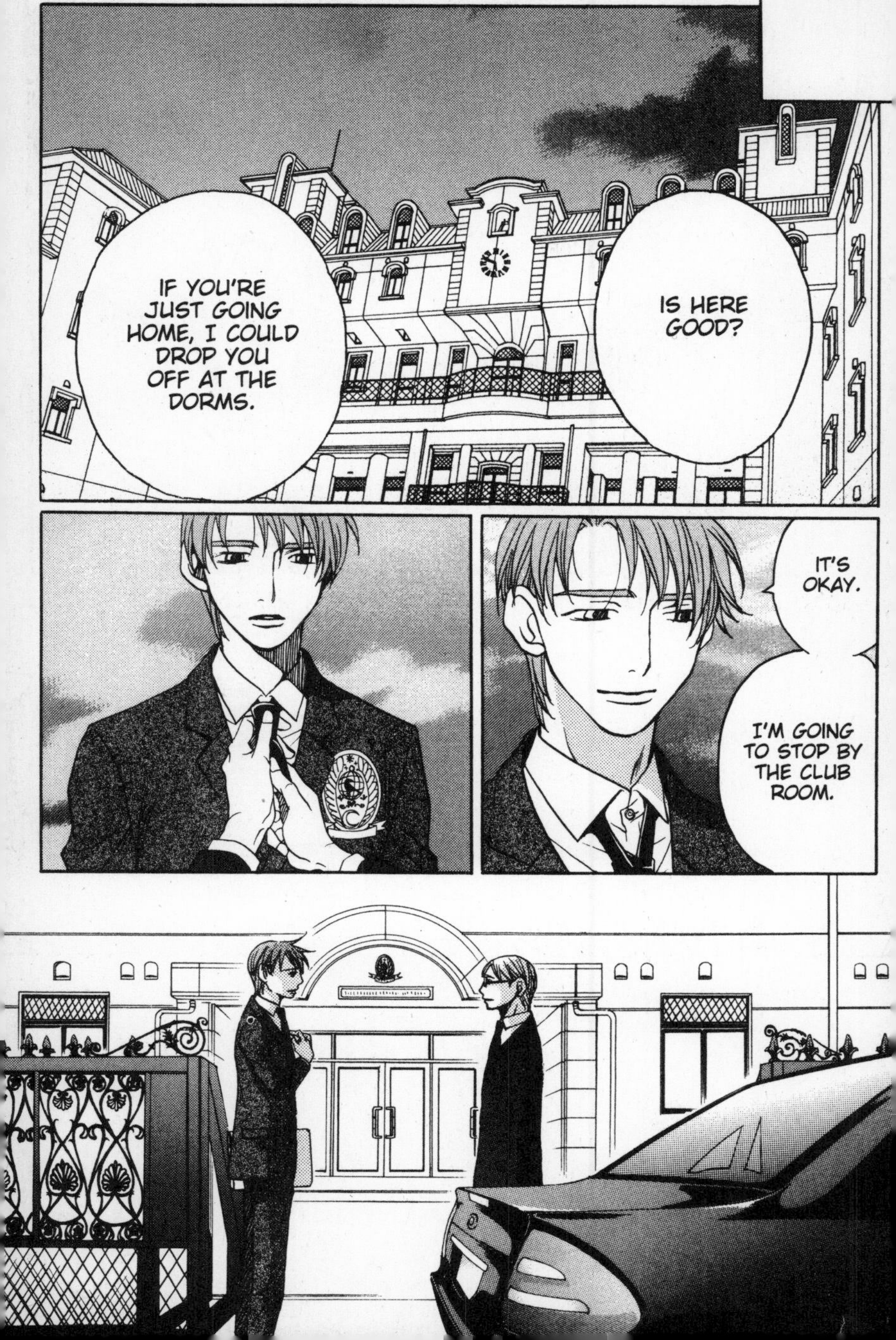
IS HERE GOOD?
IF YOU'RE JUST GOING HOME, I COULD DROP YOU OFF AT THE DORMS.
IT'S OKAY.
I'M GOING TO STOP BY THE CLUB ROOM.

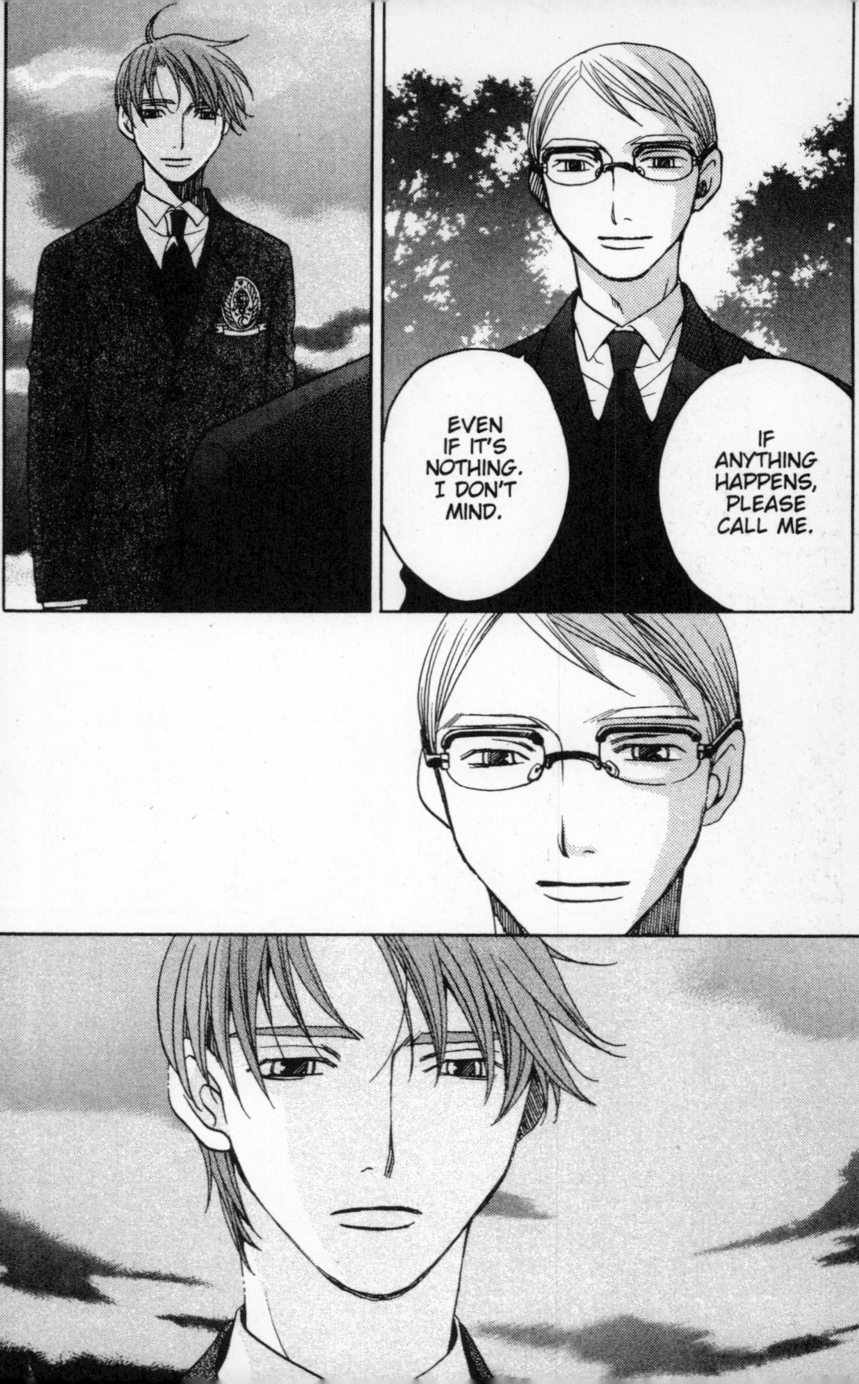
IF ANYTHING HAPPENS, PLEASE CALL ME.
EVEN IF IT'S NOTHING. I DON'T MIND.

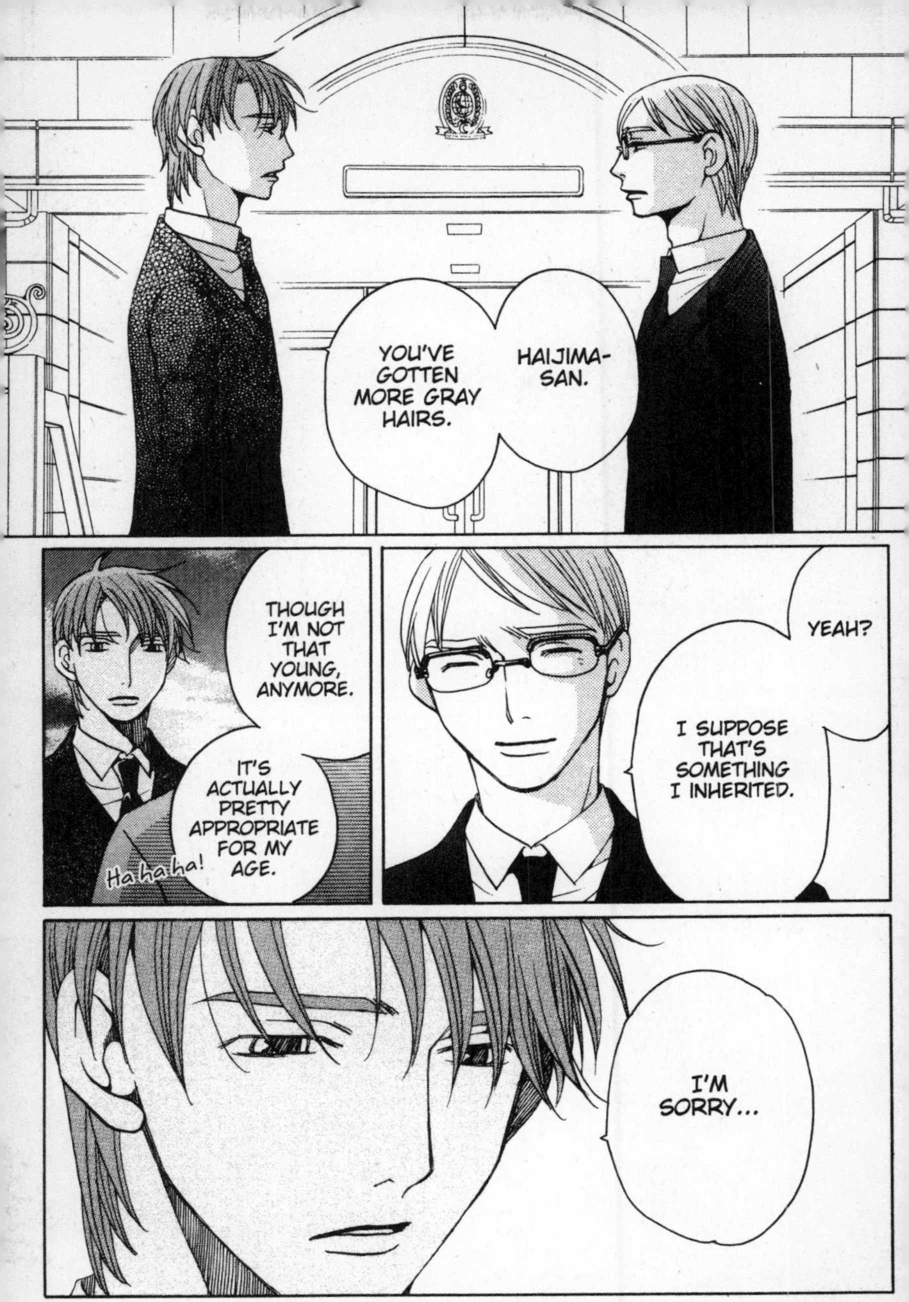
HAIJIMA-SAN.
YOU'VE GOTTEN MORE GRAY HAIRS.
YEAH?
I SUPPOSE THAT'S SOMETHING I INHERITED.
THOUGH I'M NOT THAT YOUNG, ANYMORE.
IT'S ACTUALLY PRETTY APPROPRIATE FOR MY AGE.
Ha ha ha!
I'M SORRY...

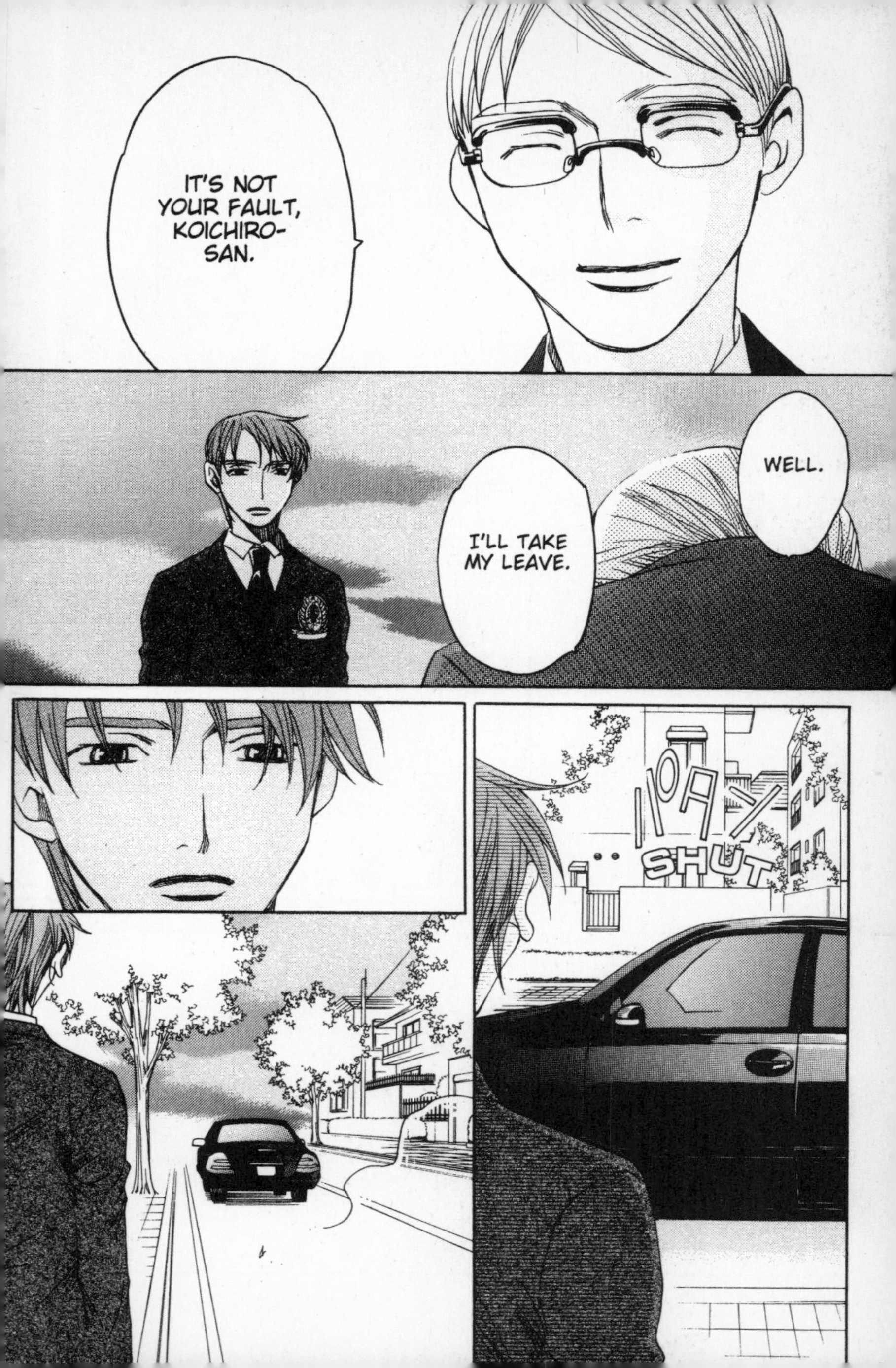
IT'S NOT YOUR FAULT, KOICHIRO-SAN.
WELL.
I'LL TAKE MY LEAVE.
SHUT

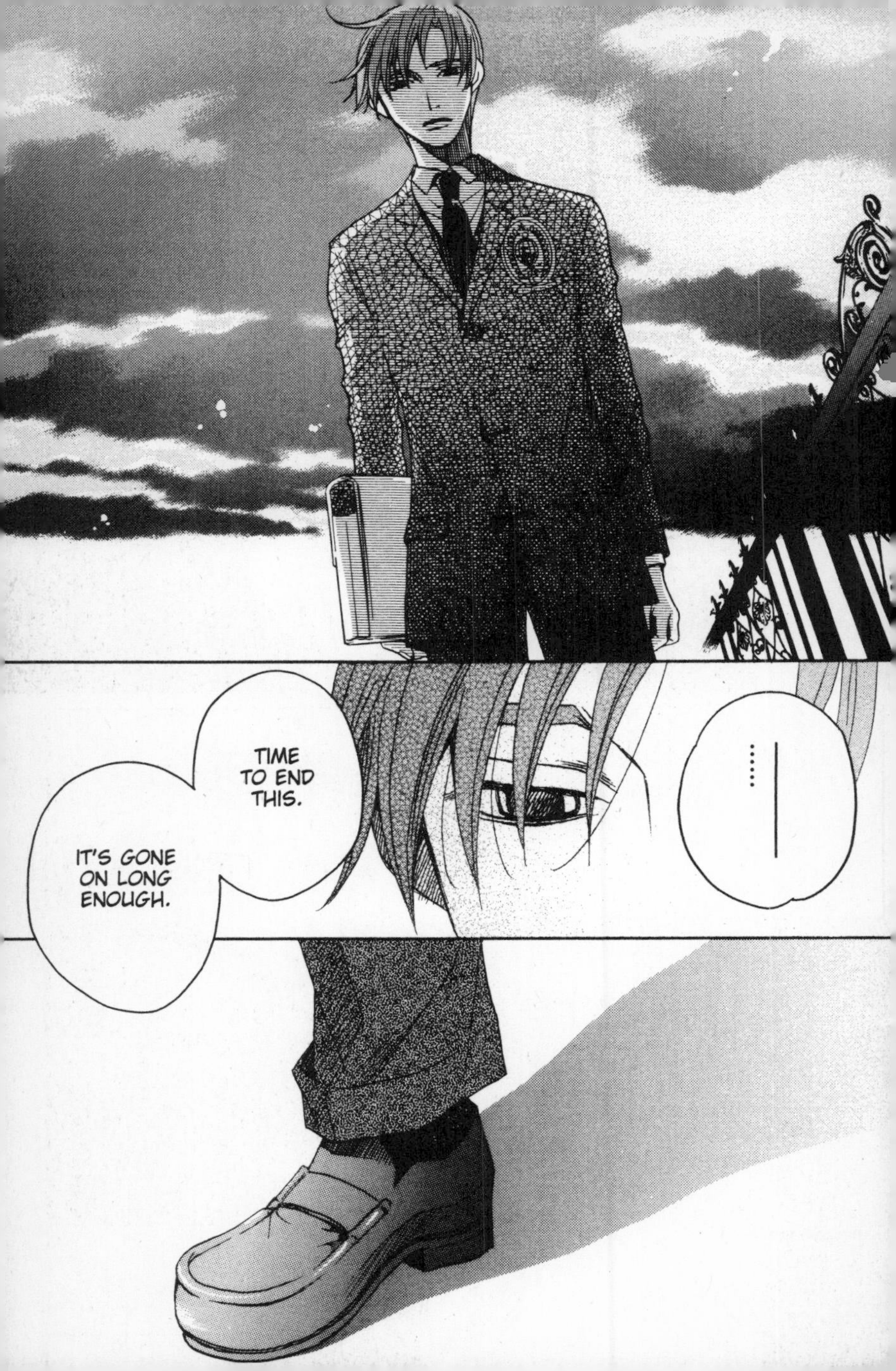
……—
TIME TO END THIS.
IT'S GONE ON LONG ENOUGH.

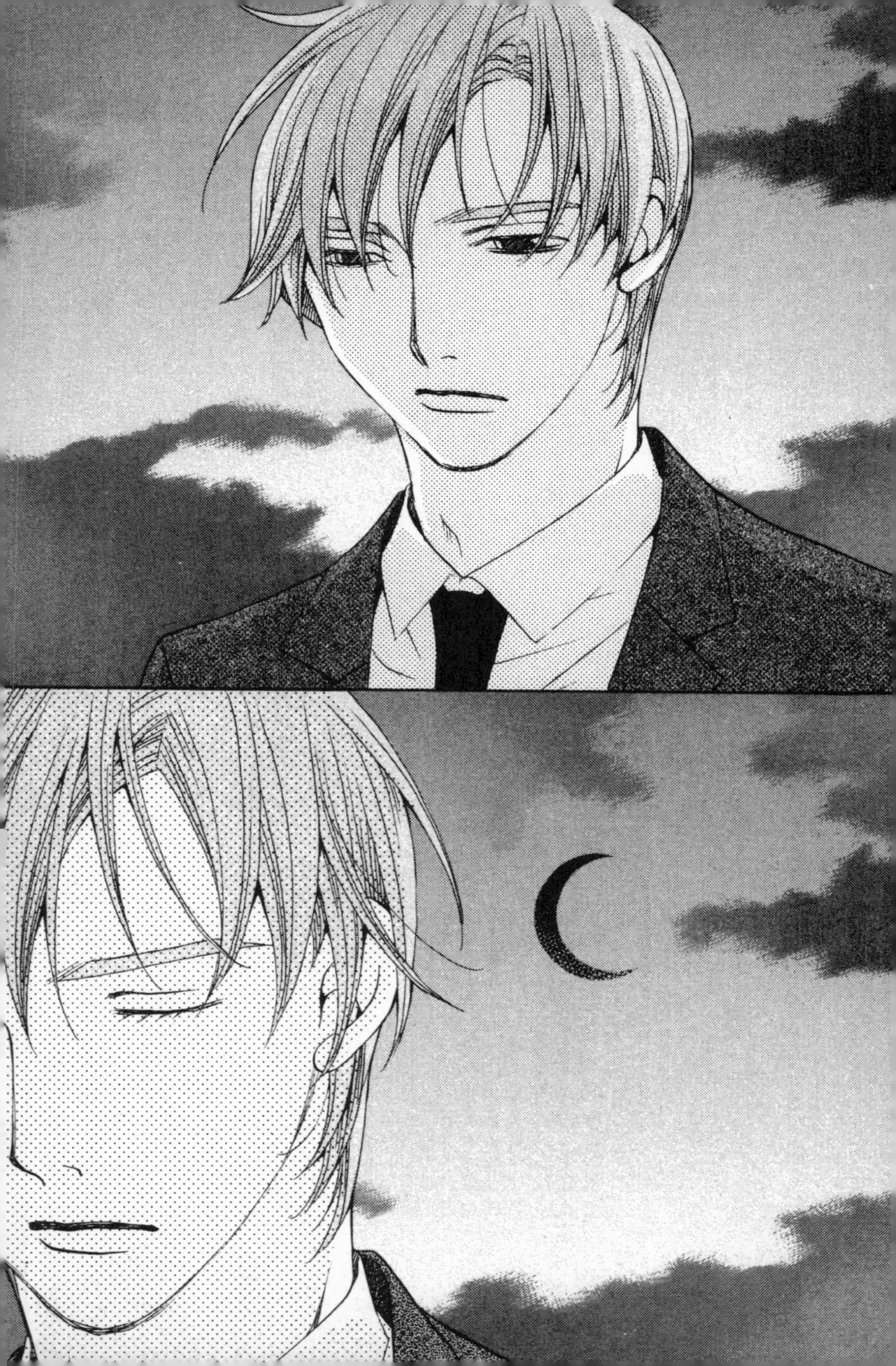

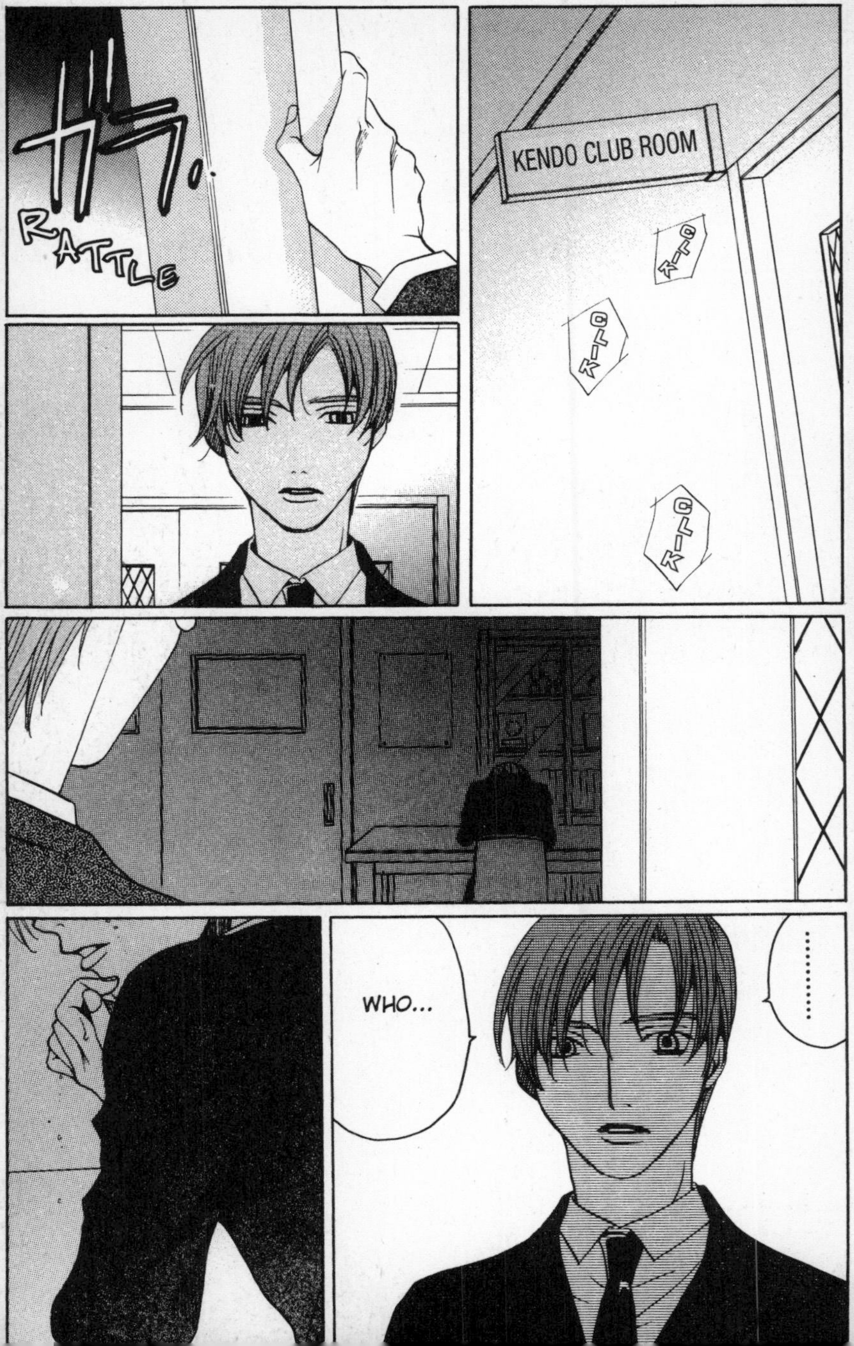
KENDO CLUB ROOM
CLIK
CLIK
CLIK
ガラ
RATTLE
......
WHO...

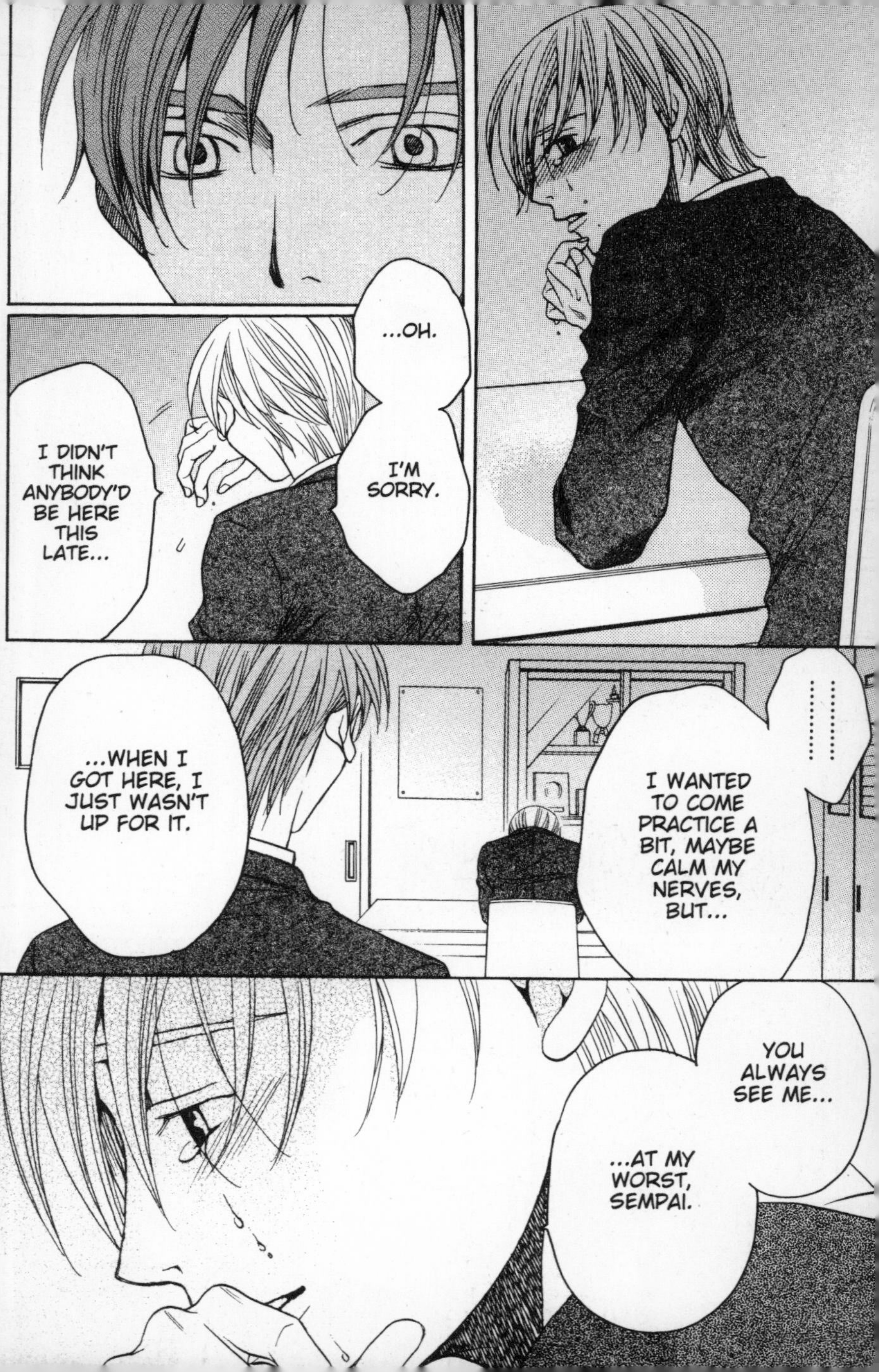
...OH.
I'M SORRY.
I DIDN'T THINK ANYBODY'D BE HERE THIS LATE...
......
I WANTED TO COME PRACTICE A BIT, MAYBE CALM MY NERVES, BUT...
...WHEN I GOT HERE, I JUST WASN'T UP FOR IT.
YOU ALWAYS SEE ME...
...AT MY WORST, SEMPAI.

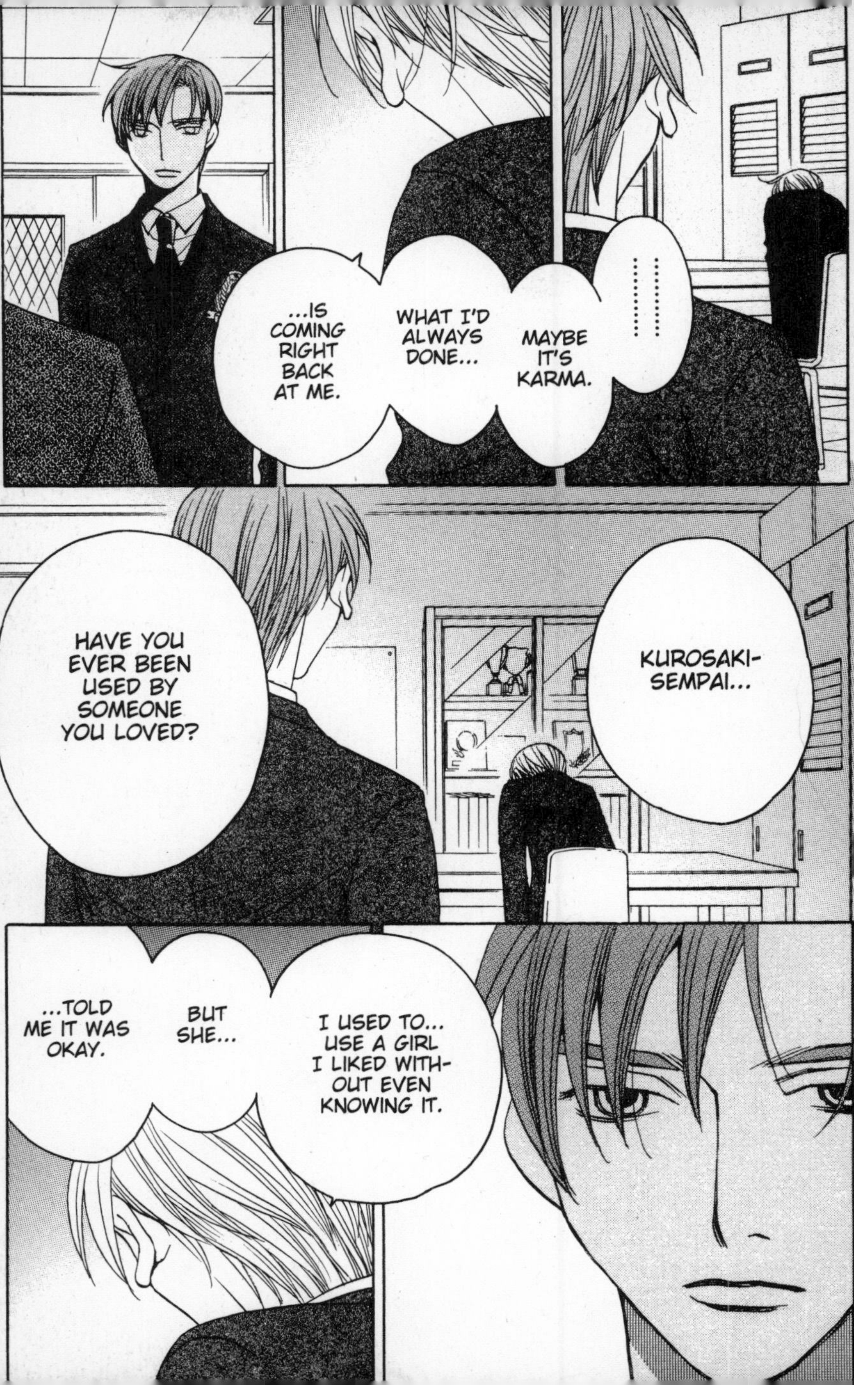
......
MAYBE IT'S KARMA.
WHAT I'D ALWAYS DONE...
...IS COMING RIGHT BACK AT ME.
KUROSAKI-SEMPAI...
HAVE YOU EVER BEEN USED BY SOMEONE YOU LOVED?
I USED TO... USE A GIRL I LIKED WITH-OUT EVEN KNOWING IT.
BUT SHE...
...TOLD ME IT WAS OKAY.

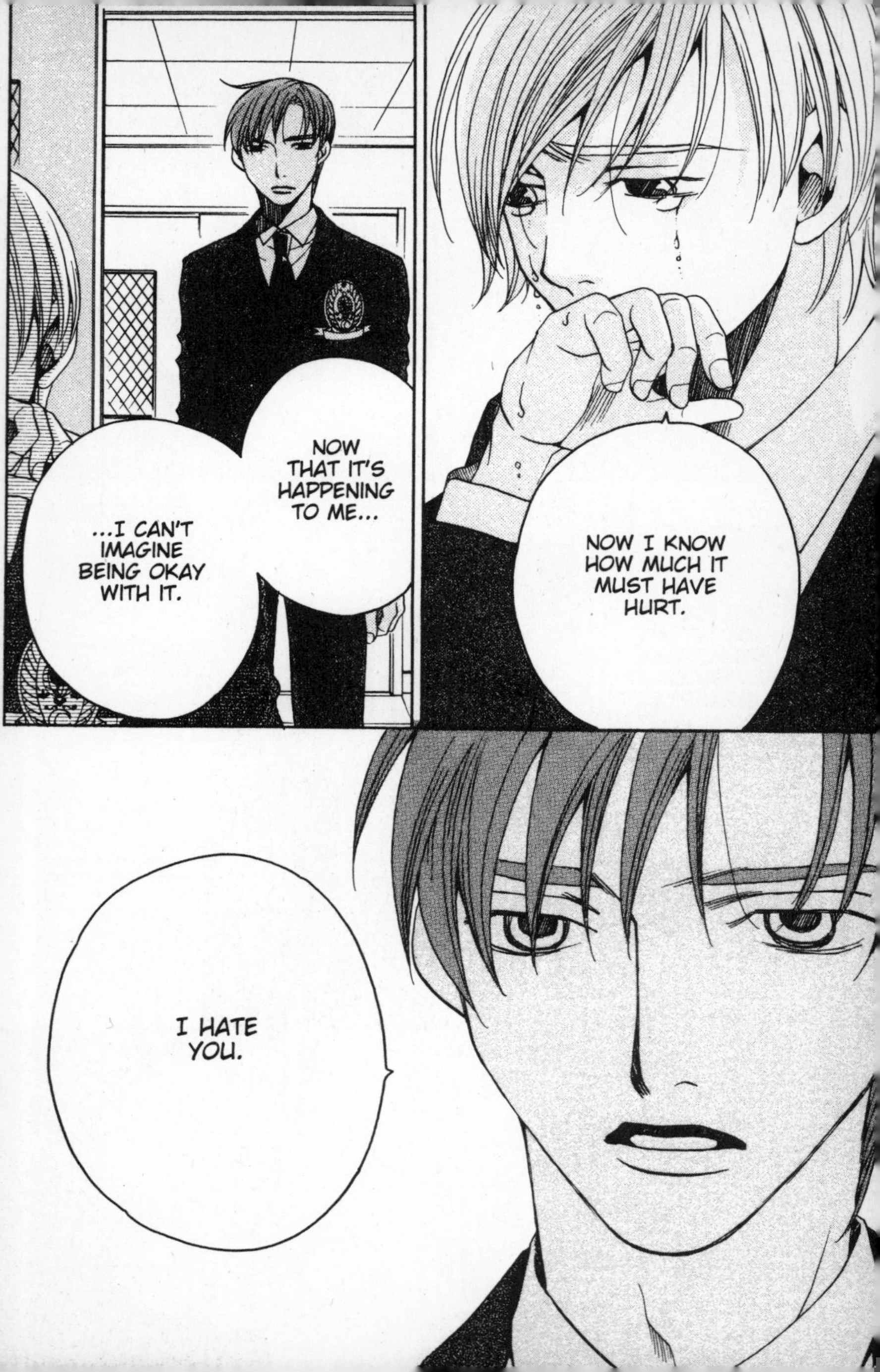
NOW I KNOW HOW MUCH IT MUST HAVE HURT.
NOW THAT IT'S HAPPENING TO ME...
...I CAN'T IMAGINE BEING OKAY WITH IT.
I HATE YOU.

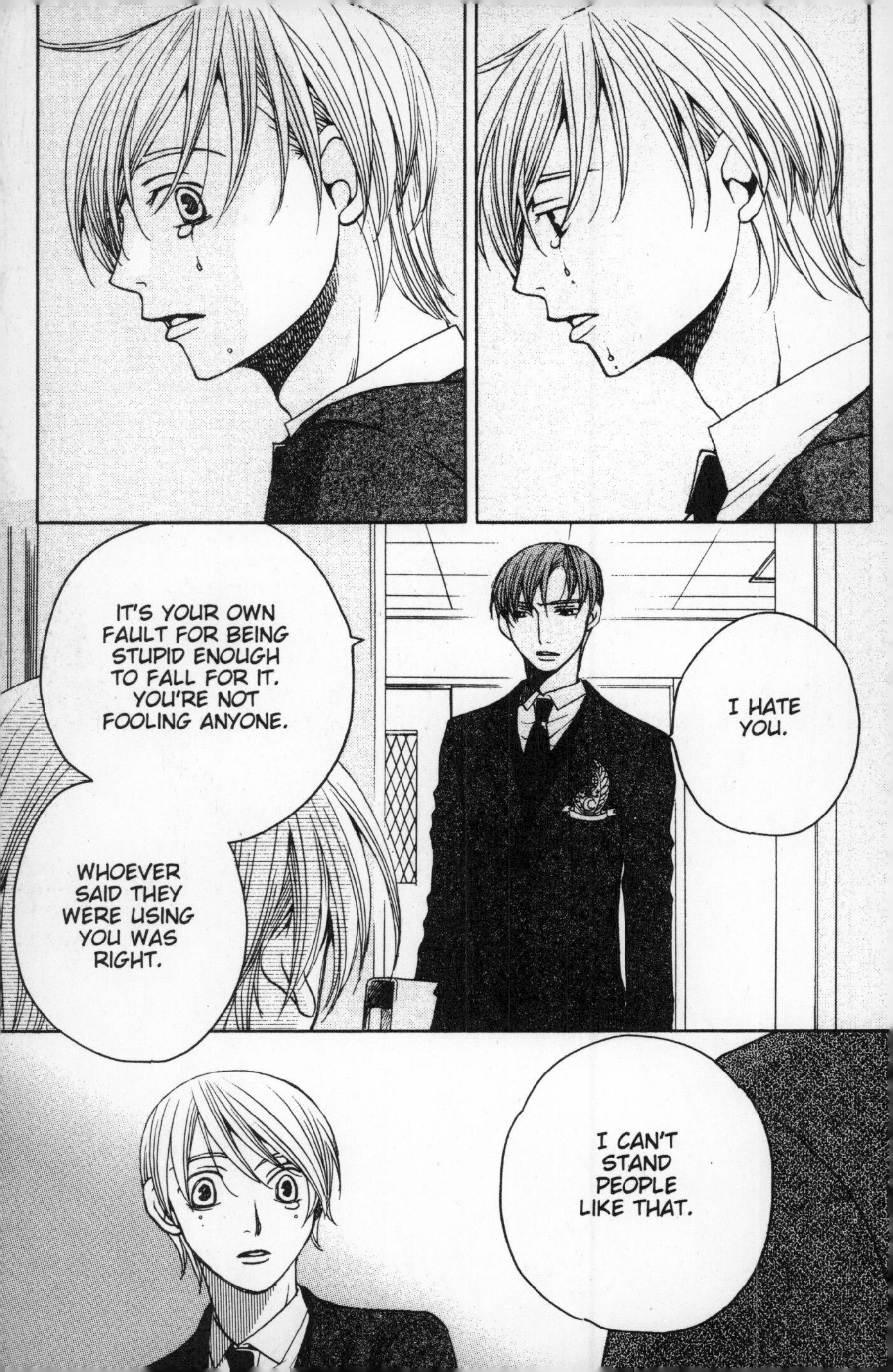
IT'S YOUR OWN FAULT FOR BEING STUPID ENOUGH TO FALL FOR IT. YOU'RE NOT FOOLING ANYONE.
WHOEVER SAID THEY WERE USING YOU WAS RIGHT.
I HATE YOU.
I CAN'T STAND PEOPLE LIKE THAT.

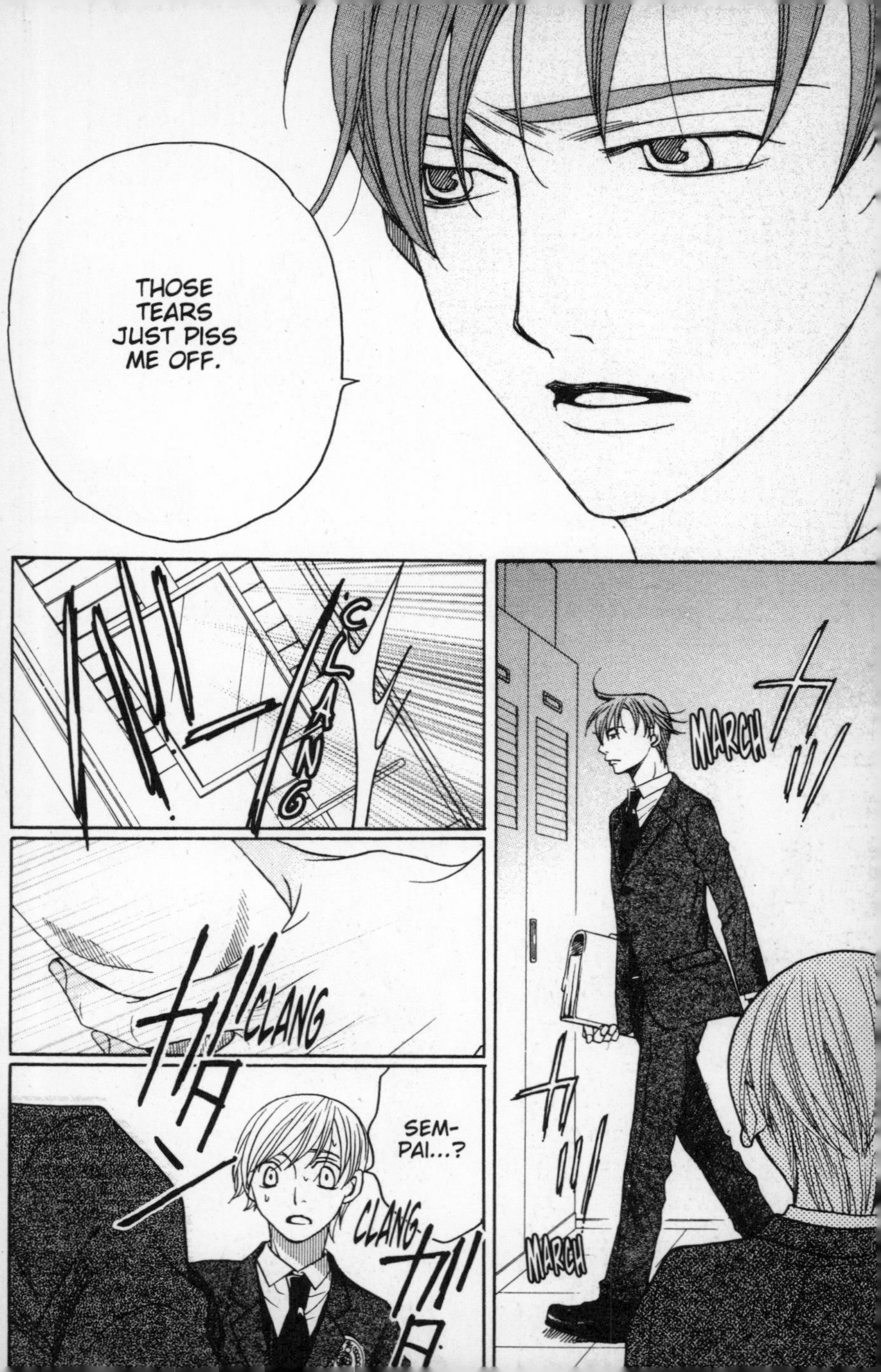
THOSE TEARS JUST PISS ME OFF.
MARCH
MARCH
CLANG
CLANG
SEM-PAI...?
CLANG

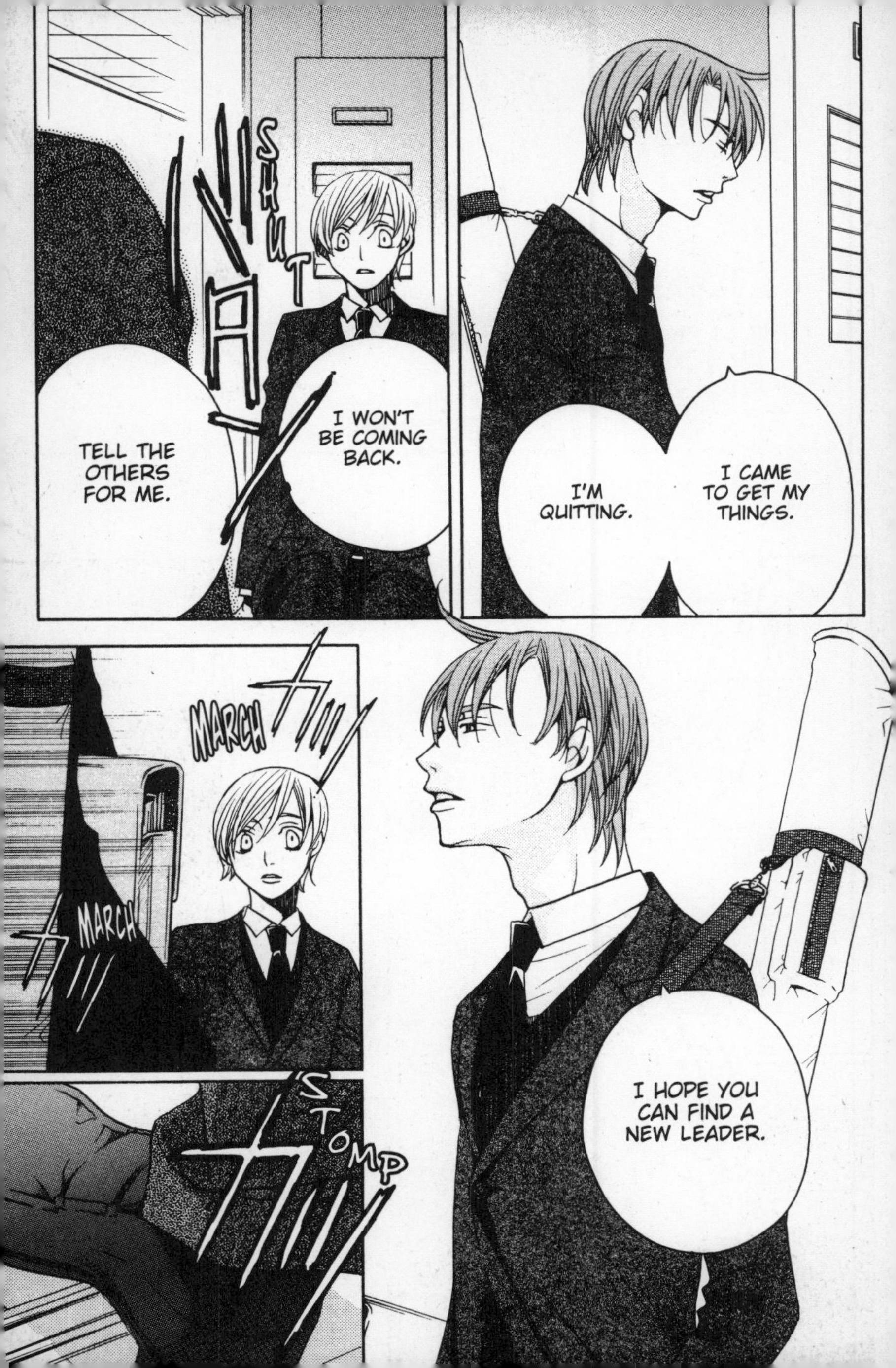
I CAME TO GET MY THINGS.
I'M QUITTING.
SHUT
I WON'T BE COMING BACK.
TELL THE OTHERS FOR ME.
I HOPE YOU CAN FIND A NEW LEADER.
MARCH
MARCH
STOMP

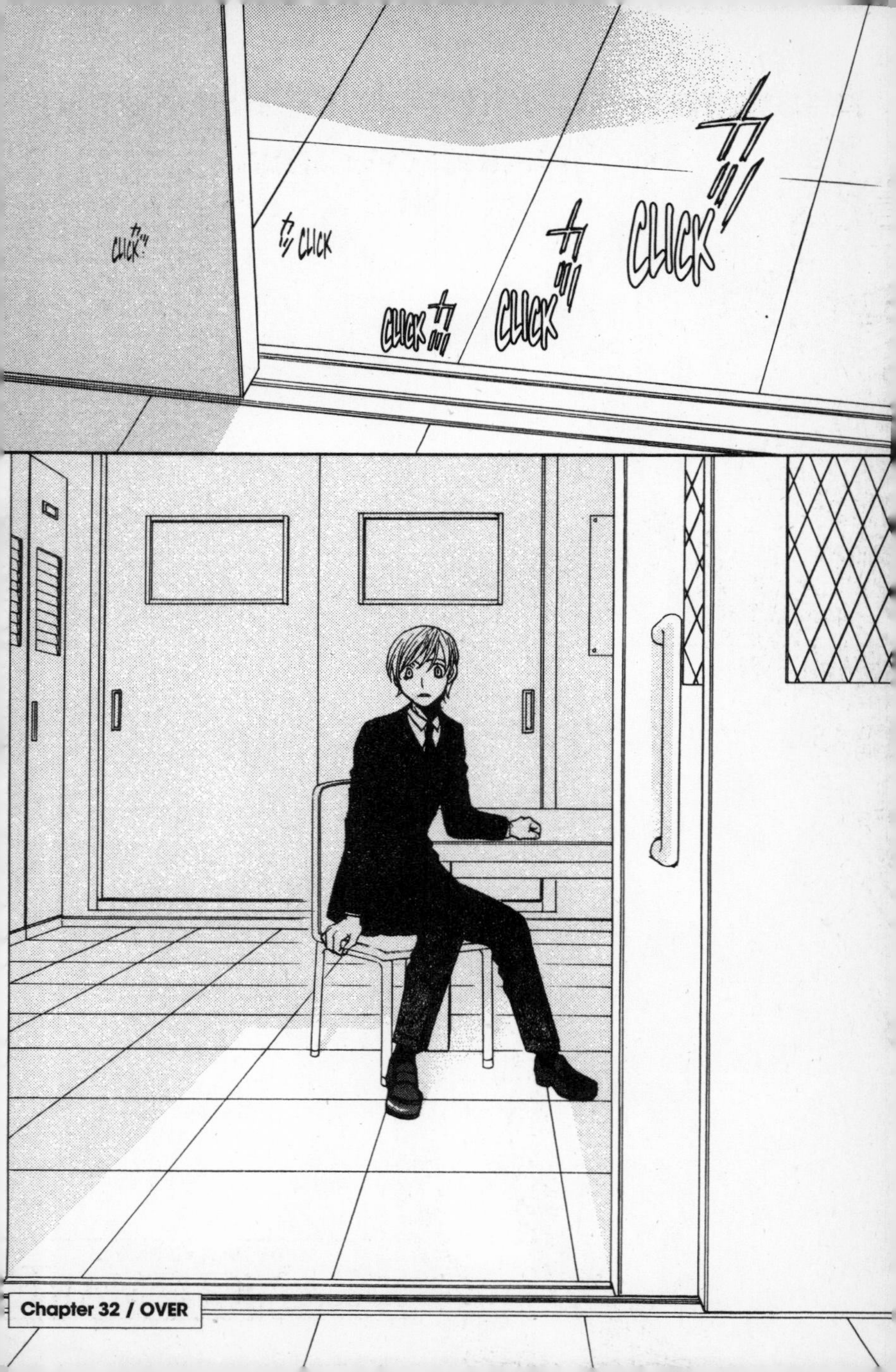
CLICK
CLICK
CLICK
CLICK
CLICK
Chapter 32 / OVER

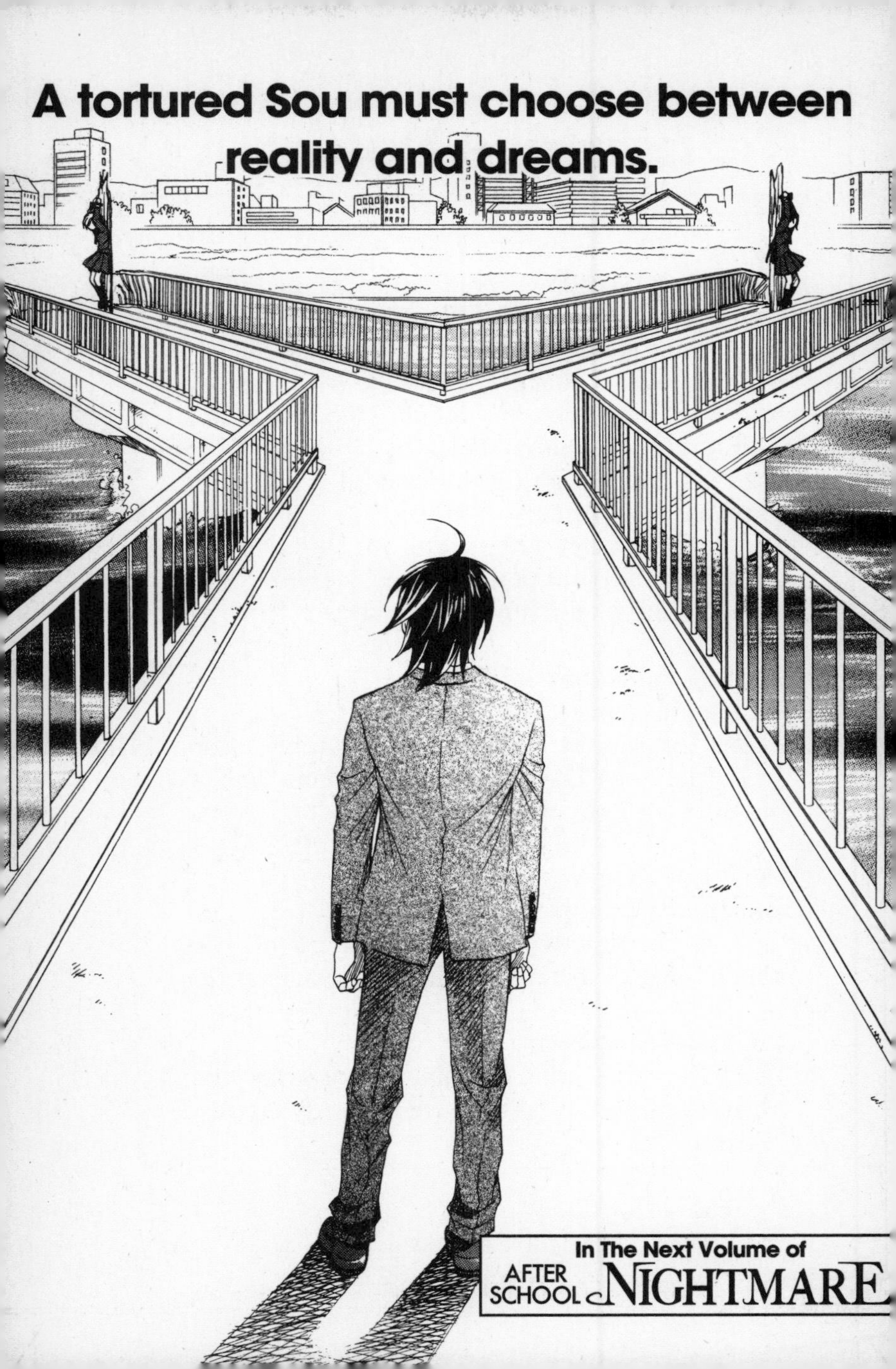
A tortured Sou must choose between reality and dreams.
In The Next Volume of
AFTER SCHOOL NIGHTMARE

Translator's Notes:

Pg. 46 – *The North Wind and the Sun*
This tale by Aesop is about the wind and the sun having a contest to decide which is more effective: brute strength or gentle coaxing. The challenge is to get a man to take his coat off. The wind tries to blow it off with a raging wind, only making the man grip it tighter.

The sun gently warms the earth until it's hot enough for the man to take it off willingly. In this scene, Sou's quiet withdrawal pulled Mashiro out better than any nagging would have done.

Pg. 65 - *Tobishima and Sakurai*
More color names.
鳶島 (Tobishima) The first symbol "tobi" means "black."
桜井 (Sakurai) The first symbol "sakura" means "cherry blossom," a light pink.

Pg. 70 – *Ebizawa*
Another color name.
海老沢 The first two symbols make up the word "ebi" which means "shrimp," a pinkish orange shade.

Pg. 122 – *Kanisawa*
蟹沢 The first symbol of this name means "crab." Mashiro messed it up because he easily confused "shrimp" for "crab."

Pg. 150 – *Haijima*
灰島 The first symbol "hai" means "ash," a gray color.

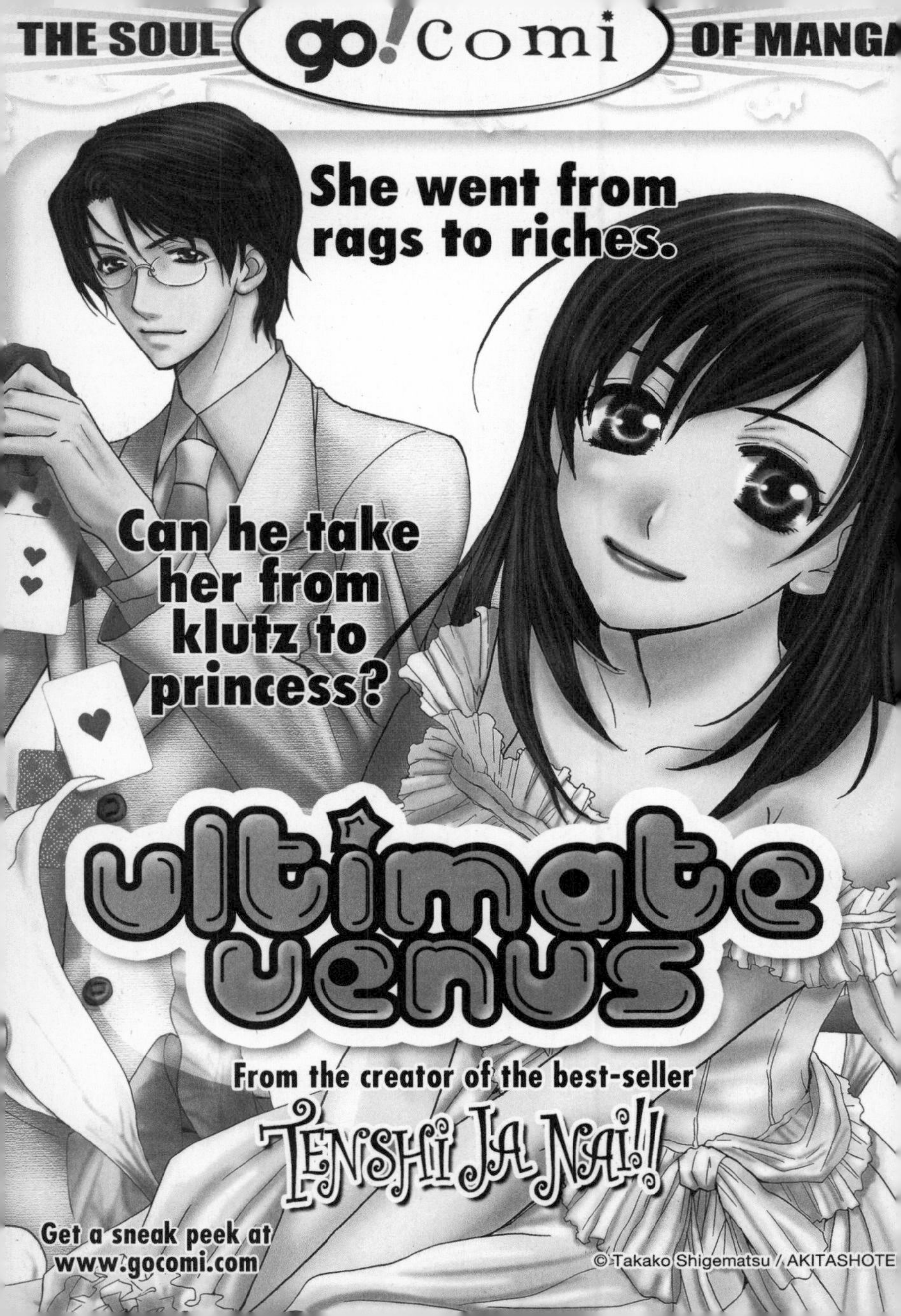

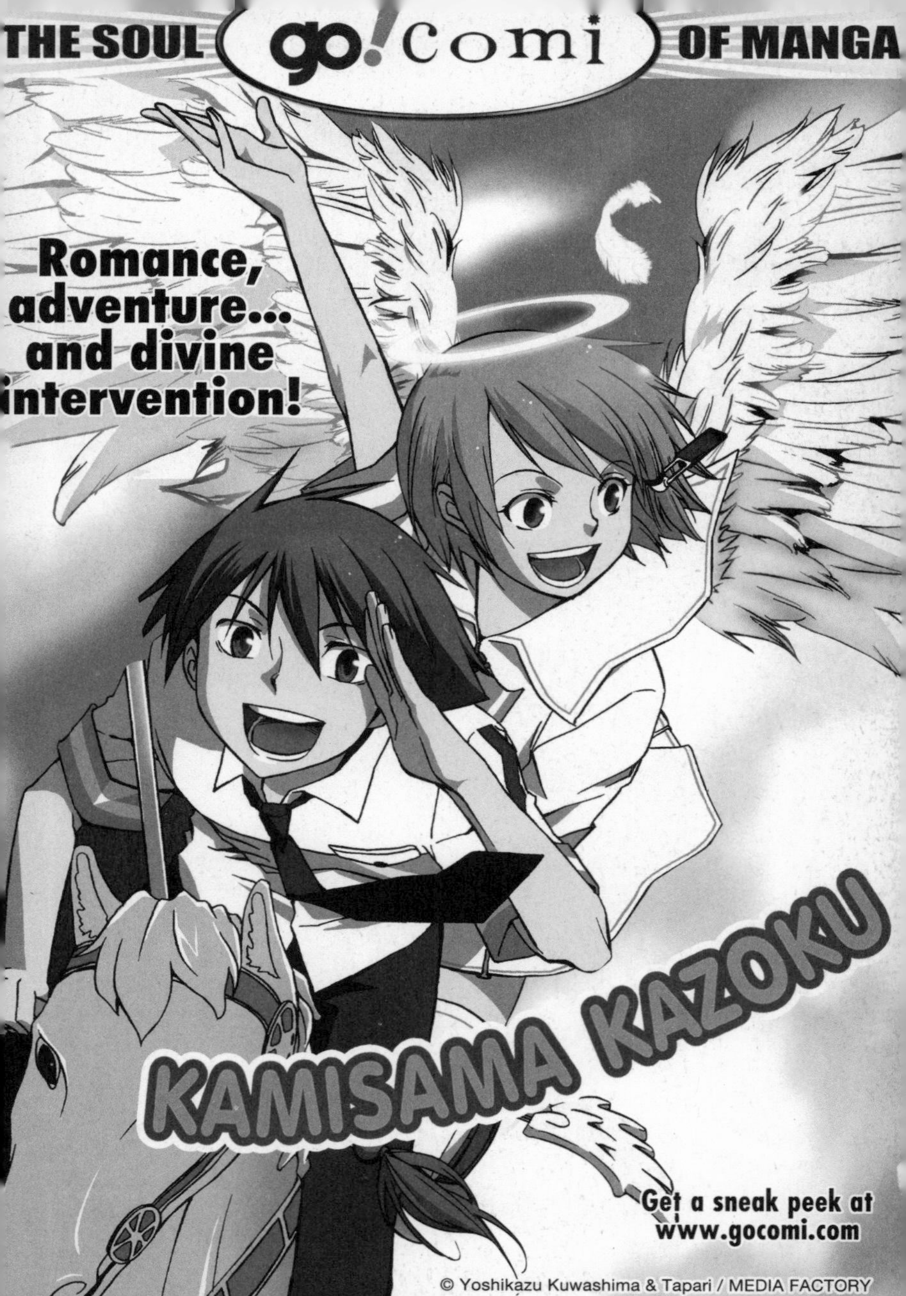
THE SOUL go! comi OF MANGA
Romance, adventure... and divine intervention!
KAMISAMA KAZOKU
Get a sneak peek at www.gocomi.com
© Yoshikazu Kuwashima & Tapari / MEDIA FACTORY

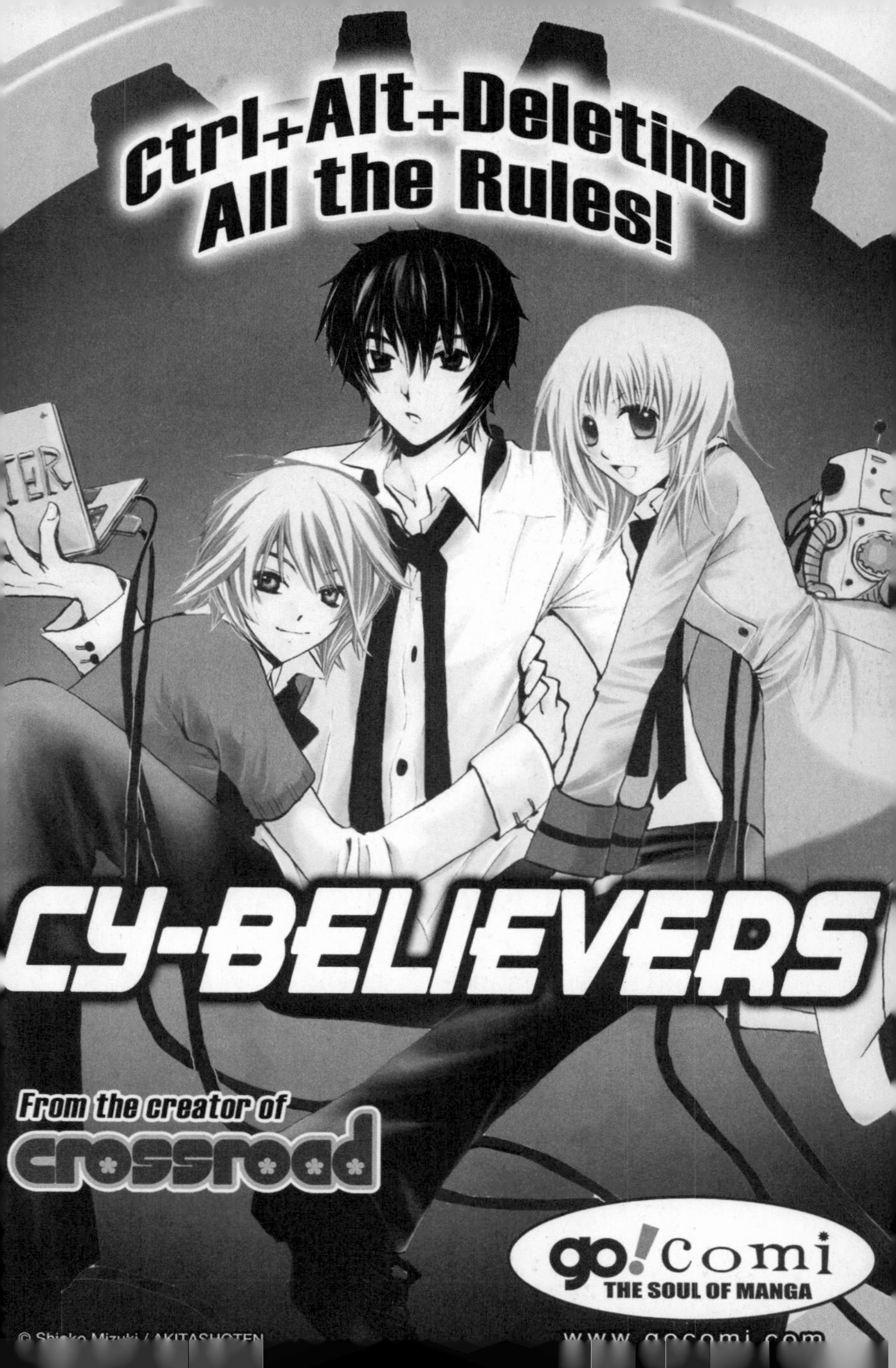

Ctrl+Alt+Deleting All the Rules!
CY-BELIEVERS
From the creator of
crossroad
go!comi
THE SOUL OF MANGA
www.gocomi.com

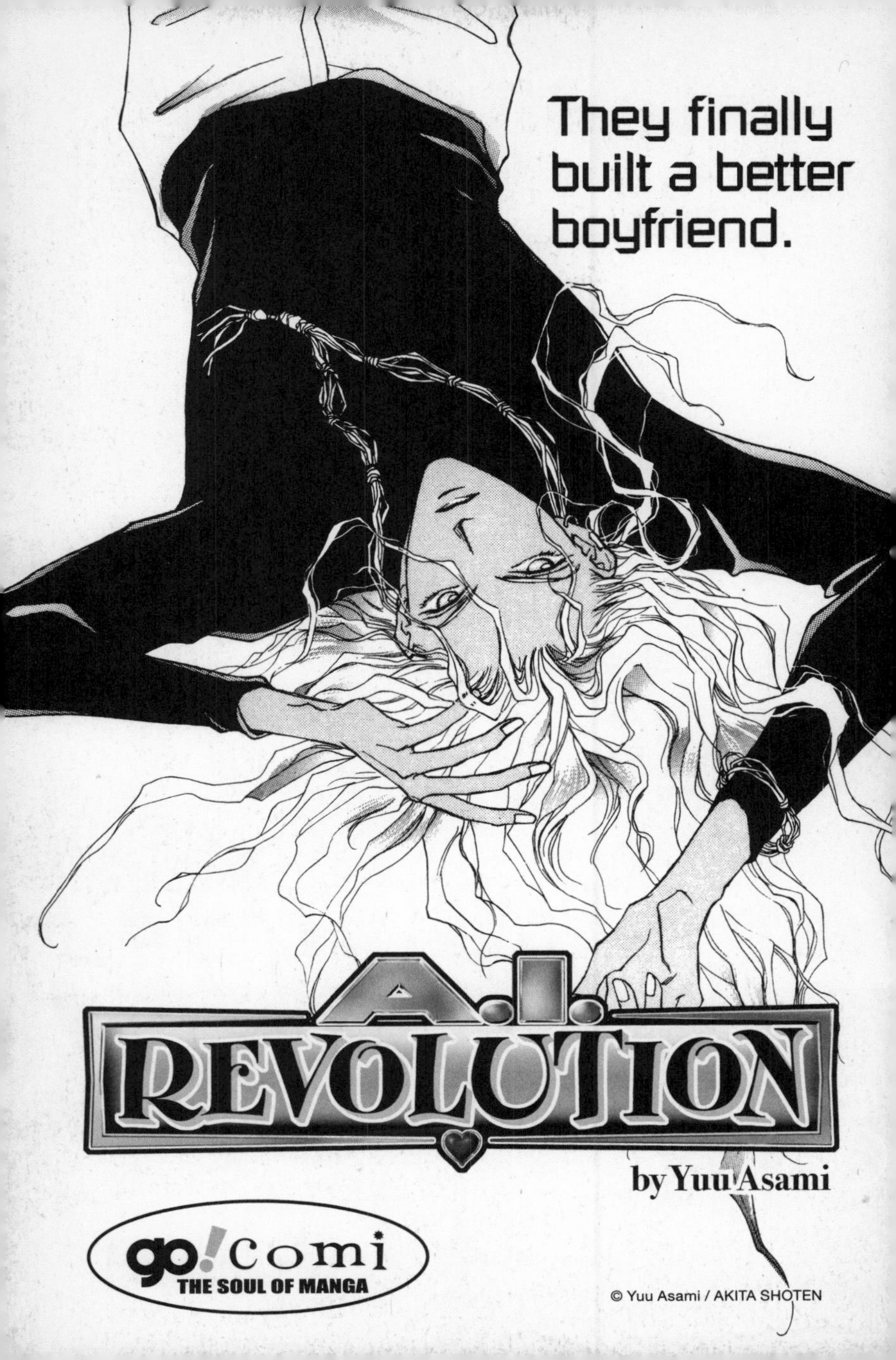

Reading. 'Riting. 'Rithmetic.

Romance.

LOVE MASTER

by Kyoko Hashimoto

A

**go!comi**
THE SOUL OF MANGA

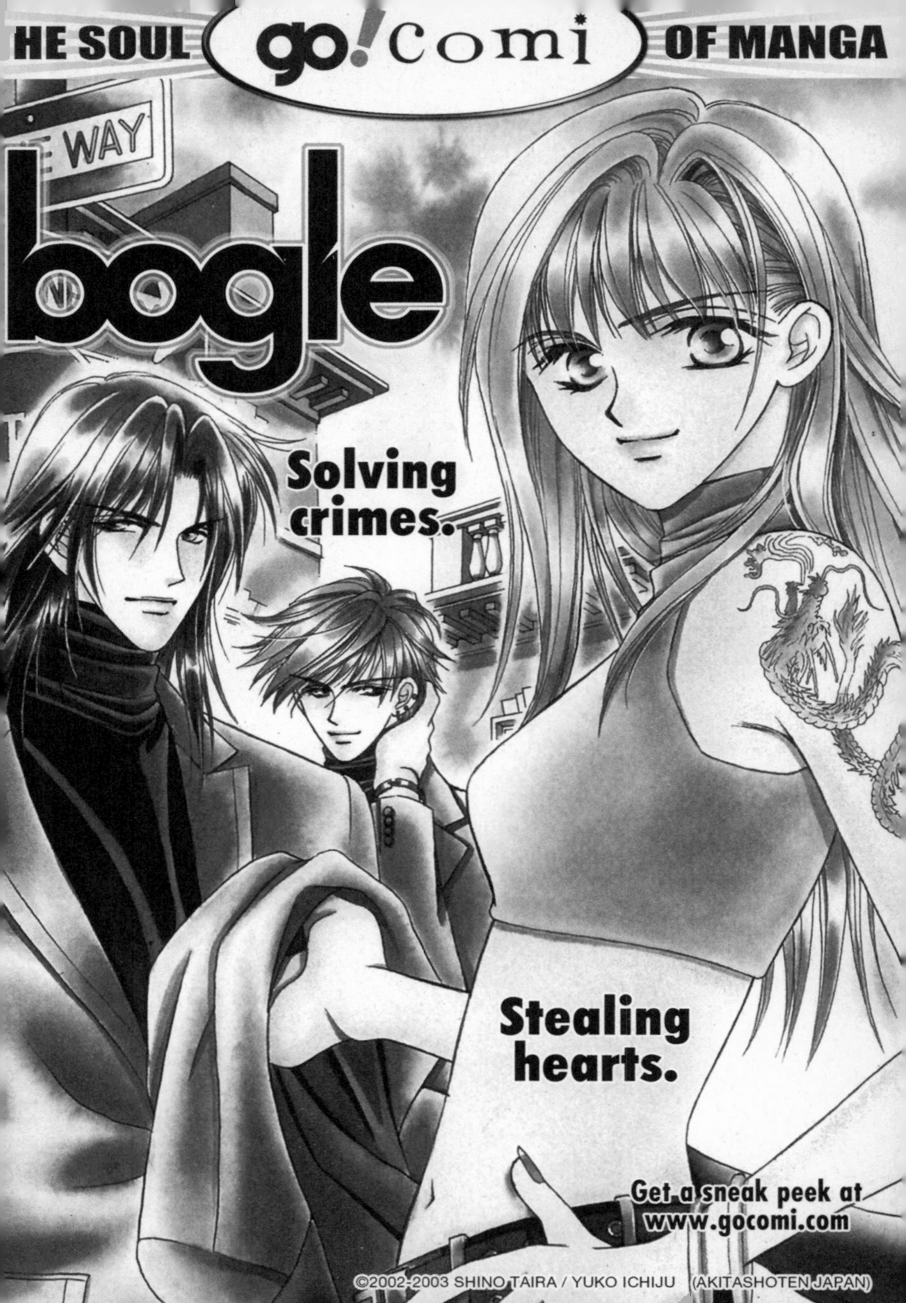
HE SOUL
go!comi
OF MANGA
WAY
bogle
Solving crimes.
Stealing hearts.
Get a sneak peek at www.gocomi.com
©2002-2003 SHINO TAIRA / YUKO ICHIJU (AKITASHOTEN JAPAN)

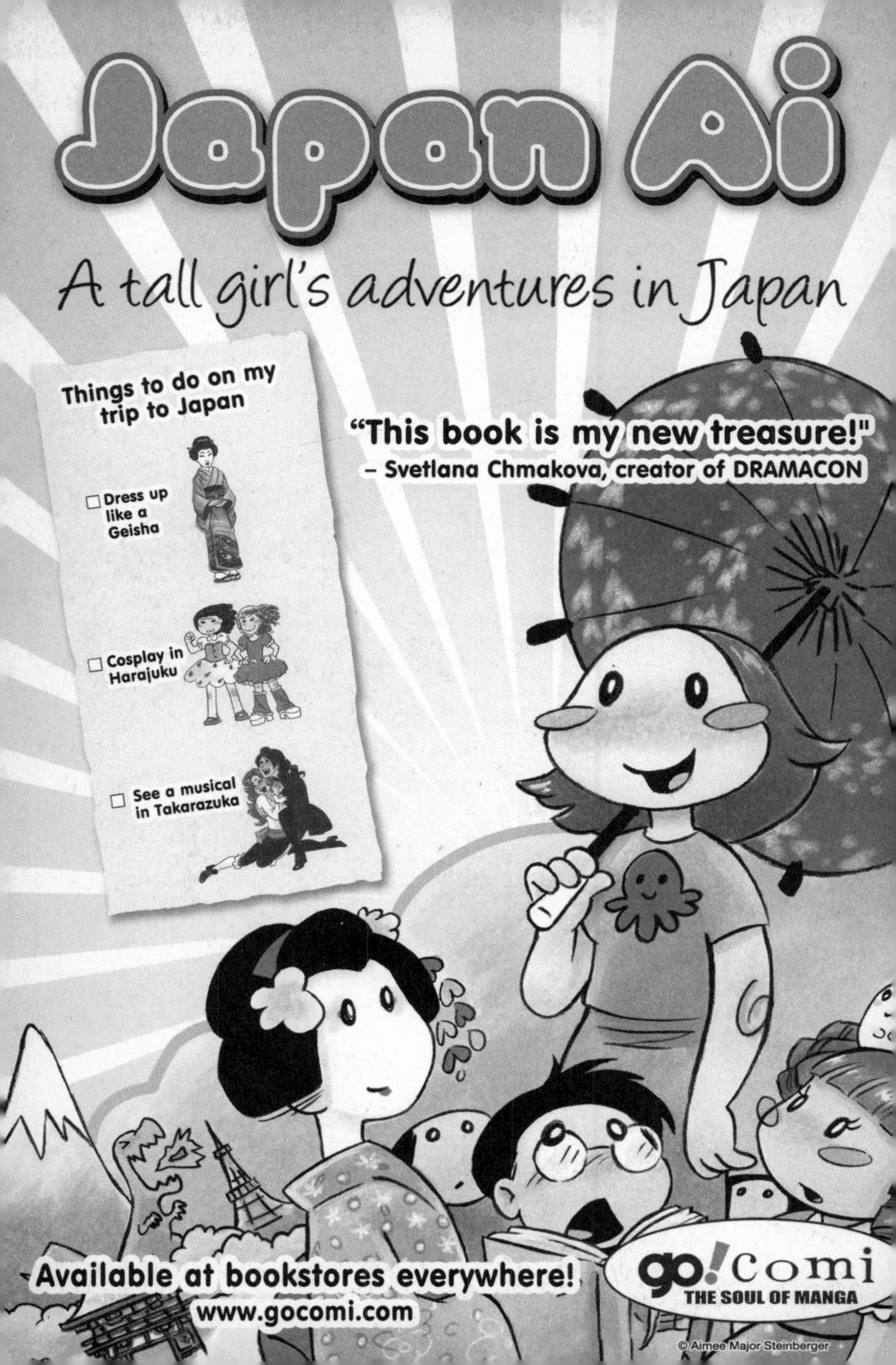
Japan Ai
A tall girl's adventures in Japan
Things to do on my trip to Japan
Dress up like a Geisha
Cosplay in Harajuku
See a musical in Takarazuka
"This book is my new treasure!"
– Svetlana Chmakova, creator of DRAMACON
Available at bookstores everywhere!
www.gocomi.com
go!comi
THE SOUL OF MANGA
© Aimee Major Steinberger

SETONA MIZUSHIRO

Until I drew this manga, I seriously had it in my head that "a plot with a short-haired girl as a heroine just won't fly." It's not like anybody told me that short just wouldn't cut it, so I figure it was just a random idea that got into my head. That's why in all the mangas I drew before ASN, my female heroines had either long or medium-length hair.

So, Mashiro is finally the first heroine I could draw with a short haircut! Mind you, there's more to why I'm calling him a "heroine," right now...

Now, including this volume, this story is going to end in three books. A lot happens in this volume, but I hope you stick with it to the very end.

ABOUT THE MANGA-KA

Setona Mizushiro's first real dabble in the world of creating manga was in 1985 when she participated in the publication of a dojinshi (amateur manga). She remained active in the dojinshi world until she debuted in April of 1993 with her short single *Fuyu ga Owarou Toshiteita* (Winter Was Ending) that ran in Shogakukan's *Puchi Comic* magazine. Mizushiro-sensei is well-known for her series *X-Day* in which she exhibits an outstanding ability to delve into psychological issues of every nature. Besides manga, Mizushiro-sensei has an affinity for chocolate, her two cats (Jam and Nene), and round sparkly objects.